¡vaya nuevo

UNIDAD			página
		Introduction	3
		Introducción	8
UNIDAD	1	Campings y albergues	10
UNIDAD	2	¡Que aproveche!	28
UNIDAD	3	Los grandes almacenes	44
UNIDAD	4	Ratos libres	60
UNIDAD	5	De compras	76
UNIDAD	6	¡A comer!	90
UNIDAD	7	Teléfonos y faxes	103
UNIDAD	8	Objetos perdidos	113
UNIDAD	9	Me siento mal	123
UNIDAD	10	Accidentes y averías	138
UNIDAD	11	Estás en tu casa	147
UNIDAD	12	El transporte público	157
UNIDAD	13	La televisión y los medios de comunicación	168
UNIDAD	14	En avión y en barco	177
UNIDAD	15	Recuerdos	186
UNIDAD	16	Dice la ley	192
UNIDAD	17	Los exámenes y después	200

Nelson 3

Michael Buckby
Michael Calvert

Thomas Nelson and Sons Ltd
Nelson House Mayfield Road
Walton-on-Thames Surrey
KT12 5PL UK

Thomas Nelson Australia
102 Dodds Street
South Melbourne Victoria 3205
Australia

Nelson Canada
1120 Birchmount Road
Scarborough Ontario
M1K 5G4 Canada

© Michael Buckby, Michael Calvert 1996

I(T)P Thomas Nelson is an International Thomson Publishing Company.

I(T)P is used under licence.

First published by Thomas Nelson and Sons Ltd 1996
ISBN   0-17-439-817-4
NPN   9 8 7 6 5 4 3 2 1

Printed in Great Britain by Hobbs the Printers.

All rights reserved. No paragraph of this publication may be reproduced, copied or transmitted save with written permission or in accordance with the provisions of the Copyright, Design and Patents Act 1988, or under the terms of any licence permitting limited copying issued by the Copyright Licensing Agency, 90 Tottenham Court Road, London W1P 9HE.

Any person who does any unauthorised act in relation to this publication may be liable to criminal prosecution and civil claims for damages.

AT-A-GLANCE

To help the teacher use these teacher's notes, certain types of activity are flagged by the following symbols:

- listening item tapescript
- oral pairwork activity
- opportunity to set homework
- source of further information
- opportunity for language game
- consolidation activity
- extension activity

Acknowledgements
María Jesús Novis Ruiz
Rita Pepper-Cano
Jorge Doce-Chambrelan

Introduction

¡Vaya Nuevo! and the communicative approach to language learning

Language learning has undergone rapid changes in recent years. Work carried out by the Council of Europe has resulted in syllabuses and examinations that reflect the language needs of learners who wish to communicate in everyday social and public situations. **¡Vaya Nuevo!** has been written to meet the urgent need for a course in Spanish which will satisfy the requirements of the National Curriculum, Standard Grade and new GCSE examinations and to help teachers to work along the lines recommended by OFSTED.

The Structure of ¡Vaya Nuevo!

The course is made up of three stages leading up to public examinations at 16+. **Stage 1** is based in Malaga and aims to provide the students with the language necessary for a holiday in Spain. In National Curriculum terms it goes up to and includes level 4 in all skill areas. **Stage 2** is set in Santander and deals mainly with situations students are likely to meet while on a extended holiday or exchange visit. It covers levels 1–6. **Stage 3** is also based on the northern coast of Spain and will prepare students for an extended stay in Spain for work or study. It covers the remainder of the levels and includes preparation for the examinations. Each stage comprises:

- Students' Book
- Teacher's Notes
- Copymasters (for copying onto paper and/or OHTs)
- Cassettes
- Assessment Support Pack

In addition there are flashcards, computer software and Language Master Cards for some stages.

Each stage is designed to motivate the students and provide them with a sense of achievement at all levels of linguistic competence. Throughout the course, background information is given on the language, country and people of Spain; this is supplemented in the Teacher's Notes. In Book 3, there is information on Latin America and its people.

How to use the course

¡Vaya Nuevo! is aimed at students studying Spanish as a first or second language and care has been taken to provide material at a variety of levels to meet the needs of students of different abilities and ages. The Teacher's Notes provide a wide variety of suggestions for exploitation of the students materials from which you may select the activities best suited for the age and ability of your students. Supplementary material is available in the form of Copymasters. These can be used for extension work in class and allow students of different abilities to work independently from the teacher, and from each other.

Pair work and group work

¡Vaya Nuevo! is based on a communicative approach to language learning and it is therefore not possible to use the course successfully without extensive oral work. In a classroom situation pair work and group work are the only practical ways of ensuring sufficient practice in speaking for each student. This demands careful preparation, but it is well worth the effort. Some suggestions for organising these activities are given below:

- Before attempting pair work or group work for the first time, establish the students pairs or groups and ask them to keep to these where possible. Organise a system for distributing cue cards, aim for the minimum reorganisation of furniture, and devise a means of reporting when a task has been completed.
- Always explain the task carefully and work through one example, either between yourself and a student, or two students, before leaving a class to work alone.
- Make sure that the students know who is asking or answering the questions.
- With exercises involving cue cards make sure that all the symbols and instructions are understood.
- In information-gap activities (when one student must find out information from another's card) it is useful for the questioner to write down the information received. This serves as a check for comprehension.

In brief: before starting on pair work all students need to know what to do and how to do it.

Reading

The Students' Book introduces and practises reading skills and there is a variety of reading materials in the Students' Book and on Copymasters.

Naturally it is not possible to provide all the reading material that students need. To ensure that there is sufficient, it will be necessary to supplement what is available by providing books and magazines which can be displayed in the classroom and used regularly by the students. Reading for pleasure and choosing what you read is very important for the students. Evidence suggests that there is insufficient reading taking place in class. Ensure that time is set aside for this and that there are materials available that will interest the students. Authentic magazines can be obtained at little expense by asking your exchange school to send material in return for your students sending magazines that they have read.

Listening practice

Listening practice is provided by the pairwork exercises and the taped material. It is not possible to teach students to communicate effectively without using the tapes and accompanying exercises. The transcripts of the scripted recordings are given in the notes for the relevant exercises.

In **¡Vaya Nuevo!** there is a variety of accents and voices from the start (Book 1 has over 100 voices). In Book 3 it is appropriate to introduce learners to Latin American language and accents. It is an important skill for them to be able to understand speakers from many countries of the Spanish-speaking world. It is not the intention to teach variations: **carro** for 'car', **camión** for 'bus/coach' but to alert students to differences in the same way that we might deal with American English. Students can be encouraged to use communication strategies to work out unfamiliar words in familiar settings, e.g. **estampilla** instead of **sello**.

Using Latin American speakers also alerts students to cultural differences (souvenirs, regional dishes, daily routine).

Writing

This forms a natural part of the activities in the Students' Book and Teacher's Notes, and numerous suggestions for activities at different levels are given throughout the course. Students are encouraged to compile a **fichero personal**, which will provide them with an accurate and useful source of information when writing to penfriends or preparing for examinations.

Ahora sé

This section can be used for reference and for revision purposes. Many activities are suggested to encourage students to be more autonomous in their learning. A knowledge of how to learn is stressed by both the National Curriculum and by OFSTED.

A ser detective

This section caters for students who will benefit from a knowledge of the underlying structure of the language they are using. It is intended to be largely self-explanatory. You are free to introduce the grammar when it seems appropriate. If a task calls for the use of a particular structure or grammar point, and you feel that the students would benefit from an explanation, it would clearly be impractical to wait for the end of the unit before giving the explanation. On other occasions, it may be valuable to revise a particular section of **A ser detective** in one unit before dealing with another unit which requires that particular grammar point, or which takes that grammar point one stage further.

Grammar Summary

A grammar summary follows the **A ser detective** section of Stage 3. The summary is cumulative, containing the grammar from Stages 1 and 2, as well as Stage 3, for the purposes of reference and revision.

Revision activities

The revision scheme is an essential part of the course, based on the regular pattern of recurrence 1, 3, 6, 12 and 24 units after the language first occurs. It follows that each unit will contain revision material from as many as four or five previous units. For reasons of pace and balance, most of the revision activities are given in the Teacher's Notes for each relevant unit, rather than in the Students' Book and we strongly recommend that they be used regularly.

Vocabulary

There is no glossary in Book 3. It is expected that the students will be able to use and have access to dictionaries. It is important that students use dictionaries intelligently and before looking up a word they ask themselves:
(a) whether the word is important for the meaning
(b) whether the meaning of the word can be deduced by using communication strategies (see below).

Communication Strategies

When communicating it is not always either appropriate or necessary to have recourse to a dictionary. There are a number of strategies for both comprehension and production which enable students to understand well and communicate effectively.

In reading comprehension it is important that students be exposed to authentic and authenticated materials and that they can deduce the meaning of words they have not met and avoid the tedium and frustration of excessive dictionary use. In speech we want students to be able to communicate with confidence and fluency and to know what to do when they 'run out of words'. The answer to both questions is to provide them with communication strategies that will both develop their wordpower and enable them to cope with a wider range of situations than they would be able to do with their existing stock of words. These strategies are not frills and some examination boards expect students to be trained in these strategies (see NEAB syllabuses).

The most common receptive strategies include the following:

- using the visual and verbal context
- using grammatical markers
- recognising features common to Spanish and English (e.g. the suffix –*ero*/*er*)

(The **Una palabra conduce a otra** section is designed to help the student with these features.)

- using the social and cultural context
- using cognates.

On the productive side learners can be trained to substitute words they know for words they do not, replacing specific words with generic terms (**flor** for **clavel**); finding paraphrases and generally keeping talking so as to answer questions 'lo más ampliamente posible' – a vital requirement in oral examinations.

Teacher's Notes

Each unit is analysed and exploited in the Teacher's Notes in the following way:

At the Head of the unit the following are listed:

- the main aim(s) of the unit
- the areas of experience covered
- the materials required for the classroom
- the language tasks of that unit
- the grammar points in the **A ser detective** section
- the productive and receptive language
- the main revision points.

The unit is divided into sections which each cover a particular task. Within each section there are suggestions for the introduction of the new language and notes on the activities in the Students' Book. In addition, there are supplementary activities for further practice using this language.

Background information is given at relevant points throughout the text.

The use of the foreign language for teaching purposes

Consistent with the need to provide instructions in the target language all the rubrics in the Students' Book are in Spanish. It is desirable that Spanish be used wherever possible in the classroom and a list of classroom expressions is given in Teacher's Notes, Stage 1 (p6).

Language games

Games play an important part in the learning of a foreign language. Not only do they give variety to the lesson, but they are also a source of enjoyment and can motivate students to concentrate on, memorise and utilise specific language. In addition, they provide a reason for practising language out of context and yet in a communicative way.

Where a game is recommended as part of the learning process it is included in the Teacher's Notes for the relevant unit; however, the games in this section can be adapted to practise almost any grammatical point or set of vocabulary items, and should be used as often as necessary. A short bibliography is provided at the end of this section.

It is recommended that all students take an active part in the games. They can take over the teacher's role as soon as it is possible, and be encouraged to prepare some of the materials. Clearly no game can work if any of the participants does not understand the rules. It may therefore be preferable to play the game in English first and then in Spanish.

Noughts and crosses

Noughts and crosses is usually played on a 3 × 3 grid and the outcome is often decided before all the squares have been occupied. We therefore recommend using a 4 × 4 grid, which allows for the practice of more material, makes for a tactically more complex and interesting game, involves high scoring contests and often means that the outcome is undecided until the last remaining square(s). A number of OHP transparencies in this course have been designed with this in mind.

The class is divided into two teams, one the noughts and the other the crosses. The object of the game is to get the greater number of rows of three symbols on the grid, whether vertically, horizontally or diagonally. Note that with the 4 × 4 grid you can score one point for three symbols in a row and an extra one of four symbols:

X	X	X	X
X	0	0	0
X	X	0	X
0	0	0	0

Score: X = 3 points, 0 = 5 points

The game can be played in a number of ways. As a memory game the students are shown 16 items of clothing, activities, words, numbers, etc., for one minute and must try to memorise as many as possible. It is advisable to prepare the items in rows of four, earlier in the lesson and gradually to build up to 16. Alternatively, you can use 9 squares at first and build up to the larger grid in subsequent lessons.

The visual stimuli are removed and a member of the class says a number between 1–16 and identifies the item which corresponds to the square. For example, if there is a jacket in the top right-hand corner a player might say: *Número cuatro – una chaqueta* and then you or a nominated student writes the team's symbol in that square.

The easiest way to play the game is to use the OHP. One transparency shows the grid in permanent ink and this is placed over another which features the visual cues. The latter is then removed leaving the grid. The noughts and crosses can then be written on the grid, using non-permanent pens. As an alternative to a memory game, the students can be asked questions and, if they answer correctly, can choose which square they would like the symbol to be put in.

¿Verdad o mentira?

This is a very simple game which gives the students a reason for repetition and can be used to check comprehension at any level. The students listen to you making certain statements. When you say something true, they repeat it. When you say something false, they remain silent. This can be a class, group or individual activity. Alternatively, the students can have two pieces of paper. On one is written **Verdad**; on the other **Mentira**. They must hold up the correct piece of paper to indicate whether the statement is true or false. You can introduce a competitive element by scoring points for each correct response; for each incorrect response you gain a point.

The statements can be presented in written form. They are shown one at a time; students have to read out a correct statement (one point) and, in the case of a false statement, have to state that it is a *mentira* (one point) and give a similar sentence that is correct for a bonus point, for example:
– *Barcelona es la capital de España.*
– *Mentira. Madrid es la capital de España.*
(two points)

¿Sí o no?

This game is similar to the one above. You ask the students questions which require yes/no answers. They hold up a card/piece of paper which has **Sí** on one side and **No** on the other. It is easy for you to see how well the class has understood the question by the number of correct responses.

The opposite of this game is to ask the students to answer questions without using **Sí** or **No**. This forces them to give full answers. To encourage the students to use interrogatives the game can be played in reverse with the students asking you questions.

El juego de Kim

Kim's game involves showing the students between 10 and 15 objects for a short time, then taking them away and asking the students to say or write down a list of the objects.

You can use this idea in different ways and at different levels. You can show them the items and then remove one or more and the class, group or individual has to tell you what is missing. You can use words or pictures instead of objects and you can ask for a greater or lesser degree of precision in the answers.

El ahorcado

Hangman is another game that is simple to set up and play. It can practise any vocabulary, as well as the pronunciation of the Spanish alphabet. Dashes are put on the board corresponding to the number of letters in the mystery word. Students have to guess which letters are used to make up the word. Each correct letter is written in, but for each incorrect letter a part of first the gallows and then the hangman body is drawn.

The complexity of the gallows and details of the victim can be varied depending on the difficulty of the vocabulary and the ability of the students, for example:
– *¿Está la letra 'f' en tu palabra?*

El ahorcado can also be played using words instead of letters. The dashes correspond to the number of words in the sentence. The students ask:
– *¿Está la palabra 'donde' en tu frase?*

Otros detalles

This game involves adding another detail to an existing string of suitable vocabulary or phrases. Begin by stating, for example,
– *En mi maleta hay un jersey...*

Students then have to add to the list and get one point for their team for each successful addition.
– *En mi maleta hay un jersey, unos pantalones...*

A correct challenge from the opposing team(s) gives them one point and removes one point from the score of the team whose member was challenged.

Simón dice

A very useful game to practise commands, actions and parts of the body. The students have to obey every command prefaced by **Simón dice** and ignore other commands. Students can be given a set number of lives and lose a life for each incorrect response.

Juegos de números

Students always need plenty of practice of numbers. Two common games are Bingo and Buzz (**Cuidado con el siete**). The former needs no explanation. The latter involves a group or a class counting upwards and avoiding saying a number which either contains or is a multiple of seven. Instead the pupil must say *chas*, e.g.

dieciséis
chas
dieciocho
diecinueve
veinte
chas

Failure to give the next number or to say **chas** at the appropriate time or undue hesitation means that the student is out. It is a good idea to have the whole class standing at the start of the game and to ask them to sit when they are eliminated.

When students become proficient at this version you can make the game more difficult by asking them to say **chas** at any number which contains a five or multiple of five as well as seven or a multiple of seven.

You can also count backwards as well as forwards.

Juego de familias

A group activity which allows you to bring in vocabulary on any topic. Ask the students to name, for example, one item of furniture. The groups confer and one member of the group should raise his/her hand.

The first group to answer correctly wins a point. Ask the students to name two sports, three articles of clothing, four rooms of the house, five parts of the body, etc.

Naufragio

The students imagine that they are on a ship which is about to sink near to a desert island and they have to salvage a set number of items (only a certain number will fit in the lifeboat). Working in pairs or in groups, the students have to decide on the most useful or desirable items to take with them on the island. They have to discuss and explain their preferences.

Pilla al intruso

Give the students a list of vocabulary items (nouns, verbs and adverbs) and the class, group or individual has to work out which is the odd one out and why. With more advanced groups there can be no 'correct' answer, but more than one item which can be considered to the odd one.

The words can be different by meaning or by a range of criteria: pronunciation, part of speech, or grammar (regular/irregular). Students can be encouraged to make up their own and have them checked by you before being used with the class or group.

For more games the following can be recommended:

Games for language learning Andrew Wright, Michael Buckby, David Butteridge (CUP, 1984)
Grammar games Mario Rinvolucri (CUP, 1985)
Take 5 Michael Carrier (Nelson, 1980)
Language games and activities Simon Greenall (Hulton, 1984)
Vocabulary John Morgan and Mario Rinvolucri (OUP, 1987)
Te toca a ti (MEC – Ministerio de Educación y Ciencia)
Five Minutes Activities Andrew Wright and Penny Ur, (CUP, 1992)

INTRODUCCION

Introducción (page 4)

Main aim
To develop insights into Spanish in Latin America.

A The students read this item and then ask you questions about anything they do not understand. If necessary, write on the board key expressions for this, e.g.

¿Qué quiere decir …?
No entiendo …

When everyone understands the text, encourage them to ask questions about things that interest them in it. You can ask questions and give more information and this can develop into a discussion.

B The students read the seven categories for the information and look for examples of each one, and read their examples aloud. You could give additional information, e.g.

Muchos mejicanos van a los Estados Unidos a encontrar trabajo. (1)

Millones de turistas van a visitar los monumentos de los Incas y de los Aztecas. (2)

Los soldados españoles robaron el oro y otros objetos de valor de los indios. (3)

Si se cortan los árboles del Amazonas, muchas plantas y animales van a desaparecer. (4)

En Perú, Argentina, etcétera el idioma oficial es el español. (5)

La comida es muy variada en América Latina. (6)

El Océano Pacífico está al oeste y el Atlántico al este. (7)

The students classify each piece of information you give (*la lengua*, etc.).

C You could base a class quiz on this, and other, information about Latin America, seeing, for example, how many questions the class can answer correctly in five minutes. There will be more informative texts on Latin America in *Libro 3* and these quizzes could become a regular feature, with the class trying always to produce a record number of correct answers.

Introduction to Latin America

It is an understatement to say that the countries of Latin America offer a contrast. The size and scale are difficult to do justice to. The length of the rivers, the sheer size of the Amazon, the vital statistics of cities such as Mexico City and Sao Paolo, the height and length of the Andes with its Indian villages that have been little changed in centuries and its modern coastal resorts along the Caribbean are difficult to comprehend. For example, the cordillera of the Andes stretches almost 8,000 km from the Eastern slopes of the Andes to the Atlantic.

Latin America includes the Central American countries. Mexico and the so-called 'banana republics' of Costa Rica and Nicaragua, etc., islands in the Caribbean and the vast land mass which is South America which stretches from well north of the Equator almost down to the Antarctic. Mexico, separated from the United States by the famous Rio Grande, is famous for its Aztec culture, its music, its revolutionaries, as well as its tourist attractions such as Acapulco and its enormous capital of 20 million people. With an incredible demographic growth rate, this figure could rise to 36 million by the turn of the century (source Fodor's *Mexico*). Four million vehicles create intolerable traffic and pollution problems and breathing in Mexico City has been equated to smoking two packets of cigarettes a day.

South America

South America is divided up into four distinct groups of countries: Colombia and Venezuela in the north; Peru, Bolivia and Ecuador – the most Indian and least developed countries on the continent, the huge Brazil which was colonised by the Portuguese and therefore does not share the Spanish language with the other countries and finally, the *cono sur*, Argentina, Paraguay, Uruguay and Chile. These are the most European and prosperous of the South American republics.

As well as the Indian tribes of the Andes and the Amazon there are *mestizos* (mixed European and Indians) and, on the northern coast particularly, a strong black or mulatto element resulting from the descendants of slaves brought across the Atlantic

INTRODUCCION

from Africa. The reference to Indians is, in fact, the fault of Columbus (Cristóbal Colón), who thought he had found Asia in 1492. In the South there are many people of European descent. In the late 19th century the arrival of refrigeration meant that the meat from the vast farms of the prairies could be transported to Europe. Many immigrants from Italy, Germany and the UK went out to make their living as farmers.

The dominant influence on most of the countries of South America has been Spain. The discovery of America was quickly followed by invasions of one country after another led by *conquistadores* such as Pizarro and Cortés. The gold-seeking excesses of these soldiers of fortune are well documented as is the violence and slaughter that accompanied the extermination of millions of Indians. The legend of *El dorado*, an empire of gold and emeralds, that would yield untold wealth to its discoverer, was the dream of many *conquistadores*, some of whom perished in the jungles and icy mountains lured by the prospect of mountains of gold. The *conquistadores* overran the native population (Pizarro took Peru with only 180 men) with ease, the natives were frightened by the appearance, firearms and dogs of the Spanish, were disunited and could not withstand the infectious diseases that the Europeans brought with them.

Colonial settlements grew up quickly and in 1535 Lima was founded as the capital of the New Viceroyalty of Peru (the seat of all power in Spanish America). The Spanish began by looking for gold, silver and precious stones and stole whatever they could find but realised that the true wealth of the New World consisted of the Indian population. The Spanish exercised a brutal regime wiping out Indian civilisations and bringing the inhabitants into slavery alongside black prisoners shipped over from Africa. Spain relied on draining the wealth from the continent to finance its endless wars in Europe. The Spanish exploited the local people in the mines and extracted high taxes.

In the 19th century, influenced by the French and North American revolutions each country in turn rose up and declared independence. The *criollos*, people of Spanish descent but born in Latin America, resented the power of Spain and the *peninsulares* (administrators from Spain) and were behind many of the revolts.

The picture of modern-day South America is a confused one of military dictatorships, left and right-wing *juntas* and democratic republics. Behind all the complexities of the individual power struggles that each country or region has undergone or is still undergoing, it could be said that one simple pattern has emerged: a relatively small but powerful elite have dominated at the expense of the powerless indigenous masses who have usually suffered much discrimination, in particular the Indians.

UNIDAD 1

Campings y albergues

Main aim
Booking and spending a holiday on a campsite or in a youth hostel.

Area(s) of experience
E – The international world

Materials
Cassette: El camping en España, Lo siento no hay, Hay que insistir, Hay problemas, Camping Municipal Bellavista, Más información, ¿Tiene una cama libre? ¿Hay camas libres? Quisiera saber …, Avisos y consejos, Ventajas y desventajas, Una tarjeta bastante rara, Radio Camping Las Arenas, Campings a la onda, Sobre gustos no hay nada escrito, Repaso: en el pueblo, Repaso: describiendo un pueblo, Repaso: describiendo las vacaciones, Repaso: en la estación de servicio
Copymasters 1–11

Tasks
Booking accommodation on a campsite or in a youth hostel
Enquiring about facilities and opening and closing times
Stating how many people (males/females) require accommodation
Understanding signs, rules and regulations
Finding out about the cost and paying the bill
Discussing holidays and making preferences

Productive language
adulto
camping
depósito
moto
niño
por persona
sábana
salón social
tienda
albergue juvenil
caravana
guardián
necesitar
por día
remitir
saco de dormir
sitio

Receptive language
alojamiento
aseos
completo
consulta médica/enfermería
cubo de basura
duchas
jornada turística
lavandería
medios de lavar la ropa
paquete de almuerzo
parcela
peluquería
precio de alquiler
servicio de lavandería
tarjeta de afiliación
toma de corriente
velocidad máxima

Revision points
Asking for places in a town
(*Libro 1, Unidad 3*)
Describing a tow
(*Libro 2, Unidad 1*)
Describing past holidays
(*Libro 2, Unidad 7*)
At a service station
(*Libro 2, Unidad 10*)

Campings y albergues (page 6)

Main aim
For the students to understand and accept the unit goals.

A Give the students three minutes to read this and to identify any words they cannot understand. Help them to develop appropriate communication strategies to understand these words, e.g.
lavandería: think of '*lavar*' and context (what you might ask for on a campsite)
letreros: the context and the examples given
albergue: the context.
Develop the habit of using strategies such as these as a first resort, and reference to a dictionary as a last resort.

B The students concentrate on the list of tasks they will learn to carry out. To help them to see how useful these are you could, e.g.
Discuss holidays in Spain, especially any camping holidays you or your students have had.
Relate the tasks here to those the students will need for their exam.

C Give orally and on the board examples of these tasks: you could start with those in this item and then adapt and go beyond these. The students categorise each example by saying which task it is an example of.

UNIDAD 1

ℹ Background information

In Spain the climate is ideal for camping. Campsites, which are subject to regulations from the tourist board, are divided into four categories: luxury, first, second and third class. They should all have an office for reception which should contain, amongst other things, a *libro de reclamaciones* in case of complaint. The price list should be on display, along with a list of rules. In order to be called a *camping*, the establishment must have drinking water, electricity, parking facilities, proper access, rubbish collection and adequate sanitation.

El camping en España (page 6)

Main aim

To meet and understand some of the key language of the unit.

A Write a few questions on the board, e.g.
¿El camping es popular en España?
¿Por qué?
Cuando llegas a un camping, ¿qué hay que hacer?
The students read and understand these questions. They then skim the text, as quickly as possible, to find the answers and to give you these orally. Clear up any problems which arise.

B The students read again the introductory text. They write a list of any words in it which they do not understand. They tell you what these are, and you help them to understand them, developing appropriate communication strategies and dictionary techniques.

C The students read the text again to find the task they have to do. Check that everyone understands this. They then work out the prices.
They now listen to the recordings to check the prices. Play each one twice and then ask a few students how much was paid. Clear up any problems and play the recording again so that everyone hears it and understands it fully. It is worth bearing in mind how often numbers are tested in exams.

El camping en España
Número 1
– Hola, buenos días.
– Buenos días, ¿hay sitio?
– Sí, sí. ¿Para cuántas personas?
– Estoy solo. Uno y una tienda.
– ¿Tiene coche?
– No, una moto.
– Vamos a ver ... una persona 475 y una moto 375 y ...
– Una tienda individual.
– 350 pesetas. Son 1.200 por día, ¿vale?
– Sí, vale.
– Rellene la ficha, por favor.

Número 2
– Buenas tardes.
– Buenas tardes, ¿tiene sitio?
– Sí, señor. ¿Para cuántas personas?
– Somos dos.
– ¿Tiene coche o caravana?
– No, una tienda solamente.
– Muy bien.
– ¿Cuánto es por día?
– Dos adultos 475 y 475 ... son 950 y una tienda 525 ... Son 1.475.
– Vale.
– Rellene la ficha, por favor.

Número 3
– Hola, buenos días.
– Buenos días. ¿Hay sitio en el camping?
– Para una caravana o coche-cama no.
– Es para un coche solamente.
– Sí, sí hay sitio. ¿Cuántos son ustedes?
– Somos tres: dos adultos y un hijo.
– Entonces, dos adultos, un niño y ¿cuántas tiendas?
– Una tienda intermedia y una tienda individual – igloo, ¿sabes?
– Sí. ¿Quiere parcela?
– Sí, pero sin agua y electricidad. ¿Cuánto es por día?
– 475 por 2 son 950, más el coche 500 son 1.450, dos tiendas 875 son 2.325 y una parcela 1.375. Son 3.700 en total.
– Vale.

D The students listen again to the recordings and choose collectively the one which they like the sound of most. Encourage them to explain why.
They listen again to the one they have chosen and repeat after the camper.
The students could listen to this dialogue as many times as they need to in order to transcribe it.

E The students read to themselves the model of the dialogue on page 7 and check that they understand

UNIDAD 1

it. They then follow the text in their books as they listen to the recording.

¿Hay sitio?
- Buenos días, ¿hay sitio?
- Sí, ¿para una tienda o una caravana?
- Para una caravana.
- ¿Cuántos son?
- Tres adultos y un niño.
- ¿Necesita electricidad?
- Sí, ¿cuánto es por día?
- Son 3.125 pesetas.
- Vale.
- Rellene la ficha, por favor.

They now listen and repeat: after the Spanish speakers and then with them, trying to maintain the same pace and pronunciation. In pairs, they practise both parts until they can act out the whole dialogue, using only the bill as a prompt. As they do this, you can move around, helping and assessing.

F Finally, the students make up dialogues based on the other two bills.

Lo siento no hay (page 7)

Main aim
Learning to cope with the unexpected.

A The students read this as quickly as possible. Check that they have understood the instructions and stress how important this is: many marks are lost in exams because the instructions were not understood or followed. This is an important thing to stress on a regular basis. You could also emphasise the importance, in exams and in real life, of learning to cope with the unexpected.

B The students try to anticipate the problems which may arise when booking in at a campsite. As they say these, note them on the board. The students then write a full list, each one putting at the top the problem which they think will occur most frequently and working down from there.

C They listen to the recording and write the number of each dialogue next to the appropriate problem in their lists. Check on these and clear up any difficulties.
They listen again to find any dialogues which contain a problem which they had not anticipated (e.g. number 3). They then listen again to this and note what the problem is.

Lo siento no hay
Número 1
- Buenos días. ¿Hay sitio?
- Sí. ¿Para cuántas personas?
- Tres, dos adultos y un niño.
- ¿Tiene tienda o caravana?
- Una tienda grande. ¿Tiene una parcela con agua y luz?
- No, lo siento. Todas las parcelas están reservadas.
- Bueno, está bien. ¿Cuánto es … ?

Número 2
- Buenos días.
- Buenos días. ¿Hay sitio para un coche-cama?
- Lo siento, está completo. No hay parcelas libres.
- Bueno, no sé qué hacer.
- Hay un camping a 200 metros. Salga de aquí y está a mano derecha.
- Vale, gracias.
- Adiós.

Número 3
- Hola, buenos días.
- ¿Hay sitio en el camping?
- Sí, sí hay.
- Quiero una parcela para una caravana y un coche.
- Mire, hay una parcela libre aquí al lado de los aseos y duchas.
- ¿No hay otra parcela?
- No, lo siento en agosto siempre hay mucha gente.
- Entonces, sí, vale.

Hay que insistir (page 8)

Main aim
Developing skills for coping with the unexpected.

A The students read this item to themselves and ask for any help they need. Praise warmly those who do ask for help and emphasise that this is how to learn effectively. Then ask them to follow the dialogues in their books as they listen to the recordings. Ask them to classify each dialogue:
el cliente no insiste
el cliente insiste un poco
el cliente insiste mucho.
When everyone is clear about this, ask them to classify the dialogues again: *al fin, el cliente (no) está satisfecho*.

UNIDAD 1

Encourage them to draw a conclusion from this: *Hay que insistir.*

B In pairs, the students play read both sorts of dialogues (insisting and not insisting) with appropriate characterisation. Encourage those who can to develop these and to create new endings.

Hay que insistir
– Buenos días. Tenemos una reserva a nombre de Hernández García.
– Hernández García ... Lo siento, no tengo la reserva. ¿Escribió usted?
– Sí, tengo la respuesta del camping aquí.
– Bueno, lo siento, no hay sitio.
– ¡Qué!
– Lo siento, no hay sitio.

continuación, versión A
– ¡Qué desastre! (se va)
– Adiós señor. Lo siento ...

continuación, versión B
– ¿Quiere mirar otra vez?
– Sí ... lo siento pero no tengo su reserva aquí.
– Pero aquí está la carta ...
– No sé nada. No está en el libro.
– ¡Qué desastre! (se va)
– Adiós señor. Lo siento ...

continuación, versión C
– ¿Quiere mirar otra vez?
– Sí ... lo siento pero no tengo su reserva aquí.
– Pero aquí está la carta ...
– No sé nada. No está en el libro.
– No hay otra parcela libre?
– A ver ... hay sitio aquí cerca de los servicios pero parcela no hay.
– No me vale. Quiero hablar con el director.
– Un momento ... Hay un bungalow libre aquí.
– Muy bien, vale.

C The students read carefully the three role-play briefs and ensure that they understand them fully. They write a few notes to prepare what they will say: this will involve anticipating what the other people may say.
They listen now to the recordings made by people in the same situations and, after each one, say how well they coped. They then listen again a few times and note down any good ideas and useful language for themselves.

Hay problemas
Número 1
– Buenos días.
– Buenos días, señor.
– He reservado una parcela.
– ¿Tienda o caravana?
– Caravana.
– ¿Su nombre, por favor?
– Bedia, B-E-D-I-A.
– Ah, sí. Aquí está. Su parcela está aquí en el plano.
– Tiene agua y electricidad, ¿verdad?
– Agua, sí, pero electricidad, no.
– Pero necesito electricidad.
– Lo siento, pero no hay.
– Bueno, adiós. Me voy. (fade)

Número 2
– Buenos días.
– Buenos días, señora.
– Tenemos una reserva a nombre de Gil.
– Sí, su parcela está aquí cerca de la piscina.
– Y cerca de los servicios también.
– Lo siento pero el camping está casi completo.
– Pero hay mucho ruido cerca de la piscina. Prefiero una parcela tranquila.
– Lo siento no hay.
– Pero reservamos en febrero y ... ¿Quiere mirar otra vez?
– Vale... Pues hay una parcela aquí. Está cerca de la recepción pero es más tranquila.
– Muy bien, vale.

Número 3
– Buenas tardes.
– Buenas tardes.
– ¿Dónde está la piscina, por favor?
– Lo siento no hay piscina. Está cerrada este año.
– ¿Y el supermercado?
– Hay una tienda cerca del camping pero no hay supermercado.
– Pero en el folleto dice que hay piscina y supermercado.
– Lo siento no hay. Si quieres pan y leche se puede comprar aquí y hay una playa muy cerca si quieres nadar.
– No voy a pagar 4.000 pesetas la noche para un camping sin piscina y supermercado. Me voy.

UNIDAD 1

D Each pair chooses one of the situations and develops it. When pairs are ready, they act it out and the others try to make helpful and constructive comments.

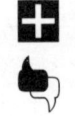

E To develop further the ability to cope with the unexpected, find two pairs which have worked on the same brief and form two new pairs: without any further preparation, they each take one of the roles and role play.

¿Tiene reserva? (page 8)

Main aim
Writing a letter to a campsite.

A Give the students one minute to read this. Then ask a few questions to check that they understand it, e.g.
¿Qué hay que hacer antes de llegar a un camping?
¿Quién escribió esta carta?
¿Cuándo la escribió?
¿Qué quiere la señora Manrique?
¿Cuántas noches quiere pasar al camping?
¿Tienen una tienda o una caravana?
¿Qué información necesita?

Make sure that the students see how the letter is set out (e.g. where addresses and dates go) and how the letter begins and ends.

B Practise adapting the letter orally: tell the class about your family and ask them to adapt the model for you, for given dates. As they do this, write on the board any key words which are needed. Base a Kim's Game on these to help the students to learn them: they study the words, then close their eyes while you erase one or two; volunteers then say what was erased and write the words back on the board, using a different colour chalk.

C For homework, the students adapt the model and write a letter for their own families. Also, as part of the homework, they could learn by heart the model letter. One technique they could use is to cover part of it by laying a ruler across it and to try to provide the words which are covered by the ruler. They then put the ruler in a different position and try again, until they know the whole letter by heart. To test this learning and to give further help, you could present a C-test on the OHP in the next lesson. This C-test consists of omitting the second half of every other word, e.g.
Muy se___ mío:
L_ ruego m_ reserve un_ parcela pa__ tres dí__ a par___ del cin__ de ab___ hasta e_ 19 d_ abril.

D To give more practice with such letters, you could give out, now or later, for revision, **copymaster 1**. The students work on this along the lines indicated, in class or at home.
The students choose one of the sites mentioned in the unit and write to book for themselves, or friends.

¿Qué hay en este camping? (page 9)

Main aim
To meet and understand more key language for camping.

A The students begin by reading this and working out, or looking up, any new words. They each produce a list of the key words and what they mean.
Help them to learn these key words, e.g.
You read aloud the words next to the symbols: the students quickly sketch the symbol.
You define or describe a place, e.g.
Vamos allí para comprar todo lo que necesitamos.
You then offer a choice of two places (e.g. *el teléfono o el supermercado*) and the students repeat the correct one.
You say a place and the students race to say the English translation. Then do this in reverse.
You and the students ask each other, *¿Qué significa …?*

B Look again at the model question and answer with the class and ensure that everyone understands it and knows what to do. You could ask where several places are and invite able students to answer. The students then continue this in pairs.

¿Dónde está? (page 9)

Main aim
To practise the key language of the unit

UNIDAD 1

A It may be useful here to revise prepositions needed for this activity, e.g.
The students mime the prepositions (e.g. left, right, next to, behind, in front of) and you say what the mime represents.
Reverse this, with you doing the mimes.
Some pairs mime the questions and answers, based on the model. The others watch and try to say what the questions and answers were.
The students then carry out the activity in pairs.

B Help the students to learn the key words on the plan of the campsite, e.g.
Each student writes the words in categories which they choose (e.g. *para limpiar, para comer, para jugar*). They compare their lists in pairs and try to identify their partners' categories.
They rank the facilities for usefulness, and again compare and discuss their lists in pairs.
Play a game of Bingo: each student chooses and writes six of the amenities, and you say them in random order.
Present this task on the board or OHP:
Haz tres listas de los servicios que a ti te parecen:
1 muy importantes
2 bastante importantes
3 sin importancia.

¿Hay en tu clase alguien de tu opinión? Sería un compañero o una compañera ideal para unas vacaciones de camping.

Pregunta a ver:
– *¿Son importantes para ti los teléfonos?*
– *Para mí son bastante importantes.*
– *¿Es importante para ti la lavandería?*
– *No, para mí no tiene importancia.*

C Look back at the unit goals with the class and encourage them to assess their progress so far.
Then revise the unit so far before going on.
You could give each student a copy of **copymaster 2**. Then play the recordings below: the students say which dialogue matches each bill. Warn them in advance that there are four dialogues and only two bills.
Solution: 2A; 4B

Camping Municipal Bellavista
Número 1
– Buenos días.
– Buenos días. Quisiera pasar tres días en el camping. ¿Hay sitio?
– ¿Tiene caravana o tienda?

– Caravana.
– Sí. ¿Para cuántos días?
– Tres.
– ¿Cuántos son?
– Dos adultos y tres niños.
– Vale ... Su documento, por favor.

Número 2
– Buenos días. ¿Hay sitio en el camping?
– Sí, señora.
– Somos dos adultos.
– ¿Tiene coche?
– Sí.
– ¿Tiene caravana?
– No, una tienda solamente.
– Vale. Son 1.975 al día.

Número 3
– Buenos días.
– Muy buenas. ¿Qué desea?
– Quisiera saber si hay sitio en el camping.
– Sí, ¿qué tiene? ¿una tienda?
– Sí.
– No hay problema. ¿Para cuántos días?
– Para cinco días. ¿Cuánto es por día?
– Pues, 475 por persona, más 500 el coche y 525 la tienda. ¿Vale?
– Sí, sí, vale.
– Su documento, por favor ...

Número 4
– Buenos días.
– Buenos días. ¿Tiene sitio para una caravana?
– Sí. ¿Cuántos son ustedes?
– Cuatro: dos adultos y dos niños.
– ¿Con coche y caravana?
– Sí, y una tienda.
– ¿Quiere toma de corriente?
– Sí.
– Muy bien ¿y su nombre ...?

Más información

C Further listening activity
The students imagine that they are at the reception desk waiting to be served. They listen to the following conversation between the receptionist and a Spanish visitor who wants to know more about the campsite.

Quieren saber:
¿Hay sitio para cuántas personas en el camping?
¿Hay más tiendas o caravanas?
¿Hay mucho sitio en el camping en verano o está lleno?
¿Se cierra el camping en invierno?

UNIDAD 1

Más información
- Disculpe. ¿Me puede decir cuántas personas caben en este camping?
- Mil quinientas. Este camping tiene capacidad para mil quinientas personas.
- En caravana y en tienda, ¿verdad?
- Bueno, normalmente hay muchas menos caravanas que tiendas. Tiendas grandes puede haber unas setecientas.
- ¿Y está siempre lleno en verano?
- Desde el veinte, veinticinco de julio hasta finales de agosto, sí.
- ¿Se cierra en invierno?
- No. Está abierto todo el año porque es un camping municipal.
- ¿Y hay mucha gente en invierno?
- No, muy pocos. Pero hay gente que viene en ferry de Plymouth. Vienen a pasar unos días.

Los campings de las Rías Bajas (page 10)

Main aim

Discussing and choosing a campsite.

A The students read the brief: check that they understand it fully.
They base a grid on the brief: do this as a class activity and write it on the board, with the criteria (*categoría, servicios, precios*) down the side and the campsites across the top. Each student copies this, adding more criteria of their own if they wish. The students study the information on the campsites and complete their grids.

B You choose one of the sites and, orally, adapt the model to say which one and explain why. The students then do this, in pairs. You could move around, listening and joining in pointing out potential drawbacks in relation to the students' choices: this will provide opportunities for giving practice in coping with the unexpected.

C In pairs, the students can practise booking into the sites they have chosen. Their partners can raise problems for them and oblige them to choose another site and then to explain why they have chosen this one.

D Conduct a quick survey to find out which sites were the most popular, and ask students to explain why they chose some and not others.

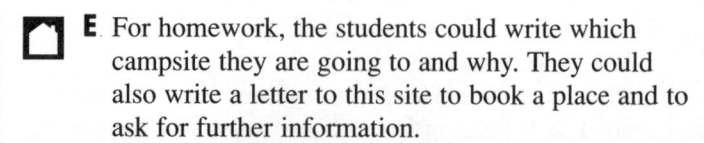

E For homework, the students could write which campsite they are going to and why. They could also write a letter to this site to book a place and to ask for further information.

F Revision of comparatives and superlative adjectives.
The students use the information they have obtained in order to answer questions about each site and finally make up their minds. You can put the questions to them orally or they can write them down, as in the example:
el más grande: el camping Samil
¿Cuál es el más grande?
¿Cuál es el más pequeño?
¿Cuál tiene la mejor situación en tu opinión?
¿Hay uno que ofrece más servicios que los otros?
¿Cuál ofrece más posibilidades deportivas?
¿Cuál es el más caro?
¿Cuál es el menos caro?
¿Cuál es el mejor en tu opinión?

Hay un error aquí (page 11)

Main aim

Developing the ability to cope with problems.

A Give the students 30 seconds to scan this and then ask them to say what it is about.

B Give more practice in rapid scanning: ask detailed questions and get them to race to find the information you asked for, e.g.
¿Cuánto cuesta un coche cama (un niño, una tienda familiar, etc.)?
¿Qué cuesta 750 (500) pesetas?

C Practise play-reading the dialogue. You could play one part and invite students to play the other. Then change your part. The students could then continue in pairs.

D Repeat this process with the other bills, making up appropriate dialogues. Encourage the students to adopt different attitudes and to act accordingly (e.g. timid, calm, angry, insistent).

E To consolidate earlier learning, the students could choose one of the bills and develop a small play, in two acts, around it. In Act 1, they arrive and book

UNIDAD 1

in, quite happily. In Act 2, they get the bill, with a mistake, and the mood changes. After some oral practice in class, the students could write their two-act plays for homework.

F Give each pair **copymaster 3**. They play this in pairs. They will need a dice and counters to mark their progress. The object of the game is to put up the tent and settle into the campsite as quickly as possible. The first person to reach 50 is the winner. The players must throw a six to start and then take it in turns to throw the dice. If they land on one of the shaded squares they must follow the instructions.

Punto información (page 11)

Main aim
To develop reading skills.

A The students use their communication and dictionary strategies to understand this short text.

B Now would be a good time to revise work on the unit so far and to discuss with the class the value and importance of regular revision. You could work on the relevant parts of *Ahora sé* (page 17) and encourage the students to use some of their favourite learning techniques.

Los albergues juveniles (page 12)

Main aim
To meet and understand some of the language needed at a youth hostel.

A Give the students just 1 minute to scan this. Then ask them to report on the gist of it. When this is clear, ask specific questions and the students race to find the answers, e.g.
¿Son baratos o caros los albergues?
¿Cuántos albergues hay en el mundo?
¿Cuántos hay en España?
¿A qué hora se cierran los albergues por la noche?
¿Cuánto cuesta la pensión completa (para un niño)?
¿Cuánto cuesta el alojamiento (para alguien con más de 26 años)?

B Use the text as a basis for a discussion of youth hostels and encourage the students to talk about any experience they have of hostels, in their own or other countries. Help and encourage the expression of ideas, opinions and points of view, with reasons.

C The students study the text and write a list of key words and expressions in it. They ensure that they understand everything in their lists. Then help them to develop their techniques for learning their words, e.g.
Associations: they write one of their words and then, next to it, a list of words which the first words suggests to them, e.g.
albergue: barato, juveniles, jóvenes, pensión, alojamiento.
They could return to this later and cover the headword: they then look at the other words and try to remember what the headword is.

D Give each student a copy of **copymaster 4**. One way of helping them not to worry about new words in a text is to ask them to put a pencil through all the words they do not know and then to try to make sense of the text. There is quite a lot of reading and you may prefer the students to read each section in turn and then ask questions. You could ask them to read the section(s) in a set time and follow this with a quiz. Divide the class into two, tell them to close their books and ask the teams alternate questions about what they have just read. Some of the vocabulary connected with the activities is difficult but the students can be encouraged to guess intelligently from the context, e.g. *montañismo* is a similar type of pursuit to pot-holing and words such as *ornitología* and *paleontología* are very similar in form to their English equivalents.
¿Cuántos albergues hay?
¿En cuántos países?
¿Qué necesitas para ir a un albergue?
¿Cuánto cuesta aproximadamente el alojamiento?
¿Se sirven comidas?
¿Los albergues son solamente para los jóvenes?
¿Qué actividades se ofrecen?

E The class can write to the address of the Spanish youth hostelling organisation given in the Students' Book to obtain more information.

UNIDAD 1

ℹ Background information

There are many youth hostels in Spain all offering inexpensive accommodation to young people mainly, but also to families who would like to spend a short time in the town or city. The accommodation is normally in dormitories and breakfast is provided. Some hostels offer other meals in addition. Sheets are provided at a small extra cost although many people prefer to bring sleeping bags. The hostels close early by Spanish standards: 11–11.30 pm but since many of the visitors are from abroad, they usually accept the early closure fairly readily. You have to belong to the International Youth Hostelling Association. Apart from the low cost, youth hostels are ideal places to meet others and offer a measure of security, especially for girls and young women travelling alone.

¿Qué sabemos de este albergue? (page 12)

Main aim

To meet and understand more key language for going to a youth hostel.

A Give the students just one minute to scan this: Then ask them to report on the gist and any interesting details they found out about.

B Go through the symbols with the class to ensure that they understand and will be able to recognise them at a later date. You take the role of a Spanish visitor asking the student (playing the warden who speaks English) what each one means.

C Give them a few minutes to look carefully at the entry for the hostel in Reinosa without looking at the text which describes it.

D Make statements about the Reinosa entry and ask the students if they are true or false, for example:
El albergue se llama Jiménez Díaz.
Reinosa está en Cantabria.
No se sirven comidas.
Hay sitio para cien personas.
La estación de autobuses y de tren está a cien metros.
Hay que reservar si va en grupo.
El número de teléfono es 924 750 561.

E Now the students can look at the Spanish description to check the information.

F They can then comment on the symbols and improve on them if they think that they are unclear. They can draw them and ask their partners to interpret them in Spanish following the Reinosa model.

G Look through the second list of symbols with the class. Ask them to close their books and show them the symbols on the OHP/board without the explanations. Ask them questions about the information given as if you were a youth hosteller asking for information at a tourist office, for example:
¿Cómo es el hostal?
¿Cuándo se abre?

H After the students have read about some other youth hostels, they choose one and prepare a description of it, using the example description of Reinosa at the bottom left of page 12. They then give the description to their partner who has to guess which youth hostel is being described. They then change over and another hostel is described.

¿Tiene una cama libre? (page 13)

Main aim

Learning how to book in at a youth hostel.

A Give the students just one minute to scan this. They then report on the gist and on any interesting details they picked up. Encourage them to ask for help with any words or phrases they do not understand, and praise those who do.

B The students listen to the recording of the model dialogue.

¿Tiene una cama libre?
- Buenas tardes. ¿Tiene camas libres?
- ¿Para cuántas personas?
- Somos dos.
- ¿Chicos o chicas?
- Un chico y una chica. ¿Hay sitio?
- ¿Tiene reserva?
- No.
- Sí hay sitio. ¿Cuánto tiempo os quedáis?

UNIDAD 1

- Tres noches.
- Bueno, ¿tenéis tarjetas de afiliación?
- Sí, tenga.
- Vale. ¿Me queréis rellenar estas fichas?
- Sí … ¿Cuánto es?
- Son 950 pesetas por persona; está incluido el desayuno. ¿Queréis alquilar sábanas?
- No gracias. Tenemos un saco de dormir.

C In pairs, the students work on the model dialogue. After a while, ask them to write the first letter only of each word and try to say the whole dialogue using only this as a prompt: they keep on practising until they can do this.

D To reinforce the dialogue, play the tape of people booking into the hostel and ask the students to work out how much each would have to pay.

¿Hay camas libres?
Número 1
- Hola, buenos días. Quería saber si hay camas libres.
- Pues … ¿cuántas sois?
- Somos dos chicas.
- Y ¿Cuánto tiempo os vais a quedar?
- Pues nos quedamos cuatro noches.
- ¿Tenéis tarjetas de afiliación?
- Sí, tome Vd.
- ¿Queréis alquilar sacos de dormir?
- Sí, ¿queríamos alquilar dos sacos de dormir.
- Bueno, pues primero, rellenad estas fichas, por favor.
- Gracias.
- Y ¿querías saber el precio?
- Sí, ¿cuánto cuesta?
- Pues son 950 pesetas por persona, por noche, más 400 pesetas por el saco de dormir.
- Gracias, adiós.

Número 2
- Hola. Quiero saber si hay camas.
- Sois … ¿cuántos, por favor?
- Somos un chico y una chica.
- Y ¿cuánto tiempo vais a estar?
- Sólo nos quedaremos una noche.
- Muy bien, ¿queréis alquilar sábanas o sacos de dormir?
- Mejor sábanas.
- Entonces el precio total serán 950 pesetas por persona, más 250 pesetas, cada uno, las sábanas.
- Muchas gracias.

Número 3
- Hola, nos queríamos quedar dos noches por favor. ¿Tenéis sitio?
- ¿Cuántos sois?
- Pues, somos dos chicos y una chica. ¿Cuánto sería?
- Tenéis tarjetas de afiliación?
- Sí, tome Vd.
- Muy bien, en ese caso, serían 950 pesetas por persona. ¿Queréis sábanas?
- Pues no, no necesitamos ni sacos ni sábanas. ¿Está el desayuno incluido?
- El desayuno está incluido, sí.

Número 4
- Hola. Queremos saber si hay sitio. Somos dos chicos.
- Sí, para dos chicos sí que hay. ¿Cuánto tiempo os vais a quedar?
- Tres noches.
- ¡Uy! Lo siento, sólo hay camas para dos noches.
- Bueno, ¿cuánto costará con desayuno y cena incluído?
- Con desayuno, cama y cena son 1.750 pesetas por persona.
- Bueno, gracias.

D Students can now prepare the three dialogues between the warden and the youth hosteller.

Quisiera saber … (page 14)

Main aim
Developing the ability to cope with the unexpected.

A Before working on this, it would be a good idea to consolidate work done on youth hostels, e.g. Working in pairs, one student reads a sentence from pages 12–13 and the other races to find it and then explain it.
Present five key sentences on the board: the students each write a dialogue which contains one or more of these sentences. They could also work in pairs and make up dialogues orally.
Present some word pairs on the board, e.g. *tienda, caravana; camping, albergue juvenil; noche, día; pensión completa, media pensión; cama, saco de dormir; ficha, tarjeta de afiliación; sábana, saco de dormir; cena, desayuno.*
The students explain the difference between the two words.

UNIDAD 1

B The students read this item and ask for any help they need. Then help them to prepare to answer the questions, e.g.

The students put the questions to you and to your foreign language assistant, if you have one.

They practise asking and answering the questions in pairs.

You and the students ask and answer the questions in the class, varying who asks and answers.

Follow a similar procedure for asking the questions suggested in the text.

C The students read carefully the instructions for the listening task: make sure that everyone understands. Then play the recording two or three times: the students try to find, and write, answers to the questions. Get students to read out, and explain, their answers. Clear up any problems and then play the recording again.

Play each dialogue once more and ask the students to report on anything they heard: ration the students to one piece of information each so as to involve as many as possible.

Quisiera saber ...
Número 1
- Oye, una pregunta. Mi amigo y yo queríamos preparar nuestra cena. ¿Hay que pagar un suplemento para usar la cocina?
- No, aquí puedes usar la cocina cuando quieras.
- ¿Está abierta ahora?
- Sí, sí, está abierta.
- Muchas gracias.

Número 2
- Vamos a salir ahora y a lo mejor no vamos a volver hasta muy tarde.
- ¿Necesitamos una llave?
- Cerramos la puerta principal a medianoche. ¿Vais a volver más tarde?
- Creo que no.
- El último autobús sale de la ciudad a las once y veinte. Llega aquí a las doce menos cuarto.
- ¿Dónde está la parada de autobús para ir al centro?
- Saliendo de aquí está a 50 metros a la derecha.
- Gracias. Hasta luego.
- ¡Qué lo paséis bien! Hasta luego.

Número 3
- ¿Para cuántas personas?
- Estoy solo.
- Y ¿te quedas cuánto tiempo?
- Una noche sólo.
- Bueno, ¿tienes tarjetas de afiliación?
- Sí, tenga. ¿Cuánto es?
- Son 950 pesetas, el desayuno incluido. ¿Quieres alquilar sábanas?
- No gracias. Tengo un saco de dormir.
- Muy bien.

Número 4
- ¿Se puede lavar la ropa aquí?
- Sí, la lavandería está enfrente del comedor al lado de los servicios.
- ¿Hay una secadora?
- No, pero puedes tender la ropa en el patio. Se seca en seguida.
- Gracias.

D For the information asked for and which is not in the recording, the students practise asking appropriate questions, e.g.

¿Hay una piscina cerca de aquí, por favor?
¿Puedo comprar un paquete de almuerzo?

¿Un albergue o un camping? (page 14)

Main aim
Understanding signs and notices in a youth hostel.

A The students write the three lists. In pairs, they tell each other what each one means. They can test each other and try to catch each other out.

B The students point to, and read aloud, relevant signs to respond to what you say, e.g.

Llego al albergue con mis dos perros.
Mi pequeño hermano quiere jugar.
¿Puedo lavar la ropa aquí?
¡Camarero! Traiga la carta, por favor.
Voy a llamar a José. ¿Tiene su número?
Tengo sed. Vamos a tomar algo.
Necesito huevos para la tortilla. ¿Quieres ir a comprar una docena?
Tengo calor. Me voy a duchar.
Cállate. Son las doce de la noche.

After a while, develop the responses into some role-play and give more practice in coping with the unexpected.

C Work orally on the notices for Spanish-speaking tourists. Then, for homework, the students could copy the symbols and write the appropriate Spanish next to each one.

UNIDAD 1

D Give each student a copy of **copymaster 5**. They could write their answers in class or at home.

Avisos y consejos (page 15)

Main aim
Developing listening skills.

A The students read the instructions and look at the signs: make sure they understand them.

B Looking at the signs, the students try to anticipate the announcements: encourage them to be inventive.

C Play the announcements: the students decide which announcement goes with which sign, and describe it to you. (There is no announcement regarding the lighting of fires.)

Avisos y consejos
1 Por favor. La noche es para dormir. Evite ruidos después de las doce. De doce a ocho descanse tranquilo. Muchas gracias.
2 Sres. conductores de coche, limiten la velocidad a 10kms/h. Piensen en los niños.
3 Visite nuestra tienda de recuerdos. Recuerdos a todos los precios y de buena calidad. La tienda está abierta de 8 a 8 todos los días.
4 Por favor, deposite la basura en los cubos. Mantenga el camping limpio.
5 No olvide que a las diez de la noche abre una discoteca para los jóvenes de 14-18. Compre sus entradas en la cafetería. Sólo 200 pesetas. Baila hasta las dos de la mañana con música fabulosa.

Ventajas y desventajas (page 15)

Main aim
To initiate and carry through a discussion about campsites and youth hostels.

A First the students have to list the main advantages and disadvantages. Although some suggestions are given, you may prefer to give them a different list and ask them to place the items in order of importance to them, coming out in favour of one type of holiday. The students can then divide up into groups depending on their preference and prepare their arguments. There can then be a class discussion and a vote. There will be more of this type of discussion as the course progresses.

B Speaking practice
The exercise can be carried out in a number of ways:
The students can work with a partner at first and ask him/her the questions and, if there is little or no agreement, ask other members of the class who might be more compatible.
They can work on one list at a time, establishing which things they think are most important and then asking other people in the class for their opinion. They can find out who agrees with them and would, therefore, make a good companion.
The students can work in groups of four. They ask each other the questions and find the most compatible member of the group.

C Listening practice
Play the tape of two young Spanish people discussing the relative merits of camping and youth hostelling. Ask them to note down the main ideas and to say who, if anyone, they agree with.

Ventajas y desventajas
- Este verano voy a hacer camping. ¿Qué te parece?
- No sé. A mí me parece más interesante quedarme en un albergue juvenil.
- ¿Por qué?
- Bueno, los prefiero porque son baratos, casi siempre están cerca del centro y además son muy cómodos.
- Yo prefiero estar al aire libre donde hay flores y árboles y tienes más libertad.
- Pero, ¿qué pasa cuando hace frío o llueve? No puedes salir, es difícil preparar las comidas …
- Sí, puede ser un poco difícil. Pero yo prefiero los campings. No me gusta volver a las once o a las doce; prefiero volver cuando quiera. Hay menos libertad.
- Yo prefiero los albergues, lo siento.
- Y yo los campings. ¡Qué lástima!

D The students listen to the recording again and note down any useful ideas and language they hear.

E If the students feel that listening to the recording has given them more ideas, they may choose to repeat the speaking practice described in **B**, above. In pairs, they discuss again the advantages and disadvantages of campsites and youth hostels,

UNIDAD 1

trying to use the ideas and language they noted in **D**, above.

F For homework, or in class, they could write two lists of the advantages and disadvantages, giving their reasons.

Una tarjeta bastante rara (page 15)

Main aim
Reading and writing postcards.

A The students read this and ask for any help they need. They then report on what their friend did on the campsite. As they do this, give any help that is needed with verb forms, etc. and write these on the board. Using these notes, the students write a brief account of what their friend did.

B The students listen to the recording and try to spot all the new information: they make brief notes as they listen and report at the end.
To help them to prepare to write a full postcard, they listen once more to the recording and then write their cards.

Una tarjeta bastante rara
– Hola, ¿qué tal lo pasaste de vacaciones?
– ¡Estupendo! Pasé dos semanas en el Camping Las Arenas.
– ¿Y qué tal es?
– Es estupendo, ideal para mí.
– ¿Por qué?
– Porque está cerca de la playa y hay mucho que hacer.
– ¿Por ejemplo?
– Por ejemplo, hay excursiones al campo y a las montañas, hay piscina abierta todo el día, hay sala de juego y de televisión, hay mini-golf ...
– ¿Qué tal el tiempo?
– Hizo muy buen tiempo; temperaturas de 30 grados casi todos los días.
– ¿Y la comida?
– Muy buena. Comí en los restaurantes de la costa. El marisco y el pescado son muy buenos.

C In class, or at home, the students design a similar multi-choice postcard for a local campsite, youth hostel or holiday resort.

Radio Camping Las Arenas (page 16)

Main aim
Developing listening skills.

A The students read, and ensure that they understand, the instructions and questions.

B Play the recording once and ask the students to report on the gist. Then play it once or twice more for them to find, and note, the answers to all the questions. Put the questions to several students and clear up any problems.

Radio Camping Las Arenas
– ¡Hola! ¿Cómo te llamas?
– Me llamo Nacho.
– Nacho, ¿de dónde eres?
– Soy de Málaga.
– ¿Y con quién estás?
– Con la familia: mis padres, mi hermana y yo.
– ¿Te gusta el camping?
– Sí, señor. Me gusta mucho.
– Bueno, ¿quieres describir un día típico para nosotros?
– Suelo levantarme a las 9.30 y voy a la tienda para comprar el pan y la leche para el desayuno. Luego me ducho y arreglo la tienda.
– ¿Sales por la mañana?
– Sí, si hace sol vamos a la playa. Si llueve vamos al hipermercado de compras.
– ¿Y por la tarde?
– Descanso. Leo un poco o juego al minigolf. Cenamos pronto, a las nueve y luego voy a la discoteca. Suelo volver a la una.
– Bueno, gracias Nacho. ¡Que lo pases bien!
– Hola, ¿tu nombre por favor?
– Me llamo Angelina.
– ¿De dónde eres?
– Soy de Perú.
– ¿De Lima?
– Sí, de Lima, la capital.
– Estás con la familia?
– No, con un amigo.
– ¿Te gusta el camping?
– Sí, mucho.
– Dime, ¿qué hiciste ayer? Hizo mucho sol, ¿no?
– Sí, ayer fue estupendo. Por la mañana fui a la piscina. Prefiero la piscina. Nadé y tomé el sol.
– ¿Te quedaste en el camping?
– No, a mediodía fuimos al pueblo a comer. Comimos en un restaurante pequeño.

UNIDAD 1

- ¿Y qué hiciste por la tarde?
- Volvimos al camping y por la tarde fuimos a una fiesta en el pueblo. Bailamos en la plaza y fuimos a los bares. Me encantó.
- Gracias, Angelina.
- De nada.

C Play the recording again, pausing it after each question: using their notes, the students try to answer for Nacho and Angelina, comparing their answers with what they hear when you let the tape play on.

D In class, practise asking and answering the questions, with the person questioned answering for her/himself. After a while, this can be continued in pairs.

E Play the recording of two radio commercials for campsites. The students listen, take notes and then make up radio commercials of their own for a campsite near them (real or imaginary). They could record these or read them aloud.

Campings a la onda
- Si vas a hacer camping este verano, ven al Camping Los Caracoles.
  A 100 metros de la playa, el camping ofrece todo lo que se necesita.
  Tiene piscina y restaurante, pistas de tenis y mini golf. Para los niños hay un salón de juegos y salón de televisión,
  El Camping Los Caracoles está en la carretera Santander-Oviedo.
  Teléfono 942 630145. Abierto de junio a setiembre.
- Camping El Molino es el camping de lujo. Situado cerca de la playa y en el campo el camping es tranquilo y limpio y muy bonito. Tiene bar y cafetería y una zona de juegos para los niños. Hay sitio para 100 caravanas y 200 tiendas y está abierto de mayo a octubre.
  Camping El Molino. Teléfono 942 393 722. Llámenos hoy.

Lo pasé muy bien (page 16)

Main aim
Describing a holiday.

A The students read the instructions carefully. They then listen again to the recording from Las Arenas and make notes about the amenities and activities which are available. Discuss these and clear up any problems.

B Put the questions listed to several students and encourage as many as possible to answer each one. The students can continue this in pairs.

C In class, or at home, the students write a description of their imaginary holiday, choosing whether to write a letter or a postcard.

D As a follow-up, each student writes nine essential requirements of a campsite or youth hostel in Spain:
a in April
b in August.

Ahora sé (page 17)

Main aim
To provide a summary of the *Unidad* and a basis for more practice and revision.

A The students can use this now or later to consolidate and revise this key language, e.g. They use another book to cover the page and, very slowly, move it down to uncover the top part of a phrase: they keep on practising until they can say each one after seeing only the top of it. They can also do this working from the bottom up. Encourage them, whenever they have a free moment (e.g. travelling to and from school, in queues, between waking up and getting up) to list in their minds:
a as many words as possible relating to a topic;
b as many phrases and sentences as possible;
c as many different conversations as possible;
d to rehearse making up, and dealing with, problems.
Give out copies of **copymaster 6**. In pairs, the students practise asking each other about the facilities available in this campsite and practise role-playing arriving and booking in at it.
Give to abler students a copy of **copymaster 7** for them to work on at home or in class.
Abler students could work on **copymaster 8**, in class or at home.

23

UNIDAD 1

Abler students who would benefit from more listening practice could work on this. Introduce the recordings, e.g.

Estás en la lavandería en el camping. Allí se oyen muchas conversaciones. No está de acuerdo la gente. ¿Sabes por qué en cada caso? ¿Con quién símpatizas?

Sobre gustos no hay nada escrito
Número 1
- Qué frío, ¿verdad?
- ¡Qué va! A mí me gusta.
- ¿Sí?
- Sí, oye. Ayer salimos de Málaga y hacía 38 grados.
- Ah, bueno.

Número 2
- Hola, ¿qué tal?
- Hola. ¿Qué te parece el camping?
- A mí me gusta – todo muy tranquilo.
- ¿Tienes hijos?
- No. ¿Por qué?
- Porque no hay nada para los jóvenes. No hay parque, ni zona infantil y la playa está a tres kilómetros.
- Sí, entiendo, pero a nosotros no nos gusta la playa.

Número 3
- Oye, ¿vienes a la discoteca esta noche?
- No gracias. No me apetece.
- ¿Por qué?
- Prefiero unas vacaciones lejos de la ciudad y las discotecas. Hay discotecas en todos sitios.
- ¿No te gustan las discotecas?
- Sí, pero de vacaciones, no.

Revision Activities

1 Asking for places in a town
(Libro 1, Unidad 3)

A Play this recording of some Spanish speakers from countries in South America who are asking the way to some places in Spain. The students note, in Spanish, where they want to go and the directions given.

Repaso: en el pueblo
Número 1
- Disculpe, ¿sabe usted cómo ir al banco?
- Sí, sube por esta calle, a la segunda calle das vuelta a la derecha. Está al lado del correo. Allí está, al lado.
- ¿No muy lejos?
- No.
- Gracias.
- Por nada.

Número 2
- Disculpa. ¿Sabes cómo llegar a la farmacia?
- Sí, mira. Sigue por esta calle. En la esquina, da vuelta a la izquierda y allí está a unos cien metros a mano derecha.
- Gracias.
- De nada.

Número 3
- ¿Me puede decir dónde está el Camping Sol?
- Sí, pase por el parque y coja la primera a la izquierda. Cuando llegue a la playa doble a la derecha.
- ¿Está muy lejos?
- No, unos cinco kilómetros.
- Muchas gracias.
- Adiós.
- Adiós.

Número 4
- Disculpa. ¿Dónde está el ayuntamiento?
- A ver. Cruza la plaza, bajas por la calle Santa Ana, y está a la izquierda.
- ¿Adónde me dijiste?
- Cruza la plaza, vas por la calle Santa Ana, toma la calle que está a mano izquierda y está enfrente del mercado. No está muy lejos.
- Ah, gracias.

B Give each student a copy of **copymaster 9**. They read and then answer this. This could be done at home.

C Make available a few copies of *Libro 1* so that students can read *Unidad 3* again and work on *Ahora sé* on page 35.

2 Describing a town
(Libro 2, Unidad 1)

A Encourage the students, when they have a few minutes to spare or when they complete another activity, to study *Ahora sé* on page 17 of *Libro 2*.

B Play this recording of two Mexicans and a Peruvian talking about the town and region they are from. The students note the main points and discuss these, comparing them with where they like and what they think of it.

Repaso: describiendo un pueblo
Número 1
- ¿Dónde vives Marta?
- En Monterrey, que está en el norte de Méjico. Es una ciudad algo grande. Tiene cinco millones de habitantes. No es muy bonito pero hay muchas cosas que hacer.
- ¿Te gusta?
- Sí. Me gusta mucho.
- ¿Por qué?
- Porque hay teatros, cafés, muchas diversiones, la gente …
- ¿Hay muchos turistas?
- No, no muchos porque hay poco que ver en realidad, pero … porque es una ciudad más bien industrial.

Número 2
- Y tú Lupita, ¿dónde vives?
- Vivo en Querétero en el centro de Méjico. Es una ciudad mediana de estilo colonial.
- ¿Cómo es, muy limpia o no?
- Sí, es muy limpia con un clima muy agradable. Es básicamente industrial pero tiene mucho comercio también.
- ¿Te gusta vivir allí?
- Sí, mucho.

Número 3
- Nashy, ¿dónde vives?
- Vivo en Lima, la capital del Perú.
- ¿Y cómo es Lima?
- Lima es muy grande y variada. Hay una parte donde hay mucha industria y otra parte que es la costa donde está la zona residencial. Las playas son lindas.
- ¿Te gusta vivir allí?
- Sí, mucho a pesar de la contaminación que hay en la ciudad.

C Give everyone a copy of **copymaster 10**.
The students read it and then make up similar headlines for advertisements for their home town which they could then send to their exchange school. The following adjectives could be useful to them:
bonito, hermoso, agradable, tranquilo, paisajístico, animado, moderno, interesante, medieval, histórico.
They could then write a few sentences to explain the suitability of their choice of adjectives, for example:
Lo histórico, lo bonito, lo interesante.

York tiene muchos monumentos y edificios históricos: castillos, murallas, iglesias. Tiene dos ríos y muchas calles estrechas y bonitas. Hay muchos sitios que visitar: museos, tiendas, galerías de arte.

3 Describing past holidays
(Libro 2, Unidad 7)

A Encourage the students to look back at this unit and especially to *Ahora sé* on page 85.

B Play this recording of Spanish speakers from Latin America describing recent holidays in the U.K. You may like to draw attention to differences in vocabulary and encourage students to use communication strategies to work them out e.g. *en carro, en carrión* cf. page 60, Revision Activity 1, cf. page 28, Revision Activity 4. The students listen, respond and discuss.

Repaso: describiendo las vacaciones
Número 1
- ¿Fuiste de vacaciones la semana pasada?
- Sí, fui por tres días.
- ¿Adónde fuiste?
- Fui a Gales, al norte, bueno, al noroeste.
- ¿Te gustó?
- Sí, me encantó. Todo estuvo muy bonito. Fuimos en carro y paramos en Chester primero y luego fuimos a un camping. Estuvimos allí dos noches.
- ¿Qué hicieron?
- Hicimos muchas caminatas, nos bañamos en el lago luego visitamos un castillo, el castillo de Conway, me parece. Y de regreso, pasamos por el parque nacional de Snowdonia. Todo estuvo estupendo.

Número 2
- ¿Adónde fuiste de vacaciones?
- Fuimos al sur de Inglaterra, a Cambridge y a Bath.
- ¿Te gustó Cambridge?
- Sí, hay la Universidad que es una de las más grandes y los edificios que están todos muy bonitos.
- ¿Y qué te pareció Bath?
- Me gustó. Me gustó mucho.
- ¿Qué hiciste?
- Visitamos los puntos más turísticos, por ejemplo los baños y caminamos por la ciudad. Fue todo en realidad.

Número 3
- ¿Adónde fuiste tú?

UNIDAD 1

- Fui a visitar Londres.
- ¿Fuiste en tren?
- No, en camión.
- ¿Cuánto tiempo estuviste?
- Dos días. Visitamos Tower Bridge y tomamos algunas fotografías.
- ¿Qué más hicieron?
- Estuvimos en un barco en el río. Fue todo muy bonito.
- ¿Y dónde se quedaron a dormir?
- En un 'bed and breakfast'.
- ¿Y qué tal?
- Bien, con el típico desayuno inglés por la mañana, riquísimo.

C Write several verbs on the board, in the first person singular of the preterite tense. Then start an account of a holiday. After a few sentences, ask a student to continue, using one of the verbs on the board. Cross off each one as it is used.

D Cut out pictures from travel brochures. As students finish other tasks, they pick up one of these at random and produce a short description of an imaginary holiday there.

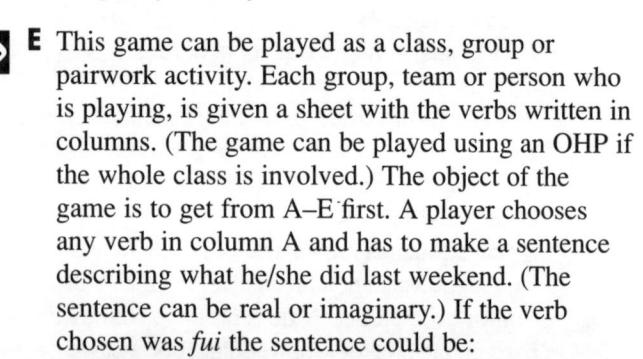

E This game can be played as a class, group or pairwork activity. Each group, team or person who is playing, is given a sheet with the verbs written in columns. (The game can be played using an OHP if the whole class is involved.) The object of the game is to get from A–E first. A player chooses any verb in column A and has to make a sentence describing what he/she did last weekend. (The sentence can be real or imaginary.) If the verb chosen was *fui* the sentence could be:

Fui a la discoteca.

If the sentence is correct, the player can choose a verb from column B which is on line with, above or below, the verb in column A (i.e. *llegué*, *compré* or *salí*). On his/her next turn that verb will have to be used to continue the story and so on. If the sentence is incorrect or does not form a logical continuation to the story the player has to go back to the column he/she was on and choose another verb. Players take it in turns and the first person to reach E is the winner.

A	B	C	D	E
pasé	salí	fui	compré	bailé
bebí	comí	cené	llegué	hice
escuché	jugué	leí	entré	cogí
pagué	tomé	subí	visité	escribí
pedí	pasé	salí	fui	compré
jugué	leí	entré	cogí	pagué
tomé	subí	visité	escribí	pedí
comí	llegué	hice	escuché	jugué
fui	compré	bailé	bebí	comí
cené	salí	leí	escribí	entré

As a development of this, the students can use the different verb endings to play the same game.

F Give out copies of **copymaster 11**. The students answer the questions in English and then write a reply to the letter, describing a real or imaginary holiday.

4 At a service station
(*Libro 2, Unidad 10*)

A Encourage the students to look back at this unit and especially to *Ahora sé* on page 117.

B Play this recording of Spanish speakers from Latin America asking for various products and help at the service station.

Repaso: en la estación de servicio
Número 1
- ¿Cuánto le pongo?
- Póngame cincuenta soles de gasolina, por favor.
- ¿Sin plomo?
- Sí, sin plomo.

Número 2
- ¿Cuánto le pongo?
- Me pone noventa pesos de gasolina, por favor.
- ¿Algo más?
- ¿Me puede checar el aceite?
- Falta un litro. ¿Se lo pongo?
- Sí, por favor.
- ¿Algo más?
- No, gracias.
- Son en total, 120 pesos.
- Gracias.

Número 3
- ¿Qué se le ofrece, señorita?
- ¿Me puede revisar la llanta, por favor? Creo que está un poco baja.

UNIDAD 1

- A ver. Déjeme ver … ¿Cuánto le pone normalmente de aire?
- Veinticuatro.
- Pues está bien.
- Gracias.
- De nada.

C Students should be able to ascertain what products or services customers are asking for. More able students could be invited to be more precise about quantities, and make remarks to the effect that there is vocabulary with which they are not familiar. Encourage these students to try and work out what unfamiliar words mean by using communication strategies, e.g. the meaning of *la llanta* can be deduced from the reference to *aire*.

UNIDAD 2

¡Que aproveche!

Main aim
Booking a meal and visiting a restaurant in Spain.

Area(s) of experience
A – Everyday activities
B – Personal and social life
C – The world around us
E – The international world

Materials
Cassette: ¡Que aproveche!, ¿Qué restaurante?, Quiero reservar una mesa, En el restaurante, ¿Qué hay en el menú del día?, ¡Escucha!, ¿Qué recomienda usted?, Sancho y Panza, ¿Qué vamos a tomar?, ¡Oiga, camarero!, El libro de reclamaciones, La cuenta, Repaso: en la oficina de turismo, Repaso: describiendo su casa, Repaso: el fin de semana en Cantabria
Copymasters 12-20
Cutlery, condiments

Tasks
Choosing a restaurant
Asking for a table and saying for how many people
Attracting a waiter's attention
Understanding a Spanish menu
Asking about the availability of food and drink
Asking for a fixed-price menu
Choosing a meal and accepting and rejecting offers giving reasons
Dealing with problems, making complaints and asking for things that are missing (e.g. glass, fork)
Asking for and paying the bill
Asking if the service charge is included

Grammar
Disjunctive pronouns

Productive language
asado
calamares
espinacas
libre
bistec (poco hecho, muy hecho)
cuchara
judías verdes
libro de reclamaciones
melocotón
menú (del día)
nombre
plato
pollo asado
rincón
tarta
tenedor
terraza
tráigame
vinagre
menestra de verduras
no me conviene
¿Para beber?
pollo al ajillo
¿Qué recomienda usted?
sardina
tarta helada
ternera
traer
verdura
zumo de fruta

Receptive language
bebidas
entremeses
¡Que aproveche!
recomendaciones

Revision points
In the tourist office (*Libro 1, Unidad 4*)
Describing your home (*Libro 2, Unidad 2*)
Talking about your interests (*Libro 2, Unidad 8*)
Camping and youth hostelling (*Libro 3, Unidad 1*)

Background information

Eating out in Cantabria
Cantabria is particularly fortunate in having a variety of sources of food within easy reach. There are mountains, rivers, lush meadows and, of course, the coastline. The fish and the seafood (cod, hake, salmon, trout, crab and squid to name but a few) come from the rivers and the sea, meat (beef and pork) and dairy produce (cheeses, butter, yogurts, etc.) from the herds of cattle, more meat (venison, wild boar) and wildfowl (pheasant) from hunting and a range of vegetables (green beans, lettuce, tomatoes) produced on the small farms.

The cuisine has a reputation for being rather austere with stews (*cocidos*) such as '*cocido montañés*' being common. However, there have been changes in recent years and the range of dishes has increased. The seafood is excellent and one of the best places to eat is in the *barrio pesquero* in Santander where the produce is so fresh. *Parrillas* and *asadores* offer the possibility of eating charcoal grilled meats and fish and roast dishes. The cheeses are made from goat, ewe and cow's milk and are very varied (smoked, veined, creamy or hard). The sweets often reflect the local produce: rice pudding is a common dish in Cantabria and Asturias; other *casero* dishes include *leche frita*, *sobaos* (a type of sponge cake) and *quesadas*.

UNIDAD 2

¡Que aproveche! (page 18)

Main aim
To understand, and want to achieve, the unit goals.

A Work on this item along the lines suggested in the notes for *Unidad 1*, page 12.

B Once the students know what all the goals are, and understand them, you could play these recordings: after each one, the students say which goal it exemplifies. The ease with which they can do this should prove highly motivating.

¡Que aproveche!

Número 1
- ¡Camarero!
- Sí, señor.
- No tengo vaso. ¿Me trae un vaso, por favor?
- Sí, señor. En seguida.

Número 2
- Restaurante Peña Prieta, dígame.
- Quisiera reservar una mesa para mañana sábado.
- ¿Para cuántas personas?
- Para tres personas.
- Vale. ¿Su nombre, por favor?
- Gutiérrez.
- Gracias, adiós.

Número 3
- ¡Camarero!
- Sí.
- El menú del día, ¿qué es?
- Sopa, chuleta y flan o fruta.
- ¿No hay tortilla?
- Lo siento, señor.

Número 4
- ¡Camarero!
- Sí.
- La cuenta por favor.
- Muy bien.

Número 5
- ¿Qué quieren, señores?
- Para mí, sopa de pescado y pollo.
- ¿Y para beber?
- Vino tinto.
- Gracias.

C You could return to this item later in the unit and do Activity **B** in reverse: you choose a goal and then ask students to make up as many different dialogues to exemplify it as possible.

¿Qué restaurante? (page 18)

Main aim
Learning how to choose a restaurant.

A Give the students one minute to scan this in order to find out which goal in *¡Que aproveche!* it helps them to learn.

B They read it again and, as a class, they could work out a strategy for using this item effectively to achieve the learning goal. This type of activity will help the students to learn how to learn, e.g.
Read and understand the dialogue and then the restaurant information.
Listen and say where the family decides to go.

¿Qué restaurante?
Madre: ¿Adónde vamos a ir?
Padre: No sé. Hay muchos restaurantes buenos.
Madre: Ramón, ¿adónde quieres ir?
Ramón: Bueno, me gusta la comida mexicana. Aquí hay uno, Mariachi. Marisol, ¿qué piensas?
Marisol: No me gusta tanto la comida mexicana. Prefiero comer marisco o pescado. Papá, ¿no tienes otra idea?
Padre: ¿Por qué no vamos a Casa José? Hay marisco fresco y postres caseros. ¡Riquísimo!
Marisol: ¿Mamá? ¿De acuerdo?
Madre: Sí, o a La Gaviota. Me encanta la paella marinera que ponen. Y a ti también, Ramón.
Ramón: ¡Sí! Entonces vamos a La Gaviota.
Padre: Vale muy bien. Voy a llamar ahora mismo, 22 11 32 …

Listen again and answer questions you put about the details, e.g.

A Marisol, ¿qué no le gusta?
Y ¿qué prefiere comer?
Y a la madre, ¿qué le gusta comer?
Y al padre, ¿qué le gusta comer?
¿Adónde van?

The students work on the restaurant advertisements. You could ask questions to practise scanning a text for specific details, e.g.

¿Qué son las especialidades de la Gaviota?
¿El restaurante Mariachi está en qué calle?
¿En qué restaurante hay postres caseros?

The students work on the dialogue, e.g. they play-read it, practising all the roles, and then complete it.

29

UNIDAD 2

As a class activity, list on the board the key words and phrases needed for choosing a restaurant: use these to help the students to adapt and extend the model dialogue, first in class with you playing a role, and then in groups of three.

Quiero reservar una mesa (page 20)

Main aim
Learning to reserve a table.

A The students could again scan this item and decide which learning goal it will help with.

B They now read it carefully and make sure they understand everything, asking about any problems.

C Help the students to practise making up appropriate dialogues, e.g.

On the board or OHP, write the questions on this page on the left and appropriate answers on the right, but in random order: the students match the questions and answers in class and then, in pairs, practise saying them to create a dialogue.
You put the questions to the class, and students answer them. Then reverse this, with the students taking turns to put the questions to you: you can vary the answers to show how the models can be adapted.

In pairs, one student could write all the questions, each one on a different piece of paper. The partner does the same thing for the answers. They turn these upside down and shuffle them. They take turns to pick one up: if they pick a question, they read it aloud and then try to answer it, and if they pick an answer, they try to say the corresponding question and then read the answer aloud.

D The students study the instructions for the listening activity and ensure that they understand them. You play the recording two or three times and the students listen, make notes appropriate to the task, and then report back. Ensure the students' notes are corrected, and play the recording once more.

Quiero reservar una mesa
Número 1
- Restaurante Santanderino. Dígame.
- Oiga. ¿Puedo reservar una mesa para el sábado día 15?
- ¿15 de setiembre?
- Sí.
- ¿A qué hora?
- A las nueve.
- ¿Para cuántas personas?
- Seis, y prefiero una mesa en un rincón.
- Lo siento, no tengo mesa para seis. Y en los rincones sólo hay mesas más pequeñas.
- ¡Vaya, vaya! Gracias pero no me conviene.
- De nada, adiós.

Número 2
- Oiga, ¿Restaurante Costa Verde?
- Sí, aquí Costa Verde.
- ¿Podría reservarme una mesa para cinco, por favor?
- ¿Para qué fecha?
- Viernes, 14 de setiembre.
- Sí, señor.
- Prefiero una mesa en la terraza si es posible.
- A ver... ¿para qué hora?
- Las nueve y media.
- No... para las diez, sí.
- Pues, sí, es igual, vale.
- ¿Su nombre, por favor?
- Puente.

Número 3
- Restaurante Cantabria.
- ¿Hay una mesa libre el domingo día 16?
- ¿Para cuántas personas?
- Para siete personas.
- Pues, sí, ¿para qué hora?
- Las ocho. Y quisiera una mesa cerca de la ventana.
- Lo siento, señor, no hay una mesa cerca de la ventana a las ocho; solo a las diez.
- ¿Hay una mesa en la terraza a las ocho?
- A las ocho y media, sí. ¿Vale?
- Sí, vale. Mi nombre es Puente.
- Muy bien Sr Puente. Está reservada.

Número 4
- Aquí Restaurante Peña Prieta.
- Quisiera una mesa para el día veinte - el jueves próximo.
- Sí, ¿para cuántas personas?
- Para cinco. Oiga, ¿Hay una mesa libre lejos de la entrada?
- Sí, ¿para qué hora?
- Para las nueve.
- Sí, señora, está reservada.
- Muchas gracias.
- ¿Su nombre, por favor?
- Puente.

– Muy bien, Sra Puente. Adiós.

E The students use their corrected notes for dialogue 3 to recreate the dialogue. This could be written at home. In the next lesson, play the recording again: the students listen and write any necessary changes to their dialogues.

F Ask the students to imagine that they have lost their voice and have to mime their request in the restaurant. The rest of the class have to interpret the mime in words.
You could also ask questions that the restaurant manager might ask and give the pupils visual clues for the replies, for example:

Dueño: ¿Para qué fecha? [Point to date on board/OHP]
Alumno: El 28 de abril.
Dueño: ¿Para cuántas personas? [Point to group of people]
Alumno: Para tres personas.
Dueño: Y ¿para qué hora? [Point to clock or watch]
Alumno: Las ocho.

G Give everyone a copy of **copymaster 12**. They could work on this at home.

¡Dígame! (page 21)

Main aim

Learning to book a table and to cope with the unexpected.

A Begin again by asking the students to scan this and to link it to one of the unit goals on page 18.

B The students read it carefully and ensure that they understand everything: help those who ask for help to develop appropriate communication strategies.

C The students practise this dialogue, e.g.
Each writes it out in full and they compare these in pairs before play reading them.
You could play one part and students take turns to play the other. Then reverse this. As this develops, you and the students can introduce, and respond to, new problems.

D As an extension to the role-play exercise the students can work out their own dialogues on similar lines. Give the students the following instructions:

Trabaja con tu pareja para hacer dos diálogos semejantes. El que hace el papel del cliente puede decir la fecha, la hora, el número de personas y la posición de la mesa deseada. El que hace el papel del director de restaurante puede decidir si estas cosas son posibles o no, y ofrecer otras posibilidades. Luego, los dos cambian de papeles.

E Give each student a copy of **copymaster 13**. The students can start this at home and practise the pairwork in class.

En el restaurante (page 21)

Main aim

Practising asking for a table and coping with the unexpected.

A Begin by revising the unit so far so as to ensure a firm base for future work. Explain the importance of this so that the students' insights into learning how to learn can be strengthened. One excellent technique is for each student to look back over the unit so far and to write a list of things they have found difficult; they then try to teach these to their partners and find that one of the best ways to learn something is to teach it to someone.

B Work with the class on this flowchart, first as a class, then in pairs and finally individually: the students practise following different routes and see how many different, and sensible, dialogues they can make up.

C Able students could make up similar flowcharts of their own. When these have been corrected, they could be used later for revision in pairs.

¿Les traigo la carta? (page 22)

Main aim

Getting a table, the menu and the wine list.

A The students scan this and link it to one of the unit goals. They then read it carefully and ensure that they understand it.

UNIDAD 2

B In pairs, they produce dialogues along the lines proposed. You could move around, listening, helping and joining in, e.g. by introducing unexpected problems. Volunteers could perform their dialogues for the class.

Mirando la carta (page 22)

Main aim
Understanding and using menus.

A The students begin again by scanning this in one minute: you could then ask them to report on the gist.

B The students read it carefully and ask about any words they cannot understand: help them to develop appropriate communication strategies, including dictionary skills.

C Present on OHT the symbols on **copymaster 14**. To help the students learn the key vocabulary, you could use these symbols in a variety of ways, e.g.
Play at ¿Verdad o Mentira?
Play at Repite si es verdad.
Play at Noughts and Crosses
Play at Bingo: each student writes five of the dishes and you select symbols at random and show them on the OHP, without saying anything.
Cover the symbols and, very slowly, reveal one: the students race to identify it.
Put a list of Spanish and English dishes on the OHP/board and, with the class divided up into two teams, ask members of the class to give the English and the Spanish version of a dish. A correct answer receives one point and the other team is asked the next question. To ensure concentration you can tell them that no repetition of any of the words is allowed, the penalty being one point awarded to the opposing side. The list could be made up of the following:

ensalada	salad
bacalao	cod
chuleta de cerdo	pork chop
pollo al ajillo	chicken with garlic
fruta del tiempo	fresh fruit (in season)
bistec	steak
chuleta de ternera	veal chop
calamares en su tinta	squid (in ink)
tarta helada	ice cream cake
merluza	hake
tortilla	Spanish omelette
judías verdes	green beans
cóctel de gambas	prawn cocktail
sopa de pescado	fish soup
sopa de cebolla	onion soup
sardinas a la plancha	grilled sardines
pollo asado	roast chicken

The translations will have to be jumbled up, of course.
This exercise is very straightforward. This basic list can be added to over a period of time and made more complicated both by the inclusion of new vocabulary and by leaving out some of the translations, e.g. putting *merluza* but not hake or putting steak but not *bistec*.
The activities can be carried out against the clock in teams, pairs, as a class activity or by individuals.
Put a list of dishes at random on the OHP/board (similar to the Spanish list above) with the different headings of the courses (*entremeses, pescado*, etc). Ask them to write up the menu with headings and dishes in the correct order. When they have finished they can add other dishes that they know to the appropriate sections. The sections will be: *entremeses, verduras, pescado, carne, postres* and *bebidas*.

Carry out an opinion poll on likes and dislikes. Make up a list with the class of ten to fifteen items and ask the students to ask five people whether they like the dishes. If students have not tried or eaten one for a long time they will say *No sé*. At the end the points can be collated and the favourite class menu decided upon. The questionnaire can be written as follows:

Plato	Me gusta mucho	Me gusta	No me gusta	No me gusta nada	No sé

You imagine you are describing a dish to your Spanish friends (the class) but the word escapes you. Give the students a definition and ask them to help you, for example:

UNIDAD 2

– *No me acuerdo de cómo se llama … es un pescado … no es merluza … se come mucho en España.*
– *A ver. ¿Cómo lo voy a describir? Vive en el mar. Se sirve en su tinta. Sabe a pescado pero no es un pescado.*

D When you are confident that they are all familiar with the vocabulary, they can then choose a dish from each section and work out the price of the meal.

E Further activities.
The students ask each other what they are ordering. Ask them if anyone is ordering the same as them. For reading practice give students a copy of **copymaster 15**. They could work on this at home.

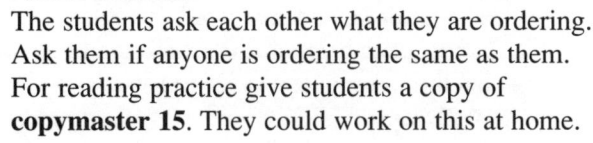

F Now look at the menu on page 22 and encourage the students to make up dialogues to order meals. You could act the part of the waitress/waiter and occasionally make a mistake to give practice in coping with the unexpected. You could also introduce problems, e.g.
No hay sardinas.
Help the students, if needs be, to ask for an alternative and then to select from what is available, e.g.
¿Hay …?
Pues, voy a tomar …

G Give out copies of **copymaster 16**.
The students read the sentences and insert them in the correct place to make the flowchart work. The solution is printed below. They can then practise the different versions of the dialogue.

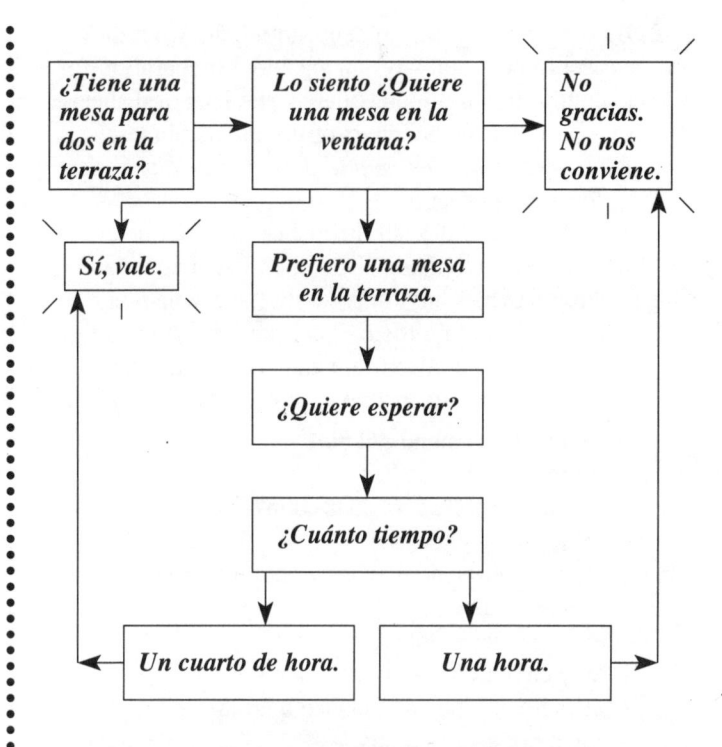

```
¿Tiene una          Lo siento ¿Quiere        No
mesa para    →      una mesa en la      →    gracias.
dos en la           ventana?                 No nos
terraza?                                     conviene.
     ↓                   ↓                      ↑
  Sí, vale.         Prefiero una mesa
                    en la terraza.
                         ↓
                    ¿Quiere esperar?
                         ↓
                    ¿Cuánto tiempo?
                    ↙           ↘
            Un cuarto de hora.   Una hora.
```

El menú del día (page 22)

Main aim
Using the menu of the day.

A The students scan this with one task: to work out the meaning of *menú del día*. They then read it carefully and check that they understand everything.

B They compare this menu with the one in the previous item and practise numbers by working out the cost of meals on the other menu and especially the cost of the same meal as on the *menú del día*. Encourage them to discuss this and to draw appropriate conclusions: you should, however, point out that the size of the portions is not necessarily the same!

¿Qué hay en el menú del día? (page 23)

Main aim
To develop listening skills.

A The students scan this to link it with the appropriate learning goal and to report on the gist.

UNIDAD 2

B Before listening, the students anticipate what they expect to hear – always an excellent preparation for listening. In ten minutes, they write lists of dishes, set out under the headings of the main courses: *entremeses, plato principal, postre*: they make these as long as they can.

They listen and tick all the dishes they can hear which they have listed. They then listen again and add to their lists anything not on them which is mentioned, writing them under the correct heading. They then listen once more and write in as many prices on their lists as they can.

¿Qué hay en el menú del día?
Número 1
- Buenos días ¿Les traigo la carta?
- ¿Hay un menú del día?
- Sí, hay ensalada, sardinas y fruta o helado.
- ¿Cuánto es?
- 900 pesetas en total.
- Muy bien. Dos menús por favor.
- ¿Les traigo vino tinto, blanco o agua?
- Agua por favor, sin gas.
- En seguida.

Número 2
- Buenos días.
- El menú del día, por favor.
- Bueno, hay ensalada o tortilla, pollo o chuleta de cerdo y para postre, flan, helado o fruta.
- Entonces ensalada o tortilla, pollo o ...
- Chuleta de cerdo.
- ... y después flan, fruta o helado.
- Eso es.

Número 3
- ¿En qué consiste el menú del día?
- Bueno, primero hay paella y después calamares y para postre helado de vainilla, fresa o chocolate.
- ¿Paella y calamares?
- Sí, señora.
- Muy bien.

C Play the dialogues again. The students listen and repeat after each client, They then listen to number **3** as many times as they need to transcribe it. Present a correct version on the board or OHP and encourage them to make any necessary corrections. For homework, the students could learn this dialogue by heart and write two variations on it.

D The students imagine they have a friend or relative who owns a restaurant in Spain and who is prepared to offer them a job in his restaurant. On the first day they are told just to follow the waiters around and make sure they will be able to understand the orders. The instructions are as follows:

Estás trabajando en el Restaurante Hamlet. Escucha a estos clientes y escribe en español lo que cada uno quiere tomar.

¡Escucha!
Número 1
- Hola. ¿Qué van a tomar Vds.?
- Bueno, pues para mí, una ensalada mixta y para él una tortilla española.
- ¿Y de beber?
- Pues, agua mineral con gas, por favor.

Número 2
- Buenas noches, señores. ¿Qué desean?
- Para mí, una chuleta de cerdo.
- ¿Y para la señorita?
- Bueno, para ella, un combinado de pescado.
- ¿Y qué van a beber?
- Pues, vamos a beber una botella de vino, gracias.

Número 3
- A ver, ¿qué van a tomar, señores?
- Y Vd. ¿qué recomienda?
- Pues, el pollo es muy bueno.
- Entonces, pues, pollo asado con patatas fritas para mí y mi amigo.
- ¿Y para beber?
- Dos cervezas, por favor.

Número 4
- ¡Oiga, camarero!
- Sí, señor. ¿Qué desea?
- Tráiganos dos chuletas de cerdo, por favor.
- ¿Y algún entremés?
- Sí, dos gazpachos.
- ¿Y para beber? ¿Qué van a querer?
- Sólo dos vasos de agua.

Número 5
- Buenas tardes, señoras.
- Buenas tardes. Para empezar, vamos a tomar sopa de cebolla, seguido de dos platos de calamares, por favor.
- Muy bien. Y ¿qué quieren para beber?
- Sí, dos zumos de fruta.
- Muy bien, señora.

Número 6
- ¡Señorita!

UNIDAD 2

– ¿Qué quería, señora?
– ¿Hay tortilla de queso?
– No, señora, sólo de champiñones, y de jamón y española también.
– Entonces, tráiganos una tortilla de jamón y una española.
– ¿Y para beber, qué querían?
– Pues, media botella de vino tinto.
– Muy bien.

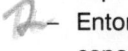

¿Qué recomienda usted? (page 23)

Main aim
To develop listening skills.

A The students read this carefully and check that they fully understand it. They should practise asking, *¿Qué es exactamente el gazpacho* (etc.)*?* and understanding your explanations of all the dishes they ask about.

B Play the recordings: the students make notes of what they are asked to find out. Check their answers, clear up any problems and play the recording again.
The students listen again and write all the different ways of asking *¿Qué recomienda usted?* Check these and clear up any problems.

¿Qué recomienda usted?
Número 1
– Camarero, por favor, ¿qué recomienda Vd.?
– Recomiendo las sardinas.
– ¿No hay otro pescado?
– No, señor, eso es todo.
– Muy bien, pues, entonces tomo las sardinas.

Número 2
– ¿Y para Vd., señora?
– Y Vd., ¿qué recomienda?
– El bistec a la pimienta es delicioso.
– Muy bien. El bistec, con patatas fritas.
– ¿Cómo quiere el bistec: muy hecho o poco hecho?
– Muy hecho, por favor.

Número 3
– Señorita, por favor, ¿cuál es la especialidad de esta casa?
– El bistec a la pimienta, señor.
– ¡Uf! No me gusta nada. Voy a tomar los calamares, y vamos a ver los postres ¿Qué otros postres hay?
– Bueno, hay pastel.

– Bien, más tarde voy a tomar un pastelito.

Número 4
– ¿Sí, señorita?
– Pues, voy a tomar el gazpacho.
– Lo siento, señorita, no hay más gazpacho. ¿Quiere Vd. probar la ensalada mixta?
– ¿No hay sopa?
– Sí, ¿para Vd. la sopa entonces?
– Sí, eso es.

Número 5
– ¿Qué me puede recomendar?
– Bueno, le recomiendo el menú, señor.
– ¿En qué consiste el menú?
– Pues, mire Vd., de primero sopa de cebolla, seguida de unas chuletas de cerdo con patatas.
– ¿Puede traerme una ensalada?
– Sí, señor, sin ningún problema.

C The students listen as you describe a number of dishes, including your opinions of them and why you hold these opinions. They write down the name of each dish.

D The students look back at the menu in *Mirando la carta* on page 22. They use the language presented in this item (*¿Qué recomienda usted?* etc.) to order a meal, working in pairs.

E Give each student a copy of **copymaster 17**, *Sancho y Panza*. After they have listened to the cartoon sequence while reading it, the students listen to Sancho narrating what happened, to a friend. Ask, for example, if he omitted anything or added anything. The students reply and then listen again to check.
Play this oral narrative again: the students note the key words. Then play it once more and pause it in the middle of sentences: the students try to complete the sentences and then listen as you let the recording run on.
The students now refer to the key words they wrote, and to the cartoon, and try to narrate the story. After doing this orally, they could write their narratives in class or at home.

Sancho y Panza
Sancho: Camarero. ¿Qué recomienda usted?
Panza: Gazpacho y Paella.
Sancho: No son platos mejicanos. Tráigame un plato típico de Méjico.
Panza: Lo siento, no hay.
Sancho: ¿Y la gran variedad de platos mejicanos?
Panza: Hay helados de fresa, vainilla, chocolate …

35

UNIDAD 2

Sancho: ¡Viva Méjico!

Sancho: Ayer fui a un restaurante mejicano que se llama Restaurante Tijuana. Leí en el letrero: 'gran variedad de platos mejicanos'. Pedí una mesa en la terraza y me senté. Pregunté al camarero: ¿Qué recomienda usted? y el camarero, el famoso Panza, recomendó ensalada y paella. Pedí un plato mejicano pero no había. Me ofreció helados de fresa, café, chocolate, vainilla pero de platos mejicanos - ¡nada! Volví a casa con mucha hambre.

F Look at the other *Sancho y Panza* cartoon on page 23. The students could read this on their own. You could also present the following joke orally or on the board. Encourage the students to tell any food or restaurant jokes they know.

Chiste
– *Y usted, ¿qué desea tomar? – dice el camarero al cliente.*
– *De momento, nada. No tengo apetito.*
– *¿Y usted? – dice el camarero al cliente de la mesa de al lado.*
– *Tráigame lo mismo, pero con patatas.*

Una palabra conduce a otra (page 23)

Main aim
To extend students' vocabulary and communication strategies.

A The students read this and discuss it with you. Encourage and help them to work out the meaning of new words: you could, for example, use the words in sentences designed to make the meaning clear.

B Present on the OHP sentences with a word missing: the students complete these with one of the words from the list, e.g.

No puedo comer la sopa. Me hace falta una _____.
(Cuchara sopera)

¿Qué hace tu padre? Es _____. Trabaja en casa.
(periodista)

Vivo en un pueblo _____.
(lejano)

Está _____. Creo que va a llover.
(nublado)

Me encanta el campo. Todo es muy _____.
(verde)

Tengo _____. Vamos a la cafetería.
(hambre)

En el bar juego al _____.
(futbolín)

Me siento _____. Tengo fiebre y me duele el estómago.
(enfermo)

No me gusta la _____. Prefiero la música clásica.
(canción)

For homework, the students could write similar sentences to be completed with words from the list.

¿Para ti? (page 24)

Main aim
To understand and use disjunctive pronouns.

A The students work on this along the lines suggested in their book. If dice are unavailable, they could use six-sided pencils with the numbers written on the sides.

B You play the part of a waitress/waiter and ask the students what they would like, e.g.

¿Para ti?
¿Para tu amigo?

The students reply appropriately, e.g.

Para mí, un…
Para él, una…

C Tell the students to look back at the menu on page 22. In pairs, they each decide what to have, and you take their orders. They must use *para mí/él/ella* in their replies. As soon as possible, a student could take over your role.

D Now would be a good time to work on *A ser detective*, page 182.

UNIDAD 2

Restaurante Costa Verde (page 24)

Main aim
Using a menu and ordering a meal.

A The students scan this and link it to the unit goals. They then read it again and check that they understand everything, asking appropriate questions, e.g.
¿Qué es exactamente la tortilla francesa (etc.)?

B In pairs, the students play-read the model dialogues and try to learn them. To help, you could present a C-test version (see page 16) of the dialogues on the OHP for them to complete.

C They practise adapting the model dialogues, with you playing one of the roles. After a while, change your role and start to introduce some unexpected problems, e.g.
Pero no hay arroz con leche (etc.).
Lo siento, pero no tenemos vino blanco (etc.).

D You could mime the part of the waiter/waitress in the second dialogue: the students guess what the mime represents. They can do this in pairs, taking turns to mime.

E To give more practice with the vocabulary, you could use two more activities:
Bingo, with each student choosing and writing five items from the menu. You could refer to the dishes in sentences which recommend, order, ask for an explanation, etc.
Categorías, with the class working together to say in 30 seconds as many things as they can in each category, e.g. *carnes, postres, verduras, entradas, sopas, pescados, bebidas*.

¿Qué vamos a tomar? (page 25)

Main aim
Ordering for yourself and others.

A Before working on this, revise the unit so far, for example by looking back at the goals on page 18 and asking the class to give as many examples as possible of each one: this should prove very encouraging.

B The students read this and check that they understand everything and know what to do.

C Now would be a good time to complete the work on, or to revise, *A ser detective* (page 182).

D The students each write out the short dialogues they have made up. They compare these in pairs, help each other to correct any errors and practise saying them. You could ask those who finish first to act theirs out for the class.

¡Camarero! ¡Hay un problema! (page 26)

Main aim
Coping with problems in a restaurant.

A The students begin by scanning this and linking it to the unit goals.

B Bring into the classroom the necessary cutlery and items that are listed. Pretend to set the table and name each item aloud. Then ask the students to identify the items.
Put a sticky label on one of the items (to show that it is dirty) and ask the students what they would say to the waiter.
Take one of the items away and ask them what they would say to the waiter. For example, if you take away a fork:
Me falta un tenedor.

C The students read this item carefully and ensure that they understand everything. They then try to learn them, e.g.
After some work on their own, they cover up the phrases but leave the pictures visible. You say the phrases, in random order, and they say or write the matching letters.
Play at *¿Verdad o mentira?* and *Repite si es verdad*. You describe a situation and the students say, or write, the sentence which best matches it, e.g.
Me siento y veo que hay una cuchara sucia.
Bebí un poco de vino, y no está bien.
Lo siento, pero no tengo tenedor.
¡Camarero! El mantel está muy sucio. ¿Lo puede cambiar?
¿Me trae aceite y vinagre para la ensalada?
¿Me puede cambiar el cuchillo?; está sucio.
Mira el vaso. No está limpio.

UNIDAD 2

¿Hay mostaza?
Me falta un plato, por favor.
El bistec está poco hecho y pedí muy hecho.

D The students study and practise the waiter's responses. They then adapt these to suit the problems you raise, e.g.

Tenemos un vaso sucio.
Nos faltan las cucharas.
¿Puede usted cambiarme este plato?
Tengo un mantel sucio.
Este flan está malo.

E If more practice is required, now or later, you could, for example:
As a class, list the new words and phrases on the board.
As a class, make up a crossword with these words, on the board, e.g.

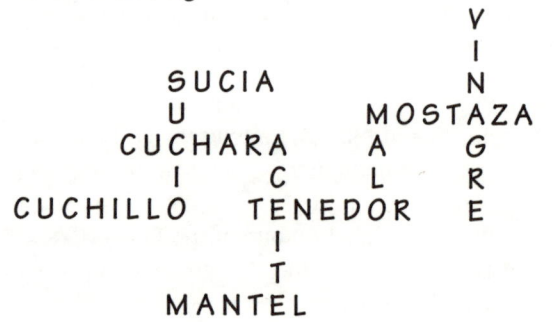

```
                              V
         S U C I A            I
         U                    N
         C U C H A R A   M O S T A Z A
         I         C       A   G
         CUCHILLO  TENEDOR  L   R
                   I        E
                   T
                   MANTEL
```

You start a drawing on the board of one of these items: the students race to identify it.
Write on the board a dash for each letter of one of the key sentences. The pupils guess the letters and, when they do so correctly, you write them in the appropriate places. They race to complete as many sentences as they can in five minutes.

¡Oiga, camarero! (page 26)

Main aim

Making complaints and coping with them.

A Go through the pictures with the class, making sure they all understand them. The students work in pairs: student A complains about an item and student B chooses the appropriate response from the list of sentences provided.

B Show the students the picture cues on **copymaster 18** on OHT and ask them what they would say to the waiter in each case. Then ask them to work in pairs and to put together the customer's query or complaint with an appropriate response from the following list:

Le traigo un tenedor limpio.
Voy a traerle otra botella.
Se los traigo en seguida.
Están al final del pasillo.
Se la traigo en seguida.
Le traigo un cuchillo ahora mismo.
¿Un plato sucio? Lo voy a cambiar.
Voy a buscarle un vaso.

A quickly sketched grid with the 9 squares lettered a-i representing the nine pictures on page 26 can be used for noughts and crosses: students must earn the right to place a 0 or X in a square by correctly saying the complaint indicated in that square.

C The students listen to this Latin American Spanish speaker doing this: they write the letter of the picture which matches each complaint. Discuss their answers, clear up any problems and play the recording again.
Solution: 1f; 2h; 3e; 4d; 5c; 6a; 7i; 8b; 9g

¡Oiga, camarero!
Número 1
– Señorita.
– ¿Sí? Dígame.
– Oiga. ¿Me podría cambiar esta copa? Está muy sucia. ¡Qué malo es este servicio!
– ¡Ah, sí! Disculpe. En seguida. ¿Qué me dijo que le fal … que le cambiara?
– Que la copa, la copa está muy sucia.
– En seguida se la cambio.
– Sí.

Número 2
– Señorita. Señorita.
– Sí, ¿qué desea?
– Disculpe, pero me está faltando aquí sal y pimienta.
– ¡Huy! Se me olvidó. Se lo traigo en seguida. No se preocupe.
– Gracias.

Número 3
– Señorita. ¡Señorita!
– Sí, dígame.
– ¿Me puede cambiar este cuchillo, por favor. Está muy sucio.
– ¿Cómo dice?
– Este cuchillo está sucio.
– ¡Ah, disculpe, sí. Le cambio por otro.
– No se demore, por favor.

UNIDAD 2

– No.

Número 4
– ¿Pero, qué pasa, señorita? El mantel está muy sucio. Cámbielo. Es imposible comer así.
– ¿Qué pasa? Disculpe, ¿qué pasa?
– El mantel está muy sucio.
– Sí, discúlpeme. Ahora mismo lo cambio.

Número 5
– Señorita, por favor. ¿Me podría cambiar este plato? Está muy sucio.
– ¡Ah, sí! ¡Cómo no! En seguida le traigo otro plato.
– Rápido, por favor.
– Sí, en seguida.

Número 6
– Disculpe, mesera.
– Dígame. ¿Qué le ofrece?
– Me falta un tenedor. ¿Me lo puede traer, por favor?
– ¡Ay! sí, claro. Disculpe. En seguida lo traigo.
– Gracias.

Número 7
– Señorita.
– Sí, dígame.
– Oiga, falta aquí el vino. ¿Me lo podría traer?
– Ah, sí, en seguida. ¿Tinto o blanco?
– Vino tinto, por favor.
– En seguida se lo traigo.

Número 8
– Señorita.
– Sí, dígame.
– Me falta una cuchara. ¿Me la podría traer, por favor?
– ¿Qué me dijo que le falta?
– Una cuchara.
– Ah. En seguida se la traigo.
– Gracias.

Número 9
– Señorita, por favor. ¿Puede venir?
– Sí. ¿Qué necesita?
– Este vino huele mal.
– ¿Cómo dice?
– Sí, huele mal. ¿Me lo puede cambiar, por favor?
– Sí, en seguida le traigo otro. Disculpe.
– Rápidamente.
– Sí.

D In class, or at home, each student writes a short play, starting with a customer reserving a table and finishing when s/he pays. They try to bring in as many problems and complaints as possible. Some of these could be acted out and also used for a wall display.

El libro de reclamaciones (page 27)

Main aim
Making written complaints.

A Background information
The *Libro de reclamaciones* has already been mentioned in the course. It is available in all hotels, cafés, restaurants, etc. The books are inspected by tourist board officials and action is taken against establishments which do not meet the standards set by the board. The penalties can be fines, downgrading of the establishment or, in extreme cases, the taking away of the licence.

B The students read the complaints and put them in order of importance. Find out whether all the class agree and compare the opinion of the class with your own: for example, you might be happy to wait between courses but highly offended by dirty cutlery.

C Invite the students to think up some more complaints that could be written in a *Libro de reclamaciones*. You could then read them out and decide upon the most serious and most trivial!

D The students listen to these recordings. After each one, they seek a comment in the book to match it: warn them that there is not a comment for each dialogue and, when this is the case, they have to write a suitable comment for the book.

El libro de reclamaciones
Número 1
– ¡Oiga, camarero!
– Sí.
– El mantel está muy sucio.
– Lo siento. Voy a ponerles otro en seguida.
– Vale.

Número 2
– Buenos días.
– Buenos días.
– Hemos reservado una mesa.
– ¿Su nombre?
– Rodríguez.
– Pasen por aquí.
– Pero reservé una mesa cerca de la ventana.
– Lo siento. No quedan mesas libres.
– No vale.
– Lo siento, pero no quedan más mesas.

39

UNIDAD 2

Número 3
- ¡Camarero!
- ¿Sí?
- No hay ni aceite ni vinagre en la mesa.
- Se los traigo en seguida.
- Vale.

Número 4
- ¡Camarero!
- Sí.
- Pedí un bistec muy hecho y me trajo un bistec poco hecho.
- Pero está muy hecho.
- Lo siento pero no está bien.
- Bueno, voy a llevarlo a la cocina.
- ¿Hay libro de reclamaciones?

E Each student chooses one of the complaints in the book and writes a dialogue to go with it. This could be done as homework.

Rompecabezas (page 27)

Main aim
To understand and use the language imaginatively.

A The students read this and check that they understand it. To demonstrate this, they give as many specific examples as possible of what Señora X likes, and does not like, to eat and drink.

B They work on the puzzle and write the answer, before discussing it in class.
Solution:
Sra. D: Sra. A no toma postre; Sra. B pide pescado y Sra. C bebe alcool.

	A	B	C	D
doesn't choose fish	✓	✗	✓	✓
orders meat	✓	✗	✓	✓
doesn't order alcohol	✓	✗	✗	✓
orders a sweet	✗	✓	✓	✓

C In class, or at home, the students write similar puzzles of their own. They can try these out on each other in another lesson.

La cuenta (page 27)

Main aim
Coping with errors when paying a bill.

A The students read this and check that they understand it.

B Set up an information gap exercise: in pairs, one student looks at this page and another at the Restaurante Costa Verde menu on page 25, and they check that all the prices on the menu are correct, e.g.

A: *En la cuenta, las gambas cuestan 1.200 pesetas. Y ¿en el menú?*

B: *Pues, en el menú también, las gambas cuestan 1.200 pesetas.*

A: *Está bien.*

C The students listen to these recordings of people receiving the bills on this page. After listening once, they say which dialogue matches which bill. They listen again to decide which waiter copes best with the situation and once more to decide which client copes best.

La cuenta
Número 1
- ¡Camarera!
- Sí.
- La cuenta, por favor.
- Sí, señor. Se la traigo en seguida.
- ¿No hay un error?
- Vamos a ver: 1.200 las gambas, 2.700, 3.050, 3.100, 3.500. No, está bien.
- Lo siento.

Número 2
- ¡Camarero!
- Sí.
- La cuenta, por favor.
- Sí, señora. Ahora mismo.
- ¿No hay un error?
- Vamos a ver. La sopa 900, el pollo 2.250, 2.550, 2.600, 2.900 pesetas.
  Sí, lo siento 2.900 pesetas.
- Pero ¿la sopa cuesta 700, verdad?
- Tiene razón. Lo siento señora: 2.700 pesetas en total.

UNIDAD 2

D The students work intensively on the model dialogue, alone and in pairs, learning it and acting it.

Ahora sé (page 28)

Main aim

To provide a summary of the *Unidad* and a basis for more practice and revision.

A Encourage the students to use familiar techniques, which they find effective, to work on this.

B You could also introduce some new ideas, e.g. In pairs, one student reads aloud one sentence from a box on the right: the partner then has 30 seconds to say as many variations as possible of that sentence.

Give out copies of **copymaster 19**. Students work on the dialogues in pairs.

Revision Activities

Wherever possible, make available copies of *Libros 1* and *2* and tell the students where to find the relevant *Ahora sé* sections.

1 In the tourist office
(Libro 1, Unidad 4)

A The students listen to this recording of a tourist in Spain. They note what he asks about and the information he is given.

Repaso: en la oficina de turismo

Número 1
- Buenas tardes. ¿Cúando se abre la catedral, por favor?
- Se abre entre las 10 y las 2 y entre las 6 y las 8 de la tarde.
- Muchas gracias, adiós.
- Adiós.

Número 2
- Buenos días.
- Dígame.
- ¿Cuándo se cierran los museos?
- Normalmente se cierran a las ocho pero los sábados a las seis.
- Gracias.
- De nada.

Número 3
- ¿Qué hay de interés en la región?
- Pues, hay playas muy bonitas, las montañas si te gustan las montañas y se puede practicar muchos deportes.
- ¿Tiene un plano de la ciudad y un horario de trenes.
- Sí, tome, el plano, un folleto y el horario de trenes.
- Gracias.
- De nada, adiós.

Número 4
- ¿Por dónde se va al Hotel Vetusta?
- ¿Vas en coche o andando?
- Andando.
- Mire, al salir de aquí, tuerza a la izquierda, tome la segunda calle a la derecha, cruce la playa y está enfrente.
- A la izquierda, segunda a la derecha, cruco la playa y ya está.
- Sí.
- Gracias.
- De nada, adiós.

Número 5
- Buenos días. ¿A qué hora empieza el espectáculo flamenco?
- Vamos a ver ... Empieza a las 22 horas.
- ¿Cuánto cuestan las entradas?
- Cuestan 1.500, 2.000 y 2.500 pesetas.
- Gracias. Adiós.
- Adiós.

B Each student writes a list of 10–15 questions a Spanish-speaking visitor to their region might ask at a local tourist office. This could be done at home. In class, they put their questions to each other and practise asking and answering them.

C You could present on the OHP a typical formal letter to a tourist office, in the form of a C-test for the students to complete and learn by heart, e.g.

Oficina de turismo

Laredo
13 de feb_____

Estimado señ____:

Voy a pasar qu_____ días e__ Laredo. L__ ruego m__ envíe u__ plano d____ pueblo y un foll_____ de infor_____ sobre l__ región. Quis_____ saber s____ hay muc_____ sitios d__ interés cer____ y q____ se pu_____ hacer e__ Laredo.

Atent_____ suyo

41

UNIDAD 2

2 Describing your home
(Libro 2, Unidad 2)

A Play these recordings of a Mexican, a Chilean and a Puerto Rican living in New York as they talk about their homes. The students listen, write notes, discuss what they have heard and draw conclusions about life in these countries.

Repaso: describiendo su casa
Número 1
- ¿Dónde dices que vives, Patricia?
- Vivo en un departamento.
- ¿Y cómo es tu departamento?
- Es bastante amplio para dos personas. Tiene dos recámaras y una sala comedor bastante amplio, la cocina y el baño. El baño no tiene bañera pero regadera, sí.
- ¿Y tiene terraza?
- No, pero tiene balcón y un pequeño patio de servicio.

Número 2
- ¿Y tú, Ana?
- Yo vivo en una casa no muy grande. La casa tiene tres habitaciones. Abajo está la sala, el comedor y la cocina. La sala y el comedor están juntos – no hay división. Detrás de la casa está el jardín y un patio. Arriba hay tres cuartos y el baño. El baño tiene ducha. Una de las habitaciones es mi estudio.

Número 3
- Lupita, ¿dónde vives?
- Vivo en una casa de una sola planta con cochera, sala comedor, una cocina muy pequeña y tres recámaras.
- ¿Y un baño, claro?
- Sí. Y un baño con una regadera únicamente.
- ¿Te gusta la casa?
- Sí, mucho.

B Each student writes a presentation to describe their homes. When you have corrected these, encourage them to produce a neat and correct version and to learn this by heart. The neat versions could be used for a wall display. Whenever you have a few minutes to spare in a lesson, you could get students to practise presenting their homes.

3 Talking about your interests
(Libro 2, Unidad 8)

A Introduce the recording, e.g.

Oyes este informe en la radio del coche. Habla de cosas que se pueden hacer este fin de semana. Apunta qué posibilidades hay para los automovilistas ingleses. Se interesan sobre todo por los deportes y los bailes.

Repaso: El fin de semana en Cantabria
- Este fin de semana tiene lugar la regata anual de Santoña. Hay concursos de vela y de traineras. Con el buen tiempo que se pronostica va a ser un paraíso para los aficionados a los deportes acuáticos.
- Y el sábado en Torrelavega empieza la Vuelta Ciclista de Cantabria. La salida está prevista para las diez de la mañana y la llegada a San Vicente, final de la primera etapa, a las cuatro y media de la tarde.
- No me lo perderé, pero sabrás por la noche hay una actuación de la Orquesta Sinfónica de Berlín que interpretará obras de Mozart y Schubert. También el sábado, a eso de las once de la noche, en el Gran Casino del Sardinero, se presenta por primera vez en España el cantante argentino Manolo Esteban.
- Cantante, por cierto, fenomenal. El domingo, a las ocho de la tarde, en un encuentro fuera de serie, el Racing de Santander se enfrentará al Real Madrid – un partido importantísimo para los dos equipos, dada su posición en la liga. Pero antes, a las cinco de la tarde y en la plaza de toros de Santander, más que un cartel, el cartelazo, porque torean Curro Romero, Espartaco y Paco Ojeda.
- Así que toros el domingo por la tarde, y por la noche bailes al aire libre en varios pueblos de la provincia, entre los cuales cabe mencionar Ontareda, Liérganes, Suances y Ampuero.
- Para los que prefieran ver una buena película recomendamos Aventura en Australia que se estrenará hoy mismo en el cine Capitol.
- Bueno, y para terminar, no se olviden del gran acontecimiento de la semana que viene: El Derby de Laredo – las únicas carreras de caballos de España que se corren por las arenas de una playa.
- Y me parece que eso es todo. Adiós a todos.
- ¡Que paséis un fin de semana estupendo!

UNIDAD 2

4 Camping and youth hostelling
(Libro 3, Unidad 1)

A Give each student a copy of **copymaster 20**.

B Looking at *Ahora sé* on page 17 of their books, the students copy the phrases in three lists: one for those which apply only when camping, one for those which apply only when youth hostelling, and one for phrases which can be used in both.

UNIDAD 3

Los grandes almacenes

Main aim
Shopping in a department store.

Area(s) of experience
A – Everyday activities
B – Personal and social life

Materials
Cassette: ¿Qué planta?, Señoras y señores, ¿Dónde puedo encontrar …?, La ropa de colegio, ¿Qué te parece a ti?, Comprando ropa de colegio, No me gusta el uniforme, ¡Son las mejores rebajas!, Sí, lo compro, Unos anuncios, ¡La gente es distinta!, El cambio, Su pasaporte, por favor, Quisiera cambiar, Repaso: comprando postales y sellos, Repaso: ¿Se echa la siesta hoy día?
Copymasters 21–29
Information from Spanish department stores (if available)

Tasks
Understanding store signs and announcements
Finding particular goods and departments within a store
Asking for items giving simple descriptions: colour, size, who for
Understanding the assistant's response
Saying you will/will not buy something, giving a reason
Asking for an article to be gift-wrapped
Checking your change
Expressing simple opinions about clothes
Describing a visit to a department store
Changing money/travellers' cheques

Grammar
Superlatives
Further practice of *lo, la, los, las*

Productive language
algodón
blusa
camisa
corbata
cheques de viaje
estéreo
lana
nilón
planta
billetero
calcetines
camiseta
chaqueta
envolver
falda
medias
pantalón
reloj
sección
sótano
walkman
seda
vaqueros
zapatillas (de deporte)

Receptive
anuncios
ganga
gran liquidación
grandes oportunidades
joyería
perfumería
rebajas
super venta
valor

Revision points
Buying postcards (*Libro 1, Unidad 5*)
Daily routine (*Libro 2, Unidad 3*)
Learning about the environment (*Libro 2, Unidad 9*)
Buying food in a restaurant (*Libro 3, Unidad 2*)

Los grandes almacenes (page 30)

Main aim
To understand the unit goals and wish to achieve them.

A Work on this along the lines suggested in the equivalent notes at the beginning of *Unidades 1* and *2*.

B To prove to the students that they can already achieve some of the unit goals, you could say aloud some varieties of the model sentences, using words which they should understand, e.g.

¿Dónde se venden los vídeos (los libros, los recuerdos, etc.), por favor?
Quisiera comprar un estéreo (una lámpara, una televisión, etc.).

Encourage the students to take over and to make up as many variations on these two sentences as they can. You can say that, by the end of the *Unidad*, they will be able to buy many more things, including clothes.

UNIDAD 3

Nueve tiendas en una (page 30)

Main aim
To understand some key shopping language.

A The students being by looking at the title and then scanning the text to find an explanation for the title. Then ask them to scan it again for 30 seconds to find which of the unit goals it will help with: looking at an item, in a textbook or elsewhere, to see how it can help is an excellent way of developing learner autonomy.

B The students read the text carefully and ask about any words they do not understand. Praise those who do ask and help them to develop good communication strategies in helping them to understand the words.

C When the students have read the information about the Laínz store, you could give some practice in ordinal numbers, e.g.

Ask seven students to come to the front and then arrange themselves in the alphabetical order of their surnames (or first names). When they are in order, you say their names and their numbers, e.g.
Primero, John Anthony.
Segunda, Mary Baker.

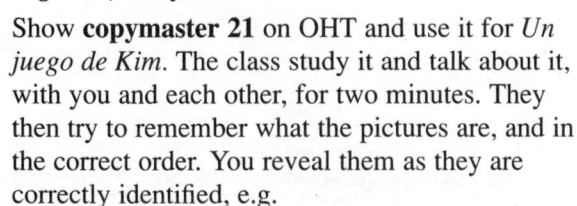

Show **copymaster 21** on OHT and use it for *Un juego de Kim*. The class study it and talk about it, with you and each other, for two minutes. They then try to remember what the pictures are, and in the correct order. You reveal them as they are correctly identified, e.g.
Primero, hay un cinturón de cuero.
La segunda cosa, es una película.

You confirm the correct identifications as you reveal the pictures, e.g.
Muy bien, es correcto. La tercera cosa, es un jersey.

D The students now do the pairs task as set out in their books, saying what they are going to buy and where. As you move around, encourage them to be adventurous and, once they have talked about everything in the list, to talk about other things, e.g.
Voy al sótano a comprar un estéreo.

E You could continue this with the whole class and ask them to say where you can buy other things in the store, e.g.
¿Dónde se venden televisiones (vídeos, libros, estéreos, etc.)?
¿Dónde puedo comprar un jersey para mi hermano (un sombrero para mi hermana, etc.)?

F If the students need more practice to learn the key words, you could use these activities:
Use **copymaster 21** on OHT to play a few games of Noughts and Crosses, displaying various combinations of 9 squares by covering up the others (e.g. 1, 2, 3, 5, 6, 9, 10, 11; 6, 7, 8, 10, 11, 12, 14, 15, 16; 2, 3, 4, 6, 7, 8, 10, 11, 12). Present these sentences on the OHP, in random order. Tell the students that they can make up three conversations between shop assistants and customers by putting them in the right order:
– *¿Dónde se venden películas, por favor?*
– *Las películas están en el sótano.*
– *Al sótano. Gracias.*

– *¿Dónde se venden los jerseys para señoras?*
– *Pues, están en la sección de confección señora, en la tercera planta.*
– *En la tercera planta. Muchas gracias.*

– *¿Dónde se venden raquetas de tenis?*
– *Se venden en la sexta planta.*
– *En la sexta planta. Muchas gracias.*

When the students have written these out and practised them in pairs, they could move around the class making up similar conversations with different students.
Show the students the drawings of **copymaster 21** on OHT. Ask them which items they would most like to buy:
a as presents
b for themselves.
After doing this orally, all the students could write their own lists and then compare and discuss their lists.

¿Qué planta? (page 31)

Main aim
To develop listening skills.

A The students read this and ensure that they understand it fully. They anticipate orally what they expect to hear people buying. After some class

UNIDAD 3

speculation and discussion, everyone writes a list of five things they expect to hear being bought. They then listen and tick the things on their lists as they hear them. Discuss their results with them.

B Play each dialogue twice: the students write what has been bought. Check that everyone has done this correctly and then ask them to find, and write down, where to buy this. Again, check the answers and clear up any problems.

C The students listen again and repeat only the sentences in which people say what they have bought. You could give the class points each time they do this correctly and take away a point each time they repeat anything else. Then see if the students can improve on this score by listening again and repeating only the greetings.

¿Qué planta?
Número 1
- Hola Francisco, ¿has ido a la sección de artículos deportivos?
- Sí, hombre.
- ¿Qué has comprado?
- He comprado una nueva raqueta de tenis.
- Muy bien.

Número 2
- Hola, ¿qué tal?
- Muy bien. ¿Qué has comprado?
- Un vídeo para mi madre. Es su cumpleaños mañana.

Número 3
- ¿Has comprado algo?
- No, fui a la cafetería a tomar algo.
- Buena idea.

Número 4
- ¿Adónde fuiste?
- Fui a comprarme un jersey para el colegio.
- ¿Un jersey?
- Sí, un jersey azul.

Número 5
- Oye Amalia. ¿Qué has comprado?
- He comprado perfume.
- ¿Para ti?
- No para un amigo.
- Un amigo, ¿eh?
- Sí.

Número 6
- Hola Paco. ¿Qué haces por aquí?
- He comprado unos sellos.
- ¿En el estanco?

- No, colecciono sellos. Tengo una colección bastante grande.
- ¿Ah, sí?

El Corte Inglés (page 31)

Main aim
Understanding signs and notices in stores.

A Give the students one minute to scan this and then ask them to say what it is about. When this is clear, they read it carefully and ask you about any words which they do not understand.

B Ask the students to read the store guide and answer the questions which follow. This could be done orally first and then written.

C Pretend to be a Spanish visitor looking for certain facilities. Ask the students (the store assistants) on what floor you can find them, for example:
Quisiera cambiar unos cheques de viaje, ¿me puede decir a qué planta tengo que ir?
He perdido mi billetero, ¿me puede decir adónde tengo que ir?
After a few minutes, see if the students can answer these, and similar, questions with their books closed. You could then reverse it: they look at the book and ask questions which you answer without looking at it.

D The students ask for help in the store and you answer their questions. Count how many questions they can ask, and you can answer, in two minutes. Then see if you can improve on this score.

¡Señoras y señores! (page 31)

Main aim
Understanding printed signs and public announcements in stores.

A Give the students one minute to scan this and then ask them to say which unit goal it will help them to learn. When this is clear, they read it carefully and ask about anything they do not understand.

UNIDAD 3

B Each student copies the signs in order of importance from the Students' Book. They compare and discuss their lists in pairs.

C Write these signs on an OHT and then reveal them, one at a time, very slowly, e.g.
starting at the end
starting at the top
starting at the bottom
starting at the beginning
The students race to identify and say the whole sign.

D To ensure that the students know how these signs are pronounced, and to prepare for the listening activity below, you could ask for information which they give you by reading aloud the relevant sign, e.g.
¿Están abiertos los viernes?
¿Cuándo abren normalmente estos almacenes?
¿Qué hay en la cuarta planta?
¿Dónde se venden las cintas?
¿Hasta qué hora están abiertos hoy?
¿Hay rebajas en la sección de confección señoras?

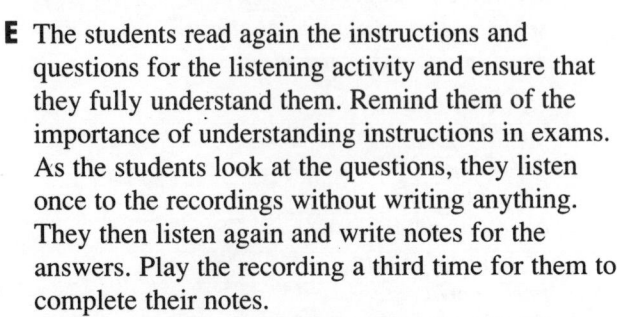

E The students read again the instructions and questions for the listening activity and ensure that they fully understand them. Remind them of the importance of understanding instructions in exams. As the students look at the questions, they listen once to the recordings without writing anything. They then listen again and write notes for the answers. Play the recording a third time for them to complete their notes.

The students write their answers in full, using the glossary or a dictionary to check their spelling. This is excellent exam practice.

Señoras y señores
Número 1
– No olviden que esta tarde nuestros almacenes están abiertos hasta las nueve y media. ¡Una oportunidad más! Les recordamos que los viernes estos almacenes permanecen abiertos hasta las diez de la noche. ¡Aun más tiempo para sus compras!

Número 2
– ¡Su atención, por favor! Recordamos a nuestros clientes que en la tercera planta hay grandes rebajas en la sección de discos y libros.

Número 3
– ¡Atención! Queremos recordar a nuestros estimados clientes que en el supermercado hay ofertas especiales de quesos y jamones.

Número 4
– Un anuncio para todos los padres de familia; en la cuarta planta van a encontrar las ofertas más sensacionales de confección para niños.

Número 5
– Señores clientes! Tienen que visitar la sección de regalos: muñecas de todo tipo, castañuelas, camisetas …

Número 6
– ¡No olviden Vds.! Si buscan artículos deportivos, en el sótano hay una gran selección de raquetas, zapatos de deporte, y mucho más.

F If more practice of this language is needed now, or later for revision, you could give students copies of **copymaster 22**. They could discuss the questions and answers in pairs and then, as homework, write their answers.

¿Dónde puedo encontrar …? (page 32)

Main aim
Finding particular goods and departments in a store.

A Begin, as usual, by asking the students first to scan this, to report on the learning objective it will help with, then to read it carefully and ensure that they understand it.

B In class, then in pairs, the students find the answers to the questions. You could follow this up by asking similar questions for them to answer, e.g.
¿Se venden lavadoras (neveras, camas, mesas, etc.) en esta planta?
¿Dónde está la librería (la sección de confección caballeros, etc.)?
¿Dónde puedo encontrar sombreros (jerseys para mi madre, cuadernos, cinturones, etc.)?
El ascensor, ¿dónde lo encuentro?
La salida, ¿dónde la encuentro?

C To consolidate some of the key vocabulary, you could play a game of *Categorías*. The students have one minute to name as many things as possible in each category you mention, e.g.
¿Qué se vende en la sección de confección caballeros?
¿Cuántas artículos de piel conocéis?

UNIDAD 3

D You say the name of an item and the students race to ask where to buy it. See how many you can do in two minutes and then try to beat this score. To extend this, and to give some variety, you could use **copymaster 21** on OHT and point at the items in random order. The students ask, e.g.

¿Dónde se venden raquetas de tenis (cámaras, películas, etc.)?

A variant on this is for the students to find and say five different ways of asking where to buy the items you point at.

E Present on the board or OHP your shopping list, e.g.
*un cinturón de piel para mí
una camiseta para mi hermana
un libro para mi padre
un sombrero para mi hermano
un bolígrafo para mí
una cinta para mi madre
un par de zapatos para mí
un vídeo
un jersey para mi hermano
una película para mi cámara
un ordenador*

The students write the list in the best order to save time while buying everything on the list. Warn them that they may have to ask at the information desk where to buy some items.

When everyone has written the list, play this recording. The students listen and check their lists to see if they agree. Encourage them to react to this narrative.

¿Dónde puedo encontrar ...?
– Ayer fui al Corte Inglés a comprarme muchas cosas. Fui a la primera planta y salí del ascensor. Fui primero a la sección de confección caballeros y compré un sombrero y un jersey para mi hermano. Luego me compré un cinturón en la sección de al lado. Me costó 6.000 pesetas pero me gusta mucho. La sección de imagen y sonido vende muchas cosas. Compré una cinta para mi madre, un vídeo, un ordenador pequeño y una película para mi cámara. Después compré unos zapatos negros y en la tienda de regalos encontré una camiseta muy buena para mi hermana. En la librería compré un libro para mi padre y al final compré un bolígrafo para mí. Cogí el ascensor y al salir de los almacenes cogí un taxi. ¡Estaba muy cansada!

F Ask the students to draw a grid like the one below. They work in pairs, imagining they are architects and managers planning the layout of the store. First of all the students have to decide which floor each department will be on and then where each would be best located on the appropriate floor. The list of departments can be taken from the store guides used previously in the unit or as follows:

3			
2			
1			
Planta baja			
Sótano			

*librería
restaurante
zapatería
cafetería
sección de confección señoras
sección de confección caballeros
sección de confección niños
joyería
recuerdos
electrodomésticos
supermercado
artículos de deporte
artículos de viaje
perfumería
CDs-cine-sonido-fotografía
servicios*
Ejemplos

– *¿Dónde vamos a poner la cafetería?*
– *En la segunda.*
– *¿Y los servicios también?*
– *Claro.*
– *¿Y el supermercado?*
– *En la planta baja. Es más fácil para los clientes.*
– *¿Vamos a poner la joyería al lado de la perfumería?*
– *Creo que sí.*

These examples will need to be written on the OHP/board and acted out by you and the language assistant or by an able student and yourself.

G Sections of the classroom are designated 'departments', each with a student in charge. The 'customer' states the item he/she wants to buy and

UNIDAD 3

the 'assistant' gives directions to that department. The customer walks there, asks for the item and is told the price by the salesperson in charge of the department. The latter may add, *Pero hay rebajas en ...*, and give further directions. The customer then either accepts or rejects the offer (*Pero no quiero ...*).

A variation on this idea is to divide the classroom into 10 departments each with an assistant who has a list of items and their prices. The remainder of the class are visitors to the store. Each has a list of items to purchase and has to make a note of the price. Some of the items are not in the department that the students might expect. Pens might be in the souvenirs section and sports accessories might be in the clothes section. The students have to try to be the first to locate each of the 10 items and note down the price. They can only ask for one item each time they talk to an assistant. The game is likely to be hectic and noisy but is very enjoyable.

La ropa de colegio (page 33)

Main aims

To meet and understand more words for clothes. Understanding and expressing opinions.

A The students scan this, report on the gist, then read it carefully and ask about anything they do not understand. Encourage the development of communication strategies and dictionary skills.

B Express your opinions about some of the clothes illustrated and encourage the students to do the same, comparing various opinions. You could present some incomplete sentences on the board for the students to complete and then to compare and discuss their answers, e.g.

Los chicos que llevan ... rojos(as) son guapos.
Las chicas que llevan faldas ... son elegantes.
Los chicos y chicas que llevan camisas ... son aburridos.
Los chicos que llevan ... azules son super inteligentes.
Las chicas que llevan ... son sofisticadas.
Los chicos que llevan chaquetas de piel son ...
Los chicos y chicas que llevan camisas ... son más guapos.

C For more practice of this key vocabulary, play at Odd-one-out (*Pilla al intruso*).

Begin with an oral game: the students listen and pick out the odd-one-out. Ask them to explain why they chose the word they chose, e.g.

una falda, una blusa, medias, una camiseta, medias, zapatos, zapatillas de deporte, un sombrero, blusas, camisetas, chaquetas, vaqueros.

The students may choose, and be able to justify, different answers: encourage this. You could then present more on the board or OHP: the students write the odd-one-out and their explanation, e.g.

una camiseta, una falda, una cinta, una blusa, vaqueros, medias, zapatos, películas, medias, zapatos, vaqueros, jersey.

D The students study again this item in their books and prepare for the listening activity. They then listen and make notes about any additional information they hear. They compare and discuss their notes and then listen again to check their notes. They report to you on the information they have noted: clear up any problems.

La ropa de colegio
– Laínz ofrece grandes rebajas en su sección de confección. Para la vuelta al colegio tenemos para las chicas: blusas blancas desde 1.400 pesetas, faldas azules y negras desde 3.300, zapatos de 2.500 a 10.000 pesetas. Para los chicos: camisetas de muchos colores, vaqueros desde 3.000 pesetas y zapatillas de deporte desde 4.000 pesetas: Nike, Adidas y Reebok. Laínz – calidad más alta, precios más bajos. Últimos días de rebajas.

You could make two photocopies of this transcript and then white out different words in each copy. Make copies of these and give one of each to the students in each pair. The students should not look at their partners' texts: they read their own and exchange information orally in order to complete both copies correctly. This information gap technique can be used with other texts.

E For homework, the students could write a similar store announcement, or radio commercial. Correct these and ask the authors of some of the best ones to read them aloud for the class.

UNIDAD 3

¿Qué te parece a ti? (page 33)

Main aim
Expressing opinions about clothes.

A The students scan this, report on the gist, and then read the text carefully and ask about anything they do not understand.

B They work on the item along the lines suggested in their books. Students could first do the activity by looking at the photos and then at the artwork in *La ropa del colegio* above, comparing the opinions in speech bubbles with their own.

C Present colour photos of people wearing different clothes, cut from magazines, and encourage the students to express and discuss their opinions. You could invite volunteers to pick a photo at random, show it to the class and then to express an opinion.

D A volunteer stands up and decides on '*una palabra secreta*', keeping it a secret. It has to be a word relating to clothes. The class asks questions to discover the word and the volunteer has to answer them fully and truthfully, but without using the '*palabra secreta*'. You could take part in the questioning to help things along, if need be. After a while, the students could continue this activity in pairs.

E The students listen to the recording and respond orally to the opinions of the two young people along the lines suggested in their books.

¿Qué te parece a ti?
- En la primera foto me gusta la camiseta pero no me gustan los pantalones. ¿Qué piensas, Luisa?
- Los pantalones son feos, no me gusta el color. Me gusta el bolso.
- Sí, y me gusta el jersey.
- ¿Qué piensas de la segunda foto, Juan?
- Me gustan los vaqueros normalmente pero éstos no.
- A mí me gusta la chaqueta y la blusa.
- ¿Y la camisa del chico?
- Está bien.

Comprando ropa para el colegio (page 34)

Main aim
To develop listening skills.

A It would be a good idea to revise and consolidate work on the unit so far. You could, for example, silently mouth some key sentences: the students watch and try to say aloud the sentences you mouth. In pairs, they could all look at a page in the unit so far and mouth sentences from it to each other for their partners to identify and say aloud.

B The students work on this along the lines suggested in their books. Work on each section at a time, get the students to give you the three pieces of information asked for, clear up any problems and play the recording again.

Comprando ropa para el colegio
- Buenos días.
- Buenos días. ¿qué desea?
- Quisiera comprar un jersey para mi niña.
- ¿Qué talla es?
- Cuarenta y dos.
- Pues aquí tenemos uno azul y otro negro.
- ¿Es de lana?
- Sí, señora.
- ¡Muy bien!
(pause)
- Y necesito una blusa gris para ella. ¿Cuánto cuestan las blusas?
- Son tres mil pesetas. A ver si tenemos.
- Mamá, no me gustan las blusas grises. Prefiero las blusas blancas.
- Ya veremos.
(pause)
- ¡Ah sí! Le hacen falta unos zapatos. ¿Hay zapatos en rebajas?
- No, lo siento señora. Pero hay unos muy bonitos por aquí. Cuestan 9.000 ptas.
(pause)
- También quisiera una falda. Le hace falta una falda.
- Mamá, me gustaría una falda roja.
- Pero, niña, es para el colegio.
- Sí, ya lo sé, pero estos colores no me gustan.
- De todos modos pruébate una falda negra como ésta.

UNIDAD 3

- – ¡Qué horror!
  (pause)
- – Finalmente unas medias negras, por favor.
- – ¿De algodón o de nilón?
- ✓ – De nilón, por favor.

C Play the recording again. The students listen and repeat only expressions of opinion. Repeat this, with the students repeating only information about prices.

D The students listen to this recording of the girl narrating her shopping trip to a friend. Whenever they hear an error, they stop you and correct the error.

No me gusta el uniforme

– Ayer fui con mi madre a los grandes almacenes. ¡Qué desastre! Primero pidió una blusa gris. ¡Qué fea! Yo dije que no, que prefiero las blusas blancas y finalmente me compró una blanca. Luego me compré un jersey de algodón. Es azul y me gusta bastante. Fuimos a comprar zapatos pero costaban demasiado, 30.000 pesetas. Yo quería una falda roja y mi madre insistió: una falda negra o nada y yo dije que nada. Pero compró la falda negra. Finalmente me compró unas medias negras de nilón. No me gusta el uniforme y esos colores son muy, muy aburridos.

E For homework, the students imagine a clothes shopping list with a parent. They can write this either as a dialogue or as a narrative.

Quisiera comprar (page 34)

Main aim

Shopping for clothes, giving clear descriptions and coping with problems.

A The students scan this, report on the gist, read it carefully and check that they understand everything.

B In class, and then in pairs, they practise adapting the model dialogue. During the classwork, show how changing the item of clothing (e.g to *una falda, medias*) necessitates changes throughout the dialogue (e.g. to adjectives, verbs and pronouns).

C Present **copymaster 23** on OHT. You could colour the clothes. In class, and then in pairs, the students make up dialogues based on these pictures. After a while, ask students to write two or three dialogues. When you have corrected these, volunteers can read a few aloud and the others match each dialogue to the relevant picture.

El uniforme (copymasters 24 and 25)

Main aim

Understanding and writing letters.

A Give each student a copy of **copymaster 24**. The students scan the letter for the gist, then read it carefully and check that they understand everything.

B They read it again and copy from it the words for any clothes they are wearing at the moment. They then do the same activity and copy the words for clothes which they wear at the weekend. They compare and discuss their lists.

C Adapt orally the paragraph in which David describes his uniform to describe what you are wearing. Then ask a few students to do this. They can also describe what their brothers and sisters wear to school, adapting the paragraph about Ana. Each student could then write these descriptions.

D Students write Juan's reply to David. This could be done at home. The corrected versions of this letter could make an interesting wall display.

E Give each student a copy of **copymaster 25**. The students read this carefully and decide which opinions are for uniforms and which are against. You could read each one aloud and the students could decide, as a class, whether it is for or against. They then write the opinions in two lists – for and against – putting them in order of importance in each list. Encourage those who can to add more opinions of their own – for or against.
With able students, you could base a class debate on these opinions.

51

UNIDAD 3

¡Son las mejores rebajas! (page 34)

Main aim
To understand and use superlatives.

A Now would be a good time to revise the unit so far. The students could look at the unit goals, say which they have done, and give examples of each. For further practice, where it is needed, you could use the following activities:
On the OHP write 10–15 words and phrases which the students should know. Practise these for one minute and then cover them up. In pairs, the students try to write them all.
You could read aloud a key sentence which appears in the Students' Book in the unit so far. The students race to find it and to say the page number. You could ask for an explanation of the sentences. After a while, this could be continued in pairs. Both these activities could be used to revise in other units.

B The students scan this item, report on the gist and then read it carefully and check that they understand it fully.

C Show pictures of items taken from a store guide or a magazine. Show them two or three types of watches, for example, and ask them which is the most elegant, expensive, practical, etc. Do the same for other articles.
Ask them to look at the descriptions given in the Students' Book. How might they describe each item? For example:

el reloj – es el más elegante/moderno
el paraguas – es el más práctico
el Seat – es el más barato
el Rolls Royce – es el más caro.

D The students ask each other the questions which accompany the pictures of the watches. They make a note of their choices. Ask the class which they prefer and see whether they agree and, if not, whether they can give reasons for their preference, for example:

Prefiero un reloj más moderno.
No me gustan los relojes elegantes.

E Play this recording to the students and elicit their opinion on the purchase, e.g.
¿Qué reloj te gusta más? ¿Por qué?

¡Son las mejores rebajas!
– ¿Puede Vd. mostrarme algunos relojes?
– Sí, señor. Tengo tres distintos: El primero es el más moderno y resulta muy económico y es el más barato. Vale 6.000 pesetas. El segundo es el más elegante: vale 10.000 pesetas solamente, una verdadera ganga. El tercero es el más caro: vale 70.000 pesetas. Es el más lujoso.
– Me gusta más el segundo.
– ¿Lo quiere Vd.?
– Sí, lo compro.
– Hay que pagar en caja.

F Give each student a copy of **copymaster 26**. They could research and answer the questions for homework.

¡Sí, lo compro! (page 35)

Main aim
Using superlatives in a shopping context.

A The students scan this quickly and report on its gist. They then read it carefully and ensure that they understand everything.

B The students listen to these dialogues and match each one to one of the pictures on the page (this includes the items with no labels). Clear up any problems and establish which pictures have no dialogue. The students' task now is to write similar dialogues to match two of these pictures: to help them in this, they listen again to the recording and make notes of any useful expressions.

¡Sí, lo compro!
Número 1
– Buenos días. Quisiera comprar una cámara.
– Sí, señor. Hay tres aquí en las rebajas.
– Quiero una cámara barata para mi hijo.
– Esta vale 8.000 pesetas. Es la mejor rebaja.
– Muy bien, la compro: ¿8.000?
– Sí. ¿Quiere usted pagar en caja?

Número 2
– ¿Se venden billeteros aquí?
– Sí, señora.
– ¿Cuánto cuestan?

- Depende. Hay de 2.000, 2.500 y 5.000.
- Es un regalo para mi marido.
- Son todos de buena calidad.
- Voy a comprar el billetero de 5.000.
- Muy bien.

Número 3
- Quisiera comprar un estéreo.
- Muy bien. Hay un modelo aquí con CD, radio y casete.
- ¿Cuánto es?
- 60.000.
- ¿Tiene uno más barato?
- El más barato vale 35.000.
- ¿Tiene CD?
- Sí.
- Bueno, lo compro.
- Muy bien.

Número 4
- Quisiera comprar un bolso.
- Cómo quiere el bolso, ¿grande o pequeño?
- Grande.
- ¿De plástico o de piel?
- De nilón, por favor.
- Aquí hay uno.
- ¿Cuánto vale?
- 3.500.
- ¿Lo tiene en negro?
- Sí.
- Me quedo con éste. Gracias.

C After you have corrected their dialogues and cleared up any problems, the students act them out in pairs, taking turns to play each role. The class then creates a model dialogue on the board, as a co-operative exercise. Practise play reading and acting this, then remove two words and continue to say the whole dialogue, then remove two more words and so on, until the dialogue has disappeared and the class can still say it all.

D The students make up labels to advertise the items at the bottom of the page. Do two or three as a class.

E If more practice is required, either now or later for revision, you could use these activities:
You describe any item on the page and eventually say something which does not match the item, or describe something which is not there. The students then stop you and correct you. They can continue this in pairs.

Give each student in a pair one part of **copymaster 27**. The students use this to practise role play, including important practice in coping with the unexpected.

¿Lo envuelvo? (page 36)

Main aim
Asking for an article to be gift wrapped.

A The students scan this, report on the gist and then read it carefully and ensure that they understand it.

B Use the pictures here, and those on **copymaster 21**, to practise the language of asking for an article to be gift wrapped. This will provide opportunities to use the full range of object pronouns, e.g.
Envuélvala, por favor.
No hace falta envolverlos.

After some practice, set the class the target of asking correctly for 10 items to be gift wrapped, then repeat this with declining an offer to gift wrap.

C Now would be a good time to work on pronouns, on page 184 in *A ser detective*.

D Return to *¿Lo envuelvo?* As a cooperative exercise, the class produces a model dialogue on the board, e.g.
- *Me gustan mucho estos zapatos. Los compro.*
- *¿Los envuelvo?*
- *No, no hace falta envolverlos. Gracias.*
- *Pues, hay que pagarlos en caja.*

Practise adapting this to buy other items which involve a range of pronouns. After some classwork on this, the students continue in pairs.

E This listening activity does not appear in the Students' Book. Give the students the following introduction:
Algunas veces es divertido ver cómo unas personas son distintas de otras. En los almacenes escuchas por casualidad a cuatro clientes bastante distintos. Escucha la cinta para decidir: cuál es cortés, cuál está de mal humor, cuál es muy difícil y cuál tiene mucha prisa. Después de escuchar a cada uno, di a tu profesor(a) cómo te parece la persona.

UNIDAD 3

¡La gente es distinta!

Número 1
- Buenos días.
- Buenos días, señora.
- Necesito una blusa de seda.
- Sí, ¿para Vd.?
- Sí, es para mí.
- ¿Qué talla?
- La 42.
- ¿De qué color?
- Rojo.
- Aquí tiene.
- No es rojo; sí, es casi amarillo.
- Sí, ¡qué color más bonito!
- De todos modos, me va bien. Me la llevo.
- ¿Se lo envuelvo como regalo?
- No, gracias.
- Hay que pagar en caja.

Número 2
- ¿Dónde puedo encontrar unos zapatos marrones de cuero?
- Pues, aquí, en esta sección.
- ¡Claro que en esta sección! ¡No soy idiota! ¿Dónde exactamente en esta sección?
- Aquí mismo, señor.
- ¿Y qué número son?
- El 44. ¿Son para Vd.?
- ¡Claro que son para mí! ¿Para quién van a ser si no?
- Son muy elegantes.
- ¡Ah! Por fin. Son muy cómodos. Me los llevo.
- Pague en caja, por favor.

Número 3
- Oiga. ¿Tiene un monedero?
- Sí, éstos son los más populares…
- Tengo prisa. Es para mi amiga. ¿Cuánto es?
- Dos mil pesetas.
- Sí, vale. Tenga. No hace falta que lo envuelva.
- Adiós.

Número 4
- Perdone, señor.
- Dígame.
- Por favor, ¿se venden aquí recuerdos de la ciudad? Son para mis padres, ¿sabe Vd.?
- Sí, ¿le interesan estos billeteros? Son muy bonitos.
- Oh, es Vd. muy amable. Sí, son perfectos. Muchas gracias. Voy a comprar éste para mi padre.
- ¿Se lo envuelvo?
- Sí, ¿puede Vd. envolvérmelo? Otra vez, muchísimas gracias. Adiós, señor.

¡Cuidado con el cambio! (page 37)

Main aims
Paying and checking change.
Describing a visit to a department store.

A This section incorporates revision of numbers with checking one's change. It may be advisable to revise the high numbers quickly before doing the excercise.
Mental arithmetic: *Seiscientos por tres son …*

Una subasta
Auction something in the classroom, starting the bidding at 1,000 pesetas and asking for bids of 50 pesetas more each time. Divide the class into two teams. The first team to make an incorrect bid loses the amount bid. The team with the most money at the end wins.

Write a number on the blackboard and ask for another number and then another. Each time ask anyone if they can say the number. See how many numbers the class can cope with, for example:

3 *tres*
34 *treinta y cuatro*
347 *trescientos cuarenta y siete*
3471 *tres mil cuatrocientos setenta y uno*
34719 *treinta y cuatro mil setecientos diecinueve*

Note: It is worth persevering with exercises of this type.

Bingo
Using all the numbers appearing on the bills, the students choose five and write them down on a piece of paper. You call them out.

Background information
All the receipts are based on original receipts from branches of the Corte Inglés in Madrid (Princesa) and Barcelona. The receipts always show the department, the cost, the change to be given and the method of payment. The word *efectivo* (cash) is used instead of *dinero* and the assistant often says, *¿Quiere pagar en efectivo?*

B First the students read the dialogue and the first bill; they then look at the other bills and produce dialogues, some of which contain calculation mistakes (as in the example dialogue) and others which don't. The partner who plays the role of the customer must try to work out whether the change given is correct or not.

C You imagine a shopping trip. The students ask you questions to find out as much about it as possible, e.g. when, where, what you bought, the cost, any problems. They take notes about your answers. You then give an oral narrative of your shopping trip. You make an occasional factual error: the students aim to spot, and correct, all of these.

D Able students could write narratives of their own, based on the bills in this item.

Sancho y Panza (page 38)

Main aim

To use language imaginatively.
You may prefer to wait to look at the cartoon with the students until after you have looked at the following activities on changing money.

A Give the students a minute to read this.

B Individually or in pairs, they change the text making up their own dialogues. Ask students to read out their own versions: the others listen, eyes closed, and try to imagine the scenes.

El cambio (page 38)

Main aims

Changing money and travellers cheques.
Understanding and producing narratives.

A The students scan this and link it to the appropriate learning goal on page 30. They then read it carefully and ask about anything they do not understand.

B Give the students three minutes to study this information and then base a *¿Verdad o mentira?* quiz on it: they repeat what is true and correct what is wrong, e.g.

Se puede cambiar dinero para el teléfono.
Para cambiar cheques de viaje, necesitas tu pasaporte.
Es fácil cambiar dinero en el Corte Inglés.
El cambio está abierto todo el día.
Se cambian monedas pero no cambian billetes.

C Check that the students all understand the useful expressions listed. They then choose the most suitable caption for each photo. They could do this orally first and then write it.
To give more practice, you could say some variations of these sentences and the students say, or write, the number of the picture which matches each one, e.g.

¿Dónde puedo cambiar cheques de viaje?
Quisiera cambiar dinero (50 libras esterlinas, 100 dólares, etc.)
¿Puede usted darme unos billetes de 500 pesetas (unas monedas de 100 pesetas, etc.)?

D Each student writes a list of the 10 most useful words for changing money. They compare their lists and try to agree on a joint list of 10. Two pairs can then compare, and justify, their lists.
  To test the lists, ask the students to make up dialogues which use them all and which are in line with a brief which you present orally or on the board, e.g.

Quieres cambiar cheques de viaje para 50 libras esterlinas. Necesitarás tu pasaporte. Quieres unos billetes de 500 pesetas y unas monedas de 100 pesetas.

E The students listen to this recording of someone narrating a visit to a *cambio*. They note the number of the picture which best matches each part of the narrative. Play it again and ask students to say the numbers of the relevant photos. Clear up any problems and play the recording again: encourage the students to make notes of any useful words and expressions.

El cambio

– En el Corte Inglés fui a cambiar unos cheques de viaje. (photo 3)
  Pregunté dónde estaba el cambio y me indicaron el ascensor y el número de la planta. (2)
  Subí y pregunté otra vez dónde estaba el cambio. (1)
  Cambié cien libras esterlinas en pesetas y pedí unos billetes de mil porque es difícil si sólo tienes billetes de cinco o diez mil. (4)
  Me cambiaron en monedas de cien porque quería llamar por teléfono. (5)
  Firmé el formulario y me fui a comprar unos regalos. (6)

UNIDAD 3

F For homework, the students write a playlet or a narrative based on these photos.

Su pasaporte, por favor (page 39)

Main aim
To develop listening skills.

A The students scan this, report on the gist and then read it carefully and ensure that they understand it.

B The students speculate orally about sentences they expect to hear. After some discussion of these, each student writes five which s/he expects to hear. They then listen and tick their sentences as they hear them: ask all those who have ticked five to read them aloud.

Su pasaporte, por favor
Número 1
- Buenos días, quisiera cambiar unos cheques de viaje.
- Vale, ¿cuánto quiere cambiar?
- 50 libras. ¿A cuánto está la libra hoy?
- A 195 pesetas.
- Vale.
- Su pasaporte, por favor ... ¿Quiere firmar aquí ...?

Número 2
- Buenos días, quisiera cambiar cien libras.
- Muy bien. Son 19.000 pesetas.
- ¿Tiene billetes de mil?
- Sí, por supuesto.
- Gracias.

Número 3
- Buenos días.
- Buenos días.
- Quisiera cambiar unos cheques de viaje.
- ¿Cuánto?
- 75 libras.
- Su pasaporte, por favor.
- Sí ... ¿Tiene monedas de cien?
- Lo siento, de momento no. ¿Quiere volver más tarde?
- Vale.

C The students now check again the information they need to find out, and listen again, making notes. Ask students to report back on the information they have found out.

D Then play number 3 as many times as necessary for the students to transcribe it: they could do this in pairs, with one transcribing the customer's lines and the other the clerk's lines. They use these to act out the dialogue. When they have done this, they practise adapting it: encourage them to introduce, and to practise coping with, the unexpected.

Quisiera cambiar (page 39)

Main aim
Changing money and coping with the unexpected.

A Before working on this, revise with the class the previous two items, e.g.
Read a dialogue, or relate a narrative, and stop occasionally before a key word or phrase: the students try to continue orally or in writing.
  Describe a situation involving someone changing a traveller's cheque: the students draw pictures to illustrate your description. They compare these. Ask some able students to use their pictures to describe the situation to you: you then draw a picture on the OHP.

B Work on this item along the lines suggested.

Quisiera cambiar
Ejemplo:
- Buenos días, quisiera cambiar unos cheques de viaje.
- Sí, ¿Cuántos?
- 150 libras.
- Muy bien. Su pasaporte por favor.
- Aquí tiene. ¿Puede usted darme billetes de 5.000, por favor?
- Sí, señor. Firme aquí, por favor.
- Gracias, adiós.

C As students complete **B**, give them a copy of **copymaster 28**. They match each text to the appropriate summary; they then choose the best title for the texts, and they finally compete the sentences with information taken from the texts.

Fui de compras (page 40)

Main aim

To understand and write letters, including narratives.

A As usual, the students begin by scanning this, reporting on the gist, then reading it carefully and ensuring that they understand it.

B You adapt the letter orally to describe a recent shopping trip you made. The students listen, write notes and then report back on what you did. You correct any errors and clear up any problems.

C In class, or at home, the students each answer the letter, using as much as possible from the stimulus letter.

Una palabra conduce a otra (page 40)

Main aim

To develop communication strategies.

A Work on this along lines which have previously proved successful.

B The students could take part in a team game, finding more words which follow this pattern. They could use dictionaries to do this.

C You could present some sentences with similar words in. The students use their communication strategies to work out what these mean, e.g.

Si no sé la definición de una palabra busco en un diccionario.
La estación está muy cerca.
La participación de los espectadores fue tremenda.
No es auténtico – es cuero de imitación.
Las negociaciones terminaron a las dos de la madrugada.

D Present more sentences which the students can complete with one of the words in this list, e.g.

1 *La ... en el brazo le dolió mucho.*
2 *Fue a la oficina de turismo a buscar ... sobre los grandes almacenes.*
3 *Compró una corbata en la ... de caballeros.*
4 *Tiene una ... de más de cinco mil.*
5 *Compró el reloj pero no leyó las ...*
6 *Dejó sus maletas en la r... del hotel.*
7 *Cuando habló a los policías dio una ... muy completa del reloj que había perdido.*
8 *La ... en los colegios españoles es muy diferente.*

Ahora sé (page 41)

Main aim

To provide a summary of the *Unidad* and a basis for more practice and revision.

A Work on this along lines which have previously proved successful.

B Other activities which you could use include, e.g. You begin a chain, e.g.

Fui a los grandes almacenes y compré unas zapatillas de deporte.

A student takes this up and extends it, e.g.

El/la profesor(a) fue a los grandes almacenes y compró unas zapatillas de deporte. Yo fui al mercado y compré un jersey de lana.

See how long a chain can be produced.
Use any text from the *Unidad* which your students need more work on. Make two photocopies and white out different words in each one. Without looking at their partners' texts, they exchange information orally and both try to produce complete texts.
Present this on the board or OHP for students to work on in pairs:

Quieres comprar regalos para miembros de tu familia. Mira lo que dices cuando hablas con tu amigo español (tu pareja) sobre un regalo para tu padre:

Tú: Tengo que comprar un regalo para mi padre.
Tu pareja: ¿Qué vas a comprar para él?
Tú: Pues, un billetero.
Tu pareja: Vamos a la sección de regalos entonces.

Prepara diálogos con tu pareja para comprar regalos para tu familia (hermano, madre y abuelos) cambiando las palabras subrayadas.

UNIDAD 3

Revision Activities

1 Buying postcards and stamps
(Libro 1, Unidad 5)

A Encourage the class to work on *Ahora sé* (page 53, *Libro 1*).

B Play this recording of someone buying postcards and stamps in Mexico. The students listen, take notes about the main points, and report back. Clear up any problems and then get the students to use their notes to make up a dialogue to buy the same things in Spain.

Repaso: comprando postales y sellos
Número 1
- Por favor, ¿puede darme unas estampillas para España?
- ¿Cuántas quiere?
- Tres, de primera clase, por favor.
- Aquí tiene. ¿Algo más?
- Sí, también déme una estampilla para Colombia, es para postal. ¿Cuánto es?
- Cinco pesos.
- Gracias.

Número 2
- ¿Tiene postales de la Ciudad de Méjico?
- Sí. ¿Cuántas necesita?
- Mm, necesito cuatro. ¿Pero puede mostrarme primero?
- Sí, por supuesto.
- Me da también las estampillas para mandarlas, por favor.
- ¿Adónde.
- A los Estados Unidos.
- Son diez pesos.
- Aquí tiene.

C The students prepare a pack of cards. On some, they write speech balloons containing sentences used when buying postcards and stamps. For each of these, they write a card with a matching narrative sentence, e.g.
Alguien quiere dos sellos para Inglaterra.

They use these to play Pelmansim: in pairs they take turns to pick up two cards and, if they form a pair, the player keeps them and has another go. If they do not form a pair, the player puts them back. The winner is the one with the most pairs.

2 Daily routine
(Libro 2, Unidad 3)

A Encourage the students to work on *Ahora sé*, *Libro 2*, page 36.

B This listening excercise revises daily routine and the impersonal *se*. Tell the pupils to note down which of the speakers has a *siesta* and what people's reasons are for having a *siesta* (or not, as the case may be).

¿Se echa la siesta hoy día?
Entrevistador: Hoy en Onda Madrid 101.3 FM presentamos, como siempre, cada semana, un aspecto de la vida cotidiana e invitamos a todos los oyentes a decirnos lo que opinan. Si Vd., Vd. misma, quiere expresar su opinión, o Vd. caballero, llame al 88 77 66, repetimos, el 88 77 66. Hoy vamos a hablar de la siesta … esta costumbre tan importante en la vida española. Vivimos en una época de cambio; ¿se echa la siesta hoy en día? Y para eso vamos a preguntar a nuestros oyentes … Las líneas están abiertas … ya tenemos una llamada en la línea uno. ¿Con quién hablo? Por favor, dígame.
Pepe: Me llamo Pepe, yo trabajo en una fábrica. Trabajo desde las ocho hasta las tres o las cuatro. Yo no tengo tiempo para siesta.
Entrevistador: ¡Qué pena, qué pena, Pepe! Pero, en fin, quizás en otra ocasión. En la línea dos tenemos a Marisa. ¿Marisa?
Marisa: Hola, muy buenas. Mire Vd., yo soy una anciana y me echo la siesta todos los días de tres a cuatro, y claro es que es una costumbre, mire Vd., desde antes de la guerra. Pero además es que lo necesito porque en el verano, mire Vd., hace mucho calor.
Entrevistador: Tiene Vd. razón, señora, hace mucho calor, es verdad, qué mejor momento para echarse una siesta. En la línea cuatro tenemos a Liliana. ¿Liliana?
Liliana: Hola, soy una alumna del Colegio Santander. Tengo clases de nueve a una y de cuatro a seis. Al llegar a casa, pues no tengo mucho tiempo,

	me gusta mucho ver la televisión, especialmente el programa del equipo 1 que sale después de comer. Está muy bien, ¿eh?
Entrevistador:	Claro, que así no se puede Vd. echar la siesta. Vamos a ver, en la línea uno tenemos a Isabel.
Isabel:	Hola, buenas. Bueno, yo soy de profesión dependienta y trabajo en unos grandes almacenes, y claro, como no cierran a mediodía, no me puedo echar la siesta y llego a casa, pues, cansadísima.
Entrevistador:	¡Qué pena, qué pena! No trabaje Vd. tanto, señora. En la línea tres tenemos a Francisco.
Francisco:	Hola. Yo nunca echo la siesta. Hoy en día no se hace. Es una cosa del pasado. Además, no hace tanto calor en el norte del país.
Entrevistador:	Es verdad, tiene razón, Francisco. La siesta es totalmente mediterránea y del sur, Andalucía. Bueno, con Francisco terminamos el programa por hoy y esperamos que mañana nos sintonice de nuevo en Onda Madrid.

C Each student produces a written presentation of their own daily routines. They copy neatly the corrected version of this and learn it by heart. Add this to the repertoire of presentations which you ask them to make when there are a few minutes to spare in a lesson.

3 The environment
(Libro 2, Unidad 9)

A The students work on *Ahora sé* on page 106 of *Libro 2*.

B Present on the board or OHP a list of facts and opinions about the environment.

Siete por ciento de la selva amazónica ha desaparecido.

Cincuenta por ciento de los millón y media especias (plantas, insectos, etc.) viven en las selvas tropicales.

Una solución posible es crear parques naturales para proteger la selva – lo que se llama el ecoturismo.

La construcción de una carretera de un lado del continente al otro afecta, y en unos casos destruye, la vida de las tribus.

Los usos medicinales de las plantas los saben los habitantes de la selva. Si desaparecen los nativos, desaparecen los secretos de los usos.

La destrucción de las selvas afecta la capa de ozono.

Los importadores de madera no tienen interés en la ecología de la selva amazónica.

Los gobiernos de unos países de América Latina no se ocupan de la educación de los agricultores.

El turismo es negativo. Los hoteles, carreteras etcétera causan muchos problemas.

First of all, the students separate the facts from the opinions, an important reading skill. Clear up any problems and discuss the facts and opinions, e.g. encourage the students to compare this with their own countries and to draw conclusions.

C Each student writes some facts and opinions about the environment in Spain and in their own country. They practise presenting these to each other in pairs and discuss them. They then do this in class.

4 Buying food in a restaurant
(Libro 3, Unidad 2)

A The students work on *Ahora sé* on page 28.

B The students work on **copymaster 29**.

C For writing practice on food and dishes, students match up the half words on **copymaster 30**.

UNIDAD 4

Ratos libres

Main aim
Talking about free time and entertainment

Area(s) of experience
A – Everyday activities
B – Personal and social life
C – The world around us
D – The world of work

Materials
Cassette: ¿Cuánto recibes y quién te da el dinero?, ¿En qué trabajan los jóvenes?, ¿Qué estás haciendo?, Encuesta, En busca de la aventura, ¿Qué sueles hacer en tu tiempo libre?, ¿Qué película prefieres?, ¿Qué te pareció el concierto?, De alquiler, Repaso: comprando recuerdos, Repaso: en el colegio.
Copymasters 31-41

Tasks
Saying how much pocket money they get and how they spend it and whether they have enough money Saying whether they have a spare time job - if so, what job, working hours, how much they earn
Giving, seeking and understanding opinions and preferences about hobbies and interests (including membership of clubs and organisations)
Buying tickets for the cinema, theatre, etc.
Understanding simple preferences and alternatives for going out
Asking for and giving information about times and prices at places of entertainment
Asking and giving an opinion and describing the entertainment
Describing recent leisure activities
Hiring equipment: videos, etc.

Grammar
Suelo (+ infinitive)
Present continuous
Gerund

Productive language
ahorrar   alquilar
aventura   buenísimo
ciencia-ficción emocionante
empleo   entradas
equipo   espectáculo
ganar   gastar
película   regular
revistas   ser socio
sesión
  de tarde/noche
tebeos

Receptive language
cartelera
día del espectador
sesión continua
taquilla
taquillero

Revision points
Buying souvenirs
(Libro 1, Unidad 6)
School *(Libro 2, Unidad 4)*
Obtaining services at a petrol station *(Libro 2, Unidad 10)*
Visiting a department store
(Libro 3, Unidad 3)

Ratos libres (page 42)

Main aim
For the students to understand and wish to achieve the unit goals.

A Work on this along the lines suggested for earlier units.

B The students aim to work out the meaning of all the new words, using communication strategies. Where necessary, help them to do this.

C You (and your language assistant) could talk about yourselves and your families, using and adapting the model sentences. The students use the unit goals to categorise what you say, e.g.
Mi hijo trabaja los sábados en unos grandes almacenes.
Hablar sobre el trabajo.

D Discuss this topic with the class and encourage them to see how interesting and useful it is, e.g. for making friends and having a good time with them.

UNIDAD 4

El dinero (page 42)

Main aim
To understand and use the language needed to discuss pocket money.

A The students scan this, report on the gist, then read it carefully and ensure that they understand it.

B Help the class to extract the interesting information from this pie chart by asking questions, e.g.
¿En qué gastan más los jóvenes españoles?
¿En qué gastan menos?
¿Crees que gastan más los españoles en ropa o menos que los ingleses/irlandeses?
¿Ahorran mucho o poco?
¿En qué gastas más?
¿En qué cosas en la encuesta no gastas nada?
¿Cuánto dinero gastas en juegos de ordenador/ropa/tebeos?
¿Cuánto cuesta una entrada a un partido de fútbol de primera división?

C A useful exercise is to help the students to express the information in the pie chart in written form. To help them, you could present a C-test on the board for part, or all, of the information, e.g.
El doce por ciento del dinero de los jóvenes españoles se gas_ en comp_ juegos d_ ordenador y víd_ .
El 11 por ci_ del dinero se ga_ en tebeos, re_ y libros. Se gasta muc_ en cara_ y chocolate, ve_ por cie_ del din_ . Sólo el nueve p_ ciento s_ gasta en ro_ .

D The students study the instructions for the pairwork task.
In pairs, the students now do the pairwork task, discussing how they spend their pocket money. Encourage them to change pairs and to do this with several members of the class.

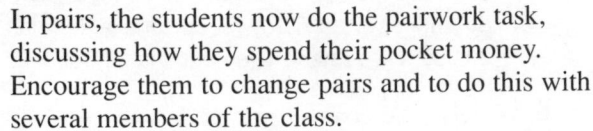

¿Cuánto recibes y quién te da el dinero? (page 43)

Main aim
To develop listening skills.

A The students scan this, report on the gist and then read it carefully and ensure that they understand it.

B They read *El dinero* again and use this information to anticipate what they are likely to hear. This can be done orally with the class and the most commonly anticipated words and phrases can be written on the board. You could then play the recordings and tick off the words on the board as you hear them.

¿Cuánto recibes y quién te da el dinero?

Número 1
– Alicia, ¿cuánto dinero recibes por semana?
– Recibo dos mil pesetas de mis padres.
– ¿En qué te lo gastas?
– Lo normal: revistas, chocolate ...
– ¿Tienes bastante dinero?
– Yo creo que sí. Mis padres me compran la ropa y pagan si quiero ir al cine o a un partido de fútbol.

Número 2
– Ana, dime, ¿cuánto dinero te dan tus padres?
– Mis padres me dan quinientas pesetas.
– ¡Quinientas pesetas!
– Sí, y mis abuelos me dan quinientas también.
– Pero mil pesetas es poco.
– De acuerdo pero trabajo los sábados en una tienda.
– ¿Te pagan bien?
– Me dan cuatro mil a la semana.
– Muy bien.
– Es bastante pero no demasiado. Me compro la ropa y me gusta la música y compro muchos CDs.

Número 3
– Alonso, ¿cuánto dinero te dan a ti?
– Mis padres me dan cinco mil pesetas y mis tíos mil.
– Pero eso es mucho.
– No, no lo es. Tengo que trabajar muchas horas en el bar que tienen mi padre y mi tío. Es poco.
– De acuerdo.

UNIDAD 4

C Study the instructions again with the class and help them to use them to produce, on the board, a grid they can use to organise their listening, e.g.

¿Cuánto?	¿De quién?	¿En qué se gasta?	¿Contentos?	¿Típicos?
1				
2				
3				
4				
5				

The students copy this and then complete it as they listen. Work on one dialogue at a time and clear up any problems before going on to the next one.

D To help the students to learn the key words, produce with them a *Word Sun* on the board based around *DINERO* (see Teacher's Book 1, page 24). When this is complete, remove one of the surrounding words and invite volunteers to say what it is and to write it back on the board. Repeat this with the others. Then erase the whole thing and see if the students can re-create it exactly in their exercise books.

¿En qué trabajan los jóvenes? (page 43)

Main aim

Understanding and using key language needed to talk about work.

A The students scan this, link it to the relevant unit goal, then read it carefully and ensure that they understand it.

B The students discuss the examples and decide which are British (number 1), which are Spanish (number 2) and which could be either (numbers 3, 4 and 5). Encourage them to explain how they can tell.
Read out the examples in random order and modify and add to them. After each one, the students say if the person is British, Spanish or either, e.g.
Reparto periódicos los domingos. Suelo levantarme a las cinco.
Vendo cintas y discos en el mercado.
Trabajo en una discoteca, vendiendo bebidas.
Ayudo a mi padre en el jardín.

C You could describe the young people in the photos (giving details of age, clothes, looks and the work they do) and the students write the relevant number and nationality.
Then write two descriptions on the board. Students adapt these orally to describe one of the others, and other students guess who. They could also describe students in the class.

D Work on the recording along the lines suggested, working on one at a time.

¿En qué trabajan los jóvenes?

Número 1
– Hola, me llamo José. Yo trabajo los sábados de 8 a 3. Trabajo en el mercado, vendiendo pescado. Suelo levantarme a las seis y media. No me gusta el trabajo pero gano bastante - 4.000 pesetas.

Número 2
– Hola, me llamo Susana. Trabajo en el bar de mis padres. Suelo trabajar de 7 a 9 de lunes a viernes y trabajo también los fines de semana. Me gusta bastante pero no gano mucho dinero. Mis padres me dan 3.000 pesetas a la semana pero no tengo que comprar ropa.

Número 3
– Me llamo Natacha. Tengo 15 años y no trabajo. Mis padres me dan 2.000 pesetas.

Número 4.
– Hola, ¿qué tal? Me presento. Soy Angeles. Trabajo en un supermercado. Suelo trabajar de 6 a 8 los jueves y viernes y de 9 a 5 los sábados. Me gusta el trabajo y me pagan 6.000 pesetas a la semana.

Número 5
– Soy Julio. Tengo 16 años. Trabajo en un camping durante el verano. Soy recepcionista. Me dan 20.000 a la semana y me encanta el trabajo.

E Write on the board, e.g.
Reparto …
Trabajo …
Ayudo …
Lavo …

As a class, the students see how many different sentences they can make up which begin with these words.
They now listen and only repeat after you the sensible sentences, ignoring others, e.g.

UNIDAD 4

Reparto en el mercado (la playa, etc.).
Lavo coches en la calle.
Trabajo los sábados.
Trabajo en un cine (un teatro, etc.)
Gano más de mil (5.000, etc.) pesetas (libras esterlinas, etc.).
Recibo mi dinero de mis padres (mi trabajo, etc.).

F For homework, the students each write the 15 words which they think are the most useful for talking about work. They also draw a picture for each word.
In class, they show their words and drawings to their partners and explain why the drawings go well with the words. They then cover up the words and see if their partners can say which word goes with each drawing. You could prepare the class for this by presenting some appropriate words and drawings of your own on the OHP. The students' words and drawings could make an attractive and useful wall display.

¿Qué haces tú? ¿Qué te gustaría hacer?
(page 44)

Main aim
To write simple texts about work and money.

A The students scan this, link it to the relevant unit goal, then read it carefully and ensure that they understand it.

B Draw the students' attention to *suelo* in number 3. Give whatever explanation is needed of the meaning and how it works. Then say a number of sentences which contain it and ask which of these young people could say each one, e.g.
Suelo ayudar a mis padres (number 2).
Suelo trabajar en una tienda (number 1).
Suelo trabajar para mis padres (number 4).
Suelo ganar 5.000 pesetas (number 3).
Suelo trabajar los sábados (number 1.).
Suelo cambiar parabrisas y neumáticos (number 4).
Suelo ir de compras para ayudar a mis padres (number 2).
Suelo vender gasolina (number 4).

Write these on the board or OHP and help the students to use them to talk about themselves, their work and their spending. Each student aims to say and write two things about themselves.

C Practise scan reading for specific information. Ask a question and encourage the students to find the answer as quickly as possible, e.g.
Suele trabajar por las tardes y el domingo: ¿quién es?
Suele trabajar en un garaje: ¿quién es?
Suele ganar cuatro mil pesetas: ¿quién es?
Suele trabajar de camarera: ¿quién es?
Suele lavar el coche e ir de compras: ¿quién es?
Suele vender cosas en una tienda: ¿quién es?

D The students try to memorise the information about these young people, in class or at home. You then base an oral quiz on it. After that, present a C-test to be completed, e.g.
Me lla_ Julia Alo_ y ten_ quince añ_ . Suelo trab_ los sába_ en un_ tienda. Ga_ cuatro mi_ pesetas y sue_ trabajar de nue_ a se_ . Me gust_ trabajar e_ un polide_ porque m_ gusta e_ deporte.

E Revise the unit so far. You could use the appropriate parts of *Ahora sé*, page 53, e.g. Write on the board or OHP 8–10 words or phrases from the list which some students are having problems with. Ensure that everyone understands them and give them one minute to 'photograph' them. Ask a student to read one aloud and then erase it. The students write it from memory. Repeat this with the others.
Present the following on the board. The students complete them orally and/or in writing to describe themselves:
Suelo trabajar ...
Suelo ayudar ...
Suelo ganar ...
Suelo comprar ...
Suelo lavar ...
Suelo ir ...
Suelo leer ...

F Now would be a good time to work on *A ser detective*, page 185.

UNIDAD 4

¿Qué estás haciendo? (page 45)

Main aim
Understanding and using the present continuous.

A As usual, the students scan this, report on the gist and then read it carefully and ensure that they understand it.

B Help the students to work out how the present continuous is formed and used. For example, once they understand all the example sentences here, you could write on the board the relevant infinitives: *hacer, jugar, preparar, escribir, ayudar, ver, lavarse*. With these, and some help, they should be able to work out how to form the present continuous.

C Present **copymaster 31**. You say an appropriate excuse for one of the pictures and the students identify which one, e.g.
Estoy jugando con juegos de ordenador.
Estoy viendo un vídeo.
Estoy leyendo un tebeo.
Estoy alquilando una bicicleta.

You can use **copymaster 31** to play at, e.g.
– ¿Verdad o mentira?
– Repite si es verdad.
– Noughts and crosses.
– Bingo (each student writing 5 numbers and crossing these off as you say the relevant sentence).

D The students prepare to do the listening activity, for example by anticipating the excuses they will hear. Play the recordings, one at a time, and the students pick out the excuse which is used. Play them again and the students say whether each excuse is true or false. Encourage them to discuss these and to say if each person wishes to go out or not, and why. This will involve inferring attitudes and drawing conclusions.
Ask the class to listen again to all the dialogues and to choose one. They then listen to this and transcribe it, and then use their transcriptions to play read the dialogue in pairs. Encourage those who can to adapt it with as many different invitations and excuses as possible.

¿Qué estás haciendo?

Número 1
– Oye Pablo ¿qué tal?
– Bien, bien. ¿Qué pasa?
– ¿Te apetece ir al partido?
– Sí, pero no puedo.
– ¿Por qué?
– Estoy haciendo mis deberes.
– ¿Y qué?
– No puedo. Mis padres no me van a dejar salir. Lo siento.

Número 2
– Dígame.
– Oye Susana.
– Sí.
– ¿Quieres ir al partido esta tarde?
– No, estoy jugando al ajedrez.
– ¿No quieres venir?
– No es eso ...
– Bueno nada, adiós.
– Adiós.

Número 3
– ¿Carmen?
– Sí.
– Oye. ¿Te apetece ir al partido conmigo?
– No puedo. Mi madre está enferma y estoy preparando la cena.
– ¡Qué lastima!
– Sí.
– Bueno, adiós.
– Adiós.

Número 4
– Oye Isabel.
– Hola, ¿qué hay?
– Voy al partido. ¿Quieres ir conmigo?
– Estoy escribiendo cartas ahora.
– ¿No quieres ir?
– No me apetece mucho.
– Adiós entonces.
– Adiós.

Número 5
– ¿Juan María?
– Sí, hombre.
– Voy al partido esta tarde. ¿Te apetece?
– Sí, pero estoy comiendo ahora.
– ¿Y qué?
– Mis abuelos y mis tíos están en casa. Es una reunión familiar. No puedo salir.
– Entiendo.
– Que lo pases bien.
– Gracias hombre. Adiós.
– Adiós.

Número 6
– ¿Alicia?
– Sí, ¿qué pasa?

UNIDAD 4

- Voy al partido. ¿Quieres ir?
- No, estoy viendo la televisión.
- Pero te gusta el fútbol, ¿no?
- Sí, pero el partido está en la televisión.
- Sí, pero ... bueno, adiós.
- Adiós.

E Now would be a good time to work with the class on the present continuous in *A ser detective*, page 185.

No suelo ofender a nadie (page 45)

Main aim

Inviting people out, refusing invitations and explaining why.

A The students scan this, report on the gist and then read it carefully and ensure that they understand it.

B You read aloud some invitations and excuses. The students say whether each one is *una invitación o una excusa*.
Then see how many they can correctly categorise in 30 seconds and, finally, see if they can improve on this score.

C Write on the board words which can describe various leisure activities, e.g.
aburrido, peligroso, interesante, cruel, estúpido, horrible, agradable, romántico, tranquilo.
Make sure that the students understand, and can say, all of these. Then present a list of activities and ask the students which adjectives they would use to describe each one and why. They could discuss them in pairs or larger groups, e.g.
la corrida de toros, ir al parque, hacer equitación, ir al cine, hacer ahorros, leer revistas, juegos de ordenador, ver vídeos, partidos de fútbol, jugar al ajedrez, escribir cartas, hacer deberes, ver la televisión, escuchar cintas, ver una película de aventuras, alquilar una bicicleta.

D Leave these activities visible while the students do the pairwork activity and encourage them to use as many of them as possible in their role playing.

E Write on the board or OHP six questions and number them, e.g.

1 *¿Te apetece ir a la playa?*
2 *¿Quieres ir a la corrida de toros?*
3 *¿Qué vas a hacer esta noche?*
4 *¿Te apetece ver la televisión esta tarde?*
5 *Voy al partido el sábado: ¿Quieres venir conmigo?*
6 *¿Quieres jugar al ajedrez conmigo?*

In pairs, the students take turns to roll a pencil, with the numbers 1–6 on the sides. They ask the question which matches the number they get and their partners answer it. Encourage them to ask for, and give, explanations.

F You could organise a few minutes of verb circle practice (see Teacher's Book 2, page 25) based on, e.g.
Estoy leyendo una revista.
Estamos viendo un partido de tenis.
Estás jugando al ajedrez.

Describiendo un fin de semana típico (page 46)

Main aim

Reading and writing a letter about leisure activities.

A Ask the students first to read the introduction and then to look at the pictures and captions. Encourage them to ask any questions to ensure that they understand the captions.
Then, working from each caption at a time, they find the part of the letter which relates to it and read it aloud. Clear up any problems.

B To give the students a clearer idea of the main points of the letter, ask them to scan it as quickly as possible to find answers to specific questions, e.g.
¿Cuándo se suele levantar el sábado?
¿Por qué va andando al centro?
¿Qué hace a las ocho?
¿A qué hora llega a casa el sábado?
¿A qué hora volvió a casa el sábado pasado?
¿Por qué llegó tan tarde?
¿Qué le gusta hacer el domingo por la mañana?
¿Cuándo ayuda a su padre?
¿Adónde va a ir el fin de semana que viene?
¿Qué va a hacer? ¿Le gusta?

C To become increasingly familiar with the content and language of the letter, the students could now

UNIDAD 4

complete these sentences which could be presented on the board or OHP, e.g.

En esta carta, Alonso va a …
El sábado, se suele …
Hace sus deberes …
Después de ir al centro …
Con sus amigos …
Llegó a casa …
Fue con sus amigos …
El domingo suele …
Observa a la gente …
Por la tarde suele …
Sus padres le van …
Le encanta …
Van a esquiar si …

D The students now read the letter very carefully and ensure that they understand it. Help and encourage them to react personally to Alonso's weekend and to express their own opinions. A good way to help them to summarise the letter is to produce, with their help, a 'mind map' on the board, e.g.

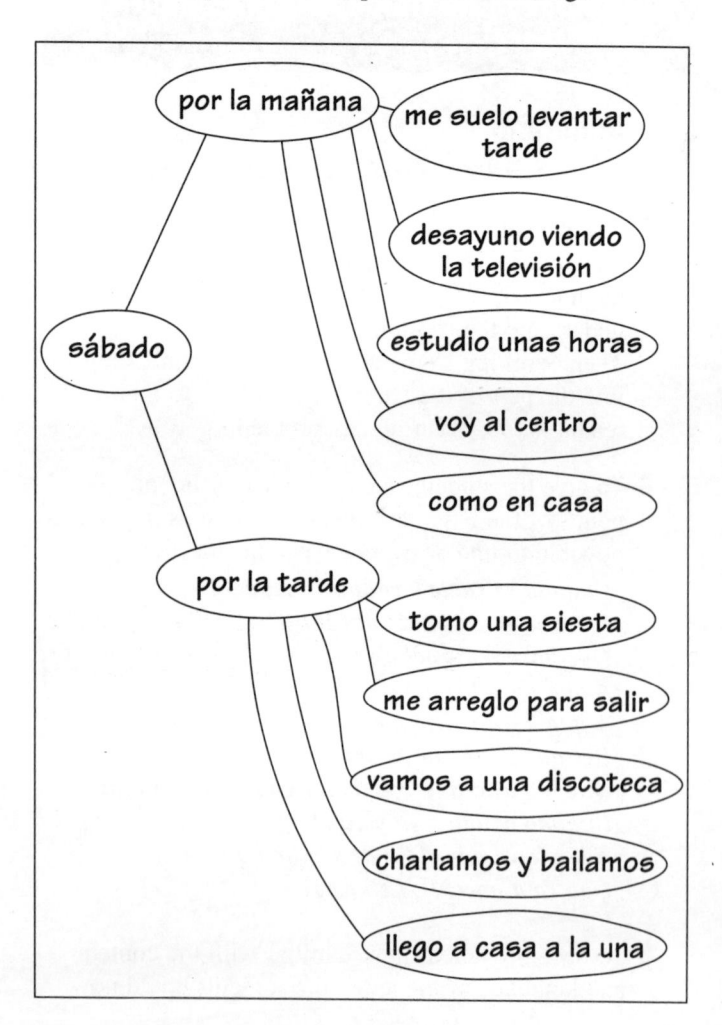

```
                  por la mañana ── me suelo levantar tarde
                        │
                        ├── desayuno viendo la televisión
                        │
                        ├── estudio unas horas
sábado ─────────────────┤
                        ├── voy al centro
                        │
                        ├── como en casa
                        │
                  por la tarde ── tomo una siesta
                        │
                        ├── me arreglo para salir
                        │
                        ├── vamos a una discoteca
                        │
                        ├── charlamos y bailamos
                        │
                        └── llego a casa a la una
```

The students could produce a similar 'mind map' for Sunday and could illustrate it. Move around as they do this, helping students as necessary.

E For homework, each student could produce a 'mind map' for their own weekends, using words and pictures. You could make OHTs of some of these and the authors could use them as the basis for oral presentations of their weekends.

You and the students could produce 'mind maps' regularly as an excellent basis for oral and written presentations: they help to organise ideas and act as a clear summary or plan.

For more ideas on 'mind maps' see *Mapping inner space – learning and teaching mind mapping*, Nancy Margulies, Hawker Brownlow Education, 1992.

F Each student now writes an answer to Alonso's letter. Encourage them to include references to past and future, and to express opinions.

¿Eres socio de algún club? (page 47)

Main aim

Talking about clubs.

A The students scan this, report on the gist and then read it carefully and ensure that they understand it.

B Work on this with the class along the lines suggested in their book.
When it is clear which person does not have a matching *agenda*, encourage the students to write a suitable *agenda* to match the activities described.

C Each student draws an empty *agenda*. They interview each other in pairs and fill in an *agenda* for their partners. To prepare them for this, you could interview your language assistant or some able students and complete an *agenda* on the OHP.

D As students complete Activity C above, ask them to help you to add to the grid which you have started on the OHP and to discuss a range of activities and clubs, e.g.
Actividad
Se hace sólo

Se hace en un club
Los dos
hacer equitación
tocar la guitarra

As you discuss this, ask students which clubs they are members of, which clubs they would like to be in, which clubs exist in the school and locally, etc.

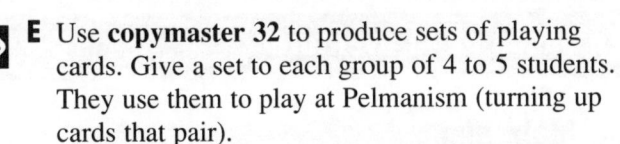

E Use **copymaster 32** to produce sets of playing cards. Give a set to each group of 4 to 5 students. They use them to play at Pelmanism (turning up cards that pair).
As students complete **copymaster 32** give each one a sentence from **copymaster 33**. Each one performs the mime and the others guess what s/he is doing.

F It would be a good idea now to revise the unit so far, e.g.
Write some controversial sentences on the board. The students write what they think about each one, e.g. *Estoy de acuerdo*, *No estoy de acuerdo*, *No sé*. After some class discussion, encourage them to discuss each sentence in small groups, e.g.

Recibo bastante dinero.
Me gustaría trabajar los domingos para ganar dinero.
Me gusta hacer mis deberes.
Paso el tiempo libre estudiando y leyendo.
Me gustaría ser miembro de un equipo deportivo.
Ahorro dinero para mis vacaciones.

After some group discussion, bring the whole class together to discuss each statement and to get an idea of who thinks what.
Draw a picture to represent a key sentence from the unit so far. The students guess until they find the sentence. They can continue this in pairs.
Say, e.g.

La clase tiene 15.000 pesetas. ¿Podéis gastarlas de tal manera que todos estén contentos?

Each student could first write their ideas and rank them. They then try to find ideas which everyone accepts. This may involve explaining, arguing and negotiating.

G Bring in as many pictures as you can of activities, cut from magazines, etc. A student chooses two, one for an activity s/he likes and another for an activity s/he does not like. The student shows the pictures to the others and explains what s/he likes and dislikes and why. The others can ask questions and express their own views.

Una palabra conduce a otra (page 47)

Main aim

To develop communication strategies and extend vocabulary.

A Work on this along lines which have previously proved successful.

B Invite the students to try to see a link between any two words in this list and to explain the link, e.g.
Esquí y esnob.
¿Por qué?
Porque las personas que hacen esquí son esnobs.

C Make a crossword on the board with these words, inviting students to add to it, e.g.

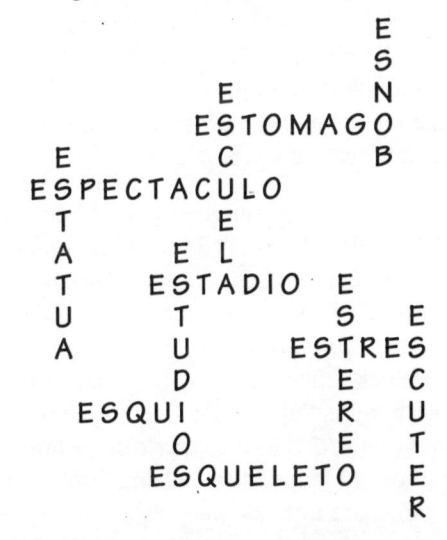

```
                              E
                              S
                    E         N
                    E S T O M A G O
       E            C         B
       E S P E C T A C U L O
       T            E
       A            E L
       T            E S T A D I O   E
       U            T               S     E
       A            U           E S T R E S
                    D               E     C
            E S Q U I               R     U
                    O               E     T
                E S Q U E L E T O         E
                                          R
```

Able students could write clues for the words in the crossword (e.g. sentences with these words omitted) and the crossword and clues could be sent to another class to do.

Encuesta (page 48)

Main aim

To develop listening and speaking skills.

A The students scan this, link it to the relevant goal on page 42, and then read it carefully and ensure that they understand it.

B Discuss the results of this survey with the class and encourage them to draw appropriate conclusions

UNIDAD 4

about the leisure activities of young Spanish people.

C Give each student a copy of **copymaster 34**. Discuss the questionnaire with the class and discuss what could be added to the lists. Encourage as many suggestions as possible, write them on the board and practise asking each other about them. Each student then adds some of these to their questionnaire and they carry out a survey, each interviewing 10 other students. They report back on their findings and you discuss the findings, for example drawing appropriate conclusions and comparing them with the Spanish findings.

D Think of some of the important sentences which arose in Activity **C** and which some students found difficult. Write on the board a dash for each letter of these sentences and work on one at a time. The students are in two teams and each in turn suggests a letter of the alphabet. If this letter occurs in the sentence, write it in, in the correct place, and then see if the team can guess what the sentence is. If not, the next team guesses a letter.

E Work on the listening activity along the lines suggested in the Students' Book. Then adapt the model to present yourself and ask your language assistant to do the same. Each student now writes a similar presentation of themselves. When you have corrected them, the students could read them aloud to each other, display them and learn them by heart. This could be added to the repertoire of oral presentations to be practised when there are a few minutes to spare in a lesson.

Encuesta

Número 1

Hola, me llamo Ignacio. En el colegio no soy miembro de ningún club. Durante el recreo suelo jugar al fútbol con amigos. Fuera del colegio soy socio de un club deportivo. Me gusta el atletismo, el voleibol y el béisbol. Voy al polideportivo dos o tres veces a la semana.

Número 2

Hola, ¿qué tal? Soy Elvira y voy a hablar de mis ratos libres. En el colegio soy miembro de tres clubes: del de ecología, del de drama y del de informática. Suelo ir una vez a la semana. Fuera del colegio no soy socia de ningún club pero tengo clases de matemáticas dos veces a la semana, los lunes y los miércoles.

Número 3

Hola, me presento. Soy Juana. En el colegio soy miembro del club de ajedrez. Me gusta mucho. Fuera del colegio soy socia de un club de equitación. Tengo un caballo y hago equitación todos los días.

En busca de la aventura (page 49)

Main aim

Planning an outing.

A The students scan this, report on the gist, and then read it carefully and ensure that they understand it.

B Play these recordings. The class explain what each couple decides to do and why. Clear up any problems and play the recording again. Then play the recordings again and concentrate on recognising opinions and attitudes.

En busca de la aventura

Número 1

– María, ¿qué te parece la Escuela de Vela en San Vicente?
– Está bien pero no me gusta el mar. Prefiero el campo.
– Entonces, ¿vamos a Unquera? Aventura en la naturaleza: hidrospeed, mountain bike, cursos de kayak alpino, rutas 4x4. ¿Está bien?
– Sí, me gustan las bicicletas. ¿Hay caballos también?
– Sí, creo que sí.

Número 2

– ¿Adónde vamos Marisol?
– Me gustan las montañas.
– Mira, Aventura en Liébana en los Picos de Europa.
– ¿Hay albergues?
– Sí, y hoteles y cabañas.
– ¿Qué se puede hacer?
– Hay muchas actividades: excursiones en caballo, rutas en mountain bike, descenso de cañones, muchas cosas.
– ¿Vamos entonces?
– Sí, ¿cómo no?

C Each student writes 8 questions s/he would like to be asked about leisure activities. They choose partners and give their questions to their partners. They interview each other, using these questions.

UNIDAD 4

On another occasion, each student could list 5 or 6 topics s/he would like to be interviewed about, e.g. **los deportes, la música, la televisión, el cine, la equitación, los juegos de ordenador, los ahorros, el chocolate, la ropa, el teatro, las discotecas, las revistas, el dinero.**

¿Qué hiciste? (page 49)

Main aim
Narrating events and expressing opinions.

A Use this text to revise the use and formation of the preterite. With these rules in mind, encourage the class to say other things they could have done, using the first person, singular and plural. Write these on the board and leave them there.

B Each student writes an account along the lines suggested.

¿Qué sueles hacer en tu tiempo libre? (page 49)

Main aim
To practise listening and note-taking skills.

A Present these recordings to the class, e.g.
Escuchas una emisión de radio. El entrevistador preguntó a unos jóvenes de Madrid – ¿qué sueles hacer en tus ratos libres?

¿Qué sueles hacer en tu tiempo libre?
Número 1
- ¿Cómo te llamas?
- Mariana.
- Mariana, ¿qué sueles hacer en tu tiempo libre?
- Primero los deberes y dos veces a la semana voy a patinar.
- ¿Dónde?
- Hay una pista a cinco minutos de mi casa. Se abre desde las 4.30 hasta las 10.30.
- ¿Vas sola?
- No, suelo ir con amigas.
- Muy bien.

Número 2
- Hola, ¿qué tal?
- Hola.
- ¿Tu nombre por favor?
- Jaime, Jaime Solano.
- Dime Jaime, ¿cómo sueles pasar tus ratos libres?
- Toco la guitarra.
- ¿En casa?
- No, en la calle delante del Corte Inglés.
- ¿Ganas mucho dinero?
- Sí, bastante. No tengo trabajo y necesito dinero para estudiar.
- ¿Sueles pasar muchas horas tocando?
- Dos horas o tres. Una hora si llueve.
- Gracias.

Número 3
- Hola. ¿Cómo te llamas?
- Me llamo Ana Gutiérrez.
- Ana, ¿cómo sueles pasar tu tiempo libre?
- Suelo ir al parque. Me gusta pasear.
- ¿Sueles ir en verano solamente o en invierno también?
- En verano y en invierno. Es más agradable en verano claro, pero me gusta - pero si llueve no voy.

Número 4
- Hola, chico, ¿cómo te llamas?
- Me llamo Nacho.
- Nacho, ¿cómo sueles pasar tu tiempo libre?
- Los fines de semana voy al campo. Hago karting y voy con mi padre.
- ¿Sueles mirar o participar?
- Yo participo y mi padre es espectador y mecánico.

B In pairs, the students prepare an alibi for yesterday evening, deciding on what they did, where they went, with whom, at what times, etc. The class then question each one in turn and try to make the two disagree and thus break the alibi.

Si vas al cine o al teatro (page 50)

Main aim
Understanding information about what is on at the cinema and theatre.

A The students scan this, report on the gist, and then read it carefully and ensure that they understand it.

B The students concentrate on the captions around the adverts and use them to help them find the answers to the questions you ask, e.g.
¿Cuál es el nombre del cine?
¿Cuántas salas hay?

UNIDAD 4

¿Cuándo empieza Abuso peligroso?
¿Cuánto cuestan las localidades en el teatro?

C Invite the students to give you any other information which they can extract from these adverts. Ration each student to one piece of information so as to involve as many as possible. Then encourage them to use this information, e.g.
¿Adónde quieres ir?
¿Por qué?
¿Cuándo empieza?
¿Hay una estación de metro cerca?
¿Cómo vas a ir?

D Each student produces a similar advert for a local cinema and theatre. These could form an attractive wall display.

En la taquilla del teatro (page 50)

Main aim
Buying tickets for the theatre and cinema.

A The students begin by scanning and reading this.

B The students role play in pairs, along the lines suggested, deciding for each one who is the *taquillero/a* and who the customer.

C The students study the model dialogue again and decide which parts of it would be relevant when buying a cinema ticket. Help them also to think what they could add, e.g.
¿Cuántas salas hay?
¿Qué películas dan?
¿A qué hora empieza / termina la película?
¿La película es interesante?

The students then role play buying a cinema ticket. For homework, they could all write a conversation for buying a cinema ticket.

D Write the following film titles on the board or OHP:
Regreso al Futuro
Ciento y un dálmatas
Loca Academia de Policía III
Blancanieves y los siete enanitos
Tiburón
El Padrino

Students try to guess the English titles. Explain that the students may need to use a dictionary

E Give each pair a copy of **copymaster 35** for them to practise coping with the unexpected in role play.

¿Qué película prefieres? (page 51)

Main aim
Expressing opinions about different types of films.

A The students begin by scanning and reading this.

B You give the Spanish titles for other films and TV programmes and the students categorise them.

C In pairs, the students play read the model dialogue and then adapt it to express their own opinions. You and your language assistant could do this first to show how it can be done.

D The students listen to these short narrative accounts of some films. After hearing each narrative twice, they categorise the film. Encourage them to disagree or agree with each other and to justify their points of view. Clear up any problems and play each one twice more. The students now pick out the main points and details about each film.

¿Qué película prefieres?
Número 1
- ¿Fuiste al cine?
- Sí, fui a la película de la noche.
- ¿Qué tal estuvo, Ana?
- Estuvo muy bien. La película se llama La locura de King George.
- ¿La locura de quién?
- La locura de King George – The madness of King George.
- Ay, ¿de qué se trata?
- Es una película histórica, claro, y se trata de la enfermedad de un rey de Inglaterra. La enfermedad ataca su sistema nervioso y se vuelve un poco loco.
- ¿Sí? ¿Y qué sucede?
- El Parlamento y su hijo están en contra de él y entonces le llevan a una casa lejos de su mujer y su familia.
- ¿Y qué tal es al final?
- Al final se recupera y vuelve a reinar.
- Mm, parece interesante.

UNIDAD 4

– Sí, es muy interesante.

Número 2
– ¿Fuiste al cine la semana pasada, Laura?
– Sí. Fui a ver Cuatro bodas y un funeral.
– ¿Qué tal estuvo?
– Muy bien, es una comedia inglesa en donde hay un grupo en el cual hay tres bodas.
– ¿Y la funeral?
– Ah sí, uno de sus amigos muere y por eso es que hay un funeral.
– ¿Y la cuarta boda?
– Ah, no se lleva a cabo porque la pareja tiene una relación bastante difícil.
– Wow, ¿y te divertiste?
– Mucho.

E The students listen once more to the narrative accounts and choose the one which they most like the sound of. They then listen to this as often as they need in order to transcribe it.

They now adapt this transcription to describe their favourite film. When you have corrected this, they could learn it by heart. From now on, encourage them to miss no opportunity in conversations to use this. They can say, e.g.

Fui anoche al cine.
Me gusta mucho ir al cine.
Soy socio de un club de cine.

The person they are talking to will respond in a way which is very likely to offer the opportunity to describe the film.

¿Qué tal fue? (page 51)

Main aim

Expressing opinions about, and describing, a film or show.

A The students begin by scanning and reading this as usual.

B When everyone understands all the questions and answers, you could ask similar questions about films, plays, concerts and TV programmes. The students reply using one of the answers on this page, or adapting one of these answers.

C The students listen to the recorded dialogues based on the pictures in this item. After each one, they write the number of the matching picture. Discuss their answers and clear up any problems.

¿Qué te pareció el concierto?
– Pili, ¿qué te pareció el concierto?
– Me pareció un concierto muy bueno.
– Mira, ¿qué me dices del primer grupo?
– El primer grupo estuvo muy bien, a mí me gustó muchísimo. Cantaron muy bien.
– ¿Y el segundo grupo?
– El segundo grupo fue aun mejor. Estaba todo fenomenal.
– Fue muy emocionante, ¿verdad?
– Fue muy emocionante y el ambiente era muy bueno, era un ambiente estupendo.
– ¿Te gusta este tipo de música?
– La verdad es que me encanta.
– Bueno, Carlos, ¿qué te pareció el concierto?
– Pues mira, nada más que regular. El primer grupo no me gustó nada. Las canciones eran muy antiguas.
– Y ¿qué pasó con el segundo?
– Bueno, el segundo grupo mejor, pero ese tipo de música no me parece muy avanzada.
– ¿Y el ambiente?
– Como dijo Pili, el ambiente estuvo fantástico.
– Bueno, muchas gracias a los dos.

D You use, or adapt, the expressions of opinion and description to react to something you have seen recently, without saying what. You keep on saying it as the students guess where you went or what you saw or did. As soon as possible, encourage students to take over your role.

E In pairs, the students work on the pictures along the lines suggested in their books. They then write these conversations. This could be done at home.

F Give one student a piece of paper with a question written on it, e.g.

¿Qué tal fue la televisión anoche?
¿Qué tal fue el partido de fútbol el sábado?
¿Qué tal fue el concierto de Celtas Cortos?
¿Qué tal fue el cine anoche?
¿Qué tal fue el club de jóvenes ayer?

The student with a question can approach any other student and put this question. They try to extend the conversation as naturally as possible and for as long as possible. This activity can be used with other topics and is excellent for giving practice in initiating and carrying through transactions.

UNIDAD 4

G Make a point of including regularly in classroom conversations questions on this topic, e.g.
¿Qué viste anoche?
¿Qué tal fue la película?
¿Qué hiciste domingo?
¿Cómo lo encontraste?

H With able students, you could use this recording to develop their listening skills. They listen to the recording and compare the reactions of the two people who are interviewed. What do they agree on? What do they disagree on?

Alquilando cosas (page 52)

Main aim

Hiring equipment, videos, etc.

A The students scan this and link it to the appropriate goal on page 42. They then read it carefully and ensure that they understand everything.

B Give each student a copy of **copymaster 36**. They help each other to name each activity or place and to write an appropriate caption for each picture. Still in pairs, they write these in groups of three or four. Emphasise that both students must agree about what goes in each group and that all the pictures must be used. Then ask pairs to present their groups and to justify them.

C The students look at all the items on **copymaster 36** and say which could be hired and where (e.g. *en la playa, en un albergue juvenil, en una tienda*). You say any number from 1 to 20 and then point to a couple. Without delay, they must make up a conversation to try to hire the object which matches the number you say.

D In pairs, the students work on this item along the lines suggested in their book.

E Play another game of Alibis (see page 69 above). This time, the alibis must include hiring something.

De alquiler (page 52)

Main aim

To develop listening and speaking skills.

A Work with the class on this item, along the lines suggested in their book.

De aquiler

Número 1
– ¡Señoras y señores! No olviden que pueden alquilar hidropedales aquí en la playa; sólo 500 pesetas por hora.

Número 2
– Hay otra facilidad que ofrece nuestra tienda; no sólo vendemos bicicletas sino que las alquilamos también, a precios muy bajos.

Número 3
¡No pierdas la oportunidad de jugar al minigolf! Puedes alquilar todo lo necesario en el quiosco central de la zona recreativa.

Número 4
¡Jóvenes! Podéis alquilar motocicletas sin problema. Hay muchas empresas en nuestra ciudad que las alquilan.

Número 5
No hay nada en la televisión. ¿Por qué no ves las últimas películas a precios muy bajos? Alquila un vídeo esta noche. Es más barato y más cómodo.

B Give the students the task of creating a radio commercial for a computer game, ski gear or a mountain bike. They should write the text and also try to record it, with appropriate music or sound effects. Play these for the class to enjoy.

C Give each pair a copy of **copymaster 37**. As they work on this, move around, helping and joining in.

Ahora sé (page 53)

Main aim

To provide a summary of the *Unidad* and a basis for more practice and revision.

A Encourage the students to use this list in different ways in line with their learning needs, and to

UNIDAD 4

concentrate on what they have not yet thoroughly learned.

B As you become aware of the learning needs of individuals or groups, you could advise them to take appropriate actions. You could use the following:
The students work in groups of six. Each one writes three questions based on this *Ahora sé*. Each student has a number, from 1 to 6. They roll a pencil with these numbers on the sides. When it stops, the number of the top indicates the number of the student who can ask one of his/her questions, choosing who in the group to put it to.
Draw on the board or OHP a river with numbered stepping stones, e.g.

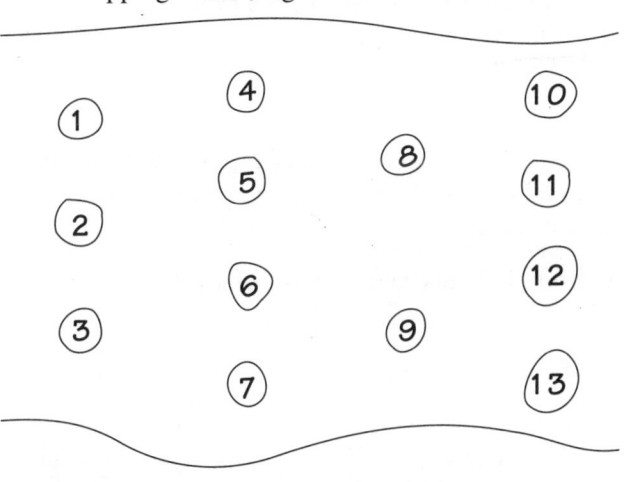

①　　④　　　　⑩
　　　⑤　⑧　⑪
②　　　⑥　　⑫
③　　　　⑨
　　　⑦　　⑬

The students play in teams. They choose which stepping stones (*pasaderas*) they will use to cross the river. To go over these, they have to answer questions correctly. If they answer correctly, they can answer another one and continue. If they answer incorrectly, they must go back and try to cross by another route. Warn them in advance that questions 8 and 9 are the most difficult, followed by questions 1, 2 and 3.
Possible questions:

1 ¿Quién te da tu dinero de bolsillo?
2 ¿Cómo pasas el tiempo libre?
3 ¿Qué te gustaría hacer para ganar dinero?
4 ¿Qué estás haciendo?
5 ¿Cuánto dinero recibes a la semana?
6 ¿En qué gastas tu dinero?
7 ¿Tienes empleo?
8 ¿Qué tal la película que viste anoche?
9 ¿Dónde puedo alquilar bicicletas cerca de aquí?
10 ¿Eres socio de algún club?
11 ¿Eres miembro de algún equipo?
12 En el cine, ¿hay descuento para estudiantes?
13 ¿Qué películas te gustan?

Revision Activities

1 Buying souvenirs
(Libro 1, Unidad 6)

A Encourage the students to work on *Ahora sé*, page 64 of *Libro 1*, using their own preferred techniques.

B Play these dialogues of tourists in México and Peru buying souvenirs. For each one, the students note three things:
1 what is recommended
2 what the tourist buys
3 how much they paid.

Repaso: Comprando recuerdos

Número 1
– Señorita, quisiera comprar algún recuerdo de Méjico. ¿Me puede sugerir algo?
– Claro que sí. Tengo tequila, es algo muy típico de aquí.
– ¿Y para un niño, qué podría llevar?
– Ah, un sombrero.
– Sí, y el tequila ¿tiene botellas chicas o grandes?
– Tengo de todos tamaños: grandes, chicas. ¿Cuál le gustaría?
– Deme una mediana. ¿Cuánto es?
– Son veinte pesos en total.
– Gracias, adiós.
– Adiós.

Número 2
– Querría llevar un recuerdo típico de Perú. ¿Me podría recomendar algo?
– Claro que sí. Mire, algo típico puede ser una chompa de alpaca o algo de plata o alguna cerámica ...
– ¿Una chompa?
– Sí, un suéter.
– Ah, sí, un suéter. ¿Hay otras cosas que me podría recomendar?
– Pues claro, tenemos cerámica muy bonita: como ceniceros, floreros ...
– Quiero la chompa de alpaca. ¿Qué precio tiene?
– Sólo cuesta cincuenta soles.
– Ah, sí, lo llevo... Gracias.

UNIDAD 4

Check the students' answers and clear up any problems. In pairs, the students now use their notes to recreate the dialogues, recommending and buying the same things.

C Give students a copy of **copymaster 38**. They work on this in pairs.

2 School
(Libro 2, Unidad 4)

A The students work on *Ahora sé*, page 47 of *Libro 2*.

B Play these three recordings. They are narrative accounts of typical days in schools in Mexico, Guatemala and Spain. The students listen twice and take notes about the main points. Go over their notes with them and discuss the main points with them, encouraging them to compare the three accounts and to draw conclusions about life in school in the three countries. They could also compare all of these with their own school.

Repaso: En el colegio

Número 1
– ¿Cómo es tu colegio en Méjico?
– Pues, es bastante grande. No sé cuántos alumnos hay.
– ¿A qué hora empiezas por la mañana?
– Voy de las siete de la mañana a las doce o la una.
– Si empiezas a las siete, ¿a qué hora sales de casa?
– A las seis, seis y media.
– ¿Vas en autobús?
– Bueno, los pequeños van en autobús, pero yo voy en carro.
– ¿Comes en el colegio?
– Sí, unas papas fritas y una Coca-Cola. Y cuando salgo, voy a comer a mi casa.
– ¿Qué haces por la tarde?
– Estudio tareas en casa.
– ¿Y cuánto tiempo dura cada clase?
– Unos cincuenta minutos.

Número 2
– ¿Cómo es tu colegio en Guatemala?
– Pues, muy grande con unos dos mil alumnos y está dividida en la parte primaria y la parte secundaria.
– ¿A qué hora entras?
– Entramos a eso de las ocho y salimos a las dos y cincuenta o a las tres.
– ¿Comes en el colegio?
– Tomamos un refrigerio a las doce y media y hay un recreo por la mañana
– Muy bien.

Número 3
– ¿Cómo es tu colegio en España?
– Pues, no es muy grande. Somos pocos alumnos.
– ¿A qué hora empiezas por la mañana?
– A las ocho y media.
– ¿Cómo vas al colegio?
– Pues voy andando porque vivo cerca del colegio.
– ¿Y tienes algún recreo?
– Sí, hay dos recreos de veinte minutos.
– ¿Y dónde comes?
– Como en mi casa. Cuando salgo a las dos como en mi casa.
– ¿Regresas al colegio por la tarde?
– No, no hay clase por la tarde.
– Muy bien.

C Give each student a copy of **copymaster 39**. They could read, and write an answer to, this letter at home.

3 Obtaining services at a petrol station
(Libro 2, Unidad 10)

A The students work on *Ahora sé*, page 117 of *Libro 2*.

B Play a game of *Categorías*: the students listen to you and categorise everything you say as *Cliente* or *Empleado*, depending on who would say it. Count how many they categorise correctly in 30 seconds and then challenge them to beat this score. You could use page 117 of *Libro 2* and the whole *Unidad* as a source.

C Present these incomplete sentences on the board or OHP and play a game of *El juego de los blancos*:
1 *¿Me pone veinte litros de … ?*
2 *Compruebe … …, por favor.*
3 *Mire … … por favor.*
4 *¿Por dónde se va a … ?*
5 *La carretera está cerrada por …*
6 *Tengo hambre. Deme … … .*
7 *Tengo sed. Deme … … .*

D Give each student a copy of **copymaster 40**. They could work on this at home.

UNIDAD 4

4 Visiting a department store
(Libro 3, Unidad 3)

A The students work on *Ahora sé*, page 185.

B Give each student a copy of **copymaster 41**. They could work on this at home.

UNIDAD 5

De compras

Main aim
Shopping for essential items

Area(s) of experience
A – Everyday activities
B – Personal and social life
C – The world around us

Materials
Cassette: En la calle, Escucha, ¿Falta algo?, ¿Cómo se dice?, Quisiera cambiar, ¡Me encantan los hipermercados!, Entrevista en la radio, Sancho y Panza, Repaso: hablando de mí, Repaso: reservando una habitación, Repaso: los campings y albergues.
Copymasters 42–52

Tasks
Understanding shop signs
Asking where particular shops are
Asking for particular items
Expressing quantity required (weight, volume, container)
Asking about and understanding non-availability
Returning unsatisfactory goods, giving reasons (asking for refund or replacement)
Understanding information about shopping habits, facilities and preferences
Discussing the advantages and disadvantages of local shops and shopping centres
Describing a shopping trip

Grammar
Demonstrative adjectives
Negatives: *ninguno*

Productive language
aquel
cepillo de dientes
chorizo
ese
estropeado
frutería
hipermercado
barra
champú
droguería
este
fresco
funcionar
jamón serrano
loción bronceadora
panadería
paquete
pastel
pastilla de jabón
tableta de chocolate
tarta
tisús
uvas
melocotón
panecillo
pasta de dientes
pastelería
tienda de comestibles
tubo

Receptive language
devolver
tendero

Revision points
Talking about myself
(Libro 1, Unidad 8)
Booking hotel accommodation
(Libro 2, Unidad 5)
Camping and youth hostelling
(Libro 3, Unidad 1)
Talking about free time
(Libro 3, Unidad 4)

De compras (page 54)

Main aim
To understand, and wish to achieve, the unit goals.

A Work on this along lines which have previously proved successful to ensure that the students understand this item. This is a topic which most students can easily see as useful. Help them to do this.

B You, and later the students, read the examples aloud and adapt them, e.g.
¿Dónde se venden películas (sellos, etc.)?
Se venden galletas (baterías, etc.) en la estación de servicio.
Deme un kilo de estas naranjas (estos plátanos, etc.)
No voy a comprar guisantes (champiñones, etc.): son demasiado caros.
No funciona esta lámpara (televisión, etc.): ¿me la puede cambiar?
Ayer fui al supermercado y compré una chuleta de cerdo (medio kilo de judías verdes, etc.).

The class listen and categorise each one, e.g. *Pedir información sobre tiendas.*

C You make up a brief oral narrative around one of the tasks exemplified in this item. The students listen and categorise each narrative, e.g.
Ayer compré una cámara. Cuando llegué a casa, descubrí que la cámara no funcionaba. Volví a la tienda y dije que mi cámara no funcionaba. Pedí otra pero no había. El dependiente me devolvió el dinero.

UNIDAD 5

¿Qué necesitas comprar si estás de vacaciones? (page 54)

Main aim

To meet and understand some of the key language of the unit.

A Use **copymaster 42** to present some of the key language. Encourage the students to develop some very useful learning techniques. They look at the pictures and ask you, or your language assistant, the Spanish word for anything. They should also ask how to spell and pronounce the words. Encourage them to write these down and to decide how best to remember what each word means (e.g. with English equivalents, drawings, Spanish definitions).
To help them to learn these words you could, e.g. Say them in random order, alone or in useful sentences. The students listen and write the matching numbers.
They read their lists and copy the words in categories. You could give the categories (e.g. *droguería, frutería, grandes almacenes, mercado, farmacia*) or leave the students to create their own. They compare and discuss their groups of words, in pairs.
Play at Bingo. Each student writes down any five of the items and ticks them off as you say them in a narrative about a shopping trip.
You say all the words aloud. The students repeat only food (or souvenirs, fruit, vegetables) that is sold in *una droguería, el mercado*, etc.

B The students now work on this item in class or at home. They aim to understand it and to learn the information in it about what is sold where. You could base a quiz on this.

C Adapt the text orally to describe what, in your country, is sold in the shops mentioned. Write any key words and phrases on the board for the students to copy. As a homework, they could then write a description, for the benefit of Spanish-speaking visitors, of what is sold where in their country. These could be illustrated and could form an attractive wall display.

D Play a version of 'My mother went to market'. See how long a sentence the students can make, each adding an item in turn to: *Ayer fui de compras y compré ...* . This is not a competition, so the students can help any student who forgets what someone bought.

E As a class activity the students could make a frieze depicting all the shops they have encountered so far with goods on display to practise finding the way, e.g.:
¿La agencia de viajes? Está al lado de la frutería.

F Shop signs
On the OHP/board show the pupils the following letters. Explain that a signwriter was about to put up some shop names but has dropped all the letters on the pavement. Ask them if they can unscramble the letters to make the names of four shops:
**TIAFPREDIAAREURAN
EEAIRGDRARTSPAIEUOL**
Two clues: The first group is made up of the letters of two words and so is the second. Count the letters first to try to find words with the same number of letters.
Solution: *frutería* and *panadería*; *pastelería* and *droguería*.

¿Dónde puedo comprar ...? (page 55)

Main aim

Asking, and saying, where specific items are sold.

A Begin by checking that the students understand all the words they will need for this, e.g.
You say a shop (e.g. *frutería*) and the class say as many things as they can, in thirty seconds, which are sold there. Repeat this with other shops and try to beat the original score.

Use **copymaster 42** again and play a game of Noughts and Crosses.
Draw one of the items in the air with a finger until a student guesses what it is. Students could soon do this and then do it in pairs.
Present the copymaster again. Ask the pupils to name each item.

As a quick game, give them the name of a shop and ask them to name an item that can be bought there and vice versa.
Give them a letter of the alphabet and ask them to think up words connected with shopping beginning with that letter, in a set time.

UNIDAD 5

Ask them where you can buy certain items and where the shop is.

B Work with the class on some of the items in the list and especially any which you think may be difficult. You could begin by asking the question, e.g.

¿Dónde puedo comprar peras (manzanas, etc.)?

Then students can ask the questions and you can answer. When they are ready, they can continue this in pairs.

C To develop fluency, you could do this activity against the clock. You ask the questions and count how many the class can answer in thirty seconds; then reverse this, with the students asking the questions and you answering; and finally divide the class into two teams, one asking and the other answering.

D Introduce this recording, e.g.

En la calle hay mucho ruido. Escucha esta conversación en la calle: algunas palabras no se oyen bien a causa del tráfico. ¿Podéis decir qué son?

En la calle
- ¿Hay un supermercado por aquí?
- ¿Supermercado? No, pero hay muchas (tiendas). ¿Qué buscas?
- ¿Dónde puedo comprar fruta?
- Hay una (frutería) en la Calle Mayor, al lado de la tienda de comestibles. Quizás es mejor ir (al mercado); muchas veces la fruta es más (fresca) allí.
- ¿Y para comprar pasteles?
- Hay una (pastelería) en la Calle Arganda, al lado de Correos.
- Muchas gracias.
- De nada, adiós.

En el hipermercado (page 56)

Main aim

Asking, and saying, where particular shops are.

A Revise the shopping vocabulary met so far, using **copymaster 42**, e.g.

The students race to identify all the items, in order. They then try to do it without any mistakes and faster.

Play at 'Half the class knows'. You show half the class a picture of one of the items and the others have to guess what it is.

B The students scan this, report on the gist and then read it and ensure that they understand it. Then present on the board a summary of it, with a few factual errors, e.g.

Un hipermercado es simplemente un supermercado grande. Contiene un mercado, claro, pero no hay otras tiendas en el complejo. Si conoces el hipermercado, tienes que pedir ayuda.

The students correct the errors orally and then in writing.

C Discuss a few of the shops on the plan and talk about what is sold there. Then choose another shop (e.g. *la farmacia, la tienda de ropa de niños*). Each student writes five things that can be bought there, using a dictionary and looking back through the book if they need to. Students read their lists aloud and give themselves 2 points for each correct item. If any student has a correct item which no other student has, this scores 10 points. Repeat this once or twice with other shops (e.g. *el supermercado, la carnicería*).

D The students can now work on the pairwork activity. You can move around, listening and helping.

En la frutería (page 57)

Main aim

To understand, and begin to use, demonstrative adjectives and *ninguno*.

A Write the following on the board: *melones, naranjas, manzanas, peras, kilo, medio kilo*. Ask the class to read this item carefully and to find the meaning of all these words. Clear up any problems and, if appropriate, develop communication strategies.
Repeat this process with: *No queda ninguno*. When everyone understands this, ask them to find another phrase in the text which has a similar meaning (*Lo siento, no hay*).
Now repeat the process with: *estos, esos, aquellos*.

B Show the students **copymaster 43** and prompt them to ask suitable questions or make suitable requests based on the phrases on page 57, e.g., showing a picture of some grapes:

UNIDAD 5

Deme un kilo de estas uvas.
Quisiera un kilo de estas uvas.
¿Cuánto son estas uvas?

C Show them two pictures of fruit. Put one picture near you and one farther away and, when they ask for the fruit, stress the difference between the ones nearer to you and those farther away and ask them to specify which they want, e.g.
Quiero medio kilo de manzanas.
Sí, señor, ¿éstas o ésas?
Quiero estas manzanas, por favor.

Practise the difference between *estos/esos*, etc. until you are sure that they understand.

D Show them **copymaster 43** again and encourage them to ask for different things: whether they are available and what the price is. Use the full range of the shopkeeper's replies given on page 57. Introduce the idea of *aquel* by making sure you are well away from the articles which you refer to in that way. Reinforce the differences between the three demonstratives by placing three pictures of the same merchandise at different distances from you and inviting the students to choose between them. They could be labelled with different prices to justify the choice, for example:
Quisiera dos kilos de manzanas.
¿Cuáles quiere? Éstas cuestan 100 pesetas, ésas 150 pesetas y aquéllas 200.
Deme un kilo de éstas; son las más baratas.

Alternatively, put three flashcards face down, one near to you, one in the middle of the room and one far away. Ask the pupils the question:
Qué tarjeta representa el melocotón? ¿Ésta, ésa o aquélla?

The pupils have to guess in Spanish.

E Present **copymaster 43** again. Volunteers come to the OHP and point at what you ask for, e.g.
Quisiera medio kilo de esos tomates (aquellas naranjas, estos melones, etc.).

You could repeat this with the picture of a market stall on page 57 of the Students' Book.

F Now would be a good time to work on *A ser detective*, page 187.

G Ensure that all the students understand the model dialogue. They can then play read it in pairs and adapt it for other shopping lists which you present on the board or OHP. As students finish this, they can write a dialogue. This could be completed at home.

Escucha (page 57)

Main aim
To develop listening skills.

A The students read this and ensure that they understand it. It is useful for them increasingly to accept responsibility for this, in preparation for exams and real life. You could check that they are all aware of the difference between *estás* and *estas*.

B The students refer back to *En la frutería* and use this to help them to anticipate what they will hear. They then listen to the first dialogue two or three times and write the answers to the three questions. Clear up any problems, play the dialogue again and go on to the next one.

Escucha
- Buenos días.
- Buenos días, señores.
- Quisiera dos kilos de manzanas.
- Muy bien. ¿Algo más?
- Sí, deme un kilo de estas naranjas.
- Aquí tiene Vd. ¿Y con eso?
- ¿No hay plátanos?
- Lo siento, plátanos no hay ninguno.
- Entonces, medio kilo de uvas.
- Aquí tiene Vd.
- ¿Cuánto es?
- Son seiscientas ochenta pesetas.
- Tenga.
- Gracias.

- Buenos días.
- Buenos días, señor. Quiero un kilo de melocotones.
- Vale. ¿Y con eso?
- Quisiera medio kilo de esas uvas.
- Muy bien. ¿Algo más?
- ¿Hay tomates?
- No, no hay tomates.
- Entonces, dos kilos de manzanas.
- Tenga. ¿Eso es todo?
- Sí. ¿Cuánto es?
- Son setecientas veinte pesetas.
- Tenga.
- Gracias. Adiós.

79

UNIDAD 5

C The students now prepare to use what they have heard to do their own shopping. They use their notes to reconstruct the dialogues and to buy the same things. Each student writes one dialogue in full.

Play the dialogues again while the students compare what they hear with what they have written. You could play the dialogues again to help them to correct their dialogues.

El cliente y el tendero (page 58)

Main aim
To develop role play skills for shopping for food.

A The students scan this, link it to the appropriate learning goal, and then read it carefully and ensure that they understand it.

B Help the class to check each shopping list against what is available on the market stall, e.g.
¿Hay uvas (plátanos, etc.)?
The students point to what you ask for and say, e.g.
Sí, hay uvas. ¿Cuántas quiere Usted?

C Play at *Repite si es verdad*, e.g.
Estos plátanos cuestan 120 pesetas el kilo. Las naranjas más baratas cuestan 150 pesetas el kilo.
The students should now be ready to do the pairwork activity described in their book.

D Encourage students to express opinions about fruits and vegetables. e.g.
They repeat what you say only if they agree, e.g.
(No) me gustan las uvas (las manzanas, etc.).
You ask individuals questions about their likes and dislikes.
Each student lists all the fruits and vegetables they know under two headings:
Me gustan
No me gustan
This could be done at home.

No gracias (page 58)

Main aim
Saying what you (do not) want and why.

A The students read this and ensure that they understand it.

B They work on it in pairs, along the lines suggested in their book.

C They could reverse this and demand only the best and most expensive fruits.

¿Falta algo? (page 58)

Main aim
To develop listening skills.

A The students scan this and report on the gist. They then read it carefully to ensure that they understand it fully. You could check that they do understand it, including the title.

B Ask if anyone in the class believes in telepathy and encourage someone to anticipate what each person has forgotten. If there are several volunteers for this, write their predictions on the board.
Play the recording and see if anyone predicted accurately.

¿Falta algo?
- Buenos días.
- Buenos días.
- Una docena de huevos.
- ¿Estos huevos o aquéllos?
- Estos; y 250 gramos de este chorizo.
- Muy bien. ¿Algo más?
- Sí, dos paquetes de esas galletas ... ¡Ah! Se me olvidó ... medio kilo de queso. Eso es todo.
- Son 950 pesetas.
- Tenga, mil.
- Y 50 de vuelta.
- Gracias. Adiós.
- De nada. Adiós.
- Hola, Miguel.
- Hola. Primero, una lata de sardinas.
- ¿Y con esto?
- Un cuarto de kilo de jamón de York, y una botella de agua mineral.

UNIDAD 5

– ¿Con gas o sin gas?
– Sin gas. También un cuarto de kilo de ese salchichón.
– Mmm, y, ¿eso es todo?
– Creo que no he olvidado nada. ¡Qué memoria! ¿Cuánto es?
– Son 880 pesetas.
– Tenga, mil.
– Y tu vuelta, 20 pesetas.
– ¿No me faltan 100?
– Oh, perdona. Ten. Hasta luego.
– Hasta luego.

Play the recording again and make sure that everyone has noted correctly the forgotten items.

C You could conduct a telepathy experiment. Write a short shopping list on the board, including items that some students are having problems with. Ask for a volunteer who believes in telepathy. S/he thinks of, and concentrates on, one of the items on the shopping list. Every other student in turn then reads aloud the item s/he thinks the 'medium' has chosen and you keep a count on the board. Find out which one the 'medium' had chosen and see how well s/he had telepathised this to the others. You can repeat this with other lists and other 'mediums'.

D Present on the board or OHP a short narrative to describe what happened to Miguel. The students race to say whether it describes Luisa or Miguel. Then begin a similar, but incomplete, narrative for Luisa, e.g.

Entró en la tienda de comestibles. Compró primero una lata de sardinas y luego jamón y agua mineral. También compró 250 gramos de salchichón. Dio mil pesetas al tendero y el hombre le dio 20 pesetas. Le dijo que había un error y el tendero le dio cien pesetas más.
Entró en la tienda de comestibles. Pidió …

The students read and complete this narrative.

E One pair of students could write a shopping list on the board and act out a dialogue associated with it, omitting or changing two details. The rest of the class should try to identify the errors.

F ¿Cuál es más barato? (**copymaster 44**)
Reading comprehension
The students have to work out which of the two shops offers the best value. Two price lists are given, with different brands of the same products at different prices. The students are given one shopping list. They have to work out the following:
a How much all the items on the shopping list would cost at each shop.
b At which shop you can buy each of the items more cheaply.
c Which shop is cheaper and by how much.

G As a class game you can appoint six shopkeepers and give each of them a list of prices for up to five items. The students work individually or in pairs trying to ascertain the prices of the five items on his/her list in the different shops. They then work out the lowest price they would have to pay for the items combined. They are only allowed to ask three questions at each shop before moving on to another to avoid long delays.
As a group activity you could have two shopkeepers and four or five customers in each group. The customers in turn ask each shopkeeper the price of each item and make a note of the price. To make the task more complicated, the shopkeepers could quote prices for different quantities (e.g. *500 gramos/1kg.*). As with the class activity, the object of the exercise is to obtain each item at the lowest price.

En la tienda de comestibles (page 59)

Main aim
Expressing opinions about food.

A The students scan this and report on the gist. They then read the introduction carefully and ensure that they understand it.

B Lead a class discussion about good picnic foods and drinks. Draw up an agreed menu for a picnic and write it on the board. Then work out the shopping list for this menu and write that on the board (not forgetting less obvious things like margarine or butter, salt, etc.).

C Practise scanning the list for drinks, meat, fish, fruit and desserts, working on one at a time.

UNIDAD 5

D Give each student a copy of **copymaster 45**. They can work on the first part individually or in pairs, at home or in class. They work on the second part in pairs, in class. Before leaving this, check that everyone now understands the meaning of *comestibles*.

En la droguería (page 59)

Main aim
Coping with the unexpected.

A The students begin by scanning and reading this. Check that they understand all the key words, e.g. *droguería, crema bronceadora, jabón*.
Practise the key vocabulary before doing the exercise. Use pictures of the items or, if possible, authentic realia to stimulate oral work. In addition, you could give the students a definition of each item as if you were a foreign customer who had just forgotten a particular word, e.g.
Quisiera … no sé cómo se llama … sirve para lavarse el pelo … (champú)
Deme un paquete de … he olvidado cómo se llaman … Tengo un resfriado … (tisús)

B You play the part of the customer and the class that of the assistant. You ask for some of the items and the class respond appropriately. The students can then continue in pairs.

¿Cómo se dice … ? (page 59)

Main aim
To develop listening and speaking skills.

A It would be a good idea to revise the unit so far, e.g. Collect a variety of items in a shopping bag. Take out the objects one at a time. For each item, the pupils see who can make the longest or best statement, giving as much information as possible on when and where it was purchased, for whom and the price paid, etc.
Discuss the advantages and disadvantages of small shops and hypermarkets. Ask the pupils which they prefer and why.

Ask students to say what sorts of shops there are in a nearby street to see how observant they are. See if the class can jointly produce a plan on the board, showing where all the shops are in the street.
Play at Twenty Questions. One student thinks of a word in *Ahora sé,* page 63 and the class has 20 questions to find it, e.g.

¿Es más grande que una uva (manzana, etc.)?
¿Puedo comerlo?
¿Tienes esto en tu casa?
¿Se vende en un supermercado (una droguería, etc.)?

The students choose a set number of items from the unit and the teacher calls them out as if asking for a long list of shopping, e.g.

Me da un kilo de uvas, por favor, cien gramos de jamón de York …

The pupils mark off any item on their list that the teacher calls out and the first to have marked them all off shouts *Bingo!*

B Work with the class on this item.
The students are required to anticipate what the shopkeeper is going to say. To do this you will have to stop the tape before the shopkeeper speaks.

¿Cómo se dice?
– Buenos días; estoy aquí de vacaciones, y quiero varias cosas. Primero, para los dientes necesito un tubo de … ¿cómo es? Un tubo de …
– … ¿pasta de dientes?
– Eso es, eso es. Y para lavarme, quiero … quiero …
– … ¿jabón?
– Jabón, sí, una pastilla de jabón. Y para el sol, un tubo de …
– … ¿crema bronceadora? Muy bien.
– Sí, eso. También, para el pelo, necesito una botella grande de … ¿cómo es?
– … champú, ¿verdad? Aquí tiene.
– Sí, sí, es casi la misma palabra. Y también tisús; necesito un … ¿cómo es?
– ¿un paquete de tisús? Sí, señora. ¿Algo más?
– Una cosa; mire, quiero un regalo para mi hermana; es una botella de … ¿cómo es?
– … de perfume. Este perfume es muy bueno.
– Gracias, esto es todo. ¿Cuánto es?
– Cinco mil seiscientas pesetas. El perfume es caro.
– Claro, sí. Gracias.
– Gracias, adiós.

You could continue to work on this until the students can provide all the missing words before the shopkeeper, without you having to pause the cassette.

C Give each student a copy of **copymaster 46**. They work on these in pairs and practise coping with the unexpected. You could move around, listening and helping.

Quisiera cambiar (page 60)

Main aim
Returning unsatisfactory goods.

A The students scan this and link it to the appropriate unit goal. They then read it carefully and ensure that they understand it.

B You could mime one of the client's sentences. The students guess which one. Repeat this with the shop assistant's sentences. The students can continue this in pairs.

C The students listen to the recording and match each dialogue to a picture. There are only four dialogues and five pictures. The students say which picture has no matching dialogue (number 1). They then write a dialogue to match this picture.

Quisiera cambiar

Número 1
– Buenos días.
– Buenos días, ¿qué desea?
– Quisiera cambiar este pescado.
– ¿Qué pasa?
– No está fresco.
– Sí, señor. Lo siento mucho.
– Gracias.

Número 2
– Buenos días. Quisiera cambiar este bolso.
– ¿Qué pasa?
– Lo compré ayer y está estropeado.
– No sé si tenemos otro.
– Pero, por favor, si no tiene otro, devuélvame el dinero.
– No sé.
– Escuche. Pagué 5500 pesetas y quiero que me devuelva el dinero.
– Vale.

Número 3
– Sí señor.
– Compré un reloj el sábado y no funciona.
– Déjeme ver. Bueno. ¿Cuánto le costó?
– Mil pesetas.
– Ah, mil pesetas.
– ¿Usted puede darme otro reloj?
– Sí, aquí están los relojes.

Número 4
– Señorita.
– ¿Sí, señora?
– Compré una blusa para mi hija y es demasiado grande. ¿Tiene una más pequeña?
– Sí, señora, un momentito. Se la voy a cambiar en seguida.

D Play the dialogues again. The students repeat only what friendly customers say.
You could base a game of *Repite si es verdad* on the pictures. You talk about one and the students repeat only what is true.

E Present **copymaster 47**. The students use as many as possible of the complaining sentences as they can for each picture. They could also base a game of Noughts and crosses on them.

F You could play at *El juego de los blancos*, e.g.
El pantalón es demasiado … .
A mí … no me gusta este champú.
… … no funciona.
Este … está estropeado.
No me gusta y quisiera … .

G You and your language assistant, or a student, could mime a complaining dialogue, based on this item. The class watch and, when you repeat the mime, provide the words. Pairs of students could prepare and perform similar mimes.

H Give each student one half of **copymaster 48**. Without looking at their partners' brief, they prepare and then perform their roles. This provides excellent practice in coping with the unexpected.

Una palabra conduce a otra (page 60)

Main aim
To develop communication strategies and extend vocabulary.

A Work on this along lines which have proved successful.

UNIDAD 5

B You could base some question and answer work on the list, e.g.

¿Dónde se vende leche?
¿Hay una lechería cerca de aquí?
¿Dónde se vende leche cerca de aquí?

C The students could look for words similar to those on the list which are not included, e.g. *croisantería, cafetería, droguería, panadería, quesería.* Encourage them to look back through the unit to find these and, if possible, give a small prize to whoever produces the longest, correct list.

D See how many different ways the students can find to complete such sentences as, e.g.

En una pastelería, se venden …
En una carnicería, se venden …
En una papelería, se venden …

¡Me encantan los hipermercados! (page 60)

Main aim

Understanding and expressing opinions.

A The students read this introduction carefully and ensure that they understand it fully. They then prepare for the listening task by anticipating the opinions they will hear and the words which will be used. To help with this, you could present some opinions and words on the board, discuss each one, and cross out those which the class does not expect to hear, e.g.

Es muy fácil. Aparcas el coche y compras todo lo que necesitas.
No me gusta la música en los hipermercados – ¡es muy mala!
Hay tantas cosas que gastas demasiado en cosas que realmente no necesitas.
Es aburrido. Miles de latas de sardinas, miles de paquetes de galletas y de botellas.
Los hipermercados son demasiado grandes. Tienes que andar kilómetros.
Me gusta porque puedo pasar un rato en las tiendas sin mis padres.
Es demasiado materialista. La idea de ir de compras como pasatiempo la odio.
Me gusta porque nunca llueve. En el mercado sí.

B With the students' help, prepare on the board a grid which will help them to organise their listening, based on the instructions:

	¿Qué opinión?	¿Por qué?
1		
2		
3		

They now copy this grid, listen to the recording and complete the grid for each person. Discuss their responses and clear up any problems. Then play the recording again and see how good their predictions in Activity **A** were.

¡Me encantan los hipermercados!

Número 1
✓ Vamos al hipermercado los sábados. Vamos todos: mis padres, mi hermano y yo. Aparcamos el coche y tomamos un café antes de hacer la compra. Mis padres van al supermercado y mi hermano y yo vamos a la tienda de música o al kiosko. Volvemos al coche y nada más. Lo pasamos bien. Me gusta.

Número 2
✗ Tengo que ir al hipermercado con mi madre los viernes. No me gusta nada. Es muy grande y hay mucha gente. Compramos toda la comida allí y me aburro muchísimo. No puedo ir a la cafetería o a la librería porque tengo que ayudar a mi madre.

Número 3
✓ Voy al hipermercado solo. Mis padres me dan una lista y voy en su coche. Me gusta porque trabajo en el supermercado los sábados y sé dónde está todo. Es fácil. Lo compro todo, pago y vuelvo a casa. Muy fácil.

C Ask about local hypermarkets, supermarkets and shops. Encourage the students to express their own opinions about them. Your language assistant could also ask for advice about good and bad shops.

D The students listen again to the recording and choose the one which is closest to their views. They listen as often as necessary to transcribe this. For homework, they could adapt this to reflect fully their own opinions about a local hypermarket or supermarket. They could learn the corrected version of this by heart and add it to their repertoire.

UNIDAD 5

En mi opinión (page 61)

Main aim
Understanding and expressing more opinions.

A The students scan this, report on the gist and then read it carefully and ensure that they understand it. They ask for help with any problems, but they take the initiative in this.

B Read each opinion aloud and discuss it with the class, e.g. where someone would say this and if the class agrees.
Then read them aloud again, first in the order in which they appear and then in random order. Students repeat only those opinions with which they agree.

C The students draw a grid in their exercise books and could complete this for homework. Back in class, they compare and discuss their grids.

D Each student writes a text, as long as possible, which begins with:
Cuando voy de compras, prefiero ir …
You, your language assistant and some students could do this orally to prepare the class for this.

Entrevista en la radio (page 62)

Main aim
Understanding and expressing opinions.

A The students read the instructions and anticipate what they will hear.

B They listen to the recording and summarise what each person says. You could help them do this by presenting a grid on the OHP which they could copy and complete.
Complete the grid for the first speaker as an example. Work on this with the class to ensure that everyone knows what to do and how to do it. Then work on the others, one at a time, clearing up any problems as you go along.

Entrevista en la radio

Número 1
– Perdón, señor. ¿Te gusta ir de compras?
– No me gusta nada, nada.
– ¿Por qué?
– Porque es aburrido. Todos los sábados. Me vuelve loco.
– Gracias.

Número 2
– ¿Le gusta ir de compras, señorita?
– Señora.
– Lo siento, señora. ¿Le gusta?
– Sí. Voy con mi marido y me gusta mucho. Prefiero el mercado porque es más barato.
– ¿Le gustan los grandes almacenes y los hipermercados?
– No, son demasiado grandes para mí.

Número 3
– ¿Le gusta ir de compras?
– Depende. Si voy a comprar discos o cintas o libros, sí, pero si compro ropa y comida, no.
– ¿Prefieres las tiendas o los supermercados?
– Prefiero las tiendas y los grandes almacenes.
– Gracias.

Número 4
– ¿Le gusta ir de compras?
– Me encanta.
– ¿Por qué?
– Porque me compro muchas cosas: ropa, regalos, todo.
– ¿Le gusta a su marido?
– ¡No!

C Listen once more to the recording. The students write the questions which are asked. Together, choose the best of these. In pairs, the students interview each other using these questions.

Una carta de Luisa (page 62)

Main aim
Reading and writing a letter about shopping.

A The students scan this, report on the gist, and then read it carefully and ensure that they understand it.

B Work on each of the preparatory questions and ask the students to find, and write, the answers. Several students read their answers aloud and you clear up any problems.

C Now ask the students to study the letter carefully and read aloud:
1 sentences which refer to the past;

85

UNIDAD 5

2 sentences which refer to the present and what generally happens;
3 sentences which refer to the future.

Use this as a basis for any necessary revision of tense usage and formation.

D You orally adapt the letter to talk about your shopping. The students take notes of the main points and report back on how you differ from Luisa. Your language assistant could also do this.

E Ask the students to find in the letter phrases and sentences which are true for them. They could write these and read them aloud.
They then find other sentences and change them to make the sentences true for them. Do this orally first, with several students, and write on the board any key words which they need. You could erase half of each word and invite the students to write them in full.
Finally, the students each write a similar letter. This could be done at home. Emphasise the importance of including references to past, present and future.

Sancho y Panza (page 62)

Main aim

To encourage imaginative uses of the language.

Work on this along lines which have previously proved successful. Point out the play on words, if appropriate: PRYCA is the name of a chain of hypermarkets, one of which is just outside Santander. This imaginary supermarket is called PERRYCA.
You could make up an oral narrative based on the cartoon. Stop from time to time and encourage the students to continue the narrative.
You could present a Cloze-test narrative on the OHP. The students write the narrative in full, adding in the missing words.

Ayer fui al hipermercado con Panza. No ( ) gusta ir con él porque siempre quiere ( ) muchas cosas. Me gusta el ( ) porque todo es más barato. Al entrar dije a (Panza) – Sólo necesitamos unas pocas cosas. Cogí ( ) o cuatro cosas de mi lista y fui a la ( ). La cajera dijo – Son 15.745 ( ). ¡Qué sorpresa! Mi amigo Panza había cogido muchas cosas y me dijo – Es mucho más ( ) en los hipermercados. ¡Barato, sí! Si ( ) vas con Panza o si paga Panza.

The students listen to this recording of *Sancho y Panza* each narrating their trip. The students compare the two versions and draw appropriate conclusions about the characters.

Sancho y Panza
– Ayer fui al Hipermercado Perryca con Sancho. Me invitó y acepté. Me gustan los hipermercados. Fuimos en coche y aparcamos delante de la entrada. A Sancho no le gusta gastar dinero. Me dijo – Sólo necesitamos unas pocas cosas. A mí me gusta comprar muchas cosas. Vi un paquete de mis galletas favoritas pero Sancho me dijo que eran demasiado caras. Y puse dos o tres cosas en el carro – las galletas, por ejemplo, pero Sancho no me vio. Llegamos a la caja y ¡qué sorpresa! La cajera dijo – Son 15.745 pesetas.
Yo estaba muy contento con mis galletas, chocolate, caramelos y helados pero Sancho no estaba contento. No sé porqué.

– Ayer invité a Panza a ir de compras conmigo. Me gustan los hipermercados porque normalmente son más baratos. Sólo quería comprar mantequilla, aceite, pan y huevos.
Llegué a la caja y tuve que pagar 15.745 pesetas. No lo entiendo. Cuando volví a casa descubrí caramelos, helados, galletas, chocolate, pasteles. No sé cómo había estas cosas en el carro.

Play this recording again. The students look at the cartoon as they listen and try to continue the narrative when you pause the cassette.

Ahora sé (page 63)

Main aim

To provide a summary of the *Unidad* and a basis for more practice and revision.

A The students work on this, now and in the future, to learn or revise this key language, taking responsibility for this and using their own favourite learning techniques.

UNIDAD 5

B You could help them to learn, and to develop their ability to learn autonomously, by introducing the following activities:

All the students involved write a sentence based on the list: these can be true or false. They read these aloud in turn and the others decide whether each sentence is true or false.

Write on the OHP a short description of something which is damaged or imperfect. The students read this and ask questions to find out what has happened, e.g.

Mi reloj está estropeado.
La radio de mi hijo no funciona.
Las gambas no están frescas.

Ask some students to prepare a one-minute talk or presentation about shopping (e.g. local shops, their views about shopping) and give them a week to prepare it. Ask them to give their talks, perhaps one or two in each lesson, and encourage the others to ask questions and express their opinions on the same topic.

Give out **copymaster 49**. The students can work on this in class or at home.

The students describe orally a simple picture which you draw on the OHP (e.g. a market stall). They then get you to remove things by saying, e.g.

No hay ninguna manzana.

You then erase the apples. You can continue until nothing is left.

Revision activities

1 Talking about myself
(Libro 1, Unidad 8)

A Each student copies this grid from the board or OHP.

	1	2	3
Nombre			
Apellido			
Dirección			
Fecha de nacimiento			
Edad			
Nacionalidad			

They now listen to these recordings and complete the grid when the relevant information is given. Warn them that some speakers may not give all this information.

Repaso: Hablando de mí

Número 1
– ¿Me puede dar alguna información, por favor?
– Sí.
– ¿Cuál es su nombre?
– Martha.
– ¿Y su apellido?
– Contreras Vásquez.
– Contreras Vásquez ... ¿y su dirección, por favor?
– Es Avenida España, 83.
– Avenida España, número, ¿qué dijo?
– 83.
– ¿Y la fecha de nacimiento, por favor?
– 29 de julio del sesenta y dos.
– ¿Del setenta y dos?
– No, sesenta y dos.
– Bueno, ¿y cuántos años tiene?
– Treinta y tres.
– Treinta y tres años. ¿y su nacionalidad?
– Mejicana.
– Muchas gracias.
– Gracias.

Número 2
– ¿Su nombre, por favor?
– María de Jesús García Hernández.
– ¿García qué?
– Hernández
– ¿Su dirección?
– Calle de Sevilla, 22B
– Calle de Sevilla, 22, ¿qué? perdón.
– B.
– B. Sí, 22B, Calle de Sevilla, Málaga.
– Málaga.
– ¿Málaga?
– Sí.
– ¿Su fecha de nacimiento?
– Diez de enero de mil novicientos setenta y tres. Tengo 22 años.
– Y finalmente, ¿su nacionalidad, por favor?
– Mejicana.

Número 3
– Necesito alguna información, por favor. ¿Cómo se llama usted?
– Me llamo Conchita Jiménez.
– Conchita Jiménez. ¿Su dirección?
– Paseo de las Américas, número 58.
– Paseo de las Américas, número ¿qué?

UNIDAD 5

– Número 58.
– ¿Su fecha de nacimiento?
– El 30 de mayo de mil novecientos ses - setenta y cinco.
– ¿Sesenta y cinco?
– No. Setenta y cinco.
– ¿Qué edad tiene?
– Tengo veinte años.
– ¿Y su nacionalidad?
– Peruana.
– Gracias.

B Using the grids, each student writes an introduction for themselves, giving all the information. Some of these could be read aloud and the others could write brief notes.

C Organise a few minutes of verb circle practice (see Teacher's Book 2, page 25), e.g.
Soy escocés.
Vive en Manchester.
Tienes quince años.
Me llamo Toni.

2 Booking hotel accommodation
(Libro 2, Unidad 5)

A Encourage the students to work on *Ahora sé*, page 60 of *Libro 2*.

B Play this recording and encourage the students to note the problems that arise, and the solutions.

Repaso: reservando una habitación
Número 1
– Buenos días, señorita.
– Buenos días. ¿Cómo puedo ayudarle?
– Me gustaría reservar tres habitaciones dobles.
– Tres habitaciones ¿Para qué fecha, por favor?
– Para el veinte de octubre.
– Para el veinte de octubre. Mm, me temo que no tenemos tres habitaciones dobles para esa fecha.
– ¿Y para el día 22?
– Para el 22, mm … sí. Para el 22 tenemos tres habitaciones dobles.
– ¿Cuál es el precio?
– El precio es de seis mil pesetas por noche. ¿Quiere reservarlas ya?
– No, me gustaría pensarlo. Llamo después para confirmar la reservación.
– Hay que llamar un día antes de la fecha.
– Perfecto, muchas gracias.
– Gracias a usted.

Número 2
– Buenos días.
– Hola, buenos días.
– Quiero una habitación doble.
– Una habitación doble, ¿para qué fecha?
– Para el quince de octubre. Tiene que tener vista al mar.
– Para el quince de octubre. Permítame un momento, voy a verlo. …Lo siento para el quince de octubre no tengo nada … mm … pero, tengo una habitación disponible muy soleada. Tiene vistas a la ciudad y está en la zona de la piscina precisamente.
– ¿No tiene con vista al mar para otra fecha?
– Mm, sí. Sí, el diecisiete. ¿Le viene bien esta fecha?
– Claro, está bien.
– El precio de la habitación es de ocho mil pesetas la noche.
– ¡Ocho mil pesetas!
– Bueno, el desayuno está incluido.
– Ah, bueno.
– ¿La reservo?
– Sí. Gracias.

Now get the students to listen again and concentrate on the language used. They write down how the problems were expressed and the solutions found.

C Give each student one half only of **copymaster 50**. They work on these in pairs and practise coping with the unexpected.

3 Camping and youth hostelling
(Libro 3, Unidad 1)

A The students work, at home or in class, on *Ahora sé*, page 16.

B Play this recording. The students listen and note the positive points and negative points in each narrative. They then decide on which family had the better holiday.

Repaso: los campings y albergues
Número 1
– ¿Qué tal fueron las vacaciones?
– Muy bien, en general. Fuimos a un camping muy bueno. Había piscina, pista de tenis, bar y restaurante, mini-golf y un salón de juegos. Tenemos una caravana y había mucho sitio para caravanas. El restaurante nos gustó pero fue algo caro; el menú del día dos mil pesetas – es mucho.

UNIDAD 5

A los niños les gustó el salón de juegos por la tarde y la piscina, claro.

Número 2
- ¿Qué tal lo pasasteis de vacaciones?
- Bastante bien. Fuimos a un camping con dos tiendas. Había muchas facilidades: piscina, tenis, bar, etcétera pero no hacía buen tiempo y es un poco difícil en una tienda. Nos gustaron el bar y el restaurante. Es mucho más fácil comer en el bar que en la tienda sobre todo cuando llueve.

The students look at **copymaster 51**, and listen to the recording again, noting anything they can use to write a similar account of a holiday on that campsite. They then write an account.

C Each student writes a letter to book for their families in this campsite, giving details of their families, dates, etc. and asking about prices.

4 Talking about free time
(Libro 3, Unidad 4)

A The students work on *Ahora sé*, page 53.

B Give each student a copy of **copymaster 52**. They could start work on this at home and discuss their answers in class.

UNIDAD 6

A comer

Main aim
Entertaining someone or being a guest in a Spanish home

Area(s) of experience
A – Everyday activities
B – Personal and social life

Materials
Cassette: Las comidas españolas, Unos platos típicos de España, Describiendo unos platos típicos, Dos platos típicos de América del Sur, ¿Te gustaría un poco más?, ¿Le puedo ayudar?, ¿Dónde pongo las servilletas? Repaso: hablando de la familia
Copymasters 53-65

Tasks
Understanding information about typical meals, meal times and eating habits
Discussing typical meals, meal times and eating habits, including differences between Britain and Spain and other Spanish-speaking countries
Discussing typical foods and how to make them
Stating/understanding a simple recipe
Expressing opinions about a meal or dish
Reacting to offers of food and drink (accepting and declining), giving reasons
Asking for a little, more, a lot, saying that one has had enough
Expressing appreciation and paying compliments
Offering to help

Grammar
Imperatives (familiar)
Absolute superlatives

Productive language
aceite de oliva   aceitunas
almendras   almuerzo
basta   cajón
cebolla   chorizo
fregadero   gaseosa
huele   lavaplatos
lechuga   mantel
mayonesa   mermelada
pimientos   poquito
probar   rico
riquísimo   sal
servilleta   zumo de tomate

Receptive vocabulary
bacalao a la vizcaína
cacerola
ensaladilla rusa
fabada asturiana
gazpacho
horno
leche frita
macedonia de frutas
queso manchego
tarta helada

Revision points
Talking about family
(*Libro 1, Unidad 9*)
Describing holidays
(*Libro 2, Unidad 6*)
Eating in a restaurant
(*Libro 3, Unidad 2*)
Buying everyday items
(*Libro 3, Unidad 5*)

¡A comer!   (page 64)

Main aim
To understand the learning goals of the *Unidad* and to want to achieve them.

A Work on this item along lines which have previously proved successful.

B You, and later the students, could adapt the examples, e.g.
   No. 1: describe a meal – the others guess which meal it is and whether it is Spanish or British.
   No. 2: describe how a dish is made – the others guess what dish it is.
   No. 3: state a difference (e.g. *Aquí se come mucho más temprano*) and the others guess the country referred to.
   No. 4: adapt this – the others say if you accept or reject.
   No. 5: express an opinion about a dish – the others guess what you have eaten.

UNIDAD 6

Las comidas españolas (page 64)

Main aim
Understanding, and giving, information about typical meals and meal times.

A Background information

As the students can see, meal times in Spain are quite different from ours. Many people have breakfast: a coffee and a roll or croissant in a bar on the way to work. Schoolchildren may have a sandwich or a pastry bought on the premises or from a nearby shop or bar during break.

Lunch is normally eaten between two and three. If you go into a restaurant at one o'clock you will usually find it quite quiet. Lunch usually consists of three courses and is the biggest meal of the day. Many bars and restaurants have a set *menú del día* which offers three courses, including bread and wine, for a very reasonable price.

Dinner is served extremely late so young people usually need a snack to keep them going. Children often take a sandwich to afternoon school which might end at six o'clock. (A bread roll with a bar of chocolate inside is a popular snack.) Adults may well have a few *tapas* in a bar on the way home: a *pincho de tortilla*, some *gambas* or *mejillones*, for example.

The evening meal is usually served around 10 o'clock. Teenagers often go out before dinner, returning about 10 o'clock to eat. Those returning later may still have a meal prepared for them if they haven't eaten.

It is important to stress that although the pattern of eating outlined above is common, there is less uniformity in eating habits as Spain changes and foreign influences take hold. Other factors which are changing lifestyles include greater affluence, more working women, different work arrangements (such as shift working) and more flexible shopping times.

B The students scan this, link it to a learning goal and then read it. Encourage them to ask for help with anything they do not understand. Then ask them to scan it again and to say which part of the text describes Spain and which part the U.K.

C Present **copymaster 53** and use it to ensure that the students understand the key food vocabulary, e.g. They read this item in order to find the name of everything illustrated and then they write each word. Ask a few students to read their words aloud and then involve everyone. You say the numbers, in random order, and point to students who should immediately name the food in that square.

As the students look at **copymaster 53**, you identify everything in turn, and then in random order. The students listen and repeat:
– only things to drink;
– only meats;
– only vegetables;
– only things with milk (sugar, salt) in;
– only things you have for breakfast (lunch, etc.).

Count round the class, but avoiding any number which can be divided by three: instead, the students say one of the things on the OHT, e.g.

uno, dos, leche, cuatro, cinco, huevo …

Make the OHP deliberately out of focus and see how many of the things the class can still identify and name.

D The students read carefully the text written by a young Spanish person. For each meal, help them to spot and discuss the similarities and differences between Spain and their country.

They then read what the young English person wrote and spot and discuss the similarities and differences between him and themselves.

E Help the students to create a grid to organise their listening to these recordings, e.g.

	Desayuno	Almuerzo	Cena	Otras comidas
1	Poco o nada	En casa 2 platos y fruta (verduras, carne, pescado)	10.00–10.30	11.30 tomo bocadillo
2	Zumo de naranja	3.00	8.00	
3	Si le apetece	1.30 a 2.30 ✓	10.00 / 10.15	7.00 Merienda
4		2.00	10.00	

As an example, you and your language assistant could describe a typical day's meals for you and complete the grid with appropriate notes.
Then work on the recordings, one at a time, correcting and clearing up problems with each one in turn.

UNIDAD 6

🏷️ **Las comidas españolas**

Número 1

Me levanto a las siete y media. Desayuno poco o nada y salgo de casa a las ocho. Las clases empiezan a las ocho y media. A las once y media tenemos recreo y tomamos algo – un bocadillo normalmente. Como en casa, dos platos y fruta. En casa comemos muchas verduras y alternamos carne un día y pescado otro.
Por la tarde descanso, estudio y hago la cena. A las diez, diez y media, empezamos a cenar. Después de cenar me acuesto sobre las 12.

Número 2

Me despierto a las siete y media y me levanto en seguida. El desayuno es normalmente un zumo de naranja que me preparo todos los días. Voy al colegio y vuelvo a las dos. Comemos a las tres. Luego duermo la siesta. A las ocho ceno y me acuesto a las diez y media.

Número 3

Vivo cerca del instituto así que me levanto a las ocho menos cuarto. Si me apetece desayuno. Vuelvo a casa a la una y media o dos y media si es miércoles, y almuerzo. Suelo almorzar a las dos y media aproximadamente. A las siete meriendo y sobre las diez, diez y cuarto ceno. Después de cenar suelo ver la televisión.

Número 4

Me levanto y entro al colegio a las nueve. Vuelvo a las dos y como. Cenamos a las diez y me voy a la cama a las once y media.

Play each recording once or twice more and help the students to assess each one in terms of the exam they are preparing for: how well would each speaker do and why? Encourage them to say which is best (number 1) and which is the least good (number 4).

F Each student writes an account of their normal eating routine, based on the models on this page of their book. This could be done at home. When you have corrected these, the students could reduce them to note form (e.g. using a purely visual 'mind map' – see page 66 above) and use their notes to give an oral presentation.

G Ask them what they have for the different meals and if what they eat is similar to the typical Spanish meal. Add more general questions about what people normally eat and drink, e.g.

¿Qué comes normalmente para desayunar?
¿Y para beber?
¿Se suele beber chocolate aquí?
¿A qué hora se come en España por lo general?
¿Y vosotros?
¿Y los fines de semana igual?
¿Qué te parece el almuerzo?
¿Es más fuerte que lo que se come aquí?

H Give each student a copy of **copymaster 54**. The students read the notices of mealtimes and memorise them. Ask them questions about when meals are served (they must not look at their book) as if you were a visitor and they were waiters in the hotel restaurant, for example:
Ya son las ocho. ¿Se puede tomar el desayuno?
Sí, señora.
¿A qué hora se puede comer?

Comparando los horarios (page 65)

Main aim

Understanding, and talking about, eating habits.

A The students scan this, link it to the relevant learning objective, and then read it carefully and ensure that they understand it.

B You present orally a typical day for you, using the verbs in this item. For every action, the students ask you the time and you tell them. They note down what you do and the times.
You now ask them at what times they do all these things, involving as many students as possible and moving quickly from one to another.

C The students work on this item in pairs, along the lines suggested in their book. You could move around, helping and joining in.

D Present on the board or OHT an account of your activities last Saturday, e.g.
Me vestí de prisa en el dormitorio.
Tomamos algo en el bar y cogimos el autobús al Sardinero.
Me reuní con mis amigos en la parada de autocares.
A las dos fuimos a comer.
Me levanté muy temprano a las siete.
Comí el menú del día en un restaurante cerca.

UNIDAD 6

Cené con la familia y me fui a la cama.
Tomé unas tostadas para el desayuno.
Cogimos el autocar para ir a la ciudad.
Por la tarde decidimos dar un paseo por el faro.
Jugamos al voleibol en la playa y tomamos el sol.
Volvimos al centro a las seis con tiempo para coger el autocar.
Salí de casa a las ocho menos cuarto.
Volví a casa a las nueve.
Llegamos a Santander a las diez y bajamos del autocar.

The students all read these sentences quietly and then re-write them, in the correct order, to produce a narrative of your day.

E With this as a model, they can all write an account of what they did on Sunday and also an account of a normal weekday. This could be done at home. If possible, they should record these accounts. When you have corrected them, the students could learn these by heart. They will form a useful addition to the 'islands of security' available to the students – chunks of Spanish which they can use with confidence whenever the opportunity arises.

¿Qué te gusta comer y beber? (page 66)

Main aim
Expressing opinions about food.

A The students look at the illustrations on page 66. Ask them if they know what each one is and, if not, explain it to them in Spanish, e.g. *gambas*:
Son mariscos bastante pequeños. Se preparan muchas veces con ajo. Se toman como tapa o primer plato. Son muy ricas.

B The students make a list similar to Miguel's showing their likes and dislikes. Invite comparisons, e.g.:
A mí me gusta el pescado pero a Miguel no le gusta.

C The students then ask their partners what they like and dislike.

D Ask them to prepare a menu to suit their guest – and hopefully one that they will both enjoy. Alternatively, they can discuss the menu as if they were cooking for themselves and could choose exactly what they wanted to eat. They can be encouraged to bring in other vocabulary for food and drink to make the menu and the exercise more varied. They have to make sure that they will both like all that is decided upon.

E As students complete Activity **D** you could ask them to write a shopping list for everything they would need for the meal they have planned. Two pairs could then come together and compare their shopping lists.

Unos platos típicos de España (page 67)

Main aim
Learning about typical Spanish dishes.

A The students scan this and report on the gist. They then read it carefully and ask about anything they do not understand and anything about which they would like more information. In answering their questions, ask them for their opinions about these dishes.

B The students study carefully the Andalusian dish. Make sure that they understand it by asking some questions, e.g.
¿Qué es el plato típico de Andalucía?
¿Qué es exactamente, el gazpacho?
¿Es un postre?
¿Se come caliente?
¿Qué hay en el gazpacho?
¿Te gustan los pimientos?
¿De qué color son los pimientos?
¿Qué es un trocito?

They then look at the text and listen to the recording, noting any new information. Ask several students to report on the differences they have found and clear up any problems. Then work on the other dishes in the same way.

Unos platos típicos de España
– Hola. Yo vivo en Sevilla en Andalucía. El plato típico más famoso es el gazpacho. Es una sopa que se sirve fría. Refresca mucho en verano cuando hace muchísimo calor. A mí no me gusta porque prefiero las sopas calientes.
– Vivo en una región que se llama la Mancha. Tiene fama por Don Quijote y el queso. El queso

UNIDAD 6

Manchego es de vaca y es muy duro. Me gusta mucho.
- En la región de Valencia se cultiva mucho arroz. Este arroz es el elemento esencial de la paella. Se hace con marisco, pescado, carne y, a veces, pollo. Se prepara en una paellera.
- Me encanta el pescado y por eso las sardinas, la merluza y el bacalao me encantan. El bacalao a la vizcaína se hace con salsa de tomate y ajo.
- En Asturias hay mucha agricultura. Se hace mucha sidra de las manzanas. La fabada es un plato típico de la región. Es muy fuerte: contiene chorizo y otra carne. Después comemos arroz con leche – otro plato típico.

Able students could now write a brief introduction to a local or national dish, or to their favourite dish. These could be illustrated and form an attractive display.
Other students could complete this C-test and illustrate it as their contribution to the display.

Es un pos_ muy típico. Consiste en ar_ , lec_ y azú_ . Se calienta en el hor_ . Se si_ caliente normal_ pero tam_ se come frío. Es riquí_ . Se co_ mucho en Gran Bre_ pero tamb_ en Ast_ y otras regi_ de Esp_ .

D For homework, the students could learn this information about Spanish dishes. You could base a quiz on it, e.g.

1 ¿Dónde está la Mancha?
2 ¿Cómo es el queso manchego?
3 ¿De dónde es la paella?
4 ¿Qué hay en una paella?
5 El bacalao a la vizcaína, ¿qué es exactamente?
6 ¿Dónde se suele beber sidra?
7 La fabada es un plato de habas, tocino y … ¿qué más?
8 Es una sopa fría, típica de Andalucía: ¿cómo se llama?
9 ¿Qué hay en el gazpacho?
10 ¿Qué plato prefieres tú y por qué?

¿En qué consiste? (page 68)

Main aim

Describing what typical dishes contain.

A The students scan this, report on the gist, and then read it and ask for any help they need. Answer their questions, spell words out for them and encourage them to write them down and to check spellings and meanings in a dictionary.

B Work on the model dialogue with the class. When everyone is happy with it, get some students to play the role of *Tú*. You play the part of the father and talk about other dishes (e.g. those in *Unos platos típicos de España*). You could reverse this and have able students play the role of the father, talking about other dishes.

C The students now work on this in pairs, discussing the other dishes on this page. Move around, listening, helping and joining in. As students finish this task, tell them to write down the ingredients for each dish.

D Each student writes an explanation of a typical dish or two, something they eat regularly, to present to a visiting Spanish speaker.
When you have corrected these, some students could read theirs aloud. The others guess what the dish is, ask relevant questions and express their own opinions about it.

¿Cómo se hace? (page 69)

Main aim

Describing how to make a typical dish.

The students scan this, report on the gist, and then read it carefully. To help them to understand and use the language of instructions you could present **copymaster 55** on the OHP and, e.g.
The students refer to their book and use this to describe each picture on the copymaster, e.g.

Número uno: corta el queso.

Show the copymaster out of focus and point to some blurred pictures. The students try to identify them. Gradually bring it into focus as the students continue to do this.
Play at Noughts and crosses.
Invite the students to make up new instructions, e.g.

Pon la cacerola en el horno.
Mezcla la leche y la mantequilla.

Then challenge them to make up a sentence with as many as possible of the words on the copymaster in it. If possible, give a small prize to the student who

UNIDAD 6

gets the most of these words in one sensible sentence.

Describiendo unos platos típicos (page 69)

Main aim
To develop listening skills.

A The students read the instructions carefully. To prepare for the listening exercise, they could anticipate what they will hear, using the available clues: for example, what dishes do they expect to hear described?

B If, in your view, the students need some help with this you could write 6–8 dishes on the board, including Yorkshire pudding, toad-in-the-hole and mushroom omelette.
The students listen and say what each speaker is describing.

Describiendo unos platos típicos
- Bueno, consiste en huevo, leche, sal y harina. Se hace en el horno. Es como un pastel. Se sirve con ternera, patatas y verduras. Es delicioso. Se toma normalmente los domingos a mediodía.
- Este plato es un poco como el primero. Se hace con harina, huevo, leche, agua y salchichas. Se hace en el horno también. Se toma a la hora de cenar.
- A mí me gustan los platos simples. Este plato se hace con huevos y champiñones. Se pone aceite de oliva en la sartén, se fríen los huevos y se añaden los champiñones.
- Se cortan la carne, las patatas y la cebolla y se ponen en una cacerola. Se prepara en el horno. Me gusta mucho.

C The students should now be ready to follow the next recording and to take notes about the main points. They report back, giving the facts and adding their own opinions.

Dos platos típicos de América del Sur
- Oye Nashy. Voy a ir a Perú y quiero saber lo que tengo que comer.
- Bueno, tendrás que comer mucho. Hay muchos platos riquísimos en Perú. Recomiendo que comas arroz con mariscos.
- ¿Y me podría decir en qué consiste?
- Sí, bueno, es a base de arroz y lleva toda clase de mariscos y también algunas verduras.
- ¿Es difícil de preparar?
- No es tan difícil.

- Deyanira, ¿qué platos me recomendarías comer en Chile?
- Si tú vas a Chile tienes que comer empanadas.
- ¿Y qué son estas empanadas?
- Las empanadas es una masa que contiene carne, aceitunas, huevo, pasas y cebolla.
- Mm, riquísimo. ¿Y lo comen todos los días?
- No exactamente todos los días. Generalmente las comemos para septiembre porque son las Fiestas Patria.
- ¿Y las puedes conseguir también en los restaurantes o en algún café?
- Sí, en los restaurantes.
- Nos vemos, chau.

¿Quieres …? (page 70)

Main aim
Reacting to offers of food and drink, giving reasons.

A Revise the unit so far, e.g.
Play a game of Twenty Questions.
Write on the board 6–8 names of foods. The students copy them in the order they prefer them. Then find out which were the most, and least, popular. Discuss these and see if the class can reach a consensus on likes and dislikes.
Write on the board the name of your favourite dish. Say what it is and why you like it. You could repeat this with your favourite drink. The students now write the names of their favourite dishes and drinks, and explain why they like them, in class and in pairs. You could also do this with what you do not like to eat and drink.

B The students scan this, link it to the relevant unit goal, and then read it carefully and ensure that they understand it. They then work on it in pairs, along the lines suggested in their book. When they have asked and answered all the questions in their book, they could make up more, similar questions and put them to each other.

UNIDAD 6

No lo he probado nunca (page 70)

Main aim

Reacting to offers of food and drink.

A The students scan this and link it to the relevant unit goal. They then read it carefully and ensure that they understand it.

B Once the students know what to do, they work on this in pairs, along the lines suggested in their book.

C Base some discussion on this, asking, e.g.

¿Quién ha estado en España?
¿Has probado churros (paella, etc.)?
¿Dónde?
¿Cuándo?
¿Te gusta la sangría (la tarta helada, etc.)?
¿Te gustan los churros (los calamares, etc.)?
¿Has probado churros alguna vez?

The students can reply:

Sí, los probé el año pasado / en casa de mi amigo / de vacaciones en Mallorca, etc.

or:

No, no los he probado nunca.

Then ask, e.g.

¿Te gustaría probar un poquito?

¡Me gustaría probarlo! (page 71)

Main aim

Understanding, and expressing, how certain dishes are made.

A The students scan this and report on the gist. They then read it carefully and check that they understand it fully.
Ask them to read the information about tortillas. Ask them questions about the ingredients. How it is served, whether they would like to try it and, if they have tried it, whether they like it.

B The students work on this in pairs along the lines suggested in their book.
They pair up the four food descriptions in the speech bubbles and practise dialogues, using the example as a model. Ask them questions, as above.

Give them a description of one of the dishes and see who can be the first to identify it, e.g.

Se come fría … se hace con patatas … huevos … y cebolla.
¿Es una tortilla?
Sí.

Then give them a number of true or false statements and ask them to say which are true and which are false.

C Give each student a copy of **copymaster 56**. They read the descriptions and name the dishes in English.
The following exercise is very difficult and involves describing English dishes in Spanish using the descriptions previously given as examples. To test whether the definition is accurate it would be a good idea to give each member of the pair four of the items and not to let them see the others. In the case of some students it may be advisable to give them a minute to look at all seven before describing four of them to their partners and working out the three definitions that the partner then makes.
The students could all write out a description of one or two of these dishes. When corrected, some of these could be read aloud and the others say what the dishes are.

¿Te gustaría un poquito más? (page 71)

Main aim

Offering food and drink, and reacting to these offers.

A The students scan this, report on the gist, and then read it carefully and check that they understand it fully.

B Divide the class into two teams. They race to identify all the food and drink illustrated. They are allowed to look things up, but this will cost time, an important point to bear in mind in exams. Each student then writes a complete list.
Base a game of *El juego de Kim* (see page 6) on these pictures.

C Practise asking and answering these questions with the class. You could put the questions to students and then invite them to put the questions to you. They can then continue this in pairs.

UNIDAD 6

D Ask the students to look at the pictures of food and drink and to give you a variety of ways in which you could ask people to have some, using the phrases and words underlined in the section above.

E Listening activity
Play number 1 through once and ask the students to make a note of what was offered or asked. Play it again. The students note if the offer was accepted or refused, or what response was made. Then play it again and ask whether the guest is being polite or impolite. This involves the skill of drawing conclusions rather than simply listening for set information.
Clear up any problems and work on the others in the same way.

¿Te gustaría un poquito más?

Número 1
– Bueno, mira, para beber, hay agua o gaseosa. ¿Qué prefieres?
– Quiero Coca-Cola.

Número 2
– ¿Tomas café después de comer?
– Sí, por favor. El café español está muy rico.

Número 3
– ¿Te gustaría más sopa?
– No, no me gusta nada. Prefiero la sopa inglesa.

Número 4
– ¿Te sirvo otro filete?
– Sí, por favor. La ternera está muy buena, me gusta mucho.

Número 5
– ¿Más macedonia de frutas?
– No gracias; está muy buena, pero no puedo más.

Número 6
– ¿Qué tal está la ensaladilla?
– Es que no la puedo comer, es horrible. Detesto la mayonesa.

Número 7
– De postre hay yogur o flan.
– No me gustan, ¿no hay otra cosa?

Número 8
– ¿Has comido bien?
– Hombre sí, he comido muy bien gracias. Todo estaba muy bueno.

Número 9
– ¿Has comido bien?
– No. No me gusta la comida española. Es mala. En Escocia comemos mejor.

F Play the tape again, stopping it after each section. Invite the students, where necessary, to improve upon what the guest said, e.g. in number 1, instead of:
Quiero Coca-Cola.
the guest could have said:
Gaseosa, por favor. Me gusta mucho.

G Give each student a copy of **copymaster 57**. They work on this in pairs.

¿Qué prefieres? (page 72)

Main aim
Expressing preferences.

A The students scan this and report on the gist. They then read it carefully and ensure that they understand it all.

B In pairs, they work on this along the lines suggested in their book.

C Put similar choices to students, using other foods and drinks, e.g.
¿Qué prefieres: champiñones o guisantes?
De postre hay flan o fruta. ¿Qué prefieres?
¿Tapas? Claro. ¿Qué quieres: tortilla española, aceitunas o almendras?
¿Tienes sed? ¿Qué quieres: agua mineral, gaseosa o zumo de naranja?

D Play a game of *El juego de los blancos*, e.g.
¿Prefieres un helado o … … ?
¿Prefieres un bocadillo de queso o … … ?
No me gusta … … .
Me gusta mucho … … .
Creo que voy a escoger … … .

E In pairs, the students ask each other questions about what they like to eat and drink. When replying, they can lie or tell the truth, and their partners guess which each time.

¿Te falta algo? (page 72)

Main aim
Asking for things at table.

97

UNIDAD 6

A The students scan this and report on the gist. They then read it carefully and check that they understand it all.

B The students use these examples to work out rules to account for the two forms of the imperative. Help them to do this and ensure that everyone understands.

C The students look at the phrases and, in pairs, take it in turns to practise asking a friend to pass them the items illustrated below:
¿Me puedes pasar la sal, por favor?

They then repeat the exercise, addressing each other as *usted*.

Ask some students to make both forms of request for a few of the items illustrated and clear up any problems. Each student could write a formal and an informal request for each item. This could be done at home.

D Now would be a good time to work again on *A ser detective*, page 189.

E Card game for two–four players
Give each pair/group 10 cards cut from **copymaster 58**. The cards are put face up on the table and the pupils memorise them. The cards are then turned over and the students in turn have to identify a card correctly. If he/she is correct the card is retained; if not, the card is replaced face down. The student with the most correct cards is the winner. To make the game fair it may be necessary to duplicate some of the cards to give a number divisible by the number of players (i.e. 12 or 16 cards for four players, 9, 12 or 15 cards for three players). If the students are playing in a group of four they can play as two pairs. One member of the pair has to ask for the item and his/her partner has to try to find it, for example:
¿Quieres pasar el pan, por favor?

Card game for two–four players
The same 10 cards are placed face down on the table. The players in turn have to turn over two cards which go together. The pairings are as follows:
Agua/Pan
Vinagre/Aceite
Fruta/Ensalada
Sal/Mostaza
Mayonesa/Salsa de tomate

If the pairing is correct, the player takes both cards; if not, the cards are put back face down on the table. The player with the most cards at the end is the winner. To make the game more difficult you can add pictures of other pairs related to the vocabulary of the unit: *tenedor/cuchillo, plato/fuente, mantel/servilleta* and *vaso/botella*.

G This would be a good time to revise the unit so far, e.g.
The students work on *Ahora sé*, using their favourite techniques.

¿Le puedo ayudar? (page 73)

Main aim
Offering to help in the house.

A The students scan this and link it to the relevant unit goal. They then read it and, with the help of their communication strategies and a dictionary, they ensure that they understand it. Give help where it is needed.

B The phrases are a mixture of those that the host and guest would say. Ask the class to look at the list for a minute and then give as many phrases as they can that the guest might say. Do the same for those that the host might say.

C The students then match numbered phrases to the pictures.

D Present the following incomplete questions on the board or OHP. See how many different and correct ways the class can find to complete each one.
¿Dónde pongo … … ?
¿Dónde están … … ?
¿Qué hago con … … ?
¿Te ayudo a … ?

¿Le ayudo a quitar la mesa? (page 73)

Main aim
Offering to help and responding to offers of help.

A Ask the class to look at the picture and memorise the items on the table. Ask them to close their

UNIDAD 6

books and see how much they can remember. The first student says:

Hay tenedores.

The second:

Hay tenedores y cuchillos.

And so on. No object may be repeated and all the objects have to be mentioned.

B In pairs, the students work on this along the lines suggested in their book. They could then work on it again, asking the same questions and, this time, answering them as they would in their own homes.

C Further activities

Aprende a ser la invitada ideal (**copymaster 59**)
Ask the students to read the magazine article on this copymaster and to see whether they would be ideal guests. Ask them which advice they think is most important and to put the sections in order of importance. Ask them whether they agree with all the advice.

¿Te gustaría cocinar a la española?
(**copymaster 60**)

The students read the recipe and, working in pairs, explain each operation to each other as if one of them were a non-Spanish-speaking person. Check their comprehension afterwards by asking key questions in English.

If the Domestic Science department were prepared to help it would be a valuable cross-curricular exercise for the students to carry out the instructions and make an omelette. Other simple recipes could also be used. The students would gain considerable confidence in carrying out instructions in this way and helping the non-Spanish speaker, in this case the cookery teacher. Failing this they could always take the recipe home and enlist their parents' help. They could then bring in their *chef d'oeuvre*!

¿Dónde pongo las servilletas? (page 74)

Main aim
Offering, and responding to offers.

A It would be a good idea to revise the unit so far, e.g. Start a vocabulary network on the board. Discuss it with the class and, with their help, add to it. Then ask the students to make their own, starting in the same way as you did, i.e.

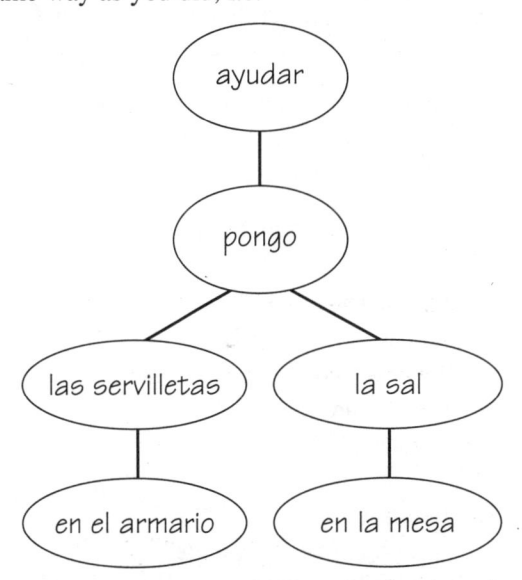

```
         ayudar
            |
          pongo
          /    \
las servilletas  la sal
     |             |
en el armario   en la mesa
```

Present this grid on the OHP. Ask who does the jobs in the students' homes and tick the appropriate boxes. They can then copy the grid and question people in the class, putting ticks in the boxes.

	Padre	Madre	Tú	Hermano/a	Otra persona
Hacer la compra					
Poner la mesa					
Preparar la comida					
Quitar la mesa					
Fregar los platos					
Limpiar el horno/el fregadero					
Limpiar la cocina					
Tirar la basura					

UNIDAD 6

Present this table on the OHP.

| El plato
El vaso
El sartén
La ensalada
Las servilletas
Las cacerolas
Los tenedores
Las cucharas | está
están | sucio.
sucia.
sucios.
sucias.
fresca.
limpio.
limpia.
limpios.
limpias. | Lo
La
Los
Las | pongo | en la nevera.
en el lavaplatos.
el el armario.
en el cajón.
en el fregadero. |

The students write as many sensible and correct sentences as they can in ten minutes with the words in the table. They can then compare their sentences.

B The students scan this item and report on the gist. They then read it carefully and check that they understand it all.

C They work on this along the lines suggested in their book.

¿Dónde pongo las servilletas?

Número 1
– ¡Oye! ¿Dónde pongo las servilletas? ¿Aquí?
– Sí, muy bien.
– ¿Está bien la mesa?
– Sí.

Número 2
– ¿Qué hago con el zumo de fruta?
– Ponlo en la nevera.
– ¿Dónde está la nevera?
– Allí en la esquina.
– Gracias.

Número 3
– ¿Te gustan los calamares?
– Sí.
– ¿Quieres más?
– No gracias. Están buenísimos pero no puedo más.
– Vale.

Número 4
– ¿Le ayudo a fregar los platos?
– No, está bien. ¿Te gustó la comida?
– Me gustó muchísimo, gracias.

D Present a list of words on the board, e.g. **cucharas, cuchillos, la mantequilla, la ensalada, el fregadero, el horno, la lechuga, la mermelada, las almendras, las aceitunas, el lavaplatos, los vasos, las cacerolas.**

The students see where each of these words could be used to replace one in the dialogues in their book and read out the relevant sentences with the new words in. They could continue this in pairs.

E As students finish Activity **D** give them a copy of **copymaster 61**. They could work on this at home to produce a written narrative.

F Give each student a copy of **copymaster 62**. They work on this in pairs.

Le escribo para agradecerle (page 74)

Main aim
Reading and writing a thank you letter.

A The students scan and then read this as usual.

B Ask students to adapt orally the model letter to meet the brief. When everyone knows what to do, they write the letter. When you have corrected these, the students write a completely correct version and learn this by heart.

C To check, and help, their learning present a C-test version of the letter on the board:
Estimada señ_ :
Le escr_ para agrade_ la ce_ de ay_ . Fue delic_ y m_ gustó muchí_ . La so_ de ceb_ fue buení_ , el bac_ a la vizc_ fue delic_ y la mace_ de fru_ fue muy ri_ .
Atentamente su_ ,

Clear up any problems. Then give a new brief and ask the students to adapt the letter again to meet this brief, e.g. *Ayer a mediodía fuiste a casa de una*

UNIDAD 6

amiga a comer. Escribe una carta para agradecer a su padre que preparó la comida. Comiste gazpacho, paella y helado de fresa.

D As students complete Activity **C** give them a copy of **copymaster 63**. They can complete this for homework.

Una palabra conduce a otra (page 74)

Main aim

To develop communication strategies and to extend vocabulary.

A Work on this along lines which have previously proved successful.

B Present some incomplete sentences on the board or OHP. The students choose a word from the list to complete each sentence, e.g.

1 *No tengo un gato, pero tengo … … .*
2 *¿Quieres … … más de sopa de mariscos?*
3 *Vivo en un piso en Madrid pero quisiera vivir en … … cerca de la costa.*
4 *Llego en seguida; ¿puedes esperar … … ?*
5 *Tengo un pez, un conejo y … … .*

C Present orally or on the board some definitions of words on the list. The students find, and write, each word, e.g.

1 *Es una silla grande.*
2 *Hablo de un coche pequeño.*
3 *Es una cuchara, pero es pequeña.*
4 *Lo que quiero no es una taza pequeña, es más grande, muy grande.*
5 *Sirve para hacer un pequeño bocadillo.*

Ahora sé (page 75)

Main aim

To provide a summary of the *Unidad* and a basis for more practice and revision.
To allow for differentiated practice and revision a number of activities can be used, e.g
All the students think of a recipe they can make and of how they would advise someone to make it. Ask some to say some dos and don'ts for their recipes.
They then write 5–8 dos and don'ts. They then form pairs and share their expertise. If some students have chosen the same dish, they could compare notes to see if they agree on how to do it.

Produce a number of cards. On each, write half a sentence of a dialogue or narrative from this unit. Give one card to each student. First, they find who has the other half of their sentence. When all the sentences have been made, they work together to make up the complete dialogue or narrative.
Present some situations on the board. The students decide how they would telephone the person to say thank you. The students could discuss each attempt and suggest how it could be improved. They then all choose one and write an appropriate thank you letter, e.g.

Comiste ayer con un amigo: la sopa estaba fría. Había demasiada sal en el pescado y no había postre. Fuiste a casa de unos amigos a comer. No había ni leche ni azúcar. Te sirvieron bocadillos de sardina que odias y sólo había una galleta para cada uno como postre.

Revision activities

1 Talking about family
(Libro 1, Unidad 9)

A Encourage the students to study page 89 of *Libro 1* and to practise all the words and sentences.

B Play this recording of three Spanish speakers presenting their families and pets. The students listen and make notes about the key facts and opinions, using a dictionary to check their notes.

Repaso: hablando de la familia

Número 1

Somos cinco en casa: mi madre, mi padre, mis dos hermanos y yo. Mis abuelos viven muy cerca. Mi hermano mayor tiene veinte años y mi hermano menor tiene diez años. No tenemos animales en casa. A mis padres no les gustan y el piso es muy pequeño y no hay mucho sitio. Me gustaría tener un perro.

Número 2

Vivo aquí con mi madre y mi abuela. Mis padres están divorciados y mi abuelo murió el año pasado. Tenemos dos gatos que se llaman Juan y Carlos. Mi madre tiene cuarenta y dos años y mi abuela sesenta y cinco.

UNIDAD 6

Número 3

Soy hijo único. Vivo aquí con mis padres y con mis abuelas. Es una casa bastante grande y hay sitio para mis abuelas. Una tiene noventa años y la otra ochenta y ocho. Tengo un perro que se llama Oscar, un conejo que se llama Bugs y un caballo que se llama Ron Rojo.

Clear up any problems about the content. Then play each one again so that the students can listen to the language used and write notes to help them with the next activity.

C Each student writes a presentation of their own family and pets. Over a number of lessons, ask a few to make their presentations orally and encourage the others to ask follow-up questions.

2 Describing holidays
(Libro 2, Unidad 6)

A The students work on page 74 of *Libro 2*, using their favourite techniques.

B The students work in pairs, taking turns to guess where the other student went on holiday by asking what s/he did and saw, e.g.

¿Fuiste a merendar en la playa?
¿Fuiste a esquiar o a patinar?
¿Hiciste windsurfing?
¿Sacaste fotos?
¿Aprendiste a pescar?
¿Saliste a una discoteca?
¿Compraste recuerdos?
¿Hizo buen tiempo?
¿Llovió?
¿Visitaste monumentos?
¿Hiciste montañismo?

You could write these model questions on the board and leave them there.

3 Eating in a restaurant
(Libro 3, Unidad 2)

A The students work on *Ahora sé*, page 28 of *Libro 3*.

B Present this narrative on the board or OHP. The students read it and then write a dialogue based on it.

El viernes tres amigos y yo decidimos ir a un restaurante por la noche. Llamamos por teléfono para reservar una mesa y llegamos a las diez y media. Pedimos cinco cosas para los cuatro: una tortilla, una ensalada, pollo al ajillo, champiñones y calamares. El camarero llegó con la ensalada y nos explicó que la electricidad no funcionaba y que sólo había cosas como ensalada. Comimos la ensalada y el pan y después unos entremeses y queso. Pagamos muy poco porque el dueño del restaurante dijo que sentía mucho el problema. Nosotros salimos muy contentos.

C Each student could write ten pieces of advice for young Spanish speakers coming to their town about eating in local restaurants.

4 Buying everyday items
(Libro 3, Unidad 5)

A The students work on *Ahora sé*, page 63. They could also read the *Unidad* again to check that they can understand everything in it.

B Give each student one of the shopping lists on **copymaster 64** and one or two of the items on **copymaster 65**. Each student aims to buy all the things on their list by moving around and asking other students. You could write a model dialogue on the board, e.g.

– *Buenos días. Quisiera medio kilo de queso.*
– *Sí, señor. Tenga. ¿Algo más?*
– *Por favor, ¿tiene latas de sardinas?*
– *Lo siento, señor, pero no tengo sardinas.*
– *Gracias, adiós.*

UNIDAD 7

Teléfonos y faxes

Main aim
Using the telephone and sending fax messages

Area(s) of experience
C – The world around us
D – The world of work
E – The international world

Materials
Cassette: Teléfonos y faxes, ¿Tiene teléfono?, ¿Quieres dejar un recado?, ¿Tienes miedo del teléfono?, ¿Quiere dejar un recado?, ¿Le digo que le llame?, ¡Qué pesado!, Repaso: las vacaciones, Repaso: anuncios en los grandes almacenes.
Copymasters 66–74

Tasks
Asking for telephone/fax services

Understanding how to use a phone in Spain
Answering a phone, stating name
Asking to speak to someone
Taking and leaving a message, including a time to call back

Grammar
cuando + subjunctive

Productive language
una conferencia con …
está comunicando
¿de parte de quién?
dígame
equivocarse de número
fax
guía telefónica
línea
llamada de cobro revertido
llamar por teléfono
mandar

número de teléfono
oiga
prefijo
recado
tarjeta telefónica
teléfono

Receptive language
auricular
descolgar
introducir (monedas)
marcar
tono

Revision points
Describing past holidays (*Libro 2, Unidad 7*)
Shopping in a department store (*Libro 3, Unidad 3*)
Eating at home as host or guest (*Libro 3, Unidad 6*)

Teléfonos y faxes (page 76)

Main aim
To understand the unit goals and to see their relevance and value.

A Work on this item along lines which have previously proved successful.

B Play these recordings and invite the students to link each one to one of the unit goals.

Teléfonos y faxes

Número 1
– Perdone, señor. ¿Hay un teléfono por aquí?
– Pues, no sé. No soy de aquí.

Número 2
– El 12.31.09, dígame.
– Buenas tardes, señora. Quisiera hablar con Miguel, por favor.
– Ah, Miguel no está. ¿De parte de quién?
– Es de parte de María. ¿Puede decirle que me llame cuando vuelva?
– Sí, por supuesto.

Número 3
– Buenos días, señor. ¿Puedo mandar un fax desde aquí?
– Sí, señorita.
– Y, ¿cuánto cuesta?

Número 4
– Oiga.
– Buenos días, señor. Quiero hablar con Juan.
– Un momento, le llamo.
– Gracias, señor.

¿Dónde puedo telefonear y mandar un fax?
(page 76)

Main aim
Asking where to obtain telephone and fax services.

UNIDAD 7

A The students read this and ask about any words which they do not understand. Wherever possible, help them to work out the meaning of these words by using appropriate comprehension strategies.

B The students follow the text of the two model dialogues, repeating each sentence after you and maintaining your speed and pronunciation. In pairs, they then act out the dialogues, playing each role in turn.

C To help students to learn the dialogues you could present them on the OHP, covering some of the words. The students, in pairs, act out the dialogue in full, adding the missing words. You could gradually cover up more and more words.

D The students adapt the model dialogues to meet the four briefs. They could do this orally, in pairs, and also write the new dialogues, in class or at home.

¿Hay un teléfono por aquí? (page 77)

Main aim

Learning the language needed to make a phone call.

A Encourage the students to work out for themselves any new words in this item and to try to do this without using a dictionary. Then work on the item along the lines suggested.

B The students cover the sentences and look at the pictures. You read the sentences aloud, in random order, and the students say or write the number of the matching picture. Give the class five minutes to learn the sentences and then cover them up again. You say the number of one of the pictures and they say or write from memory a sentence which goes with the picture.

¿Tiene teléfono? (page 77)

Main aim

To practise listening skills

Play the following recordings. The first time, ask the students to say if the person wants to phone Spain, to phone abroad or if it could be either. The second time they hear each dialogue, ask them to report on the main points and details. Then ask the students to look back over the unit so far and to write a list of the key words and sentences needed for finding and using a telephone. They then listen again to the dialogues and tick the expressions on their lists whenever they hear them. Finally, play each dialogue again and play at *¿Verdad o mentira?*

¿Tiene teléfono?

Número 1
- Buenas tardes. Quisiera una conferencia con York.
- ¿York en Inglaterra?
- Exactamente.
- Vale. ¿Con qué número?
- Es el 1904 87 58 16.
- Bien. Cuando haya una cabina libre le avisaré.

Número 2
- Oiga, ¿podría usar el teléfono?
- Sí, ¿lo pongo en la barra?
- Sí sí, está bien. ¿Tiene una guía telefónica?
- Pues no, creo que no tenemos.
- ¡Vaya! ¿Sabe el prefijo para Málaga?
- ¿Para Málaga?, pues sí. Creo que es el 95.

Número 3
- Perdone. ¿Sabe Vd. si hay un teléfono por aquí?
- Pues mire, no soy de aquí, pero me parece que hay una cabina al otro lado de la plaza.
- ¿Al otro lado de la plaza?
- Sí, cuando llegue allí verá una iglesia a la derecha y me parece que hay una cabina detrás de la iglesia.

Número 4
- ¿Podría usar el teléfono?
- ¿Adónde quiere llamar?
- A Australia.
- Pues no, lo siento, no se pueden hacer llamadas internacionales con este teléfono. Vaya a Teléfonos o a una cabina que acepte llamadas internacionales.

Número 5
- ¿Tiene teléfono?
- Sí, sí, está al lado del comedor.
- Quisiera hacer una llamada de cobro revertido.
- Pues entonces tiene Vd. que llamar a la operadora. Es el 003.

Número 6
- Bueno, gracias. ¿Cuánto es?
- Vamos a ver. Son veinte pasos registrados en el contador. Entonces son 700 pesetas.
- Tenga.

UNIDAD 7

¿Cuál es el número? (page 78)

Main aim

To learn how to ask for, and give, telephone numbers.

A Begin by revising numbers, e.g.
Play at Bingo, with each student choosing and writing five numbers from 150 to 200.
You choose a number from 0 to 999. The students try to find the number. Until someone guesses correctly, you simply say: *Más alto* or *Más bajo*.
Dictate numbers at random, noting them down as you say them. As soon as all the students have written one number, say another and see how many the class can write in one minute. Check the answers, clear up any problems and see if the class can improve on their score.
Write on the board a sequence of numbers, saying each one a few times as you write it, e.g. 0, 15, 30, 45, 60. Then rub one off and ask, e.g.

¿Qué hay que escribir aquí?

The student who gives you the answer writes the missing number on the board and rubs out another. Write a list of digits vertically on the board, e.g. 7, 3, 9, 8, 1, 4, 0, 3, 2, 5. Time the class while ten students read these digits, saying one each. Then write ten more digits in front of those on the board and time another ten students saying the two-digit numbers. Repeat this with a third row of digits, producing ten three-digit numbers for the students to say.

B Work on this item along the lines suggested.

C You can give the class further number practice in the following ways:
Write up ten Spanish telephone numbers on the board/OHP. Say a number quite quickly and ask them to pick out the one you have said or repeat it. Using the same numbers, say one of them and ask whether it is the same as one on the board/OHP or incorrect, e.g. 340 82 14:

Trescientos cuarenta, ochenta y dos, catorce.
Verdad.

729 12 56:

Setecientos veintinueve, doce, cincuenta y cinco.
Mentira.

The students can then correct the 'mistake'.

¿Qué número de teléfono tiene? (page 78)

Main aim

Asking for, and giving, telephone numbers.

A The students read this carefully and ensure that they understand it and know what to do. Practise some with the class. You ask for some of the numbers and invite students to give you them. Then reverse this so that students ask you for the numbers. They can then continue this in pairs.

B For homework, each student could produce a similar useful list in Spanish for Spanish-speaking visitors to their town.

La tarjeta telefónica (page 79)

Main aim

To develop reading skills.

A Make sure that everyone understands the instructions and the questions. Encourage students to use a dictionary if necessary.

B In pairs, the students practise asking and answering the questions. Then do this in class, with you asking the questions. After a while, put the questions in random order and see how quickly the class can answer them. Then see if they can improve on this.

C To encourage scan reading, base a *¿Verdad o mentira?* quiz on the text. After a while, continue this with the book closed, e.g.
La tarjeta telefónica se vende en estaciones de servicio (en restaurantes, etc.).
Cuesta 2.000 o 3.000 pesetas.
Es posible coleccionar tarjetas.
Puede llamar al extranjero con una tarjeta.
Es fácil comprar una tarjeta.

D Adapt the first section to talk about phone cards in your country. This could be done orally first and then written, in class or at home.

UNIDAD 7

Telefonear al extranjero (page 80)

Main aim
To understand how to use a telephone in Spain.

A The students read the text and try to work out the meaning of the words and instructions by using communication strategies such as context and world knowledge (e.g. how to use a public telephone in their country). If anyone still needs help, mime using a public phone in Spain and say the appropriate instructions.

Ask a student to use the pictures and the text to mime how to use a phone (either with coins or a card). You and the other students accompany this mime with the appropriate instructions. Then do this in reverse. One student gives the instructions and another mimes. They can continue this in pairs.

B You say the instructions aloud. The students repeat only those which apply to making a phone call within Spain.

C In class or at home, the students draw a series of pictures to show clearly how to use a telephone in Spain. They write appropriate instructions with each picture. If they draw each picture on a separate piece of paper, they can shuffle them and ask their partners to put them in the correct order and to explain how to use a phone as they do so.

D For homework, each student could adapt this text to explain how to use a public telephone to call to Spain from their own country.

E The students read *Punto información* and use this, in a class discussion, to categorise telephones, e.g. how many different sorts there are, what these are, the pros and cons of each. They could then, orally and in writing, adapt this text to match their own country.

You could base a class quiz on local telephones, e.g.

¿Dónde se venden tarjetas cerca de aquí?
¿Hay un teléfono/una cabina telefónica cerca de aquí?
¿Por dónde se va allí?
¿Qué monedas se utilizan?
¿Cuánto cuesta telefonear dentro de la ciudad?
¿Es el mismo precio todo el día?
¿Aquí hay teléfonos en los bares y cafés?
¿Dónde los hay?
¿Qué tengo que hacer si quiero llamar a X?

F Give everyone a copy of **copymaster 66**. Before they read the article and the rubric ask the students to look at the title only. Get them to say what they think the article is about, e.g.

Los teléfonos son malos pero las televisiones son buenas.
Hay más televisiones que teléfonos en España.

Do not discount any suggestion. List the responses on an OHP and give them ten seconds to accept/reject the suggestions on the list.

Ask them to read the passage, then ask questions:
¿Te ayudó el título?
¿Hay información en el artículo que no esperabas?
¿Qué se dice sobre tu país?
¿Estás de acuerdo con el artículo?

¿Quieres dejar un recado? (page 81)

Main aim
Understanding, taking and leaving messages.

A The students again begin by reading this silently and trying to work out any new words. Give them a time limit of five minutes and allow them to use dictionaries if they need to. This is excellent exam training. If anyone has not completed this in five minutes, try to find out why and give relevant advice.

B Work on this along the lines suggested, orally first and then in writing.

¿Quieres dejar un recado?

– Hola, soy yo, Marisol. Quiero hablar urgentemente contigo. Estaré en casa entre las nueve y las diez. ¿Me puedes llamar? Gracias, adiós.

– Oiga, soy la madre de Puri. Tiene un resfriado y está en la cama. No puede ir a la bolera el miércoles. Te llamará mañana si está mejor.

– Miguel al aparato. Me interesa ir a ver Celtas Cortos en la Plaza de Toros. ¿Cuándo es? Llámame hoy si puedes.

– Soy yo, Federico. No es importante ... en efecto, si puedes, llámame, ¿de acuerdo?

– Oye. Soy Andrea. ¿Quieres salir conmigo mañana? Estoy en casa a las seis. ¿Me llamas? Adiós.

UNIDAD 7

C Play the messages again. After each one, ask the class to say how urgent the message is, if at all.

D Play the messages again. With their books closed, the students listen and write appropriate messages. You could add a few new messages for the students to note, e.g.

Soy yo, Eduardo. Tengo dos entradas para el partido de fútbol. Si quieres ir, llámame. Estoy en casa de mis abuelos. Es el 23-34-45. Estaré aquí hasta las cinco.

Hola, Anita al aparato. Tengo un problema con los deberes de matemáticas. ¿Puedes llamarme cuando vuelvas?

Buenas tardes. Soy el Sr. Roldán. Le llamo para decirle que el autocar a Madrid sale a las ocho y media mañana. Sale de delante del colegio.

E Give each student one part of **copymaster 67**. They work with these in pairs.

¿Tienes miedo del teléfono? (page 81)

Main aim

Learning how to ask to speak to someone on the telephone.

A Ask the students to read and understand the instructions in exam conditions so as to develop the necessary skills.

B Play the recordings. Play each one twice and ask which person is the more nervous. Clear up any problems. The students listen to each one again and note who wishes to talk to whom. Ask several students to tell you this information and clear up any problems. Finally, play the recordings again and ask who leaves a message and what the message is.

¿Tienes miedo del teléfono?
Número 1
- Dígame.
- Buenos días. Quiero hablar con César Cordero, por favor.
- ¿De parte de quién?
- ¿Qué?
- ¿Su nombre, por favor?
- Ah, sí. Me llamo Anita Morcillo.
- ¿Cómo se escribe?
- M.O.R.C.I.L.L.O.
- Un momentito, por favor …

Número 2
- Buenos días. Dígame.
- ¿Está Miguel?
- ¿Miguel?
- Sí. Miguel Peñaranda.
- No está.
- ¿Puedes dejar un recado?
- Sí.
- Dile que Angel llamó y que me llame.
- Vale.

Número 3
- Dígame.
- Soy Angela Gómez.
- Sí.
- Quiero hablar con el director.
- Lo siento. No está. ¿Quiere dejar un recado?
- Sí, no, no sé. Voy a llamar más tarde.
- Vale, adiós.

Número 4
- Oiga. Quiero hablar con el Sr. López.
- ¿De parte de quién?
- Srta. López, su hija.
- Lo siento, señorita, pero no está en la oficina hoy.
- ¿Dónde está?
- Está en nuestra oficina en Oviedo. ¿Quiere dejar un recado?
- No, … ¿Tiene el número de teléfono de la oficina?
- Sí, 481 22 11.
- Gracias.

C You say aloud the important sentences used on the telephone. The students have two columns on a page and write each sentence in the appropriate column:

La recepcionista	El cliente

UNIDAD 7

You could use the following:
Dígame.
Lo siento, no está.
Dile que llamé y que me llame.
Me llamo López.
¿De parte de quién?
Quiero hablar con el director.
¿Quiere dejar un recado?
Buenos días.
¿Cómo se escribe?
L.O.P.E.Z.
Vale, señor López.
Gracias, señora.
Adiós.

Move around as you say each sentence, helping students where necessary.
The students could now re-write these sentences to produce a sensible telephone conversation. They could play read these, in pairs, taking turns to be nervous and confident.

D As students complete Activity **C** you could give them a copy of **copymaster 68**. They study the instructions and the form, and ensure that they understand. You play the recording and the students complete the form.

¿Quiere dejar un recado?

Número 1
- Hotel Clarín. Buenos días.
- Buenos días. Quisiera hablar con el Sr. Prieto en la habitación 706.
- ¿Prieto dice?
- Sí, P.R.I.E.T.O. en la 706.
- Un momento, por favor.
(Ringing, no reply)
- Lo siento señor, no contesta.
- ¿Le puedo dejar un recado?
- Sí señor, por supuesto.
- Dígale que me llame.
- ¿De parte de quién?
- Sr. Guerra, G.U.E.R.R.A.
- ¿Y el número de teléfono?
- 34-86-24.
- Muy bien. Le daré el recado en cuanto vuelva.
- Gracias, adiós.

Número 2
- ¿Hotel Clarín?
- Sí señora.
- Quisiera hablar con la Srta. Rodríguez en la 210.
- Lo siento, no está pero volverá a la una. ¿Quiere dejar un recado?
- Dígale que volveré a llamar a la una y cuarto.
- ¿De parte de quién?
- Ah sí, Sra. Castro.
- Muy bien, señora. Ya se lo diré cuando vuelva.
- Gracias, adiós.

Número 3
- Hotel Clarín, dígame.
- Quiero dejar un recado para el Sr. Pérez en la habitación 333.
- Sí.
- Dígale que el Sr. Martínez desea verle a las nueve y media en el hotel.
- Sr. Martínez, nueve y media, hotel.
- Sí.
- Ya se lo diré.
- Gracias.

Número 4
- Buenas tardes. Quiero hablar con Marta Alonso, por favor.
- Un momentito. No cuelge. Le voy a conectar.
(Phone rings, no reply)
- Lo siento, no contesta. ¿Quiere dejar un recado?
- Sí, voy a dejar un recado entonces.
- Muy bien.
- Dígale que me llame.
- ¿De parte de quién?
- Pablo.
- Pablo, ¿nada más?
- Nada más, gracias.

Problemas (page 82)

Main aim

Coping with the unexpected when making telephone calls.

A The students read this to themselves and ensure that they understand it. You could ask questions about the two model dialogues, e.g.
Cuando la secretaria contesta, ¿qué dice primero?
¿Con quién quiere hablar Antonio Saura?
¿Dónde está el señor Calderón?
¿Deja un recado Antonio Saura?
¿Qué quiere hacer Antonio Saura?

B The students then listen to the dialogues with their books closed.

UNIDAD 7

Problemas
- Dígame.
- Quiero hablar con El Sr. Calderón.
- ¿De parte de quién?
- De parte de Antonio Saura.
- Lo siento. El Sr. Calderón no está en la oficina hoy. ¿Quiere dejar un recado?
- Es urgente. ¿Sabe dónde está?
- Está en nuestra oficina en Madrid.
- ¿Tiene el número de teléfono?
- Sí, el 484 54 09.
- Gracias, adiós.

- Dígame.
- Quiero hablar con la Sra. Velázquez.
- ¿De parte de quién?
- De parte de Juana Fuentes.
- Lo siento, no está hoy.
- ¿Le puedo dejar un recado?
- Sí.
- ¿Puede decirle que me llame cuando vuelva?
- ¿Su número?
- 473 21 42.

C The students study the second dialogue and the message. They then cover the dialogue and, referring only to the message, play the part of the caller while you play the part of the secretary.

D Present on the board or OHP a role-play brief for the first dialogue, e.g.

Antonio Saura es arquitecto. Quiere hablar urgentemente con su cliente, el señor Calderón. Llama a su oficina.

Referring only to this brief, some students take turns to play the part of Antonio Saura while you play the part of the secretary. Keep practising until the students can do this easily. They could continue this in pairs.
Repeat this with the second model and an appropriate brief, e.g.

Eres Juana Fuentes. Necesitas hablar urgentemente con la Sra. Velásquez. Llamas a su oficina.

E The students now study the four messages and use these to make up the phone conversations. They could write these first as homework and then make up oral conversations in pairs.

F This would be a good time to work on *A ser detective*, page 192.

¿Le digo que le llame? (page 82)

Main aim
To give further listening practice and practice in taking and leaving messages.

A Play the recording. The students read the text as they listen. Ensure that they understand everything.

B In pairs the students then role play the dialogue. One student plays the receptionist, the other plays the person calling. They can then change roles.

C For further practice ask the students can invent different names and places for the conversation.

¿Le digo que le llame?
- Dígame.
- Oiga, quisiera hablar con el Sr Santos.
- ¿De parte de quién?
- Soy Raúl Carrasco.
- Lo siento, el Sr Santos está en Estocolmo.
- ¿Está en Estocolmo?
- Sí, no vuelve hasta el jueves.
- Bueno, cuando vuelva, dígale que me llame.
- De acuerdo. ¿Le puedo dejar algún recado?
- Sólo que me llame en cuanto vuelva.
- ¿Quiere decirme su nombre otra vez?
- Sí. Es Carrasco, Raúl Carrasco.
- Vale. Le diré que le llame. ¿Su número?
- Es el 408 69 43.

Quisiera mandar un fax (page 83)

Main aim
Learning how to send a fax.

A The students read this and ensure that they understand it.

B The students read the model dialogue and then follow the text. To help them to learn it, they repeat each sentence after you, maintaining the same speed and pronunciation. They then play read it in pairs, playing each part in turn.

C In pairs, they adapt the model dialogue, using the information in the table.

D As students complete Activity C to your satisfaction, give them a copy of **copymaster 69**.

109

UNIDAD 7

Ask them to find and to highlight the key sentence in each paragraph, the sentence which conveys the key information. This is a very useful reading skill. As here, informative texts usually have key sentences – usually at the start of each paragraph – with the rest of the paragraph expanding on this or giving examples. The students could use the highlighted key sentences to give brief reports on this text.

Reservando una habitación por fax
(page 84)

Main aim

How to reserve a hotel room by fax.

A The students study this silently and ensure that they understand it.

B Students adapt the model orally to make it meet different briefs which you present on the board or OHP, e.g.

Quiere reservar dos habitaciones individuales entre el 10 y 12 de julio. Va a llegar a las 21 horas.

Quiere reservar una habitación doble con ducha para el 21 de agosto. Va a llegar a las 18 horas.

Quiere reservar una habitación doble y una habitación individual para tres noches del 22 al 25 de marzo.

Quiere dos habitaciones con terraza y baño. Va a llegar a las dos de la tarde.

Quiere dos habitaciones dobles con baño para una noche. Va a llegar el 14 de noviembre por la tarde.

C The students now write the fax for the Hotel Ramiro 1. They could do this at home.

D In pairs, or on their own, the students make up a dialogue for sending their fax. They could include, e.g.
Asking where they can send a fax from.
Asking the way to the post office.
Enquiring about how to send a fax and the price.

Ahora sé
(page 85)

Main aim

To provide a summary of the *Unidad* and a basis for more practice and revision.

A The students work on this using techniques which they know work for them.

B Now, or later for revision, you could use more activities based on this summary, e.g.
You read aloud sentences from the list on page 85. The students categorise each one depending on who would say it: someone calling or someone being called.
See how good the students are at recognising voices. Ask two or three students to close their eyes. You point to someone who reads aloud any sentence in the list. The students who closed their eyes guess who spoke.

Give out copies of **copymaster 70** and play the recording. The students describe each message. Then play each one again and ask the students to note, and report on, the key points.

¡Qué pesado!
– Lo siento, no hay nadie en casa. Si quiere dejar un recado, hágalo después del tono.
– Usted ha llamado al 76 59 02. Lo siento pero en este momento ni María ni Juana están en casa. Si quiere dejar un recado hágalo después del tono y María o Juana le llamará cuando vuelva. Hable claramente y deje su nombre y el número de teléfono. Gracias.
– Hola. Soy Anita. Mamá no está en casa. Si quieres dejar un recado se lo diré. Adiós.
– Buenas días. Usted ha llamado a la Casa Blanca en Washington. El presidente no está en casa ahora pero si quiere dejar un recado, hágalo después del tono.
– Siento mucho no estar en casa. No me gusta el ansafone pero si quieres dejar un recado te llamaré cuando vuelva.

Give out a copy of **copymaster 71** to able students to work on in pairs.

110

UNIDAD 7

Revision activities

1 Describing past holidays
(Libro 2, Unidad 7)

A Give each student a copy of **copymaster 72**. They listen to the recording and complete the grid. They then draw a conclusion from the information in the grid: where they would go on holiday and why.

Repaso: las vacaciones

Número 1
- Carlos, ¿adónde fuiste de vacaciones?
- A Barcelona.
- A Barcelona, y ¿cuándo fue? ¿en verano?
- No, fui en abril.
- ¿Fuiste solo?
- No, fui con amigos, con tres amigos.
- ¿Fuisteis a un hotel?
- No, a un hostal en el centro de la ciudad cerca de la Plaza Cataluña.
- ¿Te gustó?
- Mucho. Hizo mucho calor pero con algunas nubes.
- ¿Qué hiciste?
- Visité el estadio olímpico y el parque de atracciones.
- Muy bien.

Número 2
- María, fuiste a Lima, ¿verdad?
- Sí, con mis abuelos.
- ¿Cuándo fuiste?
- En octubre. Fuimos a un hotel no muy lejos de las playas.
- ¿Por qué fuiste a Lima?
- A visitar a la familia. Tengo primos y tíos en Lima.
- ¿Qué tiempo hizo?
- Hizo mucho calor, muchísimo calor.
- ¿Hiciste algo especial?
- No, pasé mucho tiempo con mis primos en casa.

Número 3
- Luis, ¿qué tal estás?
- Muy bien.
- Oye, ¿adónde fuiste de vacaciones el año pasado?
- Fui a Málaga en junio.
- ¿Fuiste con la familia?
- No, ¡qué va! con el colegio. Fuimos a un albergue juvenil.
- ¿Cómo pasaste el tiempo?
- Pues, mucho tiempo en la playa. Hizo un tiempo maravilloso, mucho calor y mucho sol. Fuimos a discotecas, hicimos deporte: voleibol, natación …
- ¿Te gustó?
- Hombre, fue estupendo.

Número 4
- Antonia, ¿adónde fuiste de vacaciones?
- A Buenos Aires, capital de Argentina.
- ¿A Argentina?
- Sí, mi padre es argentino y mis tíos viven todavía allí.
- ¿Fuiste a verles?
- Sí.
- ¿Cuándo fuiste?
- En agosto, pasamos un mes allí.
- ¿Hacía calor?
- Sí, bastante.
- ¿Qué hiciste?
- Visité la ciudad. Es muy grande.
- ¿Te gustó?
- Sí, bastante.

B The students complete the C-test. Check their answers and clear up any problems.
They could use this as a basis for describing their imaginary holiday in the place they chose to go to in Activity **A**.

C Anyone needing more practice could work at home on **copymaster 73**.

2 Shopping in a department store
(Libro 3, Unidad 3)

A The students work on *Ahora sé*, page 41. They could do this at home.

B Give each student a copy of **copymaster 74**. They read this and work on the two activities in pairs.

El Corte Inglés
Ask the students to take turns to tell their partners as much as they can in English about what is on a particular floor. They could also use the guide as revision of role-playing dialogues. One of them asks their partner (the shop assistant) where one can buy different items. As a memory game the students could look at the guide for 30 seconds and then close their books. You could then ask for a particular thing and the students would have to remember which floor it was on, e.g.

Quisiera comprar una raqueta de tenis. ¿Me puede decir dónde se venden?
Sí, en la quinta planta.

UNIDAD 7

C Ask the students to listen to the announcements and after each one, consult with their partners to find out how much information they can put together.

Anuncios en los grandes almacenes

- Señoras y señores clientes. Por fin de temporada les ofrecemos grandes rebajas en todas las secciones. No se pierdan la oferta especial de hoy – gran liquidación de artículos de piel en nuestra sección de recuerdos y regalos. Y no se olviden nuestro servicio especial de empaquetar regalos – completamente gratis. Una ganga.
- Se ruega al dueño de un coche Seat Ibiza – color rojo – con matrícula de Madrid 21572AD que baje en seguida al aparcamiento subterránneo. Su coche está bloqueando la salida.
- Se ha encontrado a un niño de unos tres años en la tercera planta, sección confección de señoras. Dice llamarse Manolín y ha perdido a su mamá. Lleva un traje azul oscuro con pantalón largo. Tiene los ojos azules y es pelirrojo. Por favor, se ruega a su madre que pase por Información.
- Quien haya perdido un monedero con cierta cantidad de dinero diríjase, por favor, al despacho de relaciones públicas en la sexta planta.

3 Eating at home
(Libro 3, Unidad 6)

A The students work on *Ahora sé*, page 75.

B Ask the class to work in groups and to think of as many phrases as they can which would help to make a good impression, for example:
Es riquísima esta paella.
Le ayudo a fregar los platos.

In addition, as a team game, ask the students to work in groups or pairs and to try to think of as many items of food and drink as they can beginning with a particular letter of the alphabet, e.g.:
C: cerveza, calamares, Coca-Cola, cocido ...

UNIDAD 8

Objetos perdidos

Main aim
Reporting and recovering lost property.

Area(s) of experience
C – The world around us
D – The world of work
E – The international world

Materials
Cassette: ¿Por dónde se va a la oficina de objetos perdidos?, He perdido, ¿Cuándo? ¿Dónde?, Repaso: una descripción personal. Copymasters 75–85

Tasks
Reporting a loss or a theft
Saying what you have lost, when and where it was lost, left or stolen, describing the item

Grammar points
Perfect tense

Productive language
anoche
cartera
contener
dejar
dirección
llaves
oficina de
  objetos perdidos
ayer
comisaría
cuero
(de imitación)
gafas
nombre
oro
paraguas
perder
reloj
pasaporte
recompensa
tarjeta de crédito

Receptive language
marca
pérdida
rollo de película

Revision points
Describing self, family and friends (*Libro 1, Unidad 10*)
Talking about interests, plans (*Libro 2, Unidad 8*)
Talking about spending money, freetime pursuits (*Libro 3, Unidad 4*)
Using telephone/fax services (*Libro 3, Unidad 7*)

Objetos perdidos (page 88)

Main aim
To understand the unit goals and to see them as worthwhile.

A Work on this along lines which have previously proved successful. To reinforce the usefulness of this unit:
Ask for a list of things that people lose and where (e.g. an umbrella in a restaurant). You can also ask the class why people are more likely to lose things on holiday: carefree attitudes, a change of routine, items people are not used to carrying – cameras, suitcases, etc., distractions and attractions of unfamiliar places, not to mention thieves and pickpockets.
Present **copymaster 75**. Explain that these are the items most commonly asked for in lost property offices in Spain. Introduce the names of the items, e.g.
Point to each in turn and say, several times, what it is. Encourage students to complete your sentences, e.g.

El número uno, es ... .

Cover a picture and see how many students can say what it is, in twenty seconds.
Cover pictures 1, 5 and 6 and play a game of Noughts and crosses. Then cover pictures 4, 8 and 12 and play again.
Practise the vocabulary by playing Kim's Game, covering up one of the items on the OHP/board or asking the students to memorise the contents of a bag. It is preferable to use a real bag containing certain items which are often lost.

B Write the key question words on the board and check that everyone understands them, e.g.
qué, cuándo, dónde, cómo.
Say the model sentences in random order, and then adapt them, e.g.
He perdido mi pasaporte (mi billetero, etc.).
Lo he perdido ayer (a las diez aproximadamente, etc.).
Lo he perdido en el restaurante (el tren, etc.).
Mi bolso (etc.) es muy grande (rojo, etc.).

The students choose and say the relevant question word to summarise what you say. After a while, you could include two categories of information

UNIDAD 8

and the students say, or write, the relevant categories, e.g.

He perdido mi bolso en el autobús.
He perdido mi pasaporte esta mañana.
Mi billetero es de cuero.

¿Por dónde se va a la oficina de objetos perdidos? (page 88)

Main aim

Finding a lost property office.

A The students read the information and dialogue. Play a game of *¿Verdad o mentira?* as the students look at the text, e.g.

Normalmente hay una oficina de objetos perdidos en los aeropuertos (las estaciones de servicio, las estaciones grandes de la RENFE, las comisarías, los grandes almacenes, las playas, los hoteles).

In pairs, they play read the model dialogue.

B Play the tape of Spanish visitors coping with the same problems. Ask the students to listen carefully and to note down any more directions they are given.
The students check their notes and then use them to do the exercise again, giving fuller answers and using the language they have heard on the recording.

¿Por dónde se va a la oficina de objetos perdidos?

Número 1
- Perdón. ¿Hay una oficina de objetos perdidos en Laredo?
- No, hay que ir a la comisaría.
- Y, ¿por dónde se va a la comisaría?
- Pues, tome la segunda calle a la izquierda y siga todo recto. Está al lado del Banco de Santander.

Número 2
- Perdone, señora. ¿Por dónde se va a la oficina de objetos perdidos?
- No hay aquí. Hay que ir a la plaza mayor. La comisaría está allí enfrente.

Número 3
- Por favor. ¿La oficina de objetos perdidos?
- Está cerrada. Hay una comisaría bastante cerca.
- ¿Dónde está?
- Tome la segunda a la derecha y está a mano izquierda.

Número 4
- Perdone, señora. ¿Sabe Vd. dónde está la oficina de objetos perdidos?
- Está en la calle Espronceda aunque está cerrada los sábados. Pero hay una comisaría.
- ¿Por dónde se va?
- Pues, todo recto y primera a la derecha. Está enfrente del cine.

Número 5
- Perdón, señorita. ¿Me puede decir dónde está la oficina de objetos perdidos?
- Pues, siga todo recto en los semáforos y tuerza a la derecha. Está a unos doscientos metros.

Número 6
- He perdido mi cámara. ¿Hay una oficina de objetos perdidos en Santoña?
- No, hay que ir a la comisaría.
- Y, ¿dónde está?
- Pues, tome la tercera a la izquierda y siga todo recto. Está cerca de la estación.

En la oficina de objetos perdidos (page 89)

Main aim

Asking and answering questions in a lost property office.

A Revise the key vocabulary with **copymaster 75**, e.g. You say sentences containing the words. The students listen and write the numbers of the relevant pictures, e.g.

He perdido mi cámara (mi cartera, etc.).
¿De qué color es su maleta (billetero, etc.)?
¿Qué contiene su bolso (maleta, etc.)?
¿De qué marca es su reloj (cámara, etc.)?
¿Cómo es su paraguas (bolso, etc.)?

You say some appropriate sentences. The students repeat after you, but only if the object you mention is on the copymaster, e.g.

¿Qué contiene su maleta (bolso, etc.)?
¿De qué color es su abrigo (monedero, etc.)?
¿Dónde ha perdido sus llaves (su reloj, etc.)?
He perdido mis gafas (llaves, etc.).

B The students look at the illustration of objects which are frequently lost. To help them to learn the words, ask questions about them, e.g.

UNIDAD 8

¿Hay cuántas cámaras fotográficas (relojes, etc.)?
¿Dónde está la maleta (el paraguas, etc.)?
¿De qué color es la cartera (el bolso, etc.)?

Then play at *El juego de Kim*: the students write down everything they can remember with their books closed.

You could also play at *Una familia de oro* (Family Fortunes). The students guess how most Spanish people would complete the sentence: **He perdido …**

… *mi maleta: 5*
… *mi bolso: 16*
… *mi reloj: 14*
… *mi cámara: 8*
… *mi billetero: 15*
… *mi monedero: 13*
… *mi abrigo: 7*
… *mi cartera: 6*
… *mi paraguas: 10*
… *mi pasaporte: 3*
… *mis llaves: 2*
… *mis gafas: 1*

C The students read the questions and ensure that they understand them all. To help them to learn them, you could, e.g.
In random order, answer the questions. The students say, or write, the matching question, e.g.

Contiene ropa (todo mi dinero, etc.).
Mi abrigo es verde (azul, rojo, etc.).
He perdido mi reloj (maleta, etc.).
Mi cámara (etc.) vale 30.000 (etc.) pesetas.
Mi cartera (etc.) no es nueva, es vieja.
Mi reloj (etc.) es de oro (etc.).
Mi maleta (etc.) es bastante grande (etc.).
En mi bolso hay mi dinero y mi pasaporte (etc.).

Present on the board or OHP a dialogue with the questions missing. The students add the questions and complete the dialogue, orally and/or in writing, e.g.

–
– *He perdido mi bolso.*
–
– *Es bastante grande.*
–
– *Es negro y rojo.*
–
– *Contiene mi ropa, mis llaves y mi billetero.*
–
– *Es de cuero de imitación.*
–

– *No, es bastante viejo.*
–
– *Sí.*
–
– *No sé exactamente … unas veinte mil pesetas.*
–
– *Creo que es un Adidas.*

D The students concentrate now on the answers, e.g. You ask appropriate questions. They find and say, or write, the matching answers.
You ask the same questions about the students' own property (e.g. clothes, bags, watches, cameras, bikes, wallets), e.g.

¿Tienes una cámara fotográfica?
¿De qué marca es?
¿Cuánto vale?
¿Lleva tu nombre y tu dirección?
¿Es nueva?
¿Has perdido tu cámara?

Show **copymaster 75** again and ask the questions in this item about the objects illustrated.
Divide the class into two. Ask them to close their text books and, looking at **copymaster 75**, say as much as they can about the item. Each team in turn has to give one detail until they have exhausted the possibilities. Each correct sentence gains the team one point.

E Further activities
A memory game. The students look at each item on the OHP and have to recall a set number of details in order to be able to 'reclaim' it. You can prompt by asking further questions about the size, material and contents as appropriate.
As a challenge to you, the students can make five statements about a lost item. Each correct description is a point to the class and each incorrect description is a point to you. The descriptions that the class give you can be based on pictures you have given them (taken from magazines, etc.) or pictures used previously on the OHP.

El bolso (**copymaster 76**)
Two friends are sharing a bag or a suitcase. They have to discuss (in Spanish) the appearance and contents of the bag before being able to describe it fully to the assistant in the lost property office. (The descriptions become increasingly complex.) For example:

B – *¿De qué color es el bolso?*
A – *Es azul. Y, ¿cómo es exactamente?*

UNIDAD 8

B – *Bueno, grande. ¿De qué es?*
A – *Es de plástico.*
B – *¿Qué hay en el bolso?*
A – *Una chaqueta ...*
B – *Y una camiseta.*

When they have noted down all the details about each item they can then describe them to you (the employee) or to their partner who assumes the role of employee.

The students work orally on the model dialogue (*En la oficina de objetos perdidos*) and make as many adaptations of it as possible.

The students write as long a dialogue as possible, using all the questions in this item. This could be done at home.

¡Qué confusión! (copymaster 77)

The students read the questions and answers, and ensure that they understand them all. They then match up the questions and answers. In pairs, one student could read a question and the other could read the matching answer.

The students work out when to use the perfect tense and how to form it, using these questions and answers.

Now would be a good time to work with the class on *A ser detective*, page 193.

Ahora te toca a ti (page 90)

Main aim

Asking and answering questions in a lost property office.

A Ask the students to cover up the sample dialogue that accompanies the picture of a leather sports bag. Ask them the questions to prepare for the dialogue.

B Let them look at the dialogue and ask them to make up similar ones using the other three pictures as cues.

Estos señores han perdido (page 90)

Main aim

Describing lost property.

A This activity fulfils two functions: it allows for practice of the third person singular and plural of the perfect tense, and it puts the students in the important role of interpreter, helping others who are less competent at Spanish. The students read the two dialogues. Make sure that they understand.

B Draw up a list of relevant questions with the help of the class, e.g.
¿Qué ha perdido?
¿De qué es?
¿De qué marca es?
¿Es nuevo?
¿Cuánto vale?
¿Lleva su nombre?
¿Qué contiene?

The students copy these questions and in pairs make similar dialogues about the other lost objects.

He perdido (page 91)

Main aim

To develop listening skills.

A Prepare the students for the listening exercise by asking what they would say if they had to describe the lost items on page 91.

B The students listen to the recordings and match each one to one of the pictures.

C You can play the tape again and ask the class to note down what else has been lost. Stop the tape after each description.
To prepare them for this, you could write on the board, with their help, the key questions to be answered, e.g
qué, dónde, cómo, cuándo.

He perdido

Número 1

– *¡Ay madre! ¿Hay alguien aquí que hable español?*
– *Pues sí, yo misma.*
– *¡Ay hija! Escucha. He perdido mi cámara fotográfica. ¡Ay! Diós mío, ¿qué voy a hacer?*
– *Sí, señor. ¿Puede describírmela, por favor?*
– *Pues mire, ... es negra ... ¿qué más?, es que estoy muy nervioso.*
– *¿De qué marca es?*

UNIDAD 8

- ¿Qué sé yo? Espere, es una Pentax, sí eso, una Pentax.
- ¿Sólo la cámara?
- Pues, no, está en un bolso … en un bolso negro. ¿Lo tiene Vd.?
- Un momentito, por favor.

Número 2
- Perdón, señorita. Es que he perdido un paraguas.
- ¿Un paraguas?
- Sí, es de mi madre y me va a matar.
- Tranquila, señorita. ¿Cómo es este paraguas?
- Pues es rojo, amarillo, verde … y azul.
- Bueno, no se preocupe. Se entregan muchos paraguas.

Número 3
- Ayúdeme, por favor. He perdido mi bolso y contiene todo, todo, todo.
- Espere. ¿Quiere darme los detalles, por favor? ¿Cómo es este bolso?
- Es gris … es pequeño.
- ¿Es de cuero?
- No, no.
- ¿Qué contiene?
- Pues todo: mi pasaporte, mi billetero, ¡ay! todo mi dinero está en el billetero.
- ¿Lleva su nombre y su dirección?
- Sí, menos mal, menos mal …
- Un momentito, señora. Voy a ver …

Número 4
- Buenos días.
- Buenos días. ¿En qué puedo servirle?
- Pues, mire, es que he perdido mi billetero.
- Ah, y ¿cómo es?
- Pues es marrón y tiene … pues varias cosas.
- ¿Contiene dinero, tarjetas?
- Sí, eso es, no sé cuánto … unas cinco mil pesetas y mis tarjetas de crédito. ¡Ay! ¡Santo Diós!
- ¿Lleva su nombre y su dirección?
- Sí, sí.
- Bueno, bueno.

Número 5
- Buenas tardes.
- Mire, he perdido mi monedero. Iba de compras y resulta …
- Sí, señora, un momento. ¿Quiere describirlo por favor?
- Bueno, sí, es negro … bastante pequeño … es de cuero.
- ¿Me puede decir, más o menos, cuánto dinero contiene?

- Pues sí, se lo puedo decir, diez mil en billetes. Me acuerdo bien porque acababa de salir del banco con el dinero que había sacado. Sí, diez mil.
- Vale.
- Me llamará Vd. si lo entregan, ¿verdad?

Número 6
- ¿Puede ayudarme? Es que he perdido mi bolsa de deporte.
- Sí, y ¿cómo es, por favor?
- Es una de ésas grandes, de cuero.
- De cuero, y ¿qué contiene?
- Algo de ropa, ¿sabe? de deporte, y mi billetero.
- No han entregado ninguna bolsa así. Voy a ver …

Número 7
- Buenos días.
- Buenos días. Verá Vd. He perdido mi reloj y es una preciosidad de reloj ¿sabe?
- ¿Me puede decir cómo es su reloj?
- Pues sí, es un Cartier … de oro, claro.
- ¡Ay, ay, ay!
- ¿Sabe Vd. que vale más de 100.000 pesetas?
- ¡Qué pena! Si me da los detalles, por favor.
- Sí, por supuesto.

¿Qué diferencias hay? (page 91)

Main aim
Understanding and producing accurate descriptions.

A The students look at the two pictures of bags given in the example. Ask them to close their books and say whether the following sentences are true or false:

El primer bolso lleva un nombre. (False)
El segundo contiene ropa. (False)
El primero es pequeño y el segundo bastante grande. (False)
El primero contiene ropa. (True)
El segundo es gris. (False)
El segundo no contiene ropa. (True)
El primero no contiene una cámara. (True)

B The students act out dialogues in pairs using the other pictures. They should use the dialogue in the Students' Book as a guide.

C Further activities
Using the illustrations on **copymaster 78** show the students the objects and then silhouettes of the same or different objects. Ask them to identify the items as theirs or explain why they are different.

117

UNIDAD 8

Now using **copymaster 79**, show them a picture of part of an object. Then show them the whole object and ask them whether the part corresponds to the whole.

¡Es mi bolso! (page 92)

Main aim
Describing lost and stolen property.

A The students could first revise the language needed for this by working on the relevant part of *Ahora sé*, page 95, e.g.
You write on the board the first letter only of the words in the relevant sentences in the list. The students complete these orally with their books open and then close their books and complete them in writing. Correct these and clear up any problems. Then write the first letter only of the words in some slightly different sentences, e.g.

He perdido mi bolso.
Es bastante grande.
Es negro.
Contiene tres rollos de película.

The students try to guess what these new sentences are.

B The students read this and ensure that they understand it and know what to do. You could work on the first one with some able students as a model, playing each role in turn. They could then continue in pairs.

¿Cuándo y dónde? (page 92)

Main aim
Explaining when and where you lost something.

A The students read this and ensure that they understand it. You then read aloud appropriate sentences, adapting those on this page. The students categorise each one as *cuándo* or *dónde*, e.g.

He dejado mi maleta (etc.) en el tren (etc.).
Hemos dejado la cámara (etc.) en el taxi (etc.).
Perdí mis llaves (etc.) anoche (etc.).

For writing practice, the students make two columns in their exercise books, headed:

¿Dónde?
¿Cuándo?

They listen and write the sentences you say in the appropriate column.

B Refer the students back to the remaining phrases in *En la oficina de objetos perdidos* on page 89. Show them **copymaster 80** on the OHP or other pictures of the places where they might lose something. Point out an item and a place and ask them to state what they have lost and where:

¿Qué has perdido?
¿Dónde?

C Indicate a time using an overlay on the OHP or adding a time to the picture of the item. Now ask them when they lost the item.

D Work on the model dialogue with the class. You could play the role of the tourist and call on different students to play the other role. The students can continue this in pairs, changing the object, time and place.
As students complete this, ask them to write two dialogues. They could finish this at home.

E Play these recordings. After hearing each one twice, the students describe the attitude of the clerk. Clear up any problems and play the recordings again. This time the students note the details of what was lost, where and when.

¿Cuándo? ¿Dónde?

Número 1
- Oficina de Objetos Perdidos, ¿dígame?
- Buenos días, estaba cenando anoche en el restaurante del Hotel Juan Carlos, con unos amigos, y perdí mi billetero.
- ¿Aquí en Barcelona?
- Sí, aquí en Barcelona.
- ¿A qué hora?
- Serían alrededor de las nueve, de nueve a once.
- ¿Se lo ha dejado allí o se lo han robado?
- No sé.
- ¿Cuál es su nombre, por favor?
- Enrique González.
- ¿Dónde vive?
- Muntaner 33, 4ºE, Barcelona.
- Muy bien, gracias.
- Vale, gracias.

Número 2
- Oficina de Objetos Perdidos. Buenos días, ¿dígame?

UNIDAD 8

– Buenos días. Mire, acabo de perder mi pasaporte. Es importantísimo que lo encuentre porque mañana salgo para París, ¿entiende?
– Sí, señora. ¿Dónde lo ha perdido?
– En el Hotel Central.
– ¿Qué habitación?
– En la habitación 201, 201.
– ¿Sabe Vd. más o menos, a qué hora lo perdió?
– Pues mire, ayer, a eso de las tres de la tarde, aproximadamente.
– Ajá. ¿Cómo se llama Vd.?
– Soy Josefina Manresa.
– ¿Dónde vive?
– Avenida José Antonio, 14, 3er piso, Segovia.
– Muy bien, muchas gracias. Ya le enviaré información sobre esto.
– Gracias, gracias.

Número 3
– Oficina de Objetos Perdidos. Buenos días, ¿dígame?
– Hola, buenos días. Pues mire, estoy muy preocupada.
– ¿Por qué?
– Ayer perdí mi cámara en una excursión a Monserrat, y por eso llamo, a ver si alguien la ha entregado.
– ¿Dónde la perdió Vd.?
– En la cafetería.
– ¿Sobre qué hora?
– Ayer …
– ¿Por la mañana, por la tarde, por la noche?
– Más o menos a la hora de comer.
– Ajá. ¿Cómo se llama Vd.?
– Me llamo Marta Allende.
– Y, ¿dónde vive Vd.?
– En Plaza de Mayo 13, 7° piso, 2ª, Madrid.
– ¡Ah! muy bien, muchas gracias.

Número 4
– Oficina de Objetos Perdidos. Buenos días, ¿dígame?
– Hola. He perdido mi reloj de oro; y estoy preocupado porque es bastante caro.
– Y ¿dónde lo ha perdido Vd.?
– Pues lo perdí en el Hostal Residencia de Catalunya.
– ¿Recuerda Vd. el número de habitación?
– Sí, era la habitación 17.
– ¿Cree Vd. que lo perdió en la habitación del hotel?
– No … Bueno, no estoy seguro, pero, pero creo que fue en el baño.
– ¿Lo perdió Vd. hoy o ayer?
– Fue ayer.
– ¿A qué hora?

– Pues, no lo sé.
– ¿Cuál es su nombre, por favor?
– Ignacio Alfonsín.
– ¿Dónde vive Vd.?
– Vivo en la calle Buenos Aires, 25, 3°, 4ª, Alicante.
– Muy bien, muchas gracias.

Número 5
– Oficina de Objetos Perdidos. Buenos días, ¿dígame?
– Hola, buenos días. Mire Vd., que he perdido una maleta, a ver qué pueden hacer. No sé si alguien me la ha robado.
– Una maleta, ¿dónde?
– Pues la perdí en la estación, ayer por la mañana, cuando llegaba de Guadalajara, a las once, o así, más o menos.
– Ajá. ¿Cuál es su nombre, por favor?
– Me llamo Pedro López.
– Y, ¿dónde vive Vd.?
– Vivo en la calle España 24, 1°, 3ª de Valladolid.
– Muy bien, muchas gracias, señor.
– Adiós, a ver si la encuentran pronto.
– Muy bien.

F Further activity
He perdido … (**copymaster 81**)
Using the grid on **copymaster 81**, the students can generate new dialogues along the same lines.

No sé dónde lo he perdido (page 93)

Main aim
To develop role-playing skills.

A The students read this quietly and ensure that they understand everything, using a dictionary to check on anything they are not sure of. If there are still any problems, help them to see how to use the dictionary to solve them.

B Get the class to brainstorm for a few minutes to produce as many useful questions as they can for this situation. Write these on the board or OHP. Then practise asking and answering these questions.

C Using the information given, the students produce jointly an oral description of the bag and its contents, making it as detailed and accurate as possible. They could then all write this description.

UNIDAD 8

D Practise the role play in class. To start with, students ask the questions and you answer them. Then reverse this.

E The students do this role play in pairs. You could move around, listening, helping and joining in.

Un anuncio en el periódico (page 93)

Main aim
To develop reading and writing skills.

A Ask the students to look at some advertisements taken from Spanish newspapers. Point out the different ways in which you can say you have lost something and the different ways of offering a reward. (Note: although most of the advertisements are genuine, they are not representative, since nearly all ads in the lost and found columns seem to be for lost pets.)

B Ask the class to tell you what each advertisement is about.

C Ask the students to write the advertisements for the objects on page 92, in Spanish, using the small ads as a guide.

D Give each student a copy of **copymaster 82**. The students read it quietly, in school or at home, and try to work out the solution. You could present an empty grid on the board or OHP and ask questions of the class to enable you to put a tick or a cross in each box. The students then draw the conclusion that D is Señor X's case.

	ropa de señora	cámara	gafas de sol	medica-mentos	lleva un nombre	se perdió ayer	se perdió en el hotel
A							
B							
C							
D							
E							

Una carta al hotel (page 94)

Main aim
Reading and writing a letter about lost property.

A It would be a good idea to revise the unit so far, e.g. Ask the students to give examples of all the tasks presented with the unit goals on page 88 of their book.
Present two words from the unit. Students produce a sentence using both words, e.g.

objetos aquí
perdido paraguas
he gafas
es cuero
reloj oro
maleta amarilla
contiene llaves
marca cámara
nombre dirección
vale bolso
perdí ayer
dejamos metro
dejado tren

Describe any item illustrated in this unit so far. The students say what it is and find the matching picture. Then ask some students to choose and describe an item. They can continue this in pairs. Give each student a verb in the perfect tense, e.g.

he perdido, he comprado ...

They write down their verbs. You then begin a simple narrative, e.g.

Esta mañana, he ido de compras ... .

A volunteer repeats this and adds to it, using the verb you gave her/him, e.g.

Esta mañana, he ido de compras y he comprado una cámara.

A second student repeats this and adds to it. Continue this for as long as possible. When a student forgets part of the story, the others can remind him/her. At the end, ask everyone to write as much of the narrative as they can remember. Work again on *A ser detective* for this *Unidad*.

B The students read this letter and ensure that they understand it. Invite them to adapt it orally for different objects. They then all write a letter. This could be done at home.

UNIDAD 8

C Give everyone a copy of **copymaster 83**. They could work on this in class or at home.

Una palabra conduce a otra (page 94)

Main aim

To develop communication strategies and to extend vocabulary.

A Work on this along lines which have previously proved successful.

B Students could all write a dialogue or a narrative about lost property, using as many as possible of the words in this item.

Ahora sé (page 95)

Main aim

To provide a summary of the *Unidad* and a basis for more practice and revision.

A The students work on this, using their favourite techniques.

B Either now, or later for revision, you could use these activities with the summary:
Present some words on the board or OHP. The students copy these and then write any other words which come into their minds, e.g.

oficina, comisaría, cuero, billetero, color, contiene, marca, perdido.

In pairs, the students look at the summary and ask each other to choose a difficult word. They then ask questions about the word, e.g.

¿Qué significa esta palabra?
¿Cómo se escribe?
¿Cómo se dice?
¿Es una palabra útil?
¿Cuándo se dice?
¿Dónde se dice?

Each student chooses five words from the list which they are finding difficult to learn. They then try to write a short narrative which includes them all.

Give each student a copy of **copymaster 84**. They interview the others to find someone who has done everything. Check the answers after 6 minutes, e.g.
¿Quién ha ... ?
Students score a point for each correct answer.

Revision activities

1 Describing oneself, family and friends
(Libro 1, Unidad 10)

A Encourage the students to work on page 95 of *Libro 1*, either at home or school. You could base some verb circle practice with, e.g.
Soy bastante gordo pero soy guapo.
Tengo los ojos verdes y el pelo castaño.
Soy joven y llevo gafas.

B The students listen to these recordings of two young Spanish people describing themselves, their families and their friends. They begin by noting the main points and then reporting on these. Clear up any problems and play the recordings again.
The students now act as examiners and listen to the recordings again to assess them according to the exam criteria. This is a valuable way of making them familiar with what is required in an exam.

Repaso: Una descripción personal

Número 1

– Hola, me presento. Me llamo Nuria Allende. Tengo dieciséis años y vivo en Madrid. Soy alta y rubia. Tengo el pelo rubio y largo. No soy muy guapa pero no soy fea tampoco. Tengo los ojos azules y llevo gafas. Vivo en un piso con mis padres que tienen cuarenta años. Son muy simpáticos. Mi padre es artista y mi madre es enfermera. Soy hija única y vivimos los tres en un piso con dos dormitorios en el centro de la ciudad. Tengo muchos amigos y salgo con ellos por la tarde. Mi novio se llama Alberto. Es moreno, bastante delgado y no muy alto. Va al mismo colegio que yo. A Alberto le gustan la historia y la geografía. A mí me gustan el deporte y la informática.

Número 2

– Me llamo Nacho. Tengo diecisiete años. Vivo,vivo en Madrid ... Tengo tres hermanos y no tengo hermanas ... Vivo en una casa muy grande. Soy bajo y bastante gordo y tengo el pelo corto... Mi padre es director de una fábrica y mi madre no trabaja ...

UNIDAD 8

C Each student could write a presentation of themselves, their family and their friends, using the insights gained in Activity **B**. When you have corrected these, they could learn them. You could ask them to present themselves to each other, in groups, and to ask each other lots of questions.

2 Talking about interests and plans
(Libro 2, Unidad 8)

A Encourage the students to work on page 97 of *Libro 2*.

B See how many questions the class can answer about their interests and plans in 5 minutes. Then see if they can improve on this score.

3 Talking about spending money and freetime pursuits
(Libro 3, Unidad 4)

A At home or at school, the students work on page 53 of *Libro 3*.

B Give students a copy of **copymaster 85** for them to read and discuss in groups.

4 Using telephone and fax services
(Libro 3, Unidad 7)

The students work on page 85 of *Libro 3*, at home or at school.

UNIDAD 9

Me siento mal

Main aim
Coping with being ill in Spain and helping others

Area(s) of experience
B – Personal and social life

Materials
Cassette: Me siento mal, No somos todos iguales, ¿Qué te pasa?, Tienes que interpretar, ¿Puede darme hora?, Pedir hora no es siempre fácil, ¿Insisten bastante?, El médico te hace preguntas, ¿Qué me aconsejas?, ¿Me puede recomendar algo?, Te toca a ti interpretar, Repaso: hobbies y pasatiempos, Repaso: el medio ambiente, Repaso: problemas en la tienda de comestibles.
Copymasters 86–93

Tasks
Saying how you feel
Saying you would like to see a doctor or dentist
Understanding information about surgery hours
Arranging an appointment with a doctor
Saying where you have a pain or other discomfort
Reporting minor ailments and injuries
Responding to inquiries about how long an ailment or symptom has persisted
Understanding and giving advice
Understanding instructions regarding the treatment

Grammar
Perfect tense of reflexive verbs

Productive language
aconsejar   cortarse
cuello   dar hora
enfermo   a alguien
espalda   gripe
hacerse daño   hinchado
mareado   médico
muela   nariz
oído   quemarse
rodilla   romperse
roto   torcerse
urgente

Receptive language
cucharadita
enfermedad
farmacéutico
medicamento
paciente
vomitar

Revision points
Talking about sports, hobbies and pastimes (*Libro 1, Unidad 11*)
Environmental issues (*Libro 2, Unidad 9*)
Shopping for essential items (*Libro 3, Libro 5*)
Dealing with problems: lost property (*Libro 3, Unidad 8*)

Me siento mal (page 96)

Main aim
To understand the goals and to see them as worthwhile.

A Work on this along lines which have previously proved useful.

B Choose one of the pictures and narrate what happened in it, e.g.
La chica le preguntó cómo era y el niño dijo que se había roto la pierna jugando al fútbol. ¡La chica no estaba sorprendida!

The students listen and link what you say to the appropriate goal. Repeat this with the other pictures.
To give more practice in listening to narrative, you could again narrate what happened, in random order. The students listen and write the appropriate speech bubbles.

C Play this recording twice. The students listen and follow the pictures and captions. Play it again for the students to follow without looking at their book. Then play it once more, stopping it occasionally and inviting students to continue the narrative.

Me siento mal
– ¿Sabes qué me pasó? Estaba jugando al fútbol en el parque con amigos. Me caí y pensé que me había roto la pierna derecha. Mis amigos llamaron

123

UNIDAD 9

a una ambulancia y una media hora más tarde estaba aquí en el hospital. Me dolía mucho la pierna, claro. Después de esperar dos horas el médico vino y me dijo que no estaba rota pero que tenía que quedarme en la cama dos o tres días. Mi amiga Eva llamó a mis padres que van a visitarme más tarde. En el futuro voy a tomar el sol en el parque mientras que mis amigos juegan.

No somos todos iguales (page 97)

Main aim

To understand and say some of the key language related to illness.

A Present **copymaster 86** (with a blank overlay on it) and use it to present some of the key language, e.g. Point to a part of the body and ask, e.g.

¿Qué es?

When a student replies correctly, write the word in colour on the part of the body.
Put another blank overlay over the OHT. A volunteer goes to the OHT and draws a line from the label to the matching part of the body appropriate to what you say, e.g.

Me duelen los dientes (los pies, etc.).
Me duele mucho la cabeza (el estómago, etc.).
Me he roto las piernas (un diente, etc.).

With help from the class, draw a *Word Sun* on the board (see Teacher's Book 1, page 24) and work on it, based around the words *me duele*. Repeat this with *me duelen* and *me he roto*.
Draw a body on the board or OHP. Choose six parts of it and number each, from 1 to 6, e.g.

los dientes 1
las piernas y los pies 2
los oídos 3
el ojo 4
la nariz 5
la cabeza 6

You and the students now all draw a copy of the body, but without a head or legs. Use a dice or a pencil, and play a game of Beetle, drawing in the part of the body relating to the number thrown. It is necessary to throw a 6 to start. You can insist on the students naming the part of the body before they draw it.
Draw a person on the board or OHP. Write the singular words on the left and the plural words on the right. The students copy this and put arrows from the labels to the drawing. They then write 10 sentences expressing pains and symptoms, e.g.

Me duele mucho el brazo.
Me duelen también los pies.

Finally, they look at the head and say the name of the part of the body represented by each of the numbers.

B The students read this and ensure that they understand it. They then look at the pictures and listen to the recordings, judging whether each person is *valiente* or not.
Play each dialogue again and invite the students to work out who the speakers are. Then play them again and ask the students to note where each 'patient' hurts. There is no clear answer to this with number 2, so you could encourage them to speculate and argue.

No somos todos iguales

Número 1
- Oye, Pedro, levántate.
- No, mamá. Me duelen mucho los oídos.
- Pero tienes que ir al colegio.
- No puedo, mamá. ¿Tienes aspirinas, por favor?
- Tómate dos aspirinas y levántate.
- Pero, mamá …

Número 2
- Pásame el balón ¡ay!
- Paco ¿estás bien?
- Sí, sí, no te preocupes.
- Cuidado. No te muevas.
- Está bien.

Número 3
- Tienes un poco de insolación. ¿Te duele aquí?
- ¡Ay, por Diós! Sí.
- Sí, está un poco rojo.

Número 4
- ¡Cuidado con el piano!
- ¡Ay! mi brazo.
- ¿Estás bien?
- Sí.

C Present the following on the board or OHP, writing the sentences in random order. The students copy them in the correct order to produce four brief narratives. They then listen again to the above recordings and say which narrative matches which dialogue.

UNIDAD 9

No somos todos iguales

Número 1
Ayer fui a la playa solo. Me dormí y me desperté una hora más tarde. Me dolía mucho la espalda y por eso fui al médico. Me dio una crema.

Número 2
La semana pasada ayudé al padre de un amigo que va a los Estados Unidos. Tiene un piano muy grande. Tuvimos que bajarlo en el ascensor. Me hice daño en el brazo en el ascensor. Me dolía mucho el brazo.

Número 3
Esta mañana no quería ir al colegio. Me dolían mucho los oídos y no quería levantarme. Mi madre entró y me dio dos aspirinas.

Número 4
Ayer me rompí la pierna. Estaba jugando al fútbol en el patio y me caí. El profesor me llevó al hospital.

¿Qué te pasa? (page 97)

Main aim
To say where you have a pain.

A Read the captions in random order and ask students to say or point to themselves and show the area which is hurting.

B Make true and false statements about Pilar's ailments and ask the class to respond by saying *verdad* or *mentira*. Then ask the students to say what is wrong with Pilar. Allow them to look at the captions in their book if they need to.

C Now point to parts of your body. Ask the students to tell you what you are trying to say.

D The students can mime one of the pains with appropriate histrionics. The rest of the class can give the correct statement, using the captions if they need to.

E The students draw a picture of one of the parts of the body mentioned and their partner or another member of their group has to guess what is wrong, e.g.
¿Qué te pasa?
Me siento mal.
¿Te duele el estómago?
No, no me duele el estómago.
¿Te duele la nariz? ...

To prepare the students to do this in pairs, you could play each role in turn with selected students while the others watch and listen.

F Students look at the picture of Conchi and work along the same lines as the first picture but more quickly. Then ask questions about Conchi, combining the symptoms of both captions:
¿A Conchi le duele el estómago?
¿Le duele la espalda?

G Verdad o mentira
Students look at the two pictures and make true or false statements about them. The students have to note down the words *verdad o mentira* accordingly. When the statements are corrected the students can be asked to remedy the incorrect statements, e.g.
A Pilar le duele el brazo derecho.
Mentira; a Conchi le duele el brazo derecho.

They could play the same game in pairs, making five statements each and seeing which of the two is the more observant. This practice can be developed using mime. The students have to say whether the person miming is Pilar or Conchi and how they can tell, e.g.
¿Quién soy?
Eres Pilar.
¿Cómo lo sabes?
Te duele el estómago (A Pilar le duele el estómago).

H Now that the students are very familiar with the new vocabulary, you might like to try a quick game, e.g.

Simón dice
In this version the students have to touch the appropriate part of their body if Simón is mentioned, e.g.
Simón dice, me duele la espalda.

Bingo
Ask the students to draw four parts of the body and to cross them off as you mention them. To emphasise the difference between *me duele* and *le duele* you might like the students to increase the permutations by three by putting a **P** (Pilar), **C** (Conchi) or **Yo** next to each drawing. In this case, the part of the body can only be crossed off if the part and the person correspond, for example,

125

showing a picture of a neck and the letter P: *A Pilar le duele el cuello.*

Pinning the tail on the donkey
Draw on the board/OHP a body and a head. The students work in pairs – one is the guide and the other is blindfolded. The class decides what is to be 'pinned on'.
The partner guides by saying:
Le duele(n) mucho (far off)
Le duele(n) bastante (not too far)
Le duele(n) más (moving away)
Le duele(n) menos (moving closer)
Le duele(n) muy poco (near)
Ya no le duele(n) (there!)
The blindfolded student then has to draw the part of the body. This game is more exciting if there is a time limit. Begin with 20–30 seconds and then decrease it as they get better at it.

I The students now look at this page in their book and read it carefully. They try to work out the meaning of the new words. Practise these using the activities mentioned above. Point to a part of your body and say something which does not correspond, e.g. pointing to your nose:
Me duele el brazo.
The students have to correct the sentence:
Le duele la nariz.
As a variation on this game, the students can be asked to repeat phrases and remain silent if the action and the phrase do not correspond.

J Further activity
Clearly the vocabulary for the parts of the body needs lots of practice and the following idea and the above can be used over a number of lessons:

Pelmanism
This involves matching drawings of parts of the body with phrases. Give two groups of students 20 cards each **copymasters 87** and **88**. The cards are placed face down. One set of cards has 20 pictures of different parts of the body and the other has 20 sentences describing what is wrong, e.g.
Me duele el brazo.
The pupils take it in turns to pick up two cards and if they pair up the student keeps them; if not, the cards are replaced face down. The student who has the most pairs of cards at the end is the winner.

K In order to be more precise, it is necessary to specify how long the symptoms have persisted. Give the students the following examples:
¿Hace mucho que te duele?
Me duele desde hace dos horas./Me duele desde ayer.
Add different times to the OHP of the ailments, e.g. show a picture of somebody with a headache, and a length of time: 2h. Ask them to identify the illness by telling them how long it has gone on for.
You – Me duele desde hace dos horas.
Student – ¿Te duele la cabeza?
You – Sí.
Then ask them to choose an illness from those on the OHP, say what is wrong with them and how long they have had it. Practise as a 'chain game'; each person has to specify a longer time than the previous person in answer to these questions:
¿Hace mucho que no comes?
¿Hace mucho que no duermes?
¿Hace mucho que estás enfermo?
¿Hace mucho que te sientes mal?
¿Hace mucho que te duelen las muelas? etc.

L The students, in pairs, work on the exercise in their book.

M Finally, play these recordings. The students listen to each one twice and then say, or write, who the patient is. Clear up any problems as you go along.

¿Qué te pasa?
Número 1
– Buenos días. ¿Cómo estás?
– Me duelen la mano derecha, la pierna izquierda, el tobillo, las muelas …
– ¿Y qué tal te sientes?
– ¡Fantástico! ¡Superfantástico!

Número 2
– ¿Qué te pasa?
– Me duele la nariz y me duele el estómago.
– ¿Cómo te sientes?
– Muy mal.

Número 3
– ¿Qué tal estás?
– Me duelen los oídos y también la garganta y el brazo derecho.
– ¿Cómo te sientes?
– Un poco mejor.

UNIDAD 9

¿Quién es ... y qué dice? (page 98)

Main aim
Saying where you have a pain or discomfort.

A Ask questions based on the pictures, such as:
¿Qué es esto? Es una nariz/Son pies.
¿De quién es? ¿Es la nariz de Conchi?
¿Quién es? ¿Cómo lo sabes?

B Make a statement about one of the pictures and ask them to identify the square.

C As a memory game, give them a minute to memorise the 12 pictures and then repeat Activity B. Then give them a number and see if they can give you the correct statement.

D Ask them who the people are and what they would say, as shown in the example.

E Use pictures 1, 2, 3, 5, 6, 7, 9, 10, 11 for a game of Noughts and Crosses with the class. The students can continue this in pairs, using pictures 2, 3, 4, 6, 7, 8, 10, 11, 12. To be able to write a nought or a cross, a student has to say correctly what the problem with the patient is, e.g.
Le duele la nariz.

¿Qué les pasa a éstos? (page 98)

Main aim
Reporting injuries and ailments.

A Ask the students to imagine in turn that they are the patients in the pictures. In pairs, they describe their symptoms to the doctor (their partner) who then notes down (or draws) what is wrong, without looking at the text book.

B The students can now say what is wrong with the person in the picture using *le duele(n)*. This can be done without either partner looking at the text book if they have a sufficiently good memory.

C More able students may like to speculate as to how the people in the pictures came by their injuries. This can be done in the first or third person of the verb, e.g.

Ayer jugué al tenis y esta mañana me duele mucho el brazo.

You could speculate on the characters and likely pastimes of the five, e.g.

¿Son deportistas? ¿Dónde trabajan? ¿Tienen un trabajo peligroso? ¿Qué pasatiempos les gustan? ¿Cómo se hicieron daño? ¿Un accidente? ¿El chico se cayó? etc.

D You could now make up a brief narrative about how one of the patients was injured. The students listen and say which patient this was, e.g.

¿Cómo me pasó? Bueno, fui a un partido de fútbol. Yo iba a salir del estadio y Barcelona marcó un gol. Todos querían ver la acción. Caí al suelo y no sé. Me desperté en el hospital.

E Present on the board or OHP a C-test version of how patient number 3 injured herself, e.g.
Me du_ la cab_ y tam_ me du_ la ro_. Vivo en un pi_ y el asc_ no func_. Tomé la escal_ y cua_ estaba baj_ me ca_. No f_ al hosp_. He tom_ unas aspi_ y me sie_ mejor.

The students complete this in class or at home. Correct their work and clear up any problems. Able students could now use this as a model to write a short narrative to account for how one of the other patients came to be injured. When you correct these, try to work out who the patient is and give a bonus mark for this.

Tienes que interpretar (page 99)

Main aim
Reporting ailments and injuries.

A The students read this and ensure that they understand it. Remind them about how much easier listening is if you can anticipate what people will probably say in a given situation. This is a very useful exam technique. Practise this now. The students anticipate orally what the problems will be and you write these down. Play the recordings once and ask the students to say when they hear one of the problems they anticipated.

UNIDAD 9

Tienes que interpretar

Número 1
- Me siento muy mal. Me duele la cabeza, me duele la garganta y tengo fiebre. No tengo tos pero me duele mucho la garganta.

Número 2
- Me caí de mi bicicleta y me duele mucho la pierna derecha. Me duele el pie también. ¡Ay! ¡Qué dolor!

Número 3
- No sé si he comido algo malo pero me duele el estómago. ¡Ay!, me duele mucho.

Número 4
- Yo he estado trabajando en el jardín y ahora me duele mucho la espalda. Me duele muchísimo la espalda.

Número 5
- A mí me duele el brazo izquierdo y la mano izquierda. No sé qué me pasa.

B Play each recording twice more. The students write notes, in English, and then report on the problem(s). Clear up any problems and play the recording again.

C Play each recording once more. After it, the students say if the patient was *valiente* or not. They listen once more and repeat only what the brave patients say.

En el consultorio (page 99)

Main aim

Reporting minor ailments and injuries.

A The students read this carefully and try to understand it. Encourage them to use their communication strategies. They could write a list of all new words and note, in pencil, what they think they all mean. They then use a dictionary to check these. Hopefully, this will remind them that a dictionary is not usually necessary.
You could say each of the key words aloud. The students explain what it means and how they worked this out, e.g. from the visuals or the dictionary.

B The expressions in the speech bubbles all involve the use of the perfect tense of reflexive verbs. If you feel that the students need reminding of the perfect tense and would benefit from a complete presentation of the reflexive perfect, refer them to *A ser detective,* page 196.
Work on the expressions in the speech bubbles separately using activities which have previously proved successful.

C Ask the students to match up the patients with what they are saying by using the receptionist's notes. Check their answers by asking, e.g.
Buenos días, señor García. ¿Qué le pasa?
The pupils can practise likewise in pairs.

D Write the following on the board:
Me he cortado
Me he torcido
Me he hecho daño en
Me he quemado
Ask the students to find as many sensible ways of completing the sentences as possible in a set time.

E Ask the students to write down two headings: *¿Qué te pasa?* and *¿Qué te ha pasado?* Give them some short phrases which they are to write under the appropriate list, e.g.
¿Qué te pasa?
Me duelen las muelas.
¿Qué te ha pasado?
He cogido una insolación.

F The students take the roles of doctor and receptionist, and the latter has to say who is next and what the matter is. This involves changing from the first person to the third and may need some class preparation before attempting the whole activity in pairs. Refer the students to the pictures of the different injuries and ailments, and concentrate on *Se ha cortado, se ha quemado,* etc.

¿Puede darme hora? (page 100)

Main aim

Arranging an appointment with a doctor.

A The students read this to themselves and ensure that they understand it. They then listen to the recording and follow the text in their book. They then repeat, with and without the recording.

UNIDAD 9

B Adapt the model dialogue with the class. You could play the part of the receptionist and change the problems. This will give useful practice in coping with the unexpected.

C Give each student a copy of **copymaster 89**. Play each recording in turn, playing it two or three times while the students write their notes in the grid.

¿Puede darme hora?

Número 1
- Dígame.
- ¿Puede darme hora, por favor?
- ¿Qué le pasa?
- Es que hace dos días que me duele el estómago. No como, pero tengo sed. A veces me duele la cabeza y estoy mareada.
- ¿Las cinco y media?
- Vale, gracias.
- ¿Su nombre, por favor?
- Mari Carmen Candenas.

Número 2
- Buenos días.
- Buenos días. Dígame.
- Tengo tos y tengo fiebre pero no tengo frío … perdón. No quiero comer nada y me siento muy mal. ¿Puede darme hora por favor?
- ¿Su nombre, por favor?
- Micaela Muñoz.
- Vamos a ver … ¿a las seis y veinte?
- Está bien. Adiós.
- Adiós.

Número 3
- ¡Oiga! Creo que me he hecho daño en el brazo, pero no sé cómo. Me duele mucho y es muy difícil moverlo. ¿Puede darme hora hoy para una visita al médico?
- Lo siento. El médico está enfermo. ¿Puede volver mañana?
- No, no puedo volver mañana. Creo que está roto.
- Bueno. A las seis esta tarde, ¿le va bien?
- Sí, me va muy bien. Me llamo Jesús Moreno.
- Jesús Moreno. Muy bien.
- Gracias.
- De nada, adiós.

Número 4
- Oiga, me siento muy mal. Estoy constipado y creo que tengo fiebre. Además estoy muy cansado. Hace un día que no como. ¿Puede darme hora hoy o mañana?
- ¿Cómo se llama Vd?

- Enrique Alonso.
- ¿Esta tarde a las seis y diez le va bien?
- ¿No puede ser por la mañana?
- Sí, a las doce.
- Sí señora, muchas gracias.

D The students can now make up similar dialogues trying to make them as varied as possible.

E Further activity
Ask the students to suggest as many questions in Spanish as they can that a doctor might ask his/her patients, e.g.
¿Le duele mucho?
¿Dónde le duele exactamente?
¿Hace mucho que no come?
¿Duerme bien?
¿Qué comió Vd. ayer?

Write down a selection of these questions for the students to practise in pairs, making up appropriate answers.

Pedir hora no es siempre fácil (page 100)

Main aim
Coping with the unexpected.

A The students read this quietly to ensure that they understand it and how it works.

B They listen to these recordings and follow the path each one takes through the flowchart (*el diagrama de flujo*).

Pedir hora no es siempre fácil

Número 1
- Dígame.
- Oiga. ¿Puede darme hora?
- ¿Puede venir mañana a las siete?
- ¿No puede ser hoy?
- No sé. ¿Es urgente?
- No.
- Lo siento. ¿Quiere venir mañana por la tarde a las siete?
- Sí, me va bien.
- ¿Su nombre, por favor?

Número 2
- Dígame.
- Oiga. ¿Puede darme hora?
- ¿Puede venir mañana a las siete?
- Sí, me va bien.

UNIDAD 9

– ¿Su nombre, por favor?

Número 3
– Dígame.
– Oiga. ¿Puede darme hora?
– ¿Puede venir mañana a las siete?
– ¿No puede ser hoy?
– No sé. ¿Es urgente?
– Sí.
– ¿Quiere venir hoy a las cinco?
– Sí, me va bien.
– ¿Su nombre, por favor?

C In pairs, the students use the flowchart to make appointments according to the four briefs. As students finish this, you could give them some more briefs on the board, e.g.
Tienes la gripe desde hace dos días. No puedes dormir y tienes fiebre. Te sientes muy mal.
Te has cortado el dedo. Te duele mucho. ¡No eres muy valiente!

Contra-reloj (page 101)

Main aim

Using the perfect tense of reflexive verbs to report ailments and injuries.

A Now would be a good time to work on *A ser detective*, page 196.

B The students make up as many sensible sentences as they can in ten minutes. To ensure that they think about the meaning of what they write, without which the exercise will not be useful, get them to write their sentences in three categories:

Yo	me he roto	la espalda.
Mi profesor(a)	se ha torcido	el tobillo.
Mi pareja	te has cortado	el pie.

After ten minutes, ask students to read out their sentences in the three categories. Clear up any problems.

C Play at 'Do as I say, not as I do'. You point to a part of your body and report an injury. If you point to the correct part of your body, the students imitate your gesture and repeat what you say. So, you point to your left arm and say, e.g.
Me he roto el brazo izquierdo.

The students repeat this and point to their left arms. If, however, you point to your left arm and say, e.g.
Me he roto la pierna izquierda
the students do not repeat what you say. You could ask them to point at you and correct you, e.g.
¡No! Se ha roto el brazo izquierdo.

D If any students need more practice, you could organise a chain exercise. You report an injury or ailment. A student repeats this and adds to it, e.g.
Le duelen los oídos. Me he torcido el pie.

Another student repeats this and adds to it, e.g.
Le duelen los oídos. Se ha torcido el pie. Y yo, me he hecho daño en la nariz.

E You could organise a few minutes of verb circle practice, starting with, e.g.
Me he hecho daño en el ojo.
Te has cortado la rodilla.
Se ha quemado el dedo.

¿Insisten bastante? (page 101)

Main aim

Coping with the unexpected.

A Now would be a good time to revise the unit so far, e.g.
Present on the board or OHP the first and last words only of ten of the key sentences on pages 96–99. The students have five minutes to find these and to write them out in full.
Start a word association chart on the board or OHP and ask the students for ideas about how to extend it, e.g.

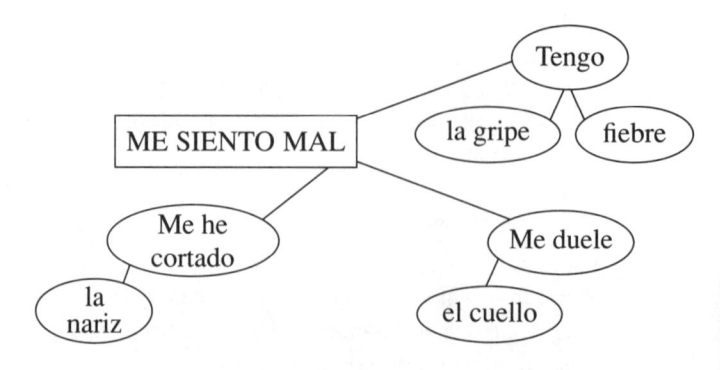

ME SIENTO MAL
– Tengo: la gripe, fiebre
– Me he cortado: la nariz
– Me duele: el cuello

UNIDAD 9

Then erase this and ask every student to produce a new one, starting from *Me siento fatal*.

Present the following on the board or OHP. Discuss what sort of words are in the circles (verbs) and what sort of words (nouns) go with them. They then all copy these and complete them:

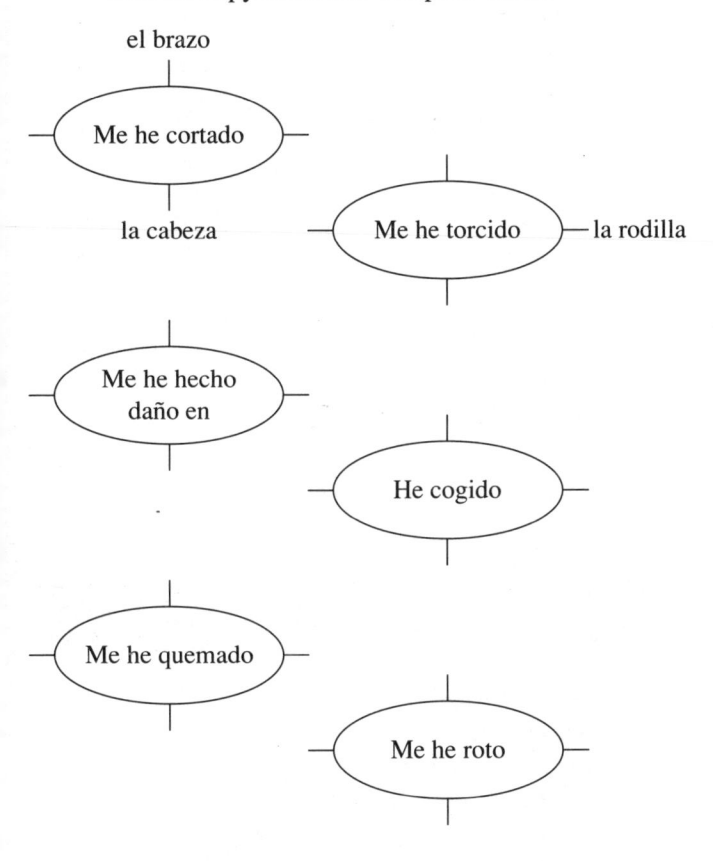

```
        el brazo
         |
    ( Me he cortado )
         |
      la cabeza        ( Me he torcido )—la rodilla

    ( Me he hecho
        daño en )
                    ( He cogido )

    ( Me he quemado )
                    ( Me he roto )
```

When everyone has done this, correct their work and clear up any problems. Then add some adjectives to your original, e.g. *el brazo izquierdo*. Check that the students understand that these are adjectives and where they can go. They could then add appropriate adjectives to their work.

B The students now read this item and, again, practise anticipating what they will hear by guessing what the problems will be. When they have found six to eight problems, they could practise appropriate responses.

¿Insisten bastante?

Número 1
- Buenos días. Quiero ver al médico.
- Lo siento, pero el médico no puede verle hoy.
- ¿Me puede dar hora para mañana?
- Sí. ¿Puede venir a las cinco?
- Sí, me va bien.

Número 2
- ¿Me puede ayudar? Me duele muchísimo el estómago y he vomitado mucho.
- Lo siento, no hay un médico libre.
- Pero es urgente. Quiero ver al médico.
- ¿Puede venir esta tarde?
- No, es urgente.
- No sé.
- Escuche. Estoy muy enferma y no puedo volver esta tarde.
- Bueno, siéntese. Vamos a ver …

Número 3
- Buenos días. ¿Me puede dar hora para ver al médico?
- Lo siento, pero el médico no está libre ahora. ¿Puede venir mañana?
- No, estoy constipado y tengo tos.
- Lo siento. No es posible.
- Pero quiero ver al médico.
- Lo siento. Tiene que volver mañana.
- Pues me viene fatal, pero bueno, vendré mañana.

C The students listen to the recordings and decide whether each patient is adequately insistent, too insistent or not insistent enough. Discuss their responses, encourage them to compare their responses, clear up any problems and play the recordings again.

D Play number 2 again and encourage the students to repeat after and then with the patient. Then play the first two lines of number 1 while the students transcribe it. Present a correct version on the board. The students use this to correct what they have written. In pairs, they now continue this, with the patient insisting more and trying to get an appointment today.

Una postal de un enfermo (page 101)

Main aim
Understanding and writing a postcard about an accident.

A The students read this and ensure that they understand it, using a dictionary if necessary.

UNIDAD 9

B They look at the drawings and choose from the card:
  a any whole sentences from the card which can be adapted and used to describe them;
  b any phrases from the card which can be adapted and used to describe them.

This provides excellent exam practice, as students need to know how to use, and to adapt, the models provided.

C Produce on the board a list of useful link words and time references which can occur in narratives, e.g.
primero, después, unos minutos más tarde, luego, finalmente, antes de + infinitive, después de + infinitive, sin embargo, sin + infinitive, a causa de, por lo tanto.

The students produce some oral narratives, based on the postcard and pictures, using as many as possible of these link words and time references. Stress the importance of these expressions for a good narrative.

D Each student writes a postcard to say where and how they are and how they came to be there, based on the four pictures. This could be done at home.

El médico te hace preguntas (page 102)

Main aim
Responding to inquiries from a doctor.

A The students read this carefully to themselves and ensure that they understand it.

B You read a question aloud and encourage students to provide an answer. Do this with the other questions.

Then reverse this. Students read aloud the questions, in any order, and you answer them. The students can continue this in pairs.

Play this recording. The students listen and compare what they hear with the brief to check that everything is covered. They then listen again and repeat each sentence after the speakers. In pairs, they then make up a role play to meet this brief, taking turns to play each role.

C The students listen to these young people and judge how well each one meets the given brief.

El médico te hace preguntas
Número 1
– ¿Qué te pasa?
– Me duele la cabeza, no puedo dormir y no puedo comer, tengo frío y tengo fiebre.
– ¿Cuándo fuiste a la playa?
– Fui a la playa a las diez. Pasé cuatro horas.
– ¿Has tomado algún medicamento?
– Sí, he tomado dos aspirinas.
– ¿Te has puesto una crema?
– No.

Número 2
– ¿Qué te pasa?
– Me duele la cabeza.
– Sí.
– No puedo dormir.
– ¿Tienes calor o tienes frío?
– Tengo frío.
– ¿Fuiste a la playa?
– A las diez.
– ¿Te pusiste alguna crema?
– No.
– ¿Cuántos años tienes?
– Tengo quince años.

Número 3
– Hola, buenas tardes.
– Buenas tardes.
– ¿Qué te pasa?
– Me duele la cabeza y no puedo ni dormir ni comer.
– ¿Cómo te sientes?
– Muy mal.
– ¿Tienes frío?
– Sí, tengo frío pero tengo fiebre también y estoy mareada.
– ¿Cuándo fuiste a la playa?
– A las diez.
– ¿Y cuánto tiempo pasaste allí?
– Pasé cuatro horas. Me dormí porque estaba cansado.
– Al volver de la playa ¿comiste algo?
– Nada.
– ¿Te pusiste alguna crema?
– No, pero tomé dos aspirinas. Me sentí muy mal en un bar y volví a casa.
– ¡Ay! Vamos a ver …

Número 4
– Buenos días.
– Buenos días, doctor.
– ¿Qué te pasa?
– He cogido una insolación.
– ¿Te duele la cabeza?

UNIDAD 9

- Me duele la cabeza, no puedo ni dormir ni comer.
- ¿Tienes frío?
- Tengo frío pero tengo fiebre y estoy mareada.
- ¿Fuiste a la playa?
- Sí.
- ¿Cuándo?
- A las diez.
- ¿Cuánto tiempo pasaste allí?
- Cuatro horas.
- ¿Te pusiste alguna crema?
- No.
- ¡Ah! ¿Comiste algo?
- No, fui al bar y me sentí muy mal. Volví a casa.
- ¿Has tomado algún medicamento?
- He tomado dos aspirinas.
- Bueno, tienes que pasar unos días en la cama. Toma esta medicina cuatro veces al día. No vas a ir a la playa esta semana, ¿verdad?
- No voy a ir nunca más a la playa.

D Play the recordings again. The students listen and note any information given which was not in the instructions.

They now listen once more as a preparation for the next activity. In pairs, they practise repeating after the speakers, taking turns to repeat after the doctor and the patient.

E In pairs, the students practise role-playing the situations described, taking turns to be the doctor and the patient. You could move around listening, helping and joining in.

F As able students complete Activity **E**, ask them to write a brief of their own, similar to those on this page, to describe an illness, how long they have had it and how it occurred. In pairs, they then interview each other to try to find all the relevant information.

¿Qué me aconsejas? (page 103)

Main aim

Understanding and giving advice.

A The students read this to themselves and ensure that they understand it all. They look at the advice that they might want to give each of the tourists. In order to familiarise the students with them, take the role of a Spanish person explaining your symptoms and needing their advice, e.g.

Me siento mareado. ¿Qué me aconsejas?
Le aconsejo sentarse un rato.
Me duelen las muelas. ¿Qué me aconsejas?
Le aconsejo pedir hora al dentista.

B Play the tape, stopping it after each section in order to give the class enough time to take a few notes and to discuss the advice they would give. Play each section twice if necessary.

¿Qué me aconsejas?

Número 1
- Hace dos días que me duele el estómago. No como, pero tengo mucha sed. ¡Ay! como me duele la cabeza y estoy mareada. ¿Qué me aconseja?

Número 2
- Tengo tos. Tengo fiebre, pero no tengo frío. No quiero comer nada. Me siento muy mal. ¿Qué me aconseja?

Número 3
- Hace dos días que me duele esta muela. No puedo comer nada y anoche no dormí. ¿Qué me aconseja?

Número 4
- Estoy constipado. Tengo tos y creo que tengo fiebre. Estoy muy cansado. Señor, ¿qué me aconseja?

Número 5
- Me duele mucho la pierna. Me duele mucho. ¡Ay! ...

C Play the tape once more and ask students to give the advice as if they were speaking to the person.

D In pairs, the students practise coping with the unexpected: one describes a new problem and the other tries to give appropriate advice.

As they finish this, ask them each to write ten problems and appropriate advice. This could be completed at home.

Sancho y Panza (page 103)

Main aim

Producing a written narrative.

A The students read the caption and ensure that they understand it.

UNIDAD 9

B As a class activity, see how many more things the class can add to what the patient cannot do.

C The students look back over the unit so far, including *A ser detective*, and write an account of what has happened to the patient in the cartoon. Encourage them to be inventive and humorous. The corrected results could make an amusing wall display.

Una palabra conduce a otra (page 103)

Main aim

To extend vocabulary and communication strategies.

A Work on this along lines which have previously proved successful.

B A very useful dictionary activity would be for the students to look these words up and to check their genders. What conclusion can they draw about words which end in *-dad* and *-tad*?
Knowing how to check the gender of nouns in a dictionary is also a useful exam technique.

¿Me puede recomendar algo? (page 104)

Main aim

Getting help from a chemist.

A Ask the students to look at the pictures of the medicines and explain to them in Spanish what each one is for, e.g.
Si te cortas el dedo, por ejemplo, hay que poner antiséptico.
Si te sientes cansado puedes tomar un tónico.

B Tell the students your imaginary symptoms and ask them to recommend one or more of the medicines, e.g.
Tengo fiebre, no duermo y me duele la cabeza.
Le aconsejo medicina 'gripe' y unas aspirinas.

C Go through the model dialogue with the students. They repeat it after you. In pairs, they practise adapting the dialogue, using as much of the language of the unit as they can.

D Play the tape of the customers in the chemist's and ask them to match them up with the pictures on page 104. Ask them to make a note of the chemist's recommendations in each case.

¿Me puede recomendar algo?

Número 1
– Buenos días. ¿Qué desea?
– Mire, me duele mucho la cabeza. ¿Me puede ayudar con algo?
– ¿Hace mucho que le duele?
– Pues, dos o tres horas por lo menos. He pasado casi todo el día al sol y yo creo que es por esto.
– Puede ser. Bueno, me parece que Vd. sólo necesita aspirinas. Y le aconsejo no salir más al sol hoy. ¿Quiere un paquete grande o pequeño?

Número 2
– Hola. ¿Qué te pasa?
– Daba una vuelta en bicicleta y me caí. Me he hecho daño en la rodilla.
– A ver, siéntate. Pues sí, es verdad, te has hecho daño en la rodilla. Te hace falta una tirita muy grande, la tirita más grande que tengo. Pero primero la vamos a lavar con un poquito de antiséptico. Espérate un momentito.

Número 3
– Buenas tardes. ¿Qué le pasa?
– No lo sé. Me siento muy mal. Me duele la cabeza, tengo fiebre, además tengo frío y estoy mareado.
– ¿Ha estado al sol hoy?
– Sí, fuimos un grupo de amigos a la playa. Nos bañamos y tomamos el sol.
– Esto. Ha cogido una insolación. Le aconsejo acostarse en seguida y tomar dos aspirinas cada cuatro horas. A lo mejor le va a hacer falta esta crema que es muy buena para la piel quemada.
– Vale. Aspirinas tengo en casa, pero deme por favor un tubo grande de esa crema. ¿Cuánto es?
– Son 560 pesetas.

Número 4
– Buenos días. ¿Qué desea?
– Tengo una tos muy mala y me duele mucho la garganta. Anoche no pude dormir por la tos.
– ¿Tiene otros síntomas aparte del dolor de garganta? ¿Tiene fiebre? ¿Ha perdido el apetito? ¿Le duele el estómago?
– Pues no, no nada de eso. Sólo esta maldita tos.
– Creo que no es nada serio. Le recomiendo este jarabe que es muy bueno para la tos, y estas pastillas para la garganta.
– A ver si es verdad. Muchas gracias. ¿Cuánto es?

UNIDAD 9

Número 5
- Buenas tardes.
- Muy buenas. Oiga. ¿Vd. me puede aconsejar?
- Bueno, lo intentaré. ¿Qué le pasa?
- Pues, me parece que tengo la gripe.
- ¿Qué síntomas tiene?
- Tengo tos y fiebre y tengo mucha sed. No como. Me duelen la cabeza, los brazos, las piernas. Estoy hecho un desastre. Me siento muy mal.
- ¿Hace cuánto tiempo se siente así?
- Hace ya varios días.
- Mire, yo le puedo dar unas aspirinas, pero me parece que lo mejor sería llamar al médico para pedir hora con él.

Número 6
- Buenos días. ¿Tiene Vd. algo para quemaduras?
- ¿De sol?
- No, no, qué va. Es que esta mañana al preparar el café para el desayuno me quemé la mano con agua caliente.
- A ver. Ah sí, no es muy serio pero supongo que le duele, ¿no?
- ¡Uy, sí! Me duele bastante.
- Tome esta crema. Es muy buena para quemaduras así. Hay que ponerla cada dos horas.

¡Ten cuidado! (page 104)

Main aim

Understanding instructions for medicines.

The instructions for the medicines should not be difficult for the students to work out. If there are any that cause problems, ask them to tell you as many instructions as they can remember for medicines they have had. Taking advantage of the context is an important strategy for them to learn. For example, if they do not understand *cucharadita* ask them either to look at the words around it or ask more directly what expressions of quantity are generally used with medicines: teaspoons, dessert spoons! …

A Ask them to tell their partner (as if he/she did not understand Spanish) what each one means and check their answers.

B The students look back at the previous item and link these instructions to the medicines in that. They then look at the illnesses outlined in the previous item, suggest a remedy and give instructions for use, e.g.

Me duele mucho la garganta. ¿Me puede recomendar algo?
Sí, aquí tengo unas pastillas que son muy buenas. Tome dos pastillas tres veces al día.

Ahora sé (page 105)

Main aim

To provide a summary of the *Unidad* and a basis for more practice and revision.

A The students work on this, in class and at home, using their preferred techniques.

B You could introduce other activities, now or later, according to the needs of different students, e.g. Give students a copy of **copymaster 90**.
Exercise 1 The students have to note down what the patient says, so the tape should be stopped after each one.

Te toca a ti interpretar

Número 1
- Hace dos días que me duele mucho el estómago. Me duele todo el tiempo, pero más si como. No puedo dormir y no quiero comer.

Número 2
- Mire Vd., doctor. Ayer me caí. Me he hecho daño en el brazo. ¡Ay! Me duele mucho y no puedo moverlo. No sé si está roto.

Número 3
- Doctor, me duele mucho la cabeza. Es decir que me duele muy a menudo. Cada día me duele. Si tomo unas aspirinas deja de dolerme unas horas pero luego empieza de nuevo. Tomo como seis o más aspirinas al día y no me gusta tomar tantas. Me parece peligroso.

Número 4
- Me siento muy mal, muy mal. No sé qué me pasa. Estoy muy cansado, no tengo ganas de hacer nada. Duermo mal y como muy poco. Me levanto tarde y ya no salgo. No sé qué hacer.

Número 5
- Fuimos a la playa ayer y creo que he cogido una insolación. Estoy mareada y tengo fiebre; y me he quemado un poquito al sol también. No he comido nada hoy.

UNIDAD 9

Número 6

– Creo que tengo la gripe. Hace dos días que me siento muy enfermo. Tengo mucha fiebre y también tengo tos. No duermo y no como casi nada, pero bebo mucho. Tengo muchísima sed. Me duele la garganta y me duele la cabeza.

Exercise 2 The students take turns at being the doctor and prepare both roles thoroughly. You can ask each student sample questions to ensure that they can answer them.

Give students a copy of **copymaster 91**. They can work on these in class or at home.

Write six numbered illnesses on the board, e.g.

1 *Te duelen los oídos.*
2 *Te duele la garganta.*
3 *Te has cortado el dedo.*
4 *Te has roto la pierna.*
5 *Estás constipado/a.*
6 *Te has quemado preparando la comida.*

The students work in pairs. Each pair has a dice or a six-sided pencil with numbers on it. They make dialogues, e.g.

Student A: Me siento fatal.
Student B: ¿Qué te pasa?
Student A: (throws no. 2) Me duele la garganta.
Student B: ¡Qué lástima! Te recomiendo estas pastillas.

You could write this dialogue on the board as a model.

Revision activities

1 Talking about sports, hobbies and pastimes
(Libro 1, Unidad 11)

A Encourage the students to work on page 105 of *Libro 1*.

B The students listen to these three oral presentations on this topic. They make notes about the main points of each one, including the attitudes and points of view expressed. Discuss their answers and clear up any problems. Then play the recordings again and ask the students to say which is the best presentation and why. Make sure that they understand the criteria for a good presentation.

Repaso: Hobbies y pasatiempos

Número 1

– María, ¿qué te gusta hacer por las tardes cuando terminas en el colegio?
– Juego al voleibol, estoy en el equipo de la escuela, entrenamos al salir de la escuela, una hora o dos. Tenemos un buen entrenador. Me gusta mucho hacerlo.
– ¿Y qué haces después?
– Vuelvo a casa y hago mis tareas. Salgo otra vez con mis amigos y jugamos en la calle.
– ¿Haces otra cosa aparte del voleibol?
– Nada más. No me queda mucho tiempo libre.

Número 2

– Angel, ¿qué haces en tus ratos libres? ¿Tienes algún hobby?
– Sí, me gusta hacer cosas tranquilas. No soy muy deportista.
– ¿Qué te gusta hacer entonces?
– Me gusta tocar música; tres veces por semana voy a clases de piano.
– ¿A clases de piano?
– Sí. Toco la flauta también.
– ¿Y qué instrumento te gusta más?
– El piano, por supuesto. Empecé a la edad de tres años y me encanta.

Número 3

– Alberto, ¿Cuál es tu pasatiempo favorito?
– Me encanta el camping. Generalmente voy con mis padres al campo y algunas veces a la playa.
– ¿Por qué te gusta el camping?
– Bueno, puedo coleccionar insectos, flores y también nadar en los lagos.
– Tienes mucha libertad cuando haces camping.
– Sí, eso sí.

C At home or at school, each student prepares an oral presentation about their hobbies and interests. Encourage them to illustrate these with photos and other visuals. Form groups of 5 or 6. In each group, the students take turns to make their presentations. You, and the other students, follow each presentation with a few minutes of question and answer.

D Give each student a copy of **copymaster 92**. They could work on this at home.

UNIDAD 9

2 Environmental issues
(Libro 2, Unidad 9)

A Encourage the students to work on page 106 of *Libro 2*, either in class or at home.

B Present these oral presentations and work on them along the lines suggested in Exercise 1, Activity B, above.

Repaso: El medio ambiente

Número 1

Vivo en una ciudad grande, Lima. Lima está dividida en varias zonas: la zona industrial y la zona de las residencias. La parte industrial obviamente tiene mucha contaminación. También hay mucho tráfico especialmente cuando es la hora punta, que es en las mañanas o en las tardes. Es increíble, insoportable. Hay mucha contaminación para la gente que vive allí desafortunadamente. Pero en las zonas residenciales todo es muy limpio. Me agrada vivir en Lima.

Número 2

Yo creo que se puede hacer más para mejorar el medio ambiente. Se puede conservar energía, por ejemplo, apagando las luces cuando no las estás usando; apagando la televisión si no la estás viendo; no utilizar tantos productos de plástico, dividir la basura, reciclar el vidrio y el papel. Se pueden hacer muchas cosas.

3 Shopping for essential items
(Libro 3, Unidad 5)

A The students work on page 63 of *Libro 3*. You could use now any activities suggested for this *Ahora sé* which you did not use at the time.

B Give the students the following introduction before playing the tape.

A veces es necesario devolver cosas en las tiendas o decir que no estás satisfecho por alguna razón. Escucha a estas personas y sabrás cómo decir lo mismo.
Estás en la cola en una tienda de comestibles y no hay más remedio que escuchar lo que dicen los clientes. Explica a alguien que no entiende la conversación lo que pasa.

Repaso: problemas en la tienda de comestibles

Número 1

– Me pone seis panecillos, por favor.
– Tenga, seis panecillos.
– Estos no me parecen muy frescos, ¿son de hoy?
– Sí, señor. El panadero los ha traido esta mañana.
– Pues, mira, a mí no me parecen muy frescos. Prefiero dejarlos. Póngame mejor dos barras de cuarto.
– Como quiera, aunque le aseguro que son fresquísimos los panecillos.

Número 2

– Dígame señora. ¿En qué puedo servirle?
– Compré esta lata de guisantes ayer. La abrí al volver a casa. A mí me huelen mal y no me gusta nada el color que tiene.
– Pues sí, tiene Vd. razón. Me sorprende mucho porque esta marca es muy famosa, tiene buena fama. ¿Quiere que le devuelva el dinero?
– No, deme otra lata. ¡A ver si tengo suerte esta vez!

Número 3

– Sí, ¿qué desea?
– Una botella de champú para cabellos secos y un tubo de pasta de dientes.
– ¿Grande o pequeño?
– El champú normal, ni muy grande ni muy pequeño – y la pasta de dientes, grande.
– Pues, tenemos esta oferta especial con el tubo super-económico: contiene el 20% más de pasta (de dientes) y también Vd. recibe, completamente gratis, este paquete de tisús.
– No quiero ningún paquete de tisús que no tengo catarro. Tampoco quiero el tubo super-económico que cuesta demasiado. Si no tiene más pequeño lo dejo por hoy.
– Entonces, ¿le envuelvo el champú?
– No, lo llevo en mi bolsa.

4 Lost property
(Libro 3, Unidad 8)

A The students work on page 95 of *Libro 3*. You could use now any activities suggested for that page.

B Give each student a copy of **copymaster 93** for them to work on in pairs.

C You could organise a few minutes of verb circle practice based on, e.g.

He perdido un reloj de oro.
Has encontrado una maleta de cuero.
Ha visto un paraguas amarillo.
Hemos dejado una cartera en el tren.
Habéis comprado una cámara muy cara.
Han escrito al hotel.

UNIDAD 10

Accidentes y averías

Main aim
Coping with road accidents and breakdowns

Area(s) of experience
E – The international world

Materials
Materials
Cassette: Accidentes y averías, ¿Me puede ayudar?, ¿Tiene sus documentos?, ¿Qué estabas haciendo?, ¿Cómo pasó?, ¿Qué le pasa?, ¿Qué le puede pasar al coche?, Quiero alquilar un coche, Repaso: comiendo en casa de otro.
Copymasters 94–101

Tasks
Reporting the location and basic details of an accident or breakdown
Giving details and describing what happened
Contacting emergency services
Getting a car repaired
Hiring a car

Grammar
Imperfect tense
Imperfect continuous tense

Productive language
accidente
alquilar
andar
autopista
batería
calzada
conducir
cruce
culpa
faro
freno
herido
  (de gravedad)
matricular
motor
peatón
remolcar
terminar
adelantar
ambulancia
atropellar
avería
calentarse
ciclista
conductor
cruzar
chocar
frenar
grave
listo
marca
mecánico
pararse
pieza de recambio
taller

Receptive language
asegurado
averiado
camión
casco
cinturón de seguridad
compañía de seguros
concesionario
hospital
límite de velocidad
moto
motociclista
paso de peatones
permiso de conducir
póliza
primeros auxilios
rueda
seguro
taxi
testigo
vehículo

Revision
Buying food in Spain (*Libro 1, Unidad 12*)
Obtaining services at a petrol station (*Libro 2, Unidad 10*)
Eating in a Spanish person's home or hosting a meal (*Libro 3, Unidad 6*)
Coping with illness (*Libro 3, Unidad 9*)

Accidentes y averías (page 106)

Main aim
To understand the unit goals and to see their usefulness.

A Work on this along lines which have previously proved successful.

B Make sure that the students understand and can say the model sentences. See how many can say each one correctly in 30 seconds. Then play these recorded narratives. The students listen and complete each one with one of the model sentences.

Accidentes y averías

Número 1
– Mi tía vive en Ribadesella e iba a visitarla. Estaba muy cerca cuando se paró el coche. Tenía mucha gasolina y no sabía qué le pasaba al coche. Bajé del coche y llamé al garaje. El mecánico llegó una hora más tarde.

Número 2
– Lo siento. Salí del parking y no lo vi. El coche chocó con el mío y no sé por qué no lo vi.

UNIDAD 10

Número 3
- Estaba en la autopista. Tuve un pinchazo y no podía cambiar la rueda. Un amigo mío es el dueño de un garaje. Le llamé y mandó a un mecánico.

Cómo evitar los accidentes de tráfico y las averías (page 106)

Main aim
To develop reading skills.

A Encourage the students to use their communication strategies, including the use of a dictionary, to understand this text.

B Look at the visuals with the class and ask students to read aloud the part of the text which goes with each visual. When it is clear that everyone knows what to do, the students could all write the letters of the visuals next to the relevant part of the text.

C Discuss the advice and ask students to say which advice is the most/least important for, e.g. cyclists, car drivers, bus drivers, old people. Each student then writes the advice in order of importance:
   a for themselves;
   b for lorry drivers.
They compare and discuss their lists.

D As abler students finish the above task, you could ask them to add some pieces of advice of their own to both lists.

¿Qué haces primero? (page 107)

Main aim
To introduce and practise some of the key language of the unit.

A The students read this to themselves, using appropriate communication strategies, including dictionary use.

B You say one of the questions aloud and encourage students to find and say the answer. Use a 'snowballing' technique. When you have practised three questions and answers, put all three questions to a student and do this after each additional question, going back over all those practised. This involves more students, maintains pace and develops confidence. After this class practice, the students can continue this in pairs, each putting all the questions to the other.

C Each student could now write a dialogue using these questions and answers. This could be done in class or at home.

D In pairs, the students develop dialogues based on the four scenarios on **copymaster 94**. You could move around helping and joining in.

¿Me puede ayudar? (page 107)

Main aim
Reporting the location and basic details of an accident or breakdown.

A The students read this to themselves and ensure that they understand it.

B They listen to the recording, first with the text to follow and then without the text. Then play the recording again. The students listen and repeat only what the travellers say. Give them two minutes to learn the travellers' lines for the first dialogue. Then play the recording again, stopping before each traveller's line and encouraging the students to say it. Then let the recording go on. Repeat this with the second dialogue.

¿Me puede ayudar?

Número 1
- ¿Dígame?
- ¿Me puede ayudar? Mi coche tiene una avería.
- ¿Qué le pasa?
- No sé.
- ¿Dónde está usted exactamente?
- Estoy a cinco kilómetros al norte de Vigo en la autopista A-9.
- ¿Qué marca de coche es?
- Es un Peugeot 405 rojo.
- ¿Y la matrícula?
- N837 TUL. ¿Puede mandar un mecánico?
- Sí, llegaremos dentro de algunos minutos.

Número 2
- ¿Dígame?
- Ha habido un accidente.
- ¿Es grave?

UNIDAD 10

- Sí, ¿puede mandar una ambulancia? El conductor está herido.
- ¿Dónde está usted exactamente?
- Estoy en la carretera N-550 a tres kilómetros al sur de Cambados
- ¿Su nombre, por favor?
- García.
- ¿Tiene coche?
- Sí, coche y caravana.
- ¿Y la matrícula?
- M503 YXL.
- Una ambulancia llegará pronto.

C The students work in pairs on the two scenarios. For homework, they could write a dialogue to go with each scenario.

Cuando llegue la policía (page 108)

Main aim

Answering a police officer's questions.

A Begin by revising the unit so far, e.g.
You say some key sentences. The students listen and categorise each one as *accidente, avería, los dos*. Repeat this and ask the students to categorise each sentence according to who would say it: *un viajero, un mecánico, la policía*.
Give each student a copy of **copymaster 95** for them to work on in pairs.

B The students read this item to themselves and ensure that they understand it.

C You play the role of the police officer and invite students to answer the questions. Then reverse this, with students putting the questions to you. They can then do this in pairs, putting the questions to each other. Encourage the students playing the part of the police officer to act accordingly.

¿Tiene sus documentos? (page 108)

Main aim

To develop listening and speaking skills.

A The students read this item carefully and prepare to listen to the recording. They then listen to it as they look at the written notes. Play the recording again and encourage the students to repeat after Ignacio Puente. Then play it again and stop the tape before Ignacio Puente speaks. Using the notes, the students play his part. Then let the recording run on so that they can hear again what he says.

¿Tiene sus documentos?
- Bueno, a ver, ¿me puede dar su nombre entonces?
- Puente González.
- ¿Y su nombre de pila, por favor?
- Ignacio.
- Ajá, Ignacio ¿y su domicilio?
- Avenida de Portugal 86, 2°F.
- Efe de Francisco, ¿verdad?
- Sí, sí.
- ¿Y dónde vive?
- En Salamanca.
- ¿Me puede dar el número de la póliza?
- Sí. El número de la póliza es … 8732/50/D.
- ¿D de Dinamarca?
- Sí, muy bien.
- ¿Con qué compañía está Vd. asegurado?
- Fénix.
- Ajá. ¿Es Vd. el asegurado? ¿A qué nombre está el seguro?
- A mi nombre.
- ¿Y qué coche es? ¿un Seat?
- Sí, sí, un Seat Panda.
- ¿Me dice la matrícula, por favor?
- La matrícula es Salamanca 708539.
- Salamanca, SA 708539.
- Exactamente.
- Vale, pues ya estaremos en contacto.

B Play the recording again and ask the students to concentrate on the questions. Encourage them to make notes if they wish. They can then use these notes to reconstruct this dialogue in pairs, referring to their own notes and to those in their book.

C In pairs, the students make up a dialogue based on the second set of notes in their book. Move around as they do this, clearing up any problems.

D In pairs, they work on the two scenarios and practise coping with the unexpected. When everyone has done this, you could play each role in turn and invite students to play the others.

UNIDAD 10

¿Qué estabas haciendo? (page 109)

Main aim
Describing what happened.

A The students read this to themselves and ensure that they understand it.

B Write on the board or OHP the key expressions, e.g.

*Yo estaba
cruzando
esperando
escuchando
frenando
conduciendo
haciendo algo*

The students try to explain what these all mean and then to work out how this construction is formed. Help them to do this and provide any additional examples to confirm and develop the rules they make. Then use these insights to say what the other four witnesses said.

C Study the visual again and ask questions about it to help the students to remember it and the language which goes with it, e.g.

*¿Dónde estaba el testigo número tres?
¿Y qué estaba haciendo?
Y las dos mujeres, ¿qué estaban haciendo?*

D The students now look at the visual as they listen to the recording. They make notes about any differences of opinion. They report on these differences and discuss them with you and the class. Clear up any problems.

¿Qué estabas haciendo?

Número 1
– Yo estaba esperando el autobús. No vi mucho. El coche pasó – no iba muy de prisa pero chocó con la bicicleta. ¡Ay! ¡Qué ruido!

Número 2
– Estaba cruzando la calle. No vi nada. Lo siento. Oí el accidente pero no vi nada.

Número 3
– Yo estaba detrás del ciclista. Yo empecé a frenar porque el cruce no estaba lejos. El ciclista no paró, no miró a la izquierda antes de salir. El coche no pudo parar.

Número 4
– Estaba hablando con mi amiga en la calle. El accidente ocurrió muy cerca. El chico con la bicicleta salió sin mirar.

Número 5
– Yo estaba conduciendo el coche que chocó con el joven. No iba de prisa. Llegué a un cruce y la bicicleta salió. Frené pero, imposible. No pude parar.

Número 6
– Estaba en la bicicleta un momento y ¡chas! al momento siguiente estaba en el suelo. Yo estaba escuchando mi walkman y no vi el coche.

E They listen once or twice more to the recording and then write a short account to describe what happened. They could finish this at home.

F Now would be a good time to work on *A ser detective*, page 200.

Describiendo un accidente (page 109)

Main aim
Giving details of an accident and describing what happened.

A The students begin by reading this to themselves and ensuring that they understand it.

B Ask the questions and encourage as many students as possible to answer each one. Use the 'snowballing' technique.

C Each student now writes the answers to the questions in their book.

D As able students finish this, ask them to develop their answers to produce a written report, describing how the accident happened.

¿Cómo pasó? (page 110)

Main aim
Giving details of an accident and describing what happened.

A The students read this and ensure that they understand it.

UNIDAD 10

B They adapt the texts to say what the two drivers could say. When doing this, they could lie. The others listen and try to spot and correct any inaccuracies.

C The students listen to the witnesses and say which, in each pair, is the better witness and why.

¿Cómo pasó?

Número 1. A
– Había un camión y un coche. El camión salió y el coche … blanco o amarillo, no paró. El coche chocó con el camión y se salió de la carretera.

Número 1. B
– El coche iba por la carretera y un camión salió en un cruce. El camión chocó con el coche y el coche se salió de la calzada.

Número 2. A
– Había dos coches, un coche azul y un coche rojo. El coche azul adelantó y ¡paf! chocó con el coche negro que se acercaba. Los dos coches se salieron de la calzada.

Número 2. B
– No sé exactamente qué pasó. Creo que el coche negro chocó con el coche azul pero no sé cómo.

Número 3. A
– Vi un taxi en el cruce y una moto. La moto iba muy rápido y chocó con el taxi.

Número 3. B
– El taxi se paró en el cruce. Luego llegó una moto, pero no se paró. La moto chocó con el taxi.

Unas preguntas de un policía (page 111)

Main aim

Reporting the details of an accident.

A In pairs, the students practise asking and answering the questions. You could move around, listening and helping.

B Each student writes an account of each accident. They could do this in class or at home.

C When you have corrected their reports, students could read them aloud. The others listen and say which accident each report refers to and if they agree with the details of the report.

Tú eres el testigo (page 111)

Main aim

Writing a description of an accident.

A The students play the part of police officers and ask you questions about the accident, in order to find out what happened.

B The students now all write a description of the accident. You could move around and give help where it is needed.

C When you have corrected these, the students could compare their different accounts.

Averiado (page 112)

Main aim

To present and practise the key language needed for reporting a breakdown.

A The students read this to themselves and ensure that they understand it.

B To help them to learn this key language you could use the following activities:
You say the phrases aloud, in random order. The students say if each one is *una pregunta* or *una explicación*.
Present pictures of cars cut from magazines. Use these to play at, e.g. *¿Verdad o mentira?* and *Repite si es verdad*. Then point to a part of a car and see which student can say first the appropriate sentence from the list.
Give the students one minute to study the page and then ask them to close their books. Test their powers of observation by asking questions about the visuals on the page.
The students open their books and watch carefully as you silently mouth one of the key phrases. They say this phrase aloud. They can continue this in pairs.

C For homework, the students learn these expressions by heart, using their favourite techniques.

UNIDAD 10

¿Qué le pasa? (page 112)

Main aim
To develop listening skills.

A The students look at each visual and, using the phrases in the previous item, try to anticipate what the travellers and mechanics will say.

B Play these recordings and work on each one separately, clearing up any problems as you go along.

¿Qué le pasa?

Número 1
- A ver, ¿qué le pasa a la moto?
- Que se me ha pinchado la rueda.
- Déjeme ver.
- ¿Podría arreglarla hoy?
- Sí. Sólo hay que sacar el neumático y lo arreglamos en seguida. Puede volver dentro de una hora.
- Bueno, volveré dentro de un par de horas, si le parece bien.
- Muy bien.

Número 2
- Hola, buenos días.
- Se me ha roto el parabrisas.
- Ah, ya veo. Vamos a ver. Está bastante mal. Tendrá que dejarlo aquí para reparar.
- ¿Tiene que poner uno nuevo?
- Sí, claro.
- ¿Y me va a resultar caro?
- ¿Tiene seguro?
- Sí.
- Pues entonces no, no muy caro.

Número 3
- Hola, ¿qué le pasa?
- No lo sé. Venía yo tranquilamente y empezó a salir humo del capó.
- Vamos a ver … Ajá, es que se ha calentado demasiado el motor. Aquí no se puede reparar. Tenemos que remolcarlo al garaje.
- De acuerdo.

Número 4
- ¿Cuál es el problema?
- Se me ha pinchado la rueda.
- ¿Y no tiene rueda de repuesto?
- Pues mire, no.
- ¿Sabe que no tiene que conducir sin rueda de repuesto?
- Ya.
- Bueno, se la reparamos en seguida.

Número 5
- ¿Qué le pasa?
- Pues se ha parado el motor del coche, no sé lo que ha pasado.
- A ver. Sencillo. Se ha quedado usted sin gasolina.
- ¡Vaya! que sea la gasolina.
- Le vamos a echar un par de litros para que llegue a la próxima gasolinera.

Número 6
- A ver, ¿Qué es lo que le pasa con el coche?
- Vengo muy disgustada porque me parece que son los frenos los que no funcionan, no responden.
- Los frenos no funcionan. A ver. Voy a echar un vistazo … Me parece que le falta líquido de frenos. Esto no es más que un momento.
- ¡Uy! Menos mal.

Número 7
- ¿En qué le puedo ayudar?
- Ay, pues mire, no sé qué hacer. No tengo luces y …
- Bueno, lo que necesita es un faro nuevo. Mire, la tienda está por allí, puede colocarlo usted misma.

C In pairs, the students make up a dialogue based on each visual. When they have finished, you could play the part of the mechanic and introduce some unexpected elements for the students to respond to, e.g.
No puedo repararlo esta semana.
No tengo parabrisas.
¿Cuándo pasó eso?
¿Y, dónde está exactamente?

D Give each student a copy of **copymaster 96** or copy it and present it on the OHP. Then play the recordings and ask the students to say each time what they think the problem is.

¿Qué le puede pasar al coche?

Número 1
- Oiga. ¿Puede mandar un mecánico?
- ¿Qué pasa?
- No sé. El motor no anda.
- ¿Dónde está usted?
- En la carretera 550 entre Nigrás y Vigo.
- Vale. Llegaremos en seguida.

Número 2
- Dígame.
- Buenos días. ¿Tiene un parabrisas para un Seat Toledo?

UNIDAD 10

- Sí, señor.
- Bueno, se me ha roto el parabrisas.
- ¿Dónde está usted?
- En la autopista A9 cerca de Vilabon.
- ¿Y la matrícula por favor …?

Número 3
- Dígame.
- Tengo un problema con el coche.
- ¿Qué le pasa?
- No sé pero creo que me he quedado sin gasolina.
- ¿No tiene gasolina?
- Creo que no.
- Bueno, ¿dónde está usted?

Número 4
- ¿Me puede ayudar por favor?
- ¿Qué pasa?
- Tengo un problema con los frenos. No funcionan.
- Ahora no tengo un mecánico libre pero en una media hora …

Número 5
- Oiga. Tengo un pinchazo y no puedo cambiar la rueda.
- ¿Un pinchazo, dice?
- Sí. ¿Puede mandar un mecánico?
- Sí, señora. ¿Dónde está usted?

¿Qué taller? (page 113)

Main aim
Getting a car repaired.

A The students read this and then say where they would go to get each problem solved.

B You read each problem aloud. The students say, for each problem, what they would say when they telephone for help. You play the part of the person answering and develop each dialogue, introducing unexpected elements as appropriate.

C In pairs, the students continue this. One chooses a problem and calls for help, and the other responds.

En el taller (page 113)

Main aim
Coping with the unexpected.

A The students read and understand this.

B In pairs, each student plays both roles in turn, for each scenario.

Quiero alquilar un coche (page 114)

Main aim
Hiring a car.

A The students read and understand this.

B Play the recording of the dialogue as the students follow the text in their book. They repeat after, with and without the recording.

Quiero alquilar un coche
- Buenos días. Quiero alquilar un coche para cuatro días.
- Bien. ¿Cómo lo quiere, pequeño, mediano o grande?
- Mejor pequeño, por favor.
- ¿Alguna marca en especial?
- Sí, un Seat.
- Vamos a ver. Tenemos un Seat Panda y un Seat Ibiza.
- ¿Cuánto cuestan por día?
- El Panda 2.300 más 19 por kilómetro y el Ibiza 2.750 más 23 por kilómetro.
- Vale, el Ibiza.
- Su carnet de conducir, por favor.
- Aquí tiene.

C You play the part of the employee and encourage several students to hire a car from you. Adjust the level of your responses to suit each student. The students then continue this in pairs, playing each role in turn.

Ahora sé (page 115)

Main aim
To provide a summary of the *Unidad* and a basis for more practice and revision.

A The students work on this list now, and later for revision, using their favourite techniques.

UNIDAD 10

B Either now or later, you could use the following activities:

Play a game of *El juego de los blancos*, e.g.

¿Puede usted …?
… no funcionan.
Quiero alquilar … .
Aquí tiene mi … .
Estaba … .

Test the students' ability to respond quickly and correctly in emergencies. Ask them what they should do and say if a Spanish visitor in their country says, e.g.

Llame a la policía.
Llame a una ambulancia.
Hay algún herido.
¿Puede usted ayudarme?
¡Ha habido un accidente!
¿Dónde está la comisaría?
Mi coche está averiado.
¿Puede usted llamar a un garaje?
Mis luces no funcionan. ¿Qué puedo hacer?
He atropellado a un ciclista.
¡Socorro! Alguien ha chocado con mi coche.
He chocado con un coche.

Present **copymaster 97** on OHP. Inform the students that you are going to see if they are good witnesses. They have two minutes to study the picture and they then answer your questions, e.g.

¿Dónde pasó el accidente?
¿Dónde estaba el autobús?
¿Qué hizo el camión unos momentos antes de atropellar al chico?
¿Qué estaban haciendo las personas cerca del autobús?
¿Dónde estaba el coche?
¿Qué hizo el coche cuando se paró el camión?
¿Qué estaba haciendo el chico cuando el camión le atropelló?
¿De dónde llamaron a una ambulancia?
¿Llegó muy rápidamente o no?

Project the copymaster again to check the students' answers and to clear up any problems. Then ask them to study it again for two minutes and to work in pairs to write a report, giving as many details as possible.

Give each student a piece of paper. At the top, each one writes a sentence from the list. They pass this to another student who writes a sentence in response to the first and then passes it on to someone else, and so on. After five or six sentences have been written, you could invite students to read aloud all the sentences on their sheet, especially if they are amusing or interesting.

Revision activities

1 Buying food in Spain
(Libro 1, Unidad 12)

A Encourage the students to look again at *Unidad 12* of *Libro 1*, and especially at page 113.

B Give each student a copy of **copymaster 98**. They can work on these in class or at home.

2 Obtaining services at a petrol station
(Libro 2, Unidad 10)

A Encourage the students to look again at *Unidad 10* of *Libro 2*, and especially at page 117.

B Give each student a copy of **copymaster 99**. They work individually on the first activity and then in pairs on the second and third.

3 Eating in a Spanish person's home or hosting a meal
(Libro 3, Unidad 6)

A The students look back over *Unidad 6*, and especially page 75, and use their favourite techniques to revise.

B Play these recordings of three Spanish speakers from different countries. The students listen two or three times and take notes. They have two main tasks:
1 To find out the speakers' attitudes to the hospitality they received.
2 To find out as much as possible about life in each of the Spanish-speaking countries.

Repaso: comiendo en casa de otro

Número 1
– ¿Qué tal cenaste anoche?
– Pues sabes que fui a casa de John.
– ¿Qué tal fue?
– Bueno, bien pero me sorprendió un poco la hora. Cenamos a eso de las seis y media y me parece muy temprano.
– ¿Y la comida?
– El postre fue riquísimo.
– Sí.

145

UNIDAD 10

– Comimos un 'crumble'. Lleva harina y fruta y …
– ¿Te gustó entonces?
– Sí, mm, todo fue riquísimo. Y también es muy buena persona.

Número 2
– Fuiste a cenar, ¿verdad?
– Sí, fue una invitación muy amable.
– ¿Y qué tal fue la cena?
– Un poco extraño para decir la verdad.
– ¿Por qué?
– Porque comimos salchichas y verduras, pero todo muy rico.
– Y de postre, ¿qué comieron?
– Fruta con 'custard', una crema que no he probado antes. Lo usan mucho aquí.

Número 3
– Oye, ¿que tal fue la cena anoche?
– Muy bien. Cenamos un bistec. Me gusta poco hecho pero me lo sirvieron muy hecho aunque me gustó igual.
– ¿Qué más?
– Unas verduras con el bistec. Y lo que más me extrañó fue que no sirvieron pan. Suelo comer pan con todas las comidas.
– ¿Comiste postre?
– Sí, una tarta acompañada de 'custard' – muy dulce pero me gustó.
– ¿Te gustó?
– Sí, perfecto.

4 Coping with illness
(Libro 3, Unidad 9)

A The students revise *Unidad 9* and especially page 105.

B You and the students mime a range of medical problems. The others guess what each mime represents, e.g.
¿Tienes algo en la pierna?
¿Te has roto el brazo?

C Present **copymaster 100** on OHP. The students orally put the sentences into a logical order to tell the story as the boy might tell it. They then imagine that this happened to them and answer your questions, e.g.
¿Adónde fuiste?
¿Qué hiciste primero?
¿Y después?
¿Te hiciste daño?
¿Qué hiciste esta mañana?

Finally, the students write the conversation which took place between the boy and the dentist.

D As students complete the task above, give them a copy of **copymaster 101**. They could complete this at home.

UNIDAD 11

Estás en tu casa

Main aim
Welcoming a Spanish guest or being a guest in a Spanish person's home.

Area(s) of experience
A – Everyday activities
B – Personal and social life
E – The international world

Materials
Cassette: Te presento ¿Qué tal el viaje?, Te presento a …, Unas fotos de la familia, Parientes, vecinos y amigos, ¿Qué te dicen estas personas?, Estás en tu casa, Hablando de las casas, ¿Te hace falta algo?, Un poco de diplomacia, Repaso: campings y albergues.
Copymasters 102–110

Tasks
Greeting someone and responding to greetings
Asking how someone is and responding to similar enquiries
Welcoming and receiving a visitor
Making and understanding informal introductions
Talking about oneself and others
Saying whether they have a room of their own or share a room
Asking where things are in the house
Saying they need, and asking others if they need, soap, toothpaste, a towel, etc.

Grammar points
Personal *a*
Possessive pronouns
Subjunctive with verbs of emotion and *querer*
Position of adjectives

Productive vocabulary
almohada	casado
compartir	despertador
divorciado	encantado
hacer falta	manta
mío	mucho gusto
parientes	en paro
primo	secador
separado	soltero
suyo	toalla
tuyo	vecinos
¿verdad?	viaje

Receptive vocabulary
amistades
estancia
gran
invitado
miembros (de la familia)
pasar
pobre
prestar

Revision points
Introducing oneself
(*Libro 1, Unidad 1*)
Eating in a restaurant
(*Libro 1, Unidad 13*)
Camping and youth hostelling
(*Libro 3, Unidad 1*)
Talking about free time
(*Libro 3, Unidad 4*)
Telephoning and faxing
(*Libro 3, Unidad 7*)
Accidents and breakdowns
(*Libro 3, Unidad 10*)

Estás en tu casa (page 116)

Main aim
To understand, and wish to achieve, the learning goals of the *Unidad*.

A Work on this along lines which have previously proved successful.

B Each student could copy out the model sentences, starting with the one they think would be the most useful and finishing with the least useful. In pairs, they compare and discuss their lists.

Te presento (page 116)

Main aims
Greeting and welcoming a visitor and responding to greetings and welcomes. Making informal introductions.

A The students all read this to themselves and ensure that they understand it, using communication and dictionary strategies as appropriate.

B They follow the conversation in their book and listen to the recording. Ask them then to close their eyes and to listen to it again, trying to visualise to themselves the people involved and what they do.

UNIDAD 11

They then open their eyes and repeat after, with and without the recording.

Te presento

Número 1
- Joanna, te presento a mi amigo Joaquín.
- Mucho gusto.
- Encantada.
- Joanna es de Edimburgo en Escocia.
- Muy bien.

Número 2
- Joanna, conoces a Ana María, ¿verdad?
- Sí, la conozco. Hola Ana.
- Hola, ¿qué tal?

Número 3
- No conoces a Isabel, una prima mía, ¿verdad?
- No, no nos conocemos.
- Bueno, te presento a mi primo Nacho.
- Mucho gusto.
- Encantado.

C Write on the board some words which could replace those in the conversation: *amigo Miguel, Londres, Inglaterra, Cristina, Carmen, mi primo Luis.* The students work out which words these could replace and act out, in pairs, the conversation with these new words.

D You and your language assistant play the part of a Spanish-speaking visitor. You greet students appropriately and they respond and introduce you to others in the class. You can adapt your responses appropriately to give the students practice in coping with the unexpected.

E The students form groups of three or four and work on the task set out in their book.

F Now would be a good time to explain and practise the use of the personal *a*. You can refer the pupils to *A ser detective*, page 203.

¿Qué tal fue el viaje? (page 117)

Main aim

Welcoming and receiving a visitor, and responding to this.

A The students read this quietly to themselves and ensure that they understand it. They prepare their answers to the questions. They then put the questions to you and to your language assistant. Try to ensure that each student asks at least two questions. They listen carefully to your answers and use what you say to improve the answers they prepared.

You and your language assistant then ask the questions, using the 'snowballing' technique. When they are ready, the students can continue this in pairs.

B The students listen to the recordings and make notes about the information given. They report on this and compare the three visitors.

Play the recordings again. This time, the students make notes about the language used by the three visitors, and again report and compare. Help them to see that the shorter answers provoke more questions. Longer answers enable the speaker to have more control over the conversation. Non-committal answers also produce more questions to be answered. As an example, play number 3 again and ask the students how the parents can respond to Isabel's *'un poco'* at the end.

¿Qué tal el viaje?

Número 1
- Hola, buenos días. Pasa, pasa … Eres Tomás, ¿verdad?
- Sí, buenos días.
- Soy la madre de Felipe. Encantada.
- ¿Qué tal?
- ¿Has estado en España antes?
- Sí.
- ¿Dónde?
- En Lloret de Mar.
- Bien, bien. ¿Qué tal fue el viaje?
- Bien.
- ¿Desde cuándo conoces a Felipe?
- Desde el año pasado.
- Estás cansado, ¿verdad?
- Sí, un poco.
- Siéntate, ¿quieres algo?, un té, café, zumo …

Número 2
- ¡Ay! ¡Qué bien! Pasa, hija. Eres Susana, ¿verdad?
- Sí, en inglés es Suzanne y en español Susana.
- ¿Cuál prefieres aquí?
- Susana.
- ¡Estupendo! Siéntate. ¿Has estado en España antes?
- Sí. Hace dos años fui a Barcelona con el colegio, y el año pasado fui con mis padres a la Costa Blanca.
- A un hotel, ¿verdad?

UNIDAD 11

- No, alquilamos un coche y fuimos a casa de unos amigos de mis padres.
- Hablas bien el español.
- Lo estudio desde hace cinco años.
- Muy bien. ¿Qué tal el viaje?
- Un poco largo. Me levanté a las cuatro y cogí el tren de las cinco para ir al aeropuerto.
- ¡Ay! Estás cansada, ¿verdad?
- No, estoy bien.
- Vamos a comer entonces. ¿Vale?
- Estupendo.

Número 3
- ¡Hola! Soy el padre de Bea. Mucho gusto en conocerte.
- Soy Isabel. Encantada.
- Buenos días, Isabel. Pasa, pasa, por favor.
- Gracias.
- ¿Has estado en España antes?
- Es la primera vez.
- Espero que te guste mucho. ¿Desde cuándo conoces a Bea?
- Desde hace un año.
- ¿Qué tal fue el viaje?
- Bien.
- ¿Estás cansada?
- Un poco.

C When the students have assessed all the visitors, play the recordings again. They repeat after the best visitor and suggest how the weakest visitor could do better.

D They study the questions at the end of this item and put them to you and your language assistant, and then to each other in pairs.

E Adapt the questions to suit your town and students, and put them to the students. Then, in pairs, they adapt the questions to suit their town and friends, and put them to each other.

Te presento a …   (page 117)

Main aim
To develop listening skills.

A It would be a good idea to prepare for this item by revising family words, e.g.
You present, on the board or OHP, a family tree for your own family, saying who each person is and writing next to each name their relationship to you (e.g. *mi abuela, mi tío*). Leave this and ask the students to produce a similar family tree of their own.

Play a game of *Pilla al intruso*. The students find an odd-one-out and explain it, e.g.

mi tía, mi prima, mi abuela, nuestros vecinos.
su padre, su madre, su abuela, su hermana.
nuestro abuelo, nuestro tío, nuestro nieto, nuestra madre.

B The students read the instructions for this item and then listen to each recording in turn, noting the information asked for. Ask several to report and clear up any problems before playing the recording again and working on the next one.

Te presento a …

Número 1
- Y ahora, te presento a mi padre.
- Mucho gusto. ¿Has tenido un buen viaje?
- Y ésta es mi hermana Francisca.
- Mucho gusto. ¿Cómo te sientes después del viaje?

Número 2
- Y no conoces a Pablo, ¿verdad? Es un buen amigo mío.
- Hola. ¿De dónde eres exactamente?

Número 3
- Pues bien, te presento a mi abuela, Luisa.
- Encantada. ¿Desde cuándo conoces a mi nieta?
- Y ahora voy a presentarte a nuestro vecino, don José. Vive en el piso de al lado.
- Encantado. ¿Cuánto tiempo vas a quedarte en España?

Número 4
- Y ésta es mi tía Ana, que vive cerca.
- Mucho gusto. ¿Habías estado antes en España?

C Play the recordings again and get the students to notice that the questions are not answered. They listen and, as you pause the recording after each question, they answer it.

Unas fotos de la familia   (page 118)

Main aims
To develop listening skills.
Talking about one's family.

UNIDAD 11

A The students read this and then anticipate what people will say about these photos. Encourage them to use a dictionary to look up any words they expect to hear. This is good examination practice. They listen once and report on what is said. Ration each student to one piece of information only so as to involve as many as possible.

Play the recordings again and ask who is the most and least interesting, and why.

Unas fotos de la familia

Número 1

– ¡Hola! Me presento. Me llamo Rafael pero mis amigos me llaman Rafa. Vivo en un piso en el séptimo piso. Me gusta el piso porque está cerca del colegio y puedo quedarme en la cama hasta muy tarde. Vivo allí con mis padres, mi hermano mayor y mi hermana menor. Mis hermanos se llaman Miguel y Susana. No tenemos animales en casa porque no se puede pero me gustan los animales.

Número 2

– Me llamo Paca y vivo aquí con mi madre, mi hermano mayor Luis que lleva la camiseta negra y mi hermano menor que se llama Andrés. Mi padre está muerto. Murió en un accidente hace dos años. Mi madre es policía y trabaja en Madrid. Mis abuelos viven cerca y se ocupan de nosotros por la tarde cuando mi madre está trabajando.

Número 3

– Me llamo Elena y vivo en una casa en las afueras de Barcelona. Mi gatito se llama Julia y vive conmigo. Mis padres compraron la casa en julio. Prefiero vivir en una casa porque los pisos son demasiado ruidosos y hay menos sitio para los animales. Tengo dos perros y un conejo también.

B Work with the class on the list of key expressions to help them to learn them, e.g.
The students work out what each means and check in a dictionary.
Ask questions based on the list, e.g.
¿Tienes un hermano?
¿Está casado?
¿Cómo se llama?
¿Cuántos años tiene?
¿Qué hace?
You tell the class about your family, using as much as possible of this language and language presented earlier. Then present, on the board or OHP, a paragraph summarising what you have said. Each student adapts this to write a paragraph about their families.

C Present on the board or OHP a mind map about your family and use this as a basis for an oral presentation of your family. Include, if possible, references to the past and the future, e.g.
Mi abuelo murió el año pasado.
Mi hermana va a tener un bebé.

The students all now prepare similar mind maps for their own families and use these to present their families. They should add this to their repertoire of presentations and you could ask students to practise them regularly.

Hablando de tu vida (page 119)

Main aim

Talking about family.

A Before working on this item, you could show how two words in Spanish can be the equivalent of five, e.g.
mis padres = mi madre y mi padre.
With this model in mind, which five words in English and Spanish can the following represent?
mis hermanos, mis tíos, mis primos, nuestros vecinos, nuestros abuelos, mis amigos, los señores.

B Present on the OHP the questions in **Conversación A** and, opposite but in random order, some appropriate answers. Practise linking these and asking and answering the questions. Then practise adapting the answers to suit your students. Then cover the answers and put the questions to the class, using the 'snowballing' technique. The students can put all the questions to each other in pairs.
You could repeat this with **Conversación B**.

C Put all the **A** questions to the class and time how long it takes them to answer. Then challenge them to beat this time with the **B** questions.

D In class or at home, each student chooses one set of questions and copies them, writing full answers for all of them.

UNIDAD 11

Parientes, vecinos y amigos (page 119)

Main aim
Talking about family and friends.

A The students read and understand this. They could then scan it to find two-word equivalents of: *mi amigo y mi amiga, nuestro amigo y nuestra amiga, nuestro vecino y nuestra vecina*.

B To help the students to learn who everyone is, ask questions about the people while the students look at the photos and the captions, e.g.
¿Cómo se llama su hermana?
¿Quién es Alfredo?
¿Carlos y Isabel tienen cuántos años?
¿Dónde están los señores de Alba?

Then get the students to cover the captions and answer your questions referring only to the photos. Finally, see if the students can answer your questions with their books closed.

C Play the following recordings. After each one, the students write the number of the photo to show who was speaking.

Parientes, vecinos y amigos

Número 1
– Este señor al lado de mi hermana es el señor Alba. Es un vecino, vive aquí al lado. Vive con su mujer. Sus hijos son mayores y no viven con ellos. Tiene sesenta y cinco años y, por eso, no trabaja. Era empleado de banco.

Número 2
– Mi hermana se llama Begoña. No trabaja en este momento pero el año que viene va a ir a la universidad. Va a estudiar francés. Tiene diecinueve años. Ha pasado mucho tiempo en Francia porque unos primos viven allí.

Número 3
– Alfonso está aquí sentado en la mesa. Tiene doce años. Es muy simpático. No habla inglés pero quiere trabajar en los Estados Unidos cuando sea mayor.

Número 4
– Alfredo es nuestro primo. Tiene veintidós años. Trabaja en el sur. Es conductor de camión. Sólo viene a vernos durante las vacaciones.

Número 5
– A la derecha están nuestros amigos Carlos e Isabel. Son supersimpáticos. Viven cerca y vienen a vernos con frecuencia.. No tienen hijos y son como tíos.

D In pairs, the students ask each other about the people, as suggested in their book. Encourage them to cover the large photo and captions as they do this.

E Now would be a good time to work with the class on possessive pronouns on page 201 of *A ser detective*.

¿Qué te dicen estas personas? (page 120)

Main aim
To develop listening skills.

A The students read and understand the instructions.

B Encourage the students to ask and answer questions about the people in the photos and write a summary of what is said about each on the board or OHP.

C Play the recordings. The students listen and compare what they hear with what they guessed. You could discuss intuition with the class and whether some people in the class are more intuitive than others and guessed more correctly about the people from their photos.

¿Qué te dicen estas personas?

– Hola, soy Santiago. A mí me gustan los idiomas. Estudio el inglés desde hace tres años pero lo encuentro bastante difícil. En los exámenes saqué buenas notas.

– Me presento. Me llamo Pedro Estrada. Soy un buen amigo de la familia. Soy de esta ciudad y vivo en la misma calle.

– ¿Qué tal? Me llamo Marcos. Soy estudiante en el mismo instituto de tu amigo. Somos buenos amigos. Nos encontramos cuando teníamos cinco años.

– Hola. Soy Elena. Me gusta conocer a gente inglesa. Tengo una amiga y su marido está trabajando en el País de Gales.

– Buenos días. Yo me llamo Sofía Pidal. Soy la profesora que te mandó la lista de chicos que quieren amigos por correspondencia.

UNIDAD 11

– Hola, ¿qué hay? Yo soy Pepita, amiga de la familia. Tengo un buen amigo que vive en la misma ciudad que tú. Iré a verle el mes que viene.

D Play the recordings again. The students report on the information given, in Spanish, again with a limit of one piece of information per student.

E The students listen once more and write notes in English about each person, noting as much as possible of the information given.

Estás en tu casa (page 120)

Main aim

Asking, and saying, where things are in a house.

A The students read this quietly and work out what everything means. Help them to learn these key expressions, e.g.
They use, and adapt, them to answer questions about the plan in their book and about their own homes.
They copy this table.

	Ventajas	*Inconvenientes*
1		
2		
3		

They then listen to what these people say about their homes, and complete the table.

Estás en tu casa

Número 1
– ¿Te gusta el piso donde vives?
– Lo bueno es que tiene cuatro dormitorios. Cuando vienen amigos pueden dormir en casa.
– ¿Y lo malo?
– Es un piso céntrico y hay mucho ruido de tráfico y el barrio es un poco sucio.

Número 2
– ¿Qué te parece tu piso?
– Me gusta mucho. Es grande y moderno y muy tranquilo.
– ¿Está en el campo?
– Sí. El único problema es que está lejos del centro y de las tiendas.
– Sí, entiendo.

Número 3
– ¿Te gusta el piso donde vives?
– El piso es demasiado pequeño, sólo tiene dos dormitorios pero está bien situado: cerca del parque, de la piscina y del polideportivo, está muy bien.

Give each student a copy of **copymaster 102**. They first work on this orally, in class and in pairs, and then write an account of what has gone, following the example.

B In pairs, the students ask and answer questions along the lines suggested.

Hablando de donde vives tú (page 121)

Main aim

Describing your room.

A The students read this item and look at the photos. Base a *¿Verdad o mentira?* quiz on the photos. When this starts to seem easy, play at *Repite si es verdad*, based on the photos, first as the students look at them and then with their books closed.

B Play a game of Chinese Whispers, with such sentences as, e.g.
Mi dormitorio me parece más grande que el tuyo.
Mi cama está delante de la ventana.

C Start a word association table on the OHP or board, e.g.

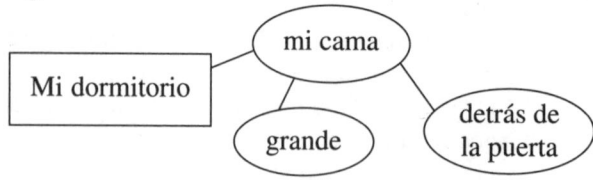

Mi dormitorio — mi cama — grande — detrás de la puerta

Add to this with help from the students. Each student then produces a similar table and uses it to describe her/his room to their partners.

D Ask students, e.g.
¿En qué habitación:
   escuchas música?
   te duchas?
   comes?
   ves la tele?

UNIDAD 11

te lavas?
duermes?
te peinas?
preparas las comidas?
escribes cartas?
te vistes?

You could also ask, e.g.

¿Dónde hay una tele en tu casa?
¿Por qué no hay una tele en el cuarto de baño?
¿Por qué no hay una alfombra en la cocina?
¿Por qué no hay una cama en el comedor?

Encourage the students to ask you, and each other, some similar questions.

E The students all write to compare the rooms, as suggested. They could do this at home.

F Now would be a good time to explain and practise adjectives. Refer the students to *A ser detective*, page 203.

Impresiones (page 122)

Main aim

Understanding descriptions of places.

A The students read this to themselves. You can ask them what almost all the phrases have in common. Ask them to explain how the possessive pronouns are formed.

B Ask the students to read the letter and to determine what impression the Spanish penfriend has of his friend's flat. They can make two columns under the headings *Mejor* and *Peor*, and write what they think the penfriend prefers or otherwise in the foreign country and in the penfriend's house.

C The students read the letter again and infer from it as much as possible about Joselito's home and town in Spain.

Hablando de las casas (page 122)

Main aim

To develop listening and writing skills.

A The students read this and, looking at the photo, anticipate what the young people who live there will say about it.

B They listen first to see how accurately they had anticipated, noting when they were right and when wrong.

Hablando de las casas

- Ahora ves donde vivimos. En un barrio muy bonito, pero el tuyo es más agradable, ¿no es cierto?
- Dime una cosa, me parece que en tu país hay muchas más casas que pisos. ¿Tengo razón?
- Hay una diferencia que se nota; en tu país las casas no tienen balcones mientras que las nuestras casi siempre los tienen, ¿verdad?
- En nuestra casa tenemos dos dormitorios; en la tuya tienes tres, ¿no es verdad?
- A causa del clima, vosotros pasáis mucho más tiempo en vuestras casas que nosotros en las nuestras; ¿tengo razón?
- En España toda la familia suele vivir en la misma casa; abuelos, padres e hijos. Eso no ocurre a menudo en tu país, ¿verdad?

C They listen again and say if each speaker is right about what s/he says about where they live.

Querido amigo (page 122)

Main aim

Writing to describe home.

A The students read and understand this. They then look and listen again to the previous item.

B Organise a chain game based on homes, e.g.

1 Mi casa es bastante grande: hay cuatro dormitorios.
2 Tu casa es bastante grande: hay cuatro dormitorios. La mía es pequeña: hay dos dormitorios.
3 Tu casa es bastante grande: hay cuatro dormitorios. La tuya es pequeña: hay dos dormitorios. En la mía, no hay comedor.
etc.

C The students all write a letter to compare their home with the flat on page 120 of their book.

UNIDAD 11

D Give each student two pictures from **copymaster 103**, one showing their old home and the other their new home. Make sure that you give out an old home to match each new home you give out. The students interview each other to find the person who is living in the home they used to live in. They ask each other to describe their present homes until they find who they are looking for.

¿Te hace falta algo? (page 123)

Main aim
Asking, and saying, what you need.

A The students read this to themselves and ensure that they understand it.

B Help them to learn the key words and expressions, e.g.
Present **copymaster 104** on the OHP and use it for a range of activities, e.g.
¿Verdad o mentira? (*El número 5, es una lámpara.*)
Repite si es verdad (*Número 7: Me falta un despertador.*)
Noughts and crosses (with pictures 1–9 and pictures 4–12) with the students saying that they need what is in the appropriate square.
In pairs, they make up requests for what is illustrated and suitable answers, e.g.
¿Te hace falta otra almohada?
Sí, por favor.
Voy a buscarte una.

C Play the recording.

¿Te hace falta algo?
– ¿Te hace falta algo?
– Me hace falta una toalla, por favor.
– Ah, sí. Voy a buscarte una. ¿Algo más?
– ¿Podrías darme otra almohada y otra manta, por favor?
– Sí, sí. Hay mantas y almohadas en el armario.
– Gracias. Y mañana tengo que levantarme a las siete. Me he olvidado mi despertador.
– Te voy a prestar el mío.
– Muchísimas gracias.

You could draw one of the items in the air with a finger. The students guess what you need, e.g.
¿Te hace falta una toalla?

They can continue this in pairs.
You paraphrase something (a useful communication strategy for your students to learn), e.g.
Me hace falta algo para despertarme mañana, porque tengo que levantarme temprano.
The students work out what you need, e.g.
Te hace falta un despertador.

¿Quieres que te traiga algo? (page 123)

Main aim
To practise asking and answering questions about personal needs

A On the board or OHP, write the questions in one column and the answers, in random order, in the other column. The students match the correct questions and responses.

B Practise with one student, then the students practise in pairs.

C Students make up other questions and responses of their own and continue the practice in pairs with these.

Un poco de diplomacia (page 124)

Main aim
To practise using polite language to solve problems.

A The students read this and understand it.

B They read the four situations and decide what they would do in each one.

C Play the recordings. The students decide which were polite and which were not. Write on the board some of the phrases used to make polite requests e.g.
¿Te molesta si…?
¿Se puede…?

D In pairs, the students role play each of the situations.

UNIDAD 11

Un poco de diplomacia

Situación 1
– Oye, ¿te molesta si yo tengo tu dormitorio?
– Bueno, es un poco difícil.
– Pero sólo es para dos semanas.

Situación 2
– Señora, me encanta la comida española pero lo siento soy vegetariano.
– ¿No comes carne?
– No, pero no te preocupes. Me gusta la tortilla y la ensalada y no es un problema para mí

Situación 3
– ¿Te molesta si cierro la ventana? No puedo dormir con el ruido.
– Yo duermo con las ventanas abiertas.
– ¿Se puede abrir la puerta y no la ventana?
– Vale.

Situación 4
– ¿Adónde vamos esta noche?
– Vamos en pandilla con los amigos de colegio.
– ¿Te molesta si me quedo en casa?
– ¿Por qué?
– Estoy un poco cansado.
– ¿No quieres venir?
– No, gracias.

Una palabra conduce a otra (page 124)

Main aim

To extend vocabulary and communication strategies.

A Work on this along lines which have previously proved successful.

B A very useful dictionary activity would be for the students to look these words up and to check their meanings. What conclusion can they draw about words which begin with *in-*? Do they always mean the opposite of the word without *in-*?

Knowing how to check the opposite of adjectives in a dictionary is a useful exam technique.

Ahora sé (page 125)

Main aim

To provide a summary of the *Unidad* and a basis for more practise and revision.

A The students use their favourite techniques to work on this.

B You could also introduce the following activities: One student is a detective and leaves the room. Another student chooses something in the room which belongs to someone but which is not easy to identify with anyone (e.g. a biro or pencil). The detective returns and tries to find who the object belongs to, e.g.

¿Este bolígrafo es tuyo?

Present **copymaster 104** again on the OHP. Tell the class that they are going on a weekend holiday and that you are moving home at the weekend. They have to say who will take which of these things, e.g.

La lámpara, ¿es la vuestra o la mía?
Es la suya.

The students study *Ahora sé* and write down all the questions in it, writing them in the order they would put them to a visitor. They then take turns to put them to their partners and to answer them.

Revision activities

1 Introducing oneself
(Libro 1, Unidad 1)

A The students revise *Unidad 1* of *Libro 1*.

B Give each student a copy of **copymaster 105** to work on.

2 Eating in a restaurant
(Libro 1, Unidad 13)

A Encourage the students to revise *Unidad 13* of *Libro 1*.

B Give the class **copymaster 106**. They work on these in pairs and then several from each group perform their work to the others.

UNIDAD 11

3 Camping and youth hostelling
(Libro 3, Unidad 1)

A The students revise *Unidad 1* and especially *Ahora sé*, page 17.

B Give each student a copy of **copymaster 107**. They can work on activities 1 and 2 at home and activity 3 in class.

Repaso: Campings y albergues
- Buenas tardes.
- Buenas tardes. ¿Tiene una cama libre, por favor?
- ¿Para cuántas noches?
- Esta noche solamente.
- ¿Y cuántos sois?
- Estoy solo.
- Sí, hay una cama libre en el dormitorio de chicos. ¿Tienes tarjeta de afiliación?
- Sí, tenga.
- Muy bien. Me dice su nombre, nacionalidad, edad.
- Me llamo Pieter van Hock, soy holandés, de Amsterdam, pero mi madre es española. Tengo dieciocho años.
- Muy bien. ¿Me quiere firmar esta ficha aquí, por favor?
- Desde luego. ¿Se puede alquilar sábanas?
- Sí. Se cobran doscientas pesetas más.
- Vale. ¿Se puede comer aquí?
- Sí, pero hay que pedir la cena antes de las cinco. El desayuno se sirve entre las siete y media y las nueve.
- Gracias. ¡Oh! ¿Dónde está el dormitorio, por favor?
- El de los chicos está en el primer piso, al final del pasillo.
- Muchas gracias.

4 Talking about free time
(Libro 3, Unidad 4)

A The students revise *Unidad 4* and especially *Ahora sé*, page 53.

B Give each student a copy of **copymaster 108**. They work on question 1 in pairs and question 2 at home.

5 Telephoning or faxing
(Libro 3, Unidad 7)

A The students revise *Unidad 7* and especially *Ahora sé*, page 85.

B Give each student a copy of **copymaster 109**. They could work on this at home.

6 Accidents and breakdowns
(Libro 3, Unidad 10)

A The students revise *Unidad 10* and especially *Ahora sé*, page 115.

B Give each student a copy of **copymaster 110**. They could work on this at home.

UNIDAD 12

El transporte público

Main aim
Using public transport in Spain.

Area(s) of experience
A – Everyday activities
C – The world around us
E – The international world

Materials
Cassette: ¿Dónde está la estación de metro?, Tomamos el metro, El metro en Madrid, ¿Qué pasa?, Avisos, En la estación, ¿Cómo se hace una reserva?, ¿Qué dijo?, ¿Está libre?, El contestador automático, ¿Cuál prefieres?, Repaso: en la farmacia.
Copymasters 111–120

Tasks
Asking for and giving information about travel by public transport
Asking if there is a bus, train, coach to a particular place
Understanding simple signs and notices
Making arrangements for travel by public transport
Buying tickets, specifying some details: destination, single/return, class, day of travel
Asking and informing about times of departure and arrival, platforms, etc.
Informing others of your time of arrival
Discussing common forms of transport

Grammar point
Future tense

Productive vocabulary
asiento
autocar
cantina
consigna (automática)
despacho de billetes
dirección
escalera mecánica
estación de autocares/ferrocarril
fumador
ida solo
ida y vuelta
libre
llegar
no fumador
ocupado
parada de autobuses/taxis
rápido
reserva
sala de espera
segunda clase
taquilla
ventanilla

Receptive vocabulary
acceso
atención
con destino a
devolver
fecha
llegada
multa
peatones
recoger
RENFE
salida
tarifa
vía
andenes
asomarse
avisos
correspondencia
expreso
horas punta
molestar
paso subterráneo
procedente de
red
retraso
taquillero
tarjeta

Revision points
Using classroom language
(*Libro 1, Unidad 2*)
Buying simple items at the chemist
(*Libro 1, Unidad 14*)
Eating in a restaurant
(*Libro 3, Unidad 2*)
Recovering lost property
(*Libro 3, Unidad 8*)
Welcoming, and being, a guest
(*Libro 3, Unidad 11*)

El transporte público (page 128)

Main aim
To understand the unit goals and wish to achieve them.

A Work on this along lines which have previously proved successful.

B The students copy the following headings from the board, one to a line: *tren, autobús, metro, autocar, taxi*. Make sure that everyone understands them. Then say a number of sentences based on those in this item: the students write the number of each in the correct category, e.g.

1 *¿A qué hora llegará el autocar (tren)?*
2 *Prefiero el metro. Es barato y rápido.*
3 *¿Hay una estación de autobuses cerca de aquí?*
4 *Quisiera un billete para ir al teatro.*
5 *Quisiera un taxi para ir al aeropuerto.*
6 *¿Hay un autocar que va a Madrid?*

UNIDAD 12

¿Cómo vamos a ir? (page 128)

Main aim
Understanding some of the key language of the unit.

A The students read this item and, with the help of a dictionary, ensure that they understand it.

B Put the first of the questions orally to the class and give the students 15 seconds to find the answer. Clear up any problems and then work on the others in the same way.

C In pairs, the students take turns to put all the questions to each other. To maintain interest, they should ask them in random order.

D To help the students to familiarise themselves with the metro, you could base some questions on the map, e.g.
Para ir a …, ¿es qué línea?
Para ir de … a …, ¿tengo que cambiar de línea?
¿Dónde tengo que cambiar?

E For homework, the students could study and learn this information. You could base a team quiz on it.

¿Dónde está la estación de metro? (page 129)

Main aim
Asking for, and giving, information about travel by metro.

A The students begin by reading this to themselves and understanding it.

B They follow the text of the dialogue and listen to the recording. They then repeat after, with and without the recording.

¿Dónde está la estación de metro?
– Buenos días. ¿Me puede decir dónde está la estación de metro más cercana? Quiero ir a la estación Alonso Martínez.
– Sí, señor. La estación es Batán. Por allí.
– ¿Es directo o hago correspondencia?
– Es directo, línea 10.
– Gracias.
– De nada.

C Present the text of the dialogue on the board or OHP. Half the class takes one role and the other half the other role. Remove one word from each sentence and encourage the students to carry on. Then remove more words and carry on until the students can perform the dialogue without any of the words.

D Present **copymaster 111** on OHP. The students read it and try to guess the missing words. Encourage them to argue about each one before providing the answer:
1 *ciento dieciséis*
2 *ciento ocho*
3 *seis*
4 *una*
5 *diez*
6 *un millón*
7 *cincuenta*

Tomamos el metro (page 129)

Main aim
Asking for, and giving, information about travel by metro.

A The students read this to themselves and ensure that they understand it.

B Use the model sentences to practise role playing, with you asking the questions and the students answering. Then change roles.

C To prepare for the listening activity, give the destination first and write it on the board: *Espanya*. The students find this on the plan and anticipate the questions and answers. Then play the recording and ask a few students to summarise the directions and to show them on the plan. Clear up any problems and work on the others along the same lines.

Tomamos el metro

Número 1
– Perdón, señor.
– Sí.
– Quiero ir a Espanya.
– Coja el metro dirección Zona Universitaria.
– Es directo.
– Sí, es la cuarta parada.
– Gracias.

158

UNIDAD 12

Número 2
- Perdón. ¿Para ir al Arc de Triomf, por favor?
- Sí, un momento, ¿Arc de Triomf?
- Sí.
- Coja el metro dirección Montbau hasta Catalunya. Luego coja la línea 1, dirección Santa Colonia.
- ¿Está lejos?
- No, es la segunda parada.

Número 3
- Buenos días. ¿Me puede decir si se puede ir a la Plaza Molina en metro?
- Sí, señora. Coja el metro a Catalunya y cambie allí.
- ¿Qué línea es?
- Es la línea 5 dirección Av. del Tibidabo.
- Gracias.
- De nada, adiós.

D Play the dialogues again and ask the students to write notes of the directions. Then play them once more, pausing them before the directions are given. The students use their notes to provide the directions, before hearing them.

Punto información (page 129)

Main aim
Learning to use the metro.

A The students read and understand this, with the help of a dictionary. They then transfer the information in this form, to another form, by copying this from the board and completing it.

El metro de Londres

el más _____
consta de _____ estaciones
abierto en _____

B As students complete this, give them a copy of **copymaster 112**. They read this and work on it in pairs. You could move around, listening, helping and joining in. When everyone is ready, play the recordings and invite the students to say if the information given is true or false. When it is false, they should correct it.

El metro en Madrid

Número 1
- Por favor, ¿por dónde se va a Banco de España?
- Mire, coja la línea 1, dirección Plaza Castilla, cambie en Sol y entonces tome la línea 2, dirección Ventas. Es la segunda estación.
- Gracias, adiós.

Número 2
- ¿Me puede ayudar, por favor? Quisiera ir a Sol.
- Bueno, coja la línea 1, dirección Portazgo y ya está. Es directo.
- Muchas gracias.
- De nada.

Número 3
- ¿Por dónde se va a Gran Vía?
- Coja la línea 2, dirección Ventas. No, no – coja Cuatro Caminos y cambie en Sol y luego es la línea 1, dirección a Cuatro Caminos.

Número 4
- Quiero ir a Bilbao, por favor.
- A ver, estamos aquí … Línea 3 hasta Sol y luego línea 1, dirección Plaza Castilla. Es la tercera estación, creo.

Número 5
- Buenos días, ¿me puede decir cómo se puede ir a Iglesia?
- Sí, señorita. Es directo. Coja la línea 1, dirección Legazpi y es la tercera estación.
- Gracias.

C Further practice
In all these dialogues there is a problem. Give the class the following introduction and play each extract once:

Estás en la Plaza Colón con tu amigo español. Tu amigo no conoce bien la red de metro y autobuses y hace preguntas a los transeúntes y empleados que encuentra. La cosa va de mal en peor. Nadie os ayuda pero, ¿por qué? Escucha lo que dice tu amigo y trata de entender lo que no va bien.

¿Qué pasa?
- Hola. ¿Me podría decir dónde está la estación de metro más cercana, por favor?
- ¡Ah! Pues mira, lo siento, no lo sé. No soy de aquí. Soy argentina.

- Buenas tardes. ¿Por dónde queda la estación de metro, por favor?
- No sé nada. Nunca cojo el metro.

- Hola. La estación de metro, ¿está cerca?
- Perdona, soy turista.

UNIDAD 12

– Hola. ¿Me puede decir cómo se llega a la estación, por favor?
– Pues mira, hay una boca del metro por esa calle pero está cerrada por obras. O sea que lo mejor es que vayas allí, más allá, al final de la calle.
– Hola. ¿Estoy lejos de la estación de metro?
– Hay huelga de metro hoy. Hay que coger el autobús.
– Un billete de diez viajes, por favor.
– Vale.
– Tome, un billete de cinco mil.
– Lo siento, no tengo cambio.

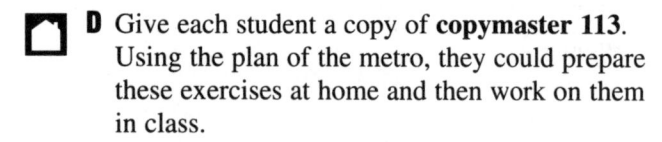

D Give each student a copy of **copymaster 113**. Using the plan of the metro, they could prepare these exercises at home and then work on them in class.

Avisos (page 130)

Main aim
To develop reading skills.

A The students begin by reading these signs and understanding them, with the help of a dictionary. They take turns to explain them to you and each other.

B Play these recordings. The students listen and write the number of the sign which goes with each conversation.

Avisos

Número 1
– ¿Su billete, por favor?
– Sí. Espere un momento … lo siento pero lo he perdido.
– ¿No sabe usted que si no tiene un billete hay que pagar una multa.
– He comprado un billete pero …
– Lo siento. Tiene que pagar 5.000 pesetas.
– ¡Cinco mil!

Número 2
– ¿Adónde voy a comprar un billete?
– Por allí. Tuerza a la izquierda y la máquina está enfrente.
– Gracias.

Número 3
– Quiero ir a la Plaza Mayor. ¿Tengo que cambiar o es directo?
– Tiene que cambiar en Cuatro Caminos. Es la tercera parada.

Número 4
– ¿Por dónde voy a coger el metro?
– La entrada está aquí.
– Pero, está cerrada.
– Ah, sí, son las once. Hay otra entrada a cien metros. Por allí.
– Gracias.

C Each student writes ten words which are on these signs and which they think are the most useful words. They compare their lists in pairs and try to agree on the twelve most useful words. They then listen as you explain or define some of the words, and write the words concerned, e.g.

entrar, automático, salir, billete, multa, correspondencia, acceso, coche, andén, precio.

Los compro cuando viajo en tren o en autobús o en metro. En unas estaciones, es posible comprarlos de la taquilla o de una máquina. En esta estación es posible cambiar.

Taxi (page 130)

Main aim
To learn the language needed to travel by taxi.

A It would be a good idea to revise now the unit so far, e.g.
Read aloud any sentence or sign on pages 128–130 of the Students' Book. The students scan quickly to find the sentence or sign and to say the number of the page it is on.
Present on the board or OHP about twenty important words from pages 128–130. Give the class one minute to study them and then ask students to make up sentences which use them. Then remove the words and see how many the students can write down correctly.

B The students read this to themselves and, with the help of a dictionary, understand it. Encourage them to respond to the gist by asking, e.g.

UNIDAD 12

¿Has viajado en taxi aquí?
¿Has viajado en taxi en España?
¿Qué piensas de los taxis?

C Work with the students on the key phrases and help them to learn them, e.g.
With long sentences, the students practise repeating them after you in smaller sections, starting from the end, e.g.
- *¿el aeropuerto?*
- *¿hasta el aeropuerto?*
- *¿desde aquí hasta el aeropuerto?*
- *¿ir desde aquí hasta el aeropuerto?*
- *¿Cuánto cuesta ir desde aquí hasta el aeropuerto?*

Adapt sentences for other destinations, e.g.
Lléveme al aeropuerto (teatro, etc.), por favor.
¿Cuánto cuesta ir desde aquí hasta la estación (playa, etc.)?

Mouth sentences silently for the others to say aloud.

D In pairs, the students work on the model dialogue. You then play the part of the traveller and adapt what you say (e.g. changing the destination and the location) to prepare the students for the unexpected. Then write notes on the board of other destinations and where each is near. In pairs, the students adapt the model dialogue to fit these.

E In pairs, the students adapt the model dialogue in line with the brief given. For homework, they could all write out this dialogue.

La RENFE (page 130)

Main aim

To present some information about the RENFE.

The students read this to themselves and understand it. They then ask you questions, either to clarify the meaning or to seek further information about train travel in Spain. The students could make notes of your replies and use the information to write a short article about la RENFE. If possible, give a small prize for the best articles. You could also create an interesting wall display with them.

Students who would find it too difficult to write an article could design an advert using the information given here. These too could be displayed.

Background information

There are two railway stations in Santander, one belonging to RENFE (*Red Nacional de Ferrocarriles Españoles*) and the other to FEVE (*Ferrocarril de Vía Estrecha*). Both companies belong to the state but are operated independently. RENFE is the national rail network whereas FEVE is restricted to the Cantabrian coast. The two types of track and rolling stock are incompatible; FEVE has track a metre wide and RENFE 1m 60. Only Spain, Portugal and the Soviet Union have the same width of track as RENFE; the rest of Western Europe has track which is 1m 40. When most other countries standardised their railway systems, Spain opted out for economic and security reasons. So, Spanish trains going to France have to use a special mechanism to change the width of the wheels. RENFE's railway network has seen great changes in recent years. Stations have been extensively modernised and services improved. RENFE has introduced new high speed trains which have cut the travelling time between Madrid and Seville from 7 to 3 hours. The new train was inaugurated in 1992 – the year of the World Exhibition held in Seville. A model of things to come is Madrid Chamartín, which has a leisure complex above the railway concourse.
FEVE too has changed from a run-down antiquated railway system to a bright, efficient service meeting the needs of people travelling along the tortuous coastal routes.

You could base a *¿Verdad o mentira?* quiz on this information, e.g.

Los mejores trenes son los Expresos.
Los trenes más rápidos son los Expresos.
Hay que pagar un suplemento para el Talgo.
Los minibuses son bastante lentos.
Los trenes Tranvía son los trenes normales.

En la estación (page 131)

Main aim

To understand station signs.

A The students first try to work out what all these signs mean, without using a dictionary. This will help them to develop other comprehension strategies.

UNIDAD 12

B Practise the vocabulary thoroughly before proceeding with the next exercises, e.g.
Using **copymaster 114** on OHP, show the railway symbols. Give the students 10–20 seconds to memorise the order. Then ask them if they can remember either the sequence of the railway symbols or give the corresponding number (1–9) to each symbol.
Show the students the symbols again.
Switch off the projector and cover up one line/symbol. Turn the machine on again and ask the students if they can remember which symbols have disappeared.
Base a game of Noughts and crosses on the symbols.

C The students look again at the signs on page 131 of their book and copy the words in order of importance. They can compare their lists and, if they wish, change them. They could also say which of these facilities are available in local stations and use this information to express an opinion about these stations. Encourage them to tell you what they think, e.g.

Para mí, es más importante la sala de espera. Si hace frío o si llueve …

D Play the tape of some conversations that take place on the station. Ask the class to draw the symbol or write down the name of the place asked for on the first hearing. Play the tape again so that they can note down some further information, such as the location.

En la estación

Número 1
- ¡Uf! Esta maleta pesa mucho. Voy a preguntar si hay una consigna.
- Vale, yo me quedo aquí.
- Oiga por favor. ¿Dónde está la consigna?
- Está ahí mismo, a la derecha, cerca del despacho de billetes.

Número 2
- Oiga, el tren para Santiago ¿de qué andén sale?
- ¿El tren de las 11.26? Andén tres vía cinco. Tiene Vd. que bajar por el paso subterráneo.
- Y eso, ¿dónde está?
- Allí mismo, enfrente de la consigna.

Número 3
- Va a salir el tren con media hora de retraso.
- ¡Vaya! Pues, voy a comprar un periódico entonces.
- Muy bien. ¿Te veo en la sala de espera?
- Pues sí, pero no sé dónde está. Voy a preguntar a este mozo … Oiga, ¿la sala de espera, por favor?
- Lo siento mucho señorita pero aquí no hay.

Número 4
- ¡Ah! Tengo que llamar a Raúl para avisarle que vamos a llegar con retraso. ¿Ves una cabina?
- Pues, no, no veo ninguna. Voy a preguntar a este señor … Oiga, por favor. ¿Me puede decir si hay un teléfono en la estación?

Número 5
- Date prisa. El tren sale dentro de cinco minutos. No tenemos billetes todavía. Oiga, oiga, ¿el despacho de billetes, por favor?
- Sí, ¿ve usted la oficina de información allí abajo? Pues, el despacho de billetes está inmediatamente después.

Número 6
- Antes de ir al restaurante tengo que cambiar dinero. Sólo tengo francos franceses. Me imagino que habrá un cambio en esta estación.
- Creo que sí pero no lo veo. Voy a preguntar en la oficina de información.
- Buenos días. ¿Hay un cambio en la estación?
- Sí, está en el andén número uno, pero está cerrado hasta las diez, eh.

¿Cómo se hace una reserva? (page 131)

Main aim
Buying tickets and reserving a seat.

A The students read this and ensure that they understand it.

B Play these recordings. After each one, the students work out which of the people in the queue was speaking.
Play the dialogues again and ask the students to repeat only what the travellers say. Then play them again and, before the travellers speak, pause the tape. The students try to act the travellers' roles.

¿Cómo se hace una reserva?

Número 1
- Quisiera un billete para Madrid.
- ¿Para cuándo?
- Para el día 23.
- ¿Primera o segunda clase?
- Segunda clase, ida solo.
- ¿Fumador?

– No, no fumador ... cerca de la ventanilla, por favor.
– Vale. El billete cuesta 2.650 pesetas. El tren sale a las 9.
– Gracias.

Número 2
– Buenos días. Quisiera reservar un billete, por favor.
– ¿Cuándo quiere viajar?
– Mañana por la tarde a Bilbao.
– ¿Ida solo o ida y vuelta?
– Ida y vuelta, segunda clase.
– ¿Quiere fumador o no fumador?
– No fumador. ¿A qué hora sale exactamente el tren?
– A las cinco y diez de la tarde.
– ¿Cuánto vale?
– 3.485 pesetas.
– Gracias.

C In pairs, the students play read the model dialogue. They then make up conversations based on what the people in the queue want. You could join in and play the role of the ticket clerk, introducing unexpected elements for the students to cope with.

D As students complete the above task, give them a copy of **copymaster 115**.

E You could present the following on the OHP. In pairs, each student takes turns to ask the questions.

Alumno A
Por favor, ¿hay un tren que va de Barcelona a Burgos?
¿A qué hora llegará a Burgos?
¿Es un tren Expreso?
¿Hay un servicio de cafetería?
Y, ¿hay coche-cama, por favor?
¿Es directo, o tendré que cambiar?
¿Tendré que pagar un suplemento?

Alumno B
Por favor, ¿a qué hora hay un tren de Zaragoza a Salamanca?
¿A qué hora llegará?
¿Es un tren Expreso?
¿Hay un servicio de cafetería?
¿Es directo, o tendré que cambiar?
¿Tendré que pagar un suplemento?
Y, ¿hay un servicio de restaurante, por favor?

UNIDAD 12

En la taquilla (page 132)

Main aim
Buying train tickets.

A The students read and understand this.

B Base a *¿Verdad o mentira?* quiz on this, e.g.
Es un billete de primera clase.
Es un billete sencillo.
Cuesta trescientas pesetas.
Es un billete para Santiago.
Es un billete de segunda clase, ida y vuelta.
Es un billete de segunda clase para Santander.

C The students practise the model dialogue in pairs and then adapt it to buy the ticket from Salou to Barcelona.

¿Qué dijo? (page 132)

Main aim
Understanding train announcements.

A The students read this and work out what the announcements mean, using a dictionary when necessary.

B Present this grid on the board or OHP. Ask the students to help you to complete it on the basis of the information in the announcements in their book.

Tipo de tren					Pueblo/Ciudad	Llegada	Salida	Vía
TER	TALGO	Exp.	Ráp.	Eléct.				

C The students copy the empty grid and listen to the recorded announcements. After hearing each one once, ask them to report on the gist. They then listen again, to each in turn, and write into the grid as much information as they can. Ask them to report back and clear up any problems before playing the announcement again and going on to the next one.

163

UNIDAD 12

¿Qué dijo?

Número 1
– Atención. Tren rápido con destino a Zamora. Sale a las 12.35. Andén primero vía dos.

Número 2
– Atención. Electrotrén con destino a León, sale a las 14.20. Andén dos vía cuatro. Faltan cinco minutos para que efectúe su salida.

Número 3
– Atención. Atlántico Expreso, con destino a La Coruña y El Ferrol. Estacionado en la vía nueve. Sale a las 22.15.

Número 4
– Atención. Tren rápido Talgo con destino a Gijón. Faltan dos minutos para que efectúe su salida, andén primero vía primera. Sale a las 16.10.

Número 5
– Atención. Tren Expreso procedente de Santiago de Compostela llega a las 6.45. Andén tres vía cinco.

Número 6
– Atención. Tren rápido procedente de Burgos tiene prevista su llegada a las 13.05. Andén cuatro vía nueve.

Número 7
– Atención. Expreso Costa Verde procedente de Madrid, tiene prevista su llegada a las 19.00 horas. Andén dos vía tres.

Número 8
– Atención. Tren rápido Ter procedente de Málaga. Tiene prevista su llegada a las 7.40. Efectuará su entrada por vía 10.

Más preguntas (page 133)

Main aim

Asking for, and giving, information about trains and platforms.

A The students read and understand this. Now would be a good time to explain the difference between *vía* and *andén*: *vía* meaning 'track' and *andén* meaning 'platform'.

B In pairs, the students practise the model dialogue. They then adapt it by matching the questions and answers in the speech bubbles, taking turns to ask the questions.

¿Está libre? (page 133)

Main aim

Asking, and saying, if seats are free or occupied.

A The students read and understand this. They all then draw a plan for eight seats and number them, listen to the recording and draw a figure in the seats which are occupied.

¿Está libre?

Número 1
– ¿Está libre este asiento?
– Sí, hijo sí, está libre.

Número 2
– Perdone, ¿está libre?
– No, está ocupado.

Número 3
– ¿Este asiento está libre?
– No, es para mi amigo. Viene ahora mismo.

Número 4
– Oiga, ¿está ocupado este asiento?
– No, no está ocupado, está libre.

Número 5
– Perdone, ¿este asiento está libre?
– No.

Número 6
– ¿Hay un asiento libre aquí?
– Este asiento está ocupado.

Número 7
– ¿Está libre?
– Me parece que sí. Sí, está libre, no hay nadie allí.

Número 8
– ¿Está ocupado este asiento?
– Bueno, de momento no, pero está reservado.
– ¿Está reservado? Bueno, voy a buscar otro.

B Give the students a copy of the information-gap exercise on **copymaster 116**. This involves asking if a seat is free and the partner answering according to the information on the seating plan.
They then write down the information they receive from their partner on the blank seating plan.

UNIDAD 12

Una palabra conduce a otra (page 133)

Main aim
To develop communication strategies and vocabulary.

A Work on this along lines which have previously proved successful.

B To give important practice in looking up words quickly in a dictionary, give the students just five minutes to look up as many of these words as they can and to note the dictionary definitions.

Un viaje en autocar (page 134)

Main aim
Informing people of arrival times.

A Now would be a good time to revise the unit so far, e.g.
Present the sentences below on the board or OHP. The students read them and say where they would expect to hear each one:
1 *¿Es directo o hago correspondencia?*
2 *Lléveme al aeropuerto, por favor.*
3 *¿Ida y vuelta, o ida solo?*
4 *¿Se puede ir a la Avenida de Tibidabo?*
5 *De segunda.*
6 *¿Está libre el taxi?*
7 *Un billete para Madrid, por favor.*
8 *Sí, señora. ¿Adónde quiere Vd. ir?*
9 *De ida y vuelta. ¿Cuánto es?*
10 *Hay que cambiar en Catalunya.*
11 *Vale. Suba Vd.*
12 *¿De primera o de segunda?*
13 *Hay que tomar la dirección Avenida de Tibidabo.*
14 *De segunda.*
15 *Son mil noventa pesetas.*
16 *Sí, coja la línea 5.*

Explain that there are three dialogues which can be made up using these sentences and give the students five minutes to write the three dialogues. They could compare these, and practise them, in pairs.

B Now would be a good time to work on the future tense in *A ser detective,* page 206.

C The students read this and ensure that they understand it. They practise the model dialogue in pairs.

D You play the part of the traveller and invite students to play the other part in the model dialogue. After doing this once or twice, begin to change some details (e.g. place and times) to show how the dialogue can be adapted. The students can then continue in pairs and produce dialogues based on the four scenarios.

E With help from the class, produce on the board a *Word Sun* around each of the following: *tren, metro, autobús, autocar, taxi.* Then remove the words and phrases surrounding these words and invite students to say what they were.

El contestador automático (page 135)

Main aim
To develop listening skills.

A The students read the instructions carefully and ensure that they understand them.

B The students listen to the messages and take notes, in English. Ask students for their messages and clear up any problems.

C Play the messages again. This time, the students look at their notes as they listen and can make notes about how to say the key points in Spanish. They then use their notes to try to re-create the messages, writing them down. Finally, they listen again to the messages and correct what they have written.

El contestador automático
- Oiga, estamos en Inglaterra, en Portsmouth. El ferry llegó hace una media hora. Saldremos de aquí muy pronto y estaremos en tu casa a las tres aproximadamente. Te llamaré más tarde si hay un problema. Hasta pronto.
- Oiga, Mariluz al aparato. Estamos en la autopista. Ha habido un accidente y la carretera está bloqueada. No se sabe cuándo llegaremos. Te llamaré en una hora. Adiós.
- Soy Antonio. Estamos en la estación en Londres. El tren sale a las 19.30 y llegará a las 21.20 h. Si no estáis en la estación cogeremos un taxi.
- Hola, soy Bea. Estamos en Londres en la estación de autocares. No cogimos el autocar de las 17.45.

UNIDAD 12

Cogeremos el de las 18.45 que llegará a las 22.00. Espero que está bien. Nos veremos pronto.

Te veré en julio (page 135)

Main aim
Writing a letter about travel plans.

A The students read this and ensure that they understand it.

B The students adapt the model letter orally to meet the demands of the brief. Clear up any problems.

C The students write their letter and can do this in class or at home.

¿Cuál prefieres? (page 136)

Main aim
To discuss common forms of transport.

A The students read this to themselves and ensure that they understand it.

B Give some practice in scan reading by asking questions and getting the students to race to find the answer, e.g.
¿Quién prefiere el metro (etc.)? ¿Por qué?
¿Cuáles son las ventajas/desventajas del autobús?
¿Quién va a su trabajo en coche?
¿Quién prefiere ir en bicicleta? ¿Por qué?

C The students listen to the recording and make notes. They compare their notes and then listen again to check. Finally, they could conduct a similar survey in class and compare their results with those expressed by the young Spanish people.

¿Cuál prefieres?
- Hola. ¿Me puedes decir cómo vienes al colegio?
① - Yo vengo andando porque es más sano. Sólo vivo tres calles más abajo.
- ¡Ajá! … Qué transporte utilizas para venir al colegio?
② - Pues yo vengo en autobús porque no vivo muy lejos. Sólo son dos paradas desde mi casa.
- ¡Ajá! En autobús. … Y ¿cómo has venido hoy al colegio?
③ - Pues yo vengo en tren. Es que vivo muy lejos y es lo más rápido.
- ¡Ah! En tren, muy bien. … Mira, ¿cómo llegas aquí?
④ - Pues yo cojo el metro porque es más rápido.
- En el metro … ¿Cómo llegas al colegio?
⑤ - Pues, en el coche porque es más cómodo.
- Muy bien. … ¿Cómo vienes a clase?
⑥ - Vengo en bicicleta, es mucho más sano.
- Ah. Muy bien. … ¿Cómo has llegado aquí esta mañana?
⑦ - Vine en el metro porque es bastante rápido, muy rápido.
- Sí, … mira, ¿en qué has venido hoy a clase?
⑧ - Pues vine en el coche porque me trajo mi padre.
- Ah, ¡qué suerte! Gracias.

D The students read again the opinions expressed on page 136. They adapt these to produce a written version of their own opinions. Correct these and then encourage the students to use them to discuss public transport, to express their own views and to answer your and each others' questions.

Ahora sé (page 137)

Main aim
To provide a summary of the *Unidad* and a basis for more practice and revision.

A The students can work independently on this, using their favourite techniques.

B Either now, or later for revision, you could use the following activities:
Encourage the students to make predictions orally (e.g. about the weather, a sports results, lottery numbers, what will happen next in a TV serial) and then to write their own predictions. In a later lesson, you could look at the predictions and talk about what, in fact, happened.
Write means of transport on the board, in pairs, e.g.
el metro – el autobús
el taxi – el tren

Encourage the students to find as many ways as they can of comparing the means of transport in each pair.
Give students a copy of **copymaster 117**. They could first answer the questions at home, and then answer and discuss them in class.

UNIDAD 12

Revision activities

1 Using classroom language
(Libro 1, Unidad 2)

A It would be a good idea to revise the rubrics commonly used in exams to ensure that all the students really understand them.

B A few minutes before the end of a lesson, ask the students to remember as many as possible of the things said earlier in the lesson and who said them.

2 Buying things at the chemists
(Libro 1, Unidad 14)

A Encourage the students to revise *Unidad 14* in *Libro 1*, and especially page 126.

B Play these recorded dialogues. The students listen and take notes, noting the illness and the medicine. When you have cleared up any problems, the students could use their notes to make up similar dialogues.

En la farmacia

Número 1
- Buenos días, ¿qué desea?
- ¿Tiene algo para la tos?
- Sí, un jarabe. ¿Algo más?
- Sí, me duele la cabeza y estoy mareado.
- Tiene que ir al médico.
- ¿Recomienda usted aspirinas?
- No, recomiendo ir al médico.
- Vale.

Número 2
- ¿Qué desea?
- No sé. Tengo la gripe.
- Recomiendo aspirinas y cama.
- No puedo tomar aspirina. Tengo alergia a las aspirinas.
- Entonces, recomiendo cama y bebidas calientes.
- Gracias.
- De nada.

Número 3
- Buenos días.
- Buenos días. ¿Qué desea?
- ¿Tiene algo para una insolación?
- Sí, hay cremas. Mire.
- ¿Cuál recomienda?
- Esta es buena pero muy cara. Aquella es más barata.
- Deme un tubo de la crema más cara.
- Son novecientas pesetas.
- ¡Ay! me duele el precio.
- Sí pero no te va a doler la espalda.
- Vale.

Número 4
- Buenas tardes.
- Buenas tardes. ¿Tiene algo para el dolor de estómago?
- ¿Qué le pasa exactamente?
- He comido demasiado y me duele el estómago.
- Recomiendo estas pastillas. Son muy buenas. En dos horas estarás muy bien.

3 Eating in a restaurant
(Libro 3, Unidad 2)

A The students revise *Unidad 2* and especially page 28.

B Give out **copymaster 118** for the students to work on in pairs. Encourage those playing the role of the waiter/waitress to introduce unexpected problems, e.g.
Lo siento, no hay más helados de fresa.

4 Recovering lost property
(Libro 3, Unidad 8)

A The students revise *Unidad 8*, and especially page 95.

B Give each student a copy of **copymaster 119** for them to read at home. you could base a quiz on it in the next lesson.

5 Welcoming, and being, a guest
(Libro 3, Unidad 11)

A The students revise *Unidad 11*, and especially page 125. You could use now any activities suggested for page 125 which you did not use at the time.

B Give everyone a copy of **copymaster 120**. They work on activities 1 and 2 in pairs, and on activity 3 on their own.

UNIDAD 13

La televisión y los medios de comunicación

Main aim
Talking about television and other media.

Area(s) of experience
A – Everyday activities
E – The international world

Materials
Cassette: ¿Cuánto tiempo pasas delante de la televisión?, ¿Qué te gusta ver?, ¿Qué pasó en las noticias?, Unas opiniones muy diferentes, Una palabra conduce a otra
Copymasters 121–125

Tasks
Stating which programmes or films they have recently seen or what music, when or where
Understanding simple information about TV programmes, etc.
Understanding and narrating simple items of news
Understanding and narrating the main features of a film, or of a television or radio programme
Asking for and giving opinions about newspapers, magazines, TV programmes and radio

Grammar points
Absolute superlatives (-ísimo)

Productive vocabulary
actualidades
cadena
comedia
contar
dibujos animados
documental
emocionante
narrar
película de acción
telenovela
aventuras
  (policíacas)
concursos
dar
divertido
emisión
historia
noticias
programa

Receptive vocabulary
emisión televisiva
experiencia
guerra
incidente
medios
personaje
publicidad
reunión de políticos
robo

Revision points
Asking for places in the town
(Libro 1, Unidad 3)
Describing your town
(Libro 2, Unidad 1)
Visiting a department store
(Libro 3, Unidad 3)
Coping with illness
(Libro 3, Unidad 9)
Using public transport
(Libro 3, Unidad 12)

La televisión y los medios de comunicación (page 138)

Main aim
To understand, and wish to achieve, the unit goals.

A Work on this along lines which have previously proved successful.

B You could give, orally, examples of each goal, in random order. The students listen and say which goal each example illustrates, e.g.
Me gusta muchísimo ver películas policíacas en la televisión.
Anoche, he visto un programa buenísimo. Era emocionante.
Cuenta la historia de un hombre pobre que va a trabajar en Nueva York. Se hace rico.
A las ocho dan las noticias y después el pronóstico meteorológico.
A mí me encantan los dibujos animados.
¿Hay algo interesante en el periódico?
El fútbol es más emocionante en el estadio que en la televisión.

C You could question the students about what they watch on TV and listen to on the radio, and when they watch and listen. Encourage them to express opinions.

D You could advise them about how to increase their chances of watching Spanish TV successfully and, if they have the chance to do this via satellite, to encourage them to do so, e.g.
Watch, or listen to, the news in their own country before watching it in Spanish. Many news items will be common to both and it is easier to

UNIDAD 13

understand something in Spanish when you already know something about it.
Watch dubbed films and soaps which they have already seen in English.
Watch any TV programmes in Spanish which have subtitles. This can be an excellent way of improving and extending your Spanish.

¿Cuánto tiempo pasas delante de la televisión? (page 138)

Main aim
Talking about watching TV.

A The students read this and use comprehension strategies, and a dictionary, to understand it. They answer the questionnaire and read the conclusions.

B You could put all the questions orally and invite several students to answer each one, comparing, and encouraging them to compare, their different answers. They could continue this in pairs, each asking the questions and then drawing the appropriate conclusions.
Discuss the results of the questionnaire with the class and discuss other activities which the students do, e.g. films, reading, sport.

C Play the recording of these young people. After each one, the students categorise the person. Encourage them to discuss their responses, and clear up any problems.
Then play the recordings again and ask the class to respond to each speaker, saying if they find them interesting, boring, etc, and why.

¿Cuánto tiempo pasas delante de la televisión?
Número 1
– ¿Cuánto tiempo pasas delante de la televisión los días de colegio?
– Tres horas aproximadamente.
– ¿Y los fines de semana?
– No sé, cinco, seis, siete, más o menos.
– ¿Es importante para ti la televisión?
– Sí, importantísimo.
– ¿Qué harías sin televisión?
– No sé. No puedo imaginarlo.

Número 2
– ¿Cuánto tiempo pasas delante de la televisión los días de colegio?
– No veo la televisión. Prefiero leer.
– ¿Y los fines de semana?
– Una hora o dos.
– ¿Es importante para ti la televisión?
– No, prefiero leer y escuchar música.
– ¿Qué harías sin televisión? Leer supongo.
– Sí, no me importaría.

Número 3
– ¿Cuánto tiempo pasas delante de la televisión los días de colegio?
– Cuatro o cinco.
– ¿Y los fines de semana?
– Todo el día.
– Es importante la televisión, ¿verdad?
– Sí.
– ¿Qué harías sin televisión?
– No sé.

D The students study this item again and extract from it what they consider to be the most important words for talking about TV. They compare and discuss their lists. They then listen again to the recordings and tick the words in their lists each time they hear them. Can they draw any conclusions about which words are useful?

Television in Spain
Spain is experiencing the same expansion in broadcasting as other countries in Western Europe. The arrival of satellite television and, in the near future, cable TV is particularly welcome in a country that does not have a very good reputation for its domestic broadcasting. In hotels it is common to find Sky and MTV with programmes in French, German and English. Spain also has regional television stations to cater for local demand and to provide entertainment in languages other than Castilian. Catalonia has its own channel as does Galicia.
Television is an important part of Spanish life. The television is often in the dining room of a Spanish home and it is often on during meal times. Spanish bars invariably have the television on irrespective of whether anyone is watching. In a restaurant in Santillana the author noted four television sets on in different parts of the room and no-one watching! The exception to this is when an important football match is on. In this case it is likely that the bar will be full of people offering their vociferous support. Sport tends to dominate the ratings. Football matches are usually shown in full as are basketball matches and some bullfights from Spain or Latin America. Game shows are a regular feature of early

UNIDAD 13

evening entertainment. Some of the game shows are direct copies of shows that have been successful in the United States or in other countries. A flop in 1995 was '*No olvides tu cepillo de dientes*' which was popular when introduced in the UK. Foreign films are popular but are often quite old.

Soap operas (*telenovelas* in Spanish), so called because they were financed originally by the advertisers, soap powder manufacturers, are popular in all countries. In Spain one is screened after the lunch time news at 3.30 when housewives mainly can sit down and follow the fortunes of their favourite characters. Some of the soap operas are imported from the USA or Australia but some are from other Spanish speaking countries like Mexico where it is a booming industry. The Mexican companies produce so many programmes that, in many cases, the actors do not have time to learn their lines. To solve the problem they wear a small device in their ear which allows them to hear their next lines. It goes some way to explaining the poor acting. The plots are always similar: blighted love, abandoned children, the child with nothing who makes his or her way in the world and achieves success.

¿Qué te gusta ver? (page 139)

Main aim
Understanding and expressing opinions about TV programmes.

A The students read this to themselves and ensure that they understand it.

B Write these two sentences on the board:
Estoy de acuerdo.
No estoy de acuerdo.

You say aloud some of the key sentences and also variations of them, e.g.
Las películas de acción me gustan muchísimo.
Los documentales son interesantes.
Prefiero las emisiones deportivas.

After each sentence, point to a student who responds at once with one of the sentences on the board. You could, after a while, do this against the clock.

C Again say aloud the key sentences and variations of them. The students repeat after you, but only those sentences with which they agree.

D You say the names of some popular TV programmes. The students categorise each one, e.g. *Es un documental*. After a while, this could be done against the clock.

E The students listen to these recordings, one at a time. To help them to organise their note-taking you could jointly produce a grid for them on the board, e.g. with three columns for each speaker:
¿Qué le gusta ver? Su opinión. ¿Por qué?
Play each one twice. The students write their notes and then report to the class. Clear up any problems.

¿Qué te gusta ver?

Número 1
– Hola, buenos días. ¿Cómo te llamas?
– Me llamo Paula y vivo en Madrid.
– Paula, dime, ¿qué te gusta ver en la televisión?
– Lo que más me gusta son las emisiones deportivos: el fútbol, el baloncesto y el atletismo. Me encantan.
– ¿Qué más?
– Las telenovelas de los Estados Unidos y de América Latina.
– ¿Por qué te gustan?
– Son divertidos. Me gustan las personajes. Siempre quiero saber qué va a pasar.
– Gracias, Paula.
– De nada.

Número 2
– Hola, buenos días. ¿Tu nombre, por favor?
– Yo me llamo Alfredo Muñoz.
– Alfredo, ¿me puedes decir qué programas te gustan a ti?
– Sí, claro. Prefiero los documentales sobre la historia o sobre la naturaleza.
– ¿Te interesan mucho?
– Muchísimo. También las noticias del día. Veo las noticias a las tres y a las 8.30.
– ¿Te gustan los concursos?
– No me gustan nada. Son aburridísimos. No veo nunca los concursos.
– Gracias Alfredo.
– Adiós.

Número 3
– Hola. ¿Cómo te llamas?
– Mariluz.
– ¿Y qué te gusta ver en la televisión?
– Muchas cosas: las películas, por ejemplo.

170

UNIDAD 13

- ¿Qué tipo de película?
- De acción, de ciencia ficción, de amor.
- ¿Qué más te gusta?
- Me gustan mucho las comedias americanas.
- ¿Por qué?
- Porque son si divertidas.
- ¿Hay algo que no te gusta?
- Detesto el deporte. No veo nunca el deporte en la televisión.
- Gracias por tu participación.
- De nada, adiós.
- Adiós.

Número 4
- Hola, buenos días. Tu nombre, por favor.
- Rafael, pero mis amigos me llaman Rafa.
- Rafa, ¿qué te gusta ver en la televisión?
- La verdad es que no suelo ver mucho la televisión.
- ¿No te gusta?
- Bueno, no es que no me gusta pero tengo muchas cosas que hacer y no tengo tiempo para ver la televisión.
- ¿No ves nunca la televisión?
- Sí, veo las noticias, una película especial, pero no suelo verla a menudo.
- Gracias, Rafa.

F Tell the students that you are going to ask them about what they watch on TV, and their opinions. Then play the recordings again and encourage the students to listen, and to note, the language used for this.
They then answer your questions, e.g.

¿Qué te gusta ver en la televisión?
¿Por qué?
¿Qué más?
¿Por qué te gustan?
¿Te interesan mucho?
¿Te gustan las actualidades (etc.)?
¿Qué tipo de película ves en la televisión?
¿Hay algo que no te gusta?

After some class discussion, write these questions on the board or OHP and, in pairs, the students take turns to put them to their partners.

Te toca a ti (page 140)

Main aim
Asking for, and giving, opinions about TV programmes.

A The students read this to themselves and ensure that they understand it.

B In pairs, they practise play reading the model dialogue and then adapting it.

C Students put the questions in the dialogue to you, and to your language assistant if you have one. You can then reverse this, with you and your language assistant putting the questions to individual students.

D Now would be a good time to work on *A ser detective*, page 207.

¿Qué vamos a ver? (page 140)

Main aim
Discussing what to watch on TV.

A The students read and understand this. They ask you what sort of programme any of those listed are, e.g.

¿Qué es exactamente, 'Buenos días'?
'Por la mañana', ¿qué tipo de programa es?

You could write these two questions on the board as a model. When you answer, you could use useful paraphrasing language and the names of programme types, e.g.

Es un documental.
Es un tipo de telenovela como 'Neighbours'.
Es como 'The Cosby Show', una comedia.

You could also express your opinions about these programmes, to give more practice in hearing and understanding opinions.

B You and your language assistant, or an able student, could discuss the programmes and what you would like to watch, to provide a model.

C The students discuss the programmes in pairs and decide what to watch. They each write a list of what they will watch, bearing in mind the roles defined for them in the instructions.

D As students finish this, they could repeat the activity, but this time act themselves and say what they would really like to watch, drawing up an agreed list.

UNIDAD 13

¿Qué tal fue el programa? (page 141)

Main aim
Talking about programmes you have seen recently.

A The students read and understand this.

B You express an opinion about something you have seen, heard or read recently. The students then ask questions to find what it was. You could then reverse this, with you finding out what the students have seen, heard or read on the basis of the opinions they express.

C In pairs, the students practise play reading the model dialogue. Present it on the board or OHP and remove a few words at a time until the students can say the dialogue by heart.

D The students adapt the dialogue to discuss programmes listed in the previous item, pretending that they watched them last night. They then do this for programmes which they have really watched recently.

¿Qué tipo de programma es? (page 141)

Main aim
Asking for, and giving, simple information about TV programmes.

A The students read and understand this.

B Practise again categorising TV programmes. You name a popular programme and the students categorise it. You could do this against the clock.

C The students work on this item along the lines suggested.

¿Qué pasó en las noticias? (page 142)

Main aim
Understanding simple news items.

A The students read the different categories of news item. Check that they understand all of these and ask them what other categories they know

B Play this recording of some other short news items. The students first categorise each one, using the categories in this item in their book. Clear up any problems.
They now listen again and draw a 'mind map' to sum up the main points of each item.
Tell them that you are going to ask them to report on each news item and play each one once or twice more so that they can listen to, and note, the language used. They then use their 'mind maps' to write a report of each news item. They could do this in class or at home.

¿Qué pasó en las noticias?
Buenas noches señoras y señores. Les presentamos las noticias de hoy, martes 19 de abril.
Hoy en Bruselas se reunieron los líderes de los países de la Comunidad Europa. Hablaron de las cuotas pesqueras. Mañana el presidente de la Comunidad va a Washington a hablar con el presidente de los Estados Unidos.

Hoy a las once de la mañana dos hombres entraron en el Corte Inglés y en el cambio pidieron 10 milliones de pesetas. Llevaban pistolas y amenazaron a los empleados que les entregaron el dinero. Escaparon de los grandes almacenes y la policía está buscando a dos hombres de 20 a 25 años con pelo rubio ...

Y finalmente, un niño de Madrid ha ganado 100 millones de pesetas en la lotería. Su abuelo le había comprado el billete para su cumpleaños. El niño dice que va a comprar una nueva bicicleta.

C Make two photocopies of the texts of the news items above. White out different words in each text. Make copies of these and give one to each student in pairs. Without looking at their partners' texts, they discuss their texts and write complete texts.

¿Qué película viste? (page 142)

Main aim
Narrating the plot of a film.

A The students could read this and identify each narration, in class or at home.

B The students report their answers and discuss them.

UNIDAD 13

C You could narrate the plots of some recent films and TV dramas. The students listen and try to identify each one.

D The students adapt the summaries in their book to narrate orally the plots of films they have seen. They can then do this in writing, at home or in class. They could illustrate their narratives (e.g. with photos from a TV magazine) and these could be displayed.

El árbol genealógico de una telenovela (page 143)

Main aim

Narrating the plot of a TV drama.

A The students read this and ensure that they understand it.

B Each student chooses one of the characters and answers your questions in role, e.g.
Buenos días. ¿Cómo se llama Vd.?
¿Puede hablarme de su familia?
¿Dónde trabaja Vd.?
¿Está usted casado(a)?
¿Cómo es usted?
¿Tiene hijos(as)?
¿Cuántos años tiene usted?
¿Cuántos años tienen sus hijos?

C Each student writes one or two paragraphs to say how they think the story begun here will develop.

D The students now create their own families for a TV drama and write an account of the story so far and of the next few episodes. Some students may also like to write a scene from the drama and act it out with some friends. If possible, video this and use it with other classes.

E Give each student a copy of **copymaster 121**. They could work on this in class or at home.

Unas opiniones muy diferentes (page 143)

Main aim

Asking for, and giving, opinions.

A The students read the instructions carefully and ensure that they understand them. Present this list of words on the board or OHP. The students copy only those which they expect to hear.
aventuras policíacas
concurso
✓*documentales*
✓*opinión*
✓*dinero*
emisión
noticias
película de acción
✓*programa*
telenovela
guerra
✓*publicidad*
reunión de políticos
robo
✓*televisión*
✓*radio*
película de amor
✓*satélite*
✓*bueno*

They listen and tick all the words in their lists as they hear them. They then listen again and add to their lists any words in your list which they did not choose.

Unas opiniones muy diferentes
– Hola, bienvenido a nuestro programa. Hoy vamos a invitar a unos jóvenes a dar su opinión sobre los medios de comunicación. En la primera línea tenemos Joaquín, ¿verdad?
– Sí. Buenos días.
– Joaquín, ¿qué opinión tienes tú?
– Muy negativa. Creo que la televisión es muy mala y la radio también.
– ¿Por qué?
– Porque compramos programas de los Estados Unidos, de Australia y del resto de Europa y no hacemos programas buenas nosotros.
– Gracias, Joaquín. En la línea 2 ...
– Maribel Carrasco de Pontevedra.
– Hola, Maribel. ¿Qué opinas tú?

173

UNIDAD 13

– Creo que la televisión es bastante buena. Hay programas regionales y hay el satélite con películas muy buenas.
– ¿Ves mucho la televisión?
– Cuatro horas diarias, más o menos.
– Gracias, Maribel. ¿Quién tenemos en la línea 3?
– Teófilo Sánchez.
– Teófilo, ¿qué piensas tú?
– Creo que todo depende de dinero. Si tienes dinero hay satélite pero, si no, tienes dos o tres cadenas bastante malas.
– ¿Qué te gustaría ver más en la televisión?
– Más drama, más documentales, más películas nuevas y menos publicidad.
– Gracias, Teófilo. Eso es todo hoy. Mañana a la misma hora hablaremos de otro tema. Adiós y buenas tardes.

B Play the recording again. They note the opinions expressed by each person, report on these to the class and then say if they agree or disagree, and why.

C Tell them to prepare to express their own opinions. They listen again to the recordings and note how these speakers do it, choosing the expressions they wish to use. You then interview as many as possible, with the help of your language assistant if you have one.

Una carta de una amiga (page 144)

Main aim

To understand, and write, a letter about the media.

A The students read and understand this.

B You put orally the questions asked in the first paragraph of the letter, using the 'snowballing' technique. Write notes on the board to summarise the students' replies. Occasionally, sum up what a few students have said and ask some able students to do this, referring to the notes on the board. For the other paragraphs, the students find the questions and put them to each other.
Stress the importance of seeking out, and answering, the questions. It is also a good idea to make up questions of your own to include in the reply. Some Exam Boards require this and give bonus marks for good questions.

C Each student writes a reply. This could be done at home.

Una palabra conduce a otra (page 144)

Main aim

To develop communication strategies and extend vocabulary.

A This activity is designed to help the students cope with words which, because of their pronunciation, are difficult to understand.
The students listen to the sentences on tape and try to work out what the new words mean. You could point out the problems caused by the dipthong *au*, the final *e* and the soft *c/g*, e.g.
autor, Laura, automóvil, Austria, capaz, noble, simple, cable, social, cero, ceremonia, civilización, gigante, generoso, generación, sociología.

Una palabra conduce a otra

Número 1
– Se ha roto el cable. ¿Dónde está el taller más cercano?

Número 2
– El autor de este libro es muy famoso.

Número 3
– Austria es un país muy bonito.

Número 4
– Laura es una chica muy generosa.

Número 5
– Me gustaría estudiar sociología en la universidad.

Número 6
– La ceremonia fue muy simple.

Número 7
– ¿Conoces a Pablo? Es un gigante.

Número 8
– ¿Eres capaz de identificar todas estas palabras?

B Work on this along lines which have previously proved successful.

C A very useful strategy when listening is to try to 'see' and to write words which are not understood: seeing them often makes the meaning clear. You could say aloud the following words to try this out:
comedia, historia, aventura, acción, drama, policíaco, satélite, robo, antena, ciencia-ficción, dibujos animados.

UNIDAD 13

D Play the recording and get the students to practise doing this in context to see if writing out difficult words helps. Also encourage them, when they hear new words, to ask, e.g.
¿Quiere Ud. repetir eso?
¿Cómo se escribe?
¿Cómo se dice?
¿Qué significa?

E Point out too that new and difficult words are often not important and can be ignored. The main thing is to read the questions carefully and to listen for the answers. They can ignore parts of the text which are not needed to answer the questions and should practise doing so. You could present the following texts and questions on the board or OHP for them to practise.

1 El robo tuvo lugar a las seis de la tarde. Los ladrones se llevaron relojes de oro, diamantes y collares que valían unos cincuenta millones de pesetas.

2 El coche del presidente estalló pocos momentos antes de llegar al palacio nacional. La bomba pesaba cinco kilos y el presidente y sus guardaespaldas murieron en el acto. La explosión se oyó a una distancia de 10 kilómetros.

3 La flota pesquera rechazó la oferta del gobierno diciendo que no pudo aceptar un acuerdo que representaría una baja del 20 por ciento en el número de barcos.

1a When did the incident take place?
   ¿Cuándo tuvo lugar el incidente?

 b How much were the items worth?
   ¿Cuánto valían los artículos mencionados?

2a Where was the car when the incident happened?
   ¿Dónde estaba el coche cuando sucedió el incidente?

 b What happened to the occupants of the car?
   ¿Qué les pasó a los ocupantes del coche?

3a Who rejected the government's offer?
   ¿Quién rechazó la oferta del gobierno?

 b What would the offer mean for the fishing fleet?
   ¿Qué representaría la oferta para la flota pesquera?

Ahora sé (page 145)

Main aim

To provide a summary of the *Unidad* and a basis for more practice.

A Encourage the students to work on this, alone and in pairs, using their favourite techniques. Organise a game of Confabulation. Give each student a card with a sentence from *Ahora sé* on it. They have to write a dialogue or a narrative which includes this sentence as naturally as possible. When these have been corrected, they can be exchanged or displayed. The others guess which sentence the writer was given.

B Give each student a copy of **copymaster 122**. They could read and prepare this in class or at home and then discuss their opinions in pairs or groups of 3–4.

Revision activities

1 Asking for places in town
(Libro 1, Unidad 3)

A Encourage the students to revise this *Unidad* and especially page 35 of *Libro 1*.

B Organise a few minutes of brainstorming on this topic and write on the board or OHP what the students say. Start with single words and then move on to sentences. This should prove very encouraging.

C Give out **copymaster 123** for the students to work on in pairs.

2 Describing your town
(Libro 2, Unidad 1)

A Encourage the students to revise this *Unidad* of *Libro 2* and especially to work on page 17.

B Divide the class into groups of 5–6. One group prepares questions to put in a TV interview, on the topic of 'Your town'. The other groups anticipate the questions which will be asked and prepare good answers. Each interviewer then interviews a group. These interviews can all be done simultaneously, or one at a time as the rest of the class listen.

UNIDAD 13

3 Visiting a department store
(Libro 3, Unidad 3)

The students revise *Unidad 3*, and especially page 41, using their own favourite techniques.

4 Coping with illness
(Libro 3, Unidad 9)

A The students revise *Unidad 9* and especially page 105.

B Give students a copy of **copymaster 124**. They could read this at home and prepare to discuss it in class. The discussion could be done in pairs and then with the whole class, when you can link eating and exercise with health.

C Choose several illnesses from *Ahora sé,* page 105. Complain that you have one of these and ask the class to advise you what to do, e.g. what to take, whether you need to see a doctor, how much time you need to take off school. The students could choose other illnesses and continue this in pairs.

5 Using public transport
(Libro 3, Unidad 12)

A The students revise *Unidad 12* and especially page 137. You could use now any activities suggested in these notes for that page which you did not use earlier.

B To revise the future tense you could use the following activities:
Ask the students to summarise recent events in popular TV soaps and then to predict what will happen next.
Almost everyone likes having their fortunes read. Form groups of 3 or 4. Each student writes the fortunes of all the others in the group. Then each student receives, reads and comments on all his/her fortunes (e.g. similarities, differences, what they really hope for).

C Give each student a copy of **copymaster 125**. In pairs, they take turns to play each role.

UNIDAD 14

En avión y en barco

Main aim
Travelling by plane and boat.

Area(s) of experience
C – The world around us
E – The international world

Materials
Cassette: En la agencia de viajes, ¡Qué pena!, ¡Atención, sres. pasajeros!, ¿Qué tiempo hará?, A bordo del avión
Copymasters 126–135

Tasks
Obtaining travel information and informing others
Making a reservation and checking the details
Understanding signs and announcements about the flight
Comparing different means of travel

Grammar point
Further practice of the future tense

Productive vocabulary
aeropuerto
avión
barco
camarote
ferry
hacer escala
suplemento
vuelo

Receptive vocabulary
crucero
embarcar
llegadas
pasajero
precipitaciones
retraso
salidas
travesía

Revision points
Going to a tourist office
(*Libro 1, Unidad 4*)
Describing where you live
(*Libro 2, Unidad 2*)
Talking about your free time
(*Libro 3, Unidad 4*)
Coping with accidents and breakdowns
(*Libro 3, Unidad 10*)
Television and the media
(*Libro 3, Unidad 13*)

En avión y en barco (page 146)

Main aim
To understand, and wish to achieve, the unit goals.

A Work on this along lines which have previously proved successful.

B With the class, you could brainstorm travel language which they already know and which they expect to be useful for plane and boat travel. Help them to adapt sentences they already know, with the words in this item, e.g. *avión*, *aeropuerto*, *ferry*, *camarote*.

C You could adapt some of the model sentences and ask the students to categorise each one, according to whether it is relevant to *un viaje en avión*, *un viaje en barco*, *los dos*, e.g.
¿A qué hora llegará el ferry a Valencia?
Quisiera reservar un asiento en el vuelo de trece horas, mañana.
Es más lento que el avión pero más tranquilo.
¿A qué hora llegará al puerto?
Me encantó el aeropuerto de Barcelona. Es muy moderno.
Quisiera reservar un camarote individual con baño.
El vuelo durará una hora.
En el aeropuerto de Málaga el cielo está nublado y la temperatura 22 grados.

D The students read the text about the unit goals and discuss it with you and each other, e.g.
¿Cómo irás en España? ¿Por qué?

España abre sus puertas (page 146)

Main aim
To read about travel to, and within, Spain.

As an introduction to the unit you may like to discuss the importance of air and sea travel for

UNIDAD 14

Spain. The class can look at the map of Spain on page 146 of the Students' Book which features all the main airports and ports, and comment on their position and importance for trade and, of course, tourism. You can mention the changes that air travel particularly has had on the modernisation of Spain. You can ask the class what they can tell you about Spain as a maritime power and of its trade links with the Americas, the countries of the Mediterranean and with Africa.

Ask them what they think particular ports are most used for: freight, passengers, fishing boats or a combination.

Ask the students if they have visited or passed through one of the airports or ports, and invite comments from them about the size and facilities available there.

It is important to state that air and sea travel tend, by their very nature, to be international and therefore signs are often bilingual and most airline and port staff with whom members of the public are likely to be in contact can speak some English. Nevertheless, it will be advantageous for them to be able to speak Spanish wherever possible since showing a willingness to speak the foreign language is generally appreciated. It is also easier to ask for information from members of the public who may well not be able to communicate in English.

A Give the students some practice in exam techniques. Ask them to study these questions on the board and then to write the answers in five minutes.

1 *Escribe el nombre de tres ciudades que tienen aeropuerto y puerto. (3)*
2 *Escribe el nombre de los tres países en el mapa. (3)*
3 *¿Cuántos viajeros llegan cada año a España en barco? (1)*
4 *¿Qué muestra este mapa? (2)*
5 *El artículo menciona dos tipos de barcos: ¿cuáles? (2)*

When discussing the students' answers, make sure that they all realise the importance of the numbers in the brackets. These indicate how many marks are available for the answers and give a very good clue about how many pieces of information each answer should contain – usually one per mark.

B Base some oral questions on the map, e.g.
¿Dónde está Alicante?
¿Cómo se llama la capital de Portugal?
¿Cuántas islas hay en el mapa?
¿Dónde están?
¿Cómo se llaman?

En la agencia de viajes (page 147)

Main aim

To understand, and start to use, some of the key language of the *Unidad*.

A The students begin by reading this and, with the help of a dictionary, understanding it.

B Read the questions aloud and ask the students to categorise them: first, according to who says them and then according to the mode of transport. You could do this first as the students look at the sentences in their books and then with their books closed.

C Divide the class into two groups. Students in one group read aloud the questions and students in the other find, and read aloud, the matching answers. Then change over and try to increase the pace by setting a target of two minutes for all the questions to be asked and answered.

D Present on the board or OHP any sentences the students are having difficulty with, but giving only the first letter of each word. The students find each sentence in their book, and say and write it. They then close their books and try to complete each sentence.

E In pairs, the students use and adapt the questions and answers to make up possible conversations between the customer and the travel agent in the photo.

F In preparation for listening to the tape you may like to revise the 24-hour clock. Here are a few suggestions for practice:

Verdad o mentira
Show the students clock times using a classroom clock, or on an OHP. Say the times using the 24-hour clock and ask them to say whether the time is correct or not.

UNIDAD 14

The game can then be reversed. Show the students times given as they would be on a timetable and then say what the time is, using a 12-hour clock with *de la mañana/de la tarde* added, e.g.

17.40 – llegará a la seis menos veinte (verdad).
19.30 – saldrá a las nueve y media (mentira).

Bingo

Put a selection of times on OHP or the board, all using the 24-hour clock. Ask them to choose six times and write them down on a piece of paper. Read out the times, incorporating phrases that they will meet later in the unit, e.g.

La hora prevista para el despegue es las trece cuarenta y cinco.
Se ruega a los señores pasajeros vuelo Sabina de las quince treinta embarquen urgentemente por la puerta número cinco.

G Play the tape and ask the students to make a note of the main details. Present the following grid to help them:

	1	2	3	4
Destino:				
Medio de transporte:				
Día/fecha:				
Hora de salida:				
Hora de llegada:				
Más información:				

Not all the details need to be asked for and you may prefer to play the tape a number of times and ask the students to pick out different facts each time they listen.

En la agencia de viajes

Número 1
– Hola, buenos días. Quiero ir a Barcelona.
– Sí, señora. ¿Cómo quiere Vd. viajar?
– En avión.
– Sí, y ¿cuándo desea hacerlo?
– Pues el lunes que viene.
– Bueno, hay cuatro vuelos diarios: dos por la mañana y dos por la tarde.
– Y ¿a qué hora sale el primer vuelo del día?
– A las 8.10.
– Bien.
– ¿Viaja Vd. sola?
– Sí, sola.
– Espere un momento que vea si queda alguna plaza en este vuelo …

Número 2
– Buenos días, ¿Qué desea?
– Hola. Quiero ir a Ibiza desde Barcelona en barco.
– Sí señor. ¿Qué fecha? Hay travesías diarias.
– Pues el miércoles, 18. ¿A qué hora sale el barco?
– A las once de la noche.
– ¿Y sabe a qué hora llegará?
– A las ocho de la mañana.
– Estupendo.
– ¿Cuántos son Vds.?
– Sólo mi mujer y yo.
– Entonces quieren un camarote para dos, con baño, ¿no?
– Sí por favor, con baño.
– Vamos a ver …

Número 3
– Buenos días. ¿Hay un vuelo para Santiago de Compostela mañana?
– Sí, sale a las 16 horas.
– Y ¿es directo o hace escala?
– Hace escala en Bilbao.
– Vale y entonces ¿cuánto tiempo dura el viaje?
– Tres horas en total. Llegará a Santiago a las 19 horas.
– Ah, muy bien.

Número 4
– Buenas tardes.
– Buenas tardes. ¿Qué desea?
– Quiero ir en ferry desde Santander a Inglaterra.
– Sí, y ¿cuándo quiere Vd. viajar? Hay travesías los lunes y los jueves desde España.
– El jueves próximo, si es posible.
– ¿Cuántas personas son Vds.?
– Pues dos adultos, dos niños y un coche. Quisiera un camarote para cuatro con cuarto de baño.
– Vale. ¿De qué marca es el coche?
– Es un Ford Fiesta. ¿Me puede decir cuánto tiempo dura la travesía?
– Sí, 24 horas. Vds. llegarán a Plymouth a las dos de la tarde.

H In class or at home, the students study the adverts. You could then base a quiz on them, e.g.

1 Iberia, ¿es la línea aérea de qué país?
2 ¿Cómo se llama la línea aéreia nacional de Gran Bretaña (Alemania, México, Francia, Suiza)?

UNIDAD 14

3 ¿Qué compañía dice que es la línea favorita del mundo?
4 ¿Cuál es la línea que nos une más?
5 Y ¿qué línea es innovadora en Europa?

Quiero ir a ... (page 148)

Main aim
Asking for, and giving, travel information.

A The students look at the dialogue on page 148. They can then cover the visual stimuli provided by the speech bubbles and try to make up a dialogue similar to the one given, changing roles after successful completion of the dialogue.

B The students then make up dialogues based on the visual cues given.

C Further practice
For highly structured information-gap practice you may prefer to give the students the cues on **copymaster 126**.

D As students complete the task above, you could ask them to adapt the model dialogue in their book to enquire about a boat to Mallorca.

Quisiera reservar ... (page 148)

Main aim
Making a reservation and checking the details.

A The students read and understand this.

B In pairs, they practise play reading these dialogues. Then present them on the board or OHP with some key words omitted and call on some volunteers to act them out.

C The students turn to page 148 in their book and revise the model dialogues. They then work in pairs to make up dialogues on the two briefs they are given, playing each part in turn.

La vida no es siempre tan fácil (page 149)

Main aim
Coping with the unexpected.

A The students read and understand these role-play briefs.

B You could play the role of the traveller in **1a**. The other role could be played by your language assistant or an able student. This could then be reversed.

C When everyone knows what to do and how to do it, they could do these role plays in pairs.

Hasta pronto (page 149)

Main aim
Reading and writing letters about travel arrangements.

A Give the students five minutes, under exam conditions, to read and answer the questions. Check their answers, clear up any problems and give any relevant advice about exam techniques.

B The students read the letter again and pick out all the examples of future tenses. Write these on the board. Ask the students to look at them and to use them to give you the rules about how the future tense is formed in Spanish. Now would be a good time to work more on *A ser detective*, page 206. You could also organise some verb circle practice with, e.g.
Iré al punto de encuentro.
Cogeré los cheques de viaje.
Llegará a las once y media.

C The students study the role-play brief in English and brainstorm the language they will need for these. You could write all their suggestions on the board or OHP. This is excellent exam practice and gives the students a very good idea for one way in which they can prepare for their orals. They could then write their letters, in class or at home.

D As a follow-up, you could give half the students one of the briefs below, giving the other brief to the other students. They could write these letters and then exchange them with students who wrote the other letter. When everyone has read these, they question each other to ensure that the recipients of the letters have understood them.

Plymouth–Santander
12th July dep: 17.30
13th July arr. 15.00
Wearing jeans, tee shirt, white jacket.
Best wishes to family.

London Heathrow–Málaga.
10th October dep: 14.30
arr: 17.50
Flight details: Iberia IB394
Wearing grey coat, black trousers.

¡Qué pena! (page 150)

Main aim

To develop listening skills.

A The students read the instructions. If necessary, they use a dictionary to understand them.

B They anticipate, as a class activity, the problems they expect to hear. They could also look back to *En la agencia de viajes* and write a list of the words there which they expect to hear.

C They listen to the recordings and tick off the words in their lists as they hear them.

¡Qué pena!

Número 1

– Oiga señorita. Me llamo Carmen García. Soy la madre de Luisa García y le llamo para decirle que lo siento pero no ha podido volar. Se ha puesto enferma esta mañana y la han llevado al hospital. Creen que se trata de apendicitis, un ataque de apendicitis. Le llamaré mañana por la mañana a ver si le puedo dar más noticias. Diga a la familia de mi parte que siento mucho que no haya podido ir … pero ¿qué sé yo? No hay otro remedio.

Número 2

– Hola. ¿Señorita Smith? Llamo de parte de Angel Ruiz. Ha perdido el avión. Dejó en casa su pasaporte y tuvo que volver a recogerlo. Creo que llegará mañana en el vuelo de la misma hora. Habrá alguien en el aeropuerto, ¿verdad?, para recogerle, digo. El es siempre así – un poco despistado …

Número 3

– Señorita. Soy Julia Montero Ibáñez. Estoy todavía en el aeropuerto de Málaga. El avión lleva casi una hora de retraso. No sé cuando despegará. Llamaré cuando sepa más. Diga a mi amigo que lo siento.

Número 4

– Oiga Señorita Smith. Llamo desde Santa Cruz de Tenerife. Me llamo Ignacio Martínez y lamento decirle que mi vuelo ha sido cancelado. Intentaré reservar un asiento en el vuelo de mañana. De todos modos llamaré más tarde para decirle lo que he podido hacer. Lo siento, ¿eh?

D Play the tape again to the class, repeating each telephone message. Ask the students to note down the most important details, namely the problem the traveller has and the action that will be taken. They can be given the names of the exchange visitors and/or a grid such as the one below in order to help them:

Nombre	*Problema*	*Acción*
Carmen García		
Angel Ruiz		
Julia Montero Ibáñez		
Ignacio Martínez		

Work on each message at a time, correct the students' answers and clear up any problems before going on to the next one.

E Tell the students that they will have to make similar calls and leave similar messages. Play the messages once or twice more so that they can listen to, and take notes about, what the speakers say. Then tell the students that they have to make similar calls to Spain on behalf of the exchange visitors who have been unable to catch the plane. Ask them to make suitable apologies and arrangements to be in contact again. Give them the following information:
Nuria Manresa: ill, has visited the doctor and will take the Saturday flight home.
Ignacio Gómez: left wallet and passport at home and missed the plane. Will catch the same plane tomorrow.
Jaime Alonso: Still at the airport. The plane will be 14 hours late because of the bad weather.

UNIDAD 14

En el aeropuerto (page 150)

Main aim
Finding facilities in an airport.

A The students read and understand this.

B They work in pairs, along the lines suggested, to ask for and give directions.

C The students test your memory! They ask the way to these facilities and you try to answer correctly without looking at the book. You could then reverse this, with you asking the questions.

Atención, sres. pasajeros (page 151)

Main aim
Understanding airport announcements.

A The students read and understand these instructions and the departure board.

B They listen to the announcements to find the one which relates to their flight. They note and report on the main points.

C You could make an OHT of **copymaster 127** or copy it and give it out. They say which announcement is relevant to which traveller and answer their questions.

Atención, sres. pasajeros
- Señores pasajeros del vuelo British Airways número 476 con destino a Londres embarquen por la puerta número 5.
- Se ruega a los señores pasajeros del vuelo Sabena número 672 con destino a Bruselas embarquen urgentemente por la puerta número 15.
- Ultimo y definitivo aviso para los señores pasajeros de Aviaco vuelo número AV103. Puerta de embarque número 2.
- Se ruega al Sr. Gómez, pasajero del vuelo Aviaco número 237 de las 15.30 con destino a Sevilla, vaya a la oficina de esa misma línea aérea donde se le entregará un recado urgente.
- Alitalia anuncia la salida de su vuelo con destino a Roma. La hora prevista del despegue es la 11.20.
- El vuelo de Iberia 312 con destino a París tiene retrasada la salida hasta las 14.50 debido a problemas técnicos.
- Salida de Air France 117 con destino a Lyon puerta 14 por favor.

¡Qué desastre! (page 151)

Main aim
Coping with the unexpected.

A The students read and understand these instructions and role-play scenarios, using a dictionary if needed. You could do this under exam conditions and impose a time limit so that the students build up the necessary skills and confidence.

B In pairs, the students practise play reading the model dialogue, playing each part in turn.

C You and your language assistant, or an able student, could work on scenario 1, as a model for the others. The students could then do these role plays lin pairs.

¿Qué tiempo hará? (page 152)

Main aim
Understanding weather forecasts.

A Present these questions on the board or OHP and give the students five minutes to find, and write, the answers, under exam conditions:
¿Qué tiempo hace en Madrid?
¿Qué tiempo hará en Mallorca?
¿Habrá precipitaciones? ¿Dónde?
¿Subirán o bajarán las temperaturas en el este?
¿En el sur de España habrá lluvia o sol?

Go over the students' answers, clear up any problems and give appropriate advice about exam techniques.

B Play this recording. The students listen and note information about the weather in Málaga and Mallorca.

UNIDAD 14

¿Qué tiempo hará?

– Buenos días, señores y señoras. Angel Díaz al micrófono. Tengo aquí el pronóstico para hoy y mañana. En todo el país se registrarán temperaturas más altas que las de ayer.
En Málaga, las temperaturas máximas serán de 25 grados y las mínimas de 15. El cielo estará despejado y sin viento.
En el este del país y en las Islas Baleares habrá nieblas matinales que darán paso a cielos despejados y soleados por la tarde. Temperaturas muy agradables, máximas de 23 grados y mínimas de 14. El mar prácticamente en calma.
Mañana en general el tiempo continuará estable pero con riesgo de lluvia en el sur de la península. Temperaturas relativamente altas para la estación.
En Málaga, vientos flojos del norte, cielo nuboso a primeras horas. Temperaturas parecidas a las de hoy, es decir, máximas de 24 grados y mínimas de 16.
En las Islas Baleares, Cataluña y los Pirineos tiempo seco y soleado.

Now present this grid on the board or OHP:

	Hoy	Mañana
Málaga		
Mallorca		

Play the recording again and ask the students to note the new information in the grid. They now compare their two sets of notes and see if having a grid like this to organise their notes is a help. What conclusions can they draw from this about what to do in exams?

C Base some questions on the map to help to increase their awareness of where major cities are in Spain, e.g.
¿Qué tiempo hará en Barcelona (etc.)?
¿Dónde lloverá (etc,)?
¿Dónde están las Islas Baleares (etc.) en el mapa?

D Give students a copy of **copymaster 128** and use it to develop useful communication strategies, e.g. They read it once and say how difficult they find it. Then ask them to make a list of words similar to English cognates and another of words which have similar known forms, for example *nublado*, known form: *nubes*.

Ask them to read the passage again and use the two strategies to work out the overall meaning of the forecast.

A bordo del avión (page 153)

Main aim
Understanding in-flight announcements.

A The students read and understand the instructions.

B Ask the students about any experience they have of air travel: where, when, who with, etc. Then encourage them to anticipate what the announcements may be about. They could use dictionaries to look up any words which they expect to hear and which would help them to understand. This is, again, excellent preparation for exams and how to use a dictionary in a listening exam.

C Present the following on the board or OHT:
El vuelo dura casi dos horas. La velocidad es 800 km/h y la altitud 10.000 metros.
No se puede fumar durante el vuelo y hay que abrocharse el cinturón.
El avión llegará en 15 minutos y en Bilbao hace mal tiempo.
El piloto y las azafatas dan la bienvenida a los pasajeros y les desea un buen viaje.

The students listen to the announcements and say which one goes with each of the above summaries. Clear up any problems and play the announcements again. Stop after each one and invite the students to explain it to the class or their partners.

A bordo del avión

– Bienvenidos a bordo del vuelo 329 con destino a Bilbao y Palma de Mallorca. El comandante y su tripulación les desean un buen viaje.

– Vamos a despegar dentro de unos momentos. Por favor no fumen durante el despegue y abróchense el cinturón.

– La duración del vuelo es 1h.50. Estaremos volando a una velocidad de 800 km/h a una altitud de 10.000 metros.

– Llegaremos al aeropuerto dentro de quince minutos. En Bilbao llueve y la temperatura es 12°.

UNIDAD 14

¿En barco o en avión? (page 153)

Main aim
Comparing and discussing different means of transport.

A Present these questions on the board or OHP and give the students three minutes to write the answers:

Complete estas frases.
1. *Es publicidad para … .(2)*
2. *En enero hay vuelos los días …, … y … .(1)*
3. *Un billete de ida y vuelta cuesta … .(1)*

Discuss the students' answers and clear up any problems.

B Practise and extend the model dialogue with the class and then in pairs.

C Adapt this to compare and discuss travel by plane and train, and coach and plane.

Una palabra conduce a otra (page 153)

Main aim
To develop communication strategies and vocabulary.

A Work on this along lines which have previously proved successful.

B Give practice in speedy dictionary use by using again the activity suggested on page 165 above.

C To ensure that the students can use this strategy when listening, say the following sentences a few times and ask for an English equivalent:

1. *En Barcelona se puede ir al aeropuerto en tren o en autobús sin dificultad.*
2. *En la tienda de recuerdos hay una gran variedad de regalos.*
3. *Si buscas regalos de calidad hay que pagar mucho.*
4. *Va a estudiar en la Universidad de Salamanca.*
5. *No sé de qué nacionalidad es.*
6. *Su padre tiene mucha autoridad en la oficina. Es director.*
7. *Hay mucha publicidad para la película en el periódico.*
8. *¿Existe la posibilidad de ir a Madrid este fin de semana?*

Ahora sé (page 154)

Main aim
To provide a summary of the *Unidad* and a basis for more practice and revision.

A The students work independently, or in pairs, with this list.

B Now, or later for revision, you could use the following activities:
Any sentences which the students find difficult to learn, they write half the sentence on one card and the other half on another card. In class and at home they practise putting these together correctly, as quickly as possible. When that becomes easy, they take a card and try to complete the sentence without looking at the other card.
Ask the students to write ten sentences about what they expect public transport to be like in the year 2100. They then read out and discuss their sentences.

Revision activities

1 Going to a tourist office
(Libro 1, Unidad 4)

A Encourage the students to look back at *Unidad 4* of *Libro 1* and especially to revise page 45.

B Each student writes a list of the sorts of documents they would send to a penfriend to prepare her/him to visit their home towns. They compare and discuss their lists.

2 Describing where you live
(Libro 2, Unidad 2)

A The students could begin by looking back at this *Unidad* and, in particular, to *Ahora sé*.

B Give each student a copy of **copymaster 129** to work on at home.

UNIDAD 14

3 Talking about your free time
(Libro 3, Unidad 4)

A The students look back at this *Unidad* and especially at page 53. You could use any activities suggested for this *Unidad* which you have not already used.

B Give each student in a pair one part of **copymaster 130**. They work on this along the lines suggested.

C Give each student a copy of **copymaster 131** for them to study at home and then discuss in class.

4 Coping with accidents and breakdowns
(Libro 3, Unidad 10)

A The students revise *Unidad 10* and you could use now any activities suggested with the *Unidad* which you have not already used.

B Give each student a copy of **copymaster 132** to read and prepare at home. They then discuss number 1 and role play numbers 2 and 3 in pairs.

C Give each student a copy of **copymaster 133**. They work on this in pairs along the lines suggested.

D You could also give out copies of **copymaster 134** for the students to work on at home.

5 Television and the media
(Libro 3, Unidad 13)

A The students revise *Unidad 13* and you could use now any activities suggested with *Unidad 13* which you have not already used.

B Give everyone a copy of **copymaster 135** for them to work on at home. In class, they compare and discuss what they considered to be important and different.

UNIDAD 15

Recuerdos

Main aim
Describing past holidays or visits in more detail.

Area(s) of experience
A – Everyday activities
B – Personal and social life
E – The international world

Materials
Cassette: ¡Felices Pascuas!, Unas fotos de las vacaciones, ¿Qué tal fue el viaje?, ¿Qué hicisteis?, Repaso: rutina diaria.
Copymasters 136–145

Tasks
Describing holidays/visits that you or others have undertaken and expressing opinions

Understanding other people talking about their holidays
Describing what the weather was like
Expressing preferences for different types of holiday.

Grammar points
Further practice of preterite of regular verbs
Pretérito grave

Productive language
adornos
alojarse
árbol de navidad
hacer una excursión en barco/en autocar
Navidad
Nochebuena
Nochevieja
Semana Santa

Receptive language
Reyes Magos
ruinas
santo

Revision points
Buying postcards and stamps
(*Libro 1, Unidad 5*)
Talking about daily routine
(*Libro 2, Unidad 3*)
Buying essential items
(*Libro 3, Unidad 5*)
Entertaining and being a guest
(*Libro 3, Unidad 11*)
Travelling by boat and plane
(*Libro 3, Unidad 14*)

Recuerdos (page 155)

Main aim
To understand, and wish to achieve, the unit goals.

A Work on this along lines which have previously proved successful.

B You describe previous holidays of your own. After each sentence the students say one of the following:
Describe sus vacaciones.
Habla del tiempo.

C Describe again past and future holidays, real or imagined. After each sentence the students say one of the following:
Habla del pasado.
Habla del futuro.

Extra vacaciones (page 155)

Main aim
Expressing preferences for different types of holiday.

A Present this grid on the board.
The students read the item and write key information in as many boxes as possible.

	¿Dónde?	¿Por qué?	¿Qué hicieron?	¿Su opinión?	¿El tiempo?
1					
2					
3					

Encourage the students to present, compare and discuss their answers.

UNIDAD 15

B Discuss with the students which of these holidays they would prefer and why.

C The students could interview their partners or other members of their group as if they were celebrities being interviewed for the magazine article. They could ask each other:
¿Adónde fuiste?
¿Por qué?
¿Qué sitios visitaste?
¿Qué cosas de interés viste?
¿Qué tal lo pasaste?

D The passages contain many examples of the first person singular and plural of the preterite. You could ask able pupils to pick out any verb forms which are different from the regular preterite forms, e.g. *fuimos, dimos, fui, hicimos, vi.* You can refer them to *A ser detective,* page 212 which deals with these verbs and others similar to them.

E You could cut from holiday brochures photos of different holiday destinations and display these in different parts of the classroom. Talk briefly about each one and ask the students to stand in front of the place they would like to go to. Ask them to say why they have chosen this destination and try to get each student to explain.

Las Navidades en España (page 156)

Main aim

Understanding about Christmas in Spain.

A The students read this to themselves and, with the help of a dictionary, answer the following questions.
1 *¿En qué día se celebra la fiesta de los Reyes Magos?* (2)
2 *¿Qué se bebe y qué se come normalmente, el seis de enero?* (2)
3 *El 5 de enero, ¿qué hay en el Parque del Retiro?* (2)
4 *¿Quién deja los regalos?* (1)
5 *La Nochebuena, ¿qué hace la familia de Jorge?* (3)
6 *Y, ¿qué hacen el 25 de diciembre?* (3)
7 *La Nochevieja, a medianoche, ¿qué suele hacer la gente?* (2)

Discuss their answers and clear up any problems.

B For homework, the students could write a summary, in English, of what happens in Spain over Christmas and the New Year. They could also find, and write down, the parts of the letter which relate to each of the drawings.

C Each student writes a list of the important words for talking about Christmas in Spain. To help them to learn these you could use the following activities: Draw on an OHP one of the items, e.g. a Christmas tree. Ask several students to say what it is. Ask one to come and write the Spanish word next to your drawing. When you have worked on several words, ask the students to make their own drawings and to label them.
The students work in pairs and use their drawings to teach the words to each other.

D The students use their new words to question you about Christmas in Spain and to find out as much as they can.

¡Felices Pascuas! (page 156)

Main aim

Talking about Christmas.

A The students read this and categorise each sentence. They then compare and discuss their answers.

B You say the sentences aloud. The students repeat only those which are true for them.

C Play these recordings. After hearing each one twice, the students note and report on the main facts. They then listen again and report on the opinions expressed. Clear up any problems.

¡Felices Pascuas!

Número 1
– A mí me encantan las Navidades. En Nochebuena comemos juntos en familia. Comemos pavo y besugo que es un pescado típico. El día de Navidad nos quedamos en casa normalmente. El año pasado fuimos a las Islas Canarias para celebrar el Año Nuevo en un hotel que tiene mi abuelo. ¡Qué bien!

Número 2
– Nosotros celebramos más el 6 de enero cuando se dan los regalos. Vivimos en Madrid y vamos a ver a

UNIDAD 15

los Reyes Magos en el Parque del Retiro. Me gusta el día de Navidad pero prefiero el 6 de enero.

Número 3

– Este año vamos a celebrar las Pascuas en Méjico. Mis tíos viven allí y nos han invitado. Vamos a pasar dos semanas. No sé qué tiempo hará pero espero que haga mejor tiempo que en España.

D Tell the class that they are going to talk about what they do at Christmas. They can listen again to the recordings and make notes of any expressions which they expect to be able to use or to adapt and use.

Using language from the recording and from page 156, the students say something about what they do at Christmas. This could be done first with the class and then in pairs. At home or in class, everyone could then write a paragraph or two about how they spend Christmas.

E Give everyone a copy of **copymaster 136**. Encourage the class to ask lots of questions to find out about the *Reyes Magos* and present-giving in Spain. They all then write a list of presents.

Una carta de una amiga (page 157)

Main aim

Reading and writing a letter about holidays.

A The students read the introduction to the letter and then read the letter to answer the questions. You could do this in exam conditions to develop exam skills.

B The students say as much as they can about each photo, using what is in the letter. Then give them two minutes to study the letter. They then cover it and talk about the photos again.

C You could base some verb circle practice on:
Decidieron ir a Asturias.
Pasamos ocho días allí.
Luego fuimos a Gijón.
Volvimos el miércoles.

D Ask students to answer Luisa's letter. Do this orally first and use the 'snowballing' technique. Then ask everyone to write an answer. This could be done at home.

Unas fotos de las vacaciones (page 158)

Main aim

Talking about past holidays.

A The students read this and ensure that they understand it. Ask questions about the photos and encourage the students to predict what the speakers will say.

B Play the tape and ask them to note down anything that they could not have found out from the photograph.

Unas fotos de las vacaciones
– ¿Adónde fuiste de vacaciones este año?
– Fuimos a Santander, mis padres y yo.
– ¿Y qué hiciste allí?
– Pasamos casi todo el día en la playa. Nos bañamos, tomamos el sol y jugamos a las palas.
– ¿Os alojasteis en un apartamento?
– No, fuimos a un hotel en el Sardinero.
– Os gustó, ¿no?
– Pues sí. Había una piscina y un restaurante muy bueno.
– ¿Comisteis mucho allí?
– Sí, todas las tardes.
– ¿Qué lugares de interés visitasteis?
– Visitamos el puerto pesquero, fuimos a Reinosa y Fuente Dé.
– ¿Lo pasasteis bien, entonces?
– Hombre, ¡estupendo!

C You can either prepare the work on the photos as a class activity or let the pairs develop their own dialogue. Ask for pairs of students to go through their dialogues and compare them with those of others.

D Invite volunteers to give an oral presentation to the class based on these photos. Some students may wish to prepare a presentation on past and future holidays. They could write these and then learn by heart the corrected version. You could practise these regularly.

UNIDAD 15

¿Qué tal fue el viaje? (page 159)

Main aim
Describing a journey.

A The students read this and ensure that they understand it.

B The students listen to the Spanish people being interviewed and note down the main facts about their journey.

¿Qué tal fue el viaje?
- Buenos días. Bienvenidos a nuestro hotel. Soy el representante de la compañía Brittany Ferries.
- ¡Ah! Buenos días.
- Quisiera hacer unas preguntas sobre su viaje. ¿Me hacen el favor de ayudarme?
- Sí, sí, por supuesto. De acuerdo.
- ¿De dónde son Vds?
- Somos de Madrid pero pasamos las vacaciones en Londres y volvemos a Madrid mañana.
- … vacaciones en Londres. ¿Cuándo empezaron Vds. el viaje?
- Salimos de nuestro hotel a las ocho.
- … a las ocho. ¿Y cómo fueron Vds. al puerto?
- En autocar desde Londres a Plymouth.
- … desde Londres a Plymouth. ¿Cuánto tiempo duró el viaje?
- Seis horas, ¿no?
- Sí, seis horas.
- … seis horas. ¿Cómo fue el viaje en barco?
- Nos gustó mucho.
- ¿Cómo pasaron Vds. el tiempo?
- Bueno, jugamos a las cartas, leímos …
- Fuimos a bailar por la tarde.
- Exacto.
- … cartas, lectura, baile. Bueno, gracias. ¡Qué lo pasen bien aquí en el hotel!

C They then look at the prompt that has been written to enable them to answer the interview questions. Practise the questions individually at first.

D The students work in pairs to produce a similar dialogue to the one they heard. You might like to repeat the dialogue before they prepare theirs in order to give them more guidance.

E At home or in class, each student could write an advertisement for a journey to a holiday destination.

¿Qué hicisteis? (page 160)

Main aim
Talking and writing about a holiday.

A Look through the diary entries and ask questions about them:
¿Qué hicieron el lunes?
¿Encontraron a sus amigos antes o después de visitar el museo?

B Then ask questions as if you were the Spanish friend asking the person who has written the diary:
¿Qué hicimos el viernes? ¿Fuimos al parque?

C Ask them to look at the diary while listening to the tape and to listen out for any discrepancies. The students could draw up a blank of the page and note down all that his/her friend says and then compare notes afterwards. If they do this you will need to stop the tape more frequently.

¿Qué hicisteis?
- ¿Qué hicisteis en Santander?
- Bueno, pues el lunes … fuimos en autocar a Altamira. Vimos las pinturas prehistóricas. El martes, mmm … ¿qué hicimos? Ah sí, fuimos a ver un partido de pelota vasca en Bilbao.
- ¿Le gustó a tu corresponsal?
- Sí, pero no sé si lo entendió todo. El miércoles, poca cosa, creo que dimos un paseo por la bahía. El jueves visitamos el Museo de Arte Moderno y nos reunimos con amigos. El sábado fuimos a casa de unos amigos.
- ¿Y el viernes?
- No sé, fuimos a la piscina me parece. y el domingo, mmm … vimos un partido estupendo en el estadio. Ganó Santander 3 a 0.

D Writing activity.
The pupils write a similar diary to the one on page 160. The activity can be practised with the whole class first; students saying what they did or writing down sentences on the board or OHP.

E You could base some verb circle practice on:
Hicimos una excursión en autocar.
Dimos un paseo por el parque.
Jugamos al tenis.
Vimos una película.

UNIDAD 15

Una palabra conduce a otra (page 160)

Main aim

To develop communication strategies and to extend vocabulary.

Work on this along lines which have previously proved successful.

¿Qué tal el tiempo? (page 161)

Main aim

Describing what the weather was like.

A The students read this and ensure that they understand it.

B They say who said each of the weather sentences. You could read some aloud and the students could argue about who said it. They could continue this in pairs.

C Present **copymaster 137** on OHP and ask the students to comment on each picture. Encourage them to express an opinion, e.g.
¡Qué desastre! Hubo niebla.

You could use the OHT to play at *Repite si es verdad* and Noughts and crosses. You could also point to a picture and ask a student, e.g.
¿Qué tal fue el tiempo?
Then ask what s/he did, e.g.
¿Qué hiciste?
The student thinks up an appropriate activity.

Unas tarjetas postales (page 161)

Main aim

Reading and writing holiday postcards.

A The students read and understand this.

B They write similar information about real or imaginary holidays. Point out the useful expressions of time: *ayer*, *por la tarde*, *esta mañana* and encourage them to mention the weather (at least once), what they did and what the accommodation was like.

C It would be a good idea to learn by heart a holiday postcard text for exam purposes.

Unas vacaciones malísimas (page 162)

Main aim

Understanding a letter about holidays.

A The students read the introduction and the advertisement. They speculate about what will be in the letter. They then read the letter to check. Ask students to report to the class and encourage discussion.

B To compare the advertisement and the reality, the students write each line of the advert on the left of a page and then, opposite it, what the letter says. Again, encourage them to compare and discuss their notes.

C Each student writes, in English, what they would tell their parents.

Ahora sé (page 163)

Main aim

To summarise the unit and provide a basis for more practice and revision.

A Alone, and then in pairs, the students work on this using their favourite techniques.

B Either now, or later for revision, you could use the following activities:
Give everyone a copy of **copymaster 138** to work on in class or at home.
Give everyone a copy of **copymaster 139**. The students use this to carry out a survey in the class. They then report on the results and compare them with the Spanish results.
Give everyone a copy of **copymaster 140**. The students study the two postcards and then write one of their own.
Ask students to write a list of 8–10 people they have sent cards to over the past year. They write

UNIDAD 15

person's name, the relationship, the date and what they wrote, e.g.

Ana – mi hermana – el 25 de diciembre – ¡Feliz Navidad!

Revision activities

1 Buying postcards and stamps
(Libro 1, Unidad 5)

A Encourage the students to look back at this *Unidad* of *Libro 1* and to revise it.

B Give everyone a copy of **copymaster 141**. They work on Activity 1 in pairs and on Activity 2 individually.

C Give everyone a copy of **copymaster 142**. They work on it in pairs.

2 Talking about daily routine
(Libro 2, Unidad 3)

A Encourage the students to look back at this *Unidad* of *Libro 2* and to revise it.

B Play this recording. The students note what the boy and girl do. They then compare the two and draw appropriate conclusions.

Repaso: rutina diaria
- ¿Qué haces tú en un día normal?
- Me levanto a las ocho. Me visto y preparo el desayuno. Después ayudo a mi madre en la cocina y voy de compras. Como, y voy al parque con mi hermano menor. Sólo tiene dos años. Por la tarde preparo la cena y después veo la televisión y me acuesto temprano, a eso de las once. ¿Y tú?
- Me levanto a las once. Voy a un bar a tomar un café y unas tostadas. Como en casa y luego salgo otra vez. Por la tarde juego al tenis o al baloncesto y ceno en casa.
- ¿No haces nada para ayudar en casa?
- No. ¿Por qué?

C Each student prepares an oral presentation about their daily routine. In groups, they perform these, discuss them and draw appropriate conclusions.

3 Buying essential items
(Libro 3, Unidad 5)

A The students revise *Unidad 5* and especially page 63.

B Give everyone a copy of **copymaster 143** for them to work on at home.

4 Entertaining, and being, a guest
(Libro 3, Unidad 11)

A The students revise *Unidad 11* and especially page 125.

B Give everyone a copy of **copymaster 144**. They work on this in pairs.

5 Travelling by boat and plane
(Libro 3, Unidad 14)

A The students revise *Unidad 14* and especially page 154.

B Give everyone a copy of **copymaster 145**. They could work on this at home.

UNIDAD 16

Dice la ley

Main aim
Dealing with regulations and crime.

Area(s) of experience
E – The international world

Materials
Cassette: Las reglas del tráfico, ¡Pues, no lo sabía!, El policía te explica, ¡Atención, por favor!, He oído en la radio, Repaso: en el café. Copymasters 146–155

Tasks
Understanding and explaining regulations and road signs
Dealing with minor traffic offences
Understanding news reports of crimes
Reporting a theft and describing the suspects

Grammar
Pluperfect tense

Productive language
aparcar
denuncia
ladrón
multa
robar
testigo
bloquear
detener
lugar
peatón
sospechoso
víctima

Receptive language
acceso
atentado
atraco
ceder el paso
crimen
denunciar
estacionamiento
evitar
infracción
ley
asesinato
atracador
bigote
circular
delincuente
escaparate
estacionar
excesivo
letrero
obligatorio
prensa
regla
relato
señales de tráfico
uso
ratero
relatar
robo
terrorista
vigilante

Revision points
Buying snacks in a café
(*Libro 1, Unidad 6*)
Asking for, and understanding, information about hotels
(*Libro 2, Unidad 5*)
Eating at someone's house
(*Libro 3, Unidad 6*)
Using public transport
(*Libro 3, Unidad 12*)
Describing past holidays
(*Libro 3, Unidad 15*)

Dice la ley (page 164)

Main aim
To understand, and wish to achieve, the unit goals.

A Work on this along lines which have previously proved successful.

B Present **copymaster 146** on OHP. The students find the words from this item in their book to complete the text, orally first and then in writing.
The missing words are: *leyes, ley, reglas, prensa, entender, crimen, describir*.

Las reglas del tráfico (page 164)

Main aim
To develop listening and speaking skills.

A Give the students one minute only to read and understand this item. Allow them to use a dictionary if they need to, but still only allow one minute. This sort of practice will be extremely useful for exams.

B The students cover up the seven sentences, and look at the pictures. You say the sentences and the students write the letter of the matching pictures.

C The students read again the instructions for the listening exercise. They look at the first picture and guess what the police officer might say. Encourage them to use their imaginations!

D Play the first recording and discuss how close the students came to guessing what would be said. Then play it again and ask the students to note, and then report on, the facts. Clear up any problems and play it again, asking the students to note, and then report on, the attitudes of the police officer and the motorist. Finally, play the recording again and ask the students to note the key language used.

UNIDAD 16

use their notes to role play the scene in pairs, taking turns to play each role. Then work on the other recordings in the same way.

Las reglas del tráfico

Número 1
- Oiga señora. No se puede pasar.
- ¿Por qué?
- Porque la calle está bloqueada.
- Vale.

Número 2
- Señor, el límite de velocidad es 90 kilómetros por hora. Usted iba demasiado de prisa.
- ¿Sí?

Número 3
- Usted no puede pasar por aquí. El acceso está prohibido.
- ¿Por qué?
- Porque es sentido único.
- No lo sabía.

Número 4
- Señor. Iba usted a una velocidad excesiva.
- No es verdad. Tenía prisa pero ...
- Usted iba a 170, ¿No es una velocidad excesiva?
- Sí, pero ...

Número 5
- ¿Señor, no sabía usted que está aparcado en una parada de autobús?
- Sí, pero ...
- El coche está aparcado en lugar prohibido y le tengo que poner una multa.
- No lo creo.

Número 6
- Mira lo que dice 'Estacionamiento prohibido'.
- Sólo fui a esta tienda a comprar pan.
- Prohibido significa prohibido.

Número 7
- Buenos días, señora. Lo siento pero hay que dar la vuelta.
- Pero vivo en esta calle.
- Lo siento pero no se puede pasar.

¡Pues, no lo sabía! (page 165)

Main aim
To develop listening and speaking skills.

A Give the students just two minutes to read and understand this, using a dictionary only if they have to.

B The students guess what the police officers said for each one. Again, encourage them to be imaginative!

C Play the recordings and ask the students to write the number of the reply which goes best with each one. Clear up any problems.

¡Pues, no lo sabía!
- Mire señor, están prohibidas las señales acústicas después de medianoche.
- Señora, es obligatorio llevar el disco en esta zona.
- Señor, ésta es una zona reglamentada.
- ¡Eh, se prohibe dar la vuelta aquí!
- Señorita, ésta prohibido estacionar delante del Ayuntamiento.
- ¡Está prohibido hacer más de 120 kilómetros por hora en esta carretera!
- ¡Eh! ¡Hay un desvío! ¿No ve Vd?
- Mire señora, hay que circular por la izquierda en esta parte de la calle.

D Play the tape again and ask the students to respond orally to the police officer, saying one of the responses in their book. They then close their books, listen again and make an appropriate response to each police officer.

El policía te explica (page 165)

Main aim
To develop listening skills.

A Give the students one minute only to read this and to ensure that they understand it.

B Play the first recording and ask the students to note, and then report on, what the driver did. Play it again and ask the students to note, and then report on, if the motorist had to pay a fine and how much. Play it again and ask the students to note, and report on, what the motorist had to do. Then play it once more and ask the students to report on all three questions. Repeat this with the other recordings.

El policía te explica
- Oiga, está Vd. aparcado delante de la entrada de este almacén e impidiendo el paso a otros

UNIDAD 16

vehículos. Haga el favor de aparcar en el lugar debido, o me obligará a ponerle una multa.
– ¿Se da Vd. cuenta de dónde ha aparcado y de que son las diez de la mañana? Como puede ver en el cartel, esto está prohibido de ocho de la mañana a seis de la tarde. La multa es de 3.000 pesetas pero serán sólo 500 si paga ahora.
– Está Vd. conduciendo a una velocidad excesiva, por lo menos a cien kilómetros por hora. El límite aquí es de ochenta, o sea, que tendrá que pagar una multa de 5.000 pesetas, o bien, de 800 si la paga ahora.
– Mire, Vd. ha conducido a través de esta calle que es de sentido único y en dirección contraria. Dé la vuelta y no le pondré multa.
– Oiga, está Vd. aparcado en el paso de peatones. Haga el favor de retirar el coche: si lo hace ahora mismo no tendrá que pagar nada.
– Mire, ha hecho una maniobra arriesgada dando la vuelta aquí en medio de la carretera. Esto no se puede hacer. Tendrá Vd. que pagar 6.000 pesetas por el peligro que esto implica.

C Revise the unit so far to ensure that the students learn the key vocabulary, e.g.
List 10 key words and give the students two minutes to copy them and to write, next to each one, the English equivalent.
Write a key word on the board, e.g. *Prohibido*. Then think of another key word which shares a letter with *Prohibido*. Give a clue to help the students to guess this word, e.g.
Es alguien que anda a pie en la ciudad.

The student who guesses *peatón* comes to the board and writes the word so that it crosses *Prohibido*, e.g.

PROHIBIDO
E
A
T
O
N

Continue along these lines and build up a crossword on the board.

Sancho y Panza (page 165)

Main aim
To use language imaginatively.

A Give students a minute to read and understand this.

B In pairs, the students try to make up their own dialogues. Ask students to read out their dialogues. The others listen and try to imagine the scene.

Más excusas (page 166)

Main aim
Dealing with minor traffic offences.

A Give the students two minutes to read and understand this, using a dictionary if necessary.

B Work with the class on the excuses. Ask them first what they think of each excuse and then what a police officer would probably think of it. Then ask them to match each excuse with one of the problems.

C Now would be a good time to work on *A ser detective*, page 214.

D Return to this item and work again, quickly, on Activities **A** and **B** above. The students then practise the model dialogue in pairs.

E The students prepare for the role play tasks, with the help of a dictionary, as they would in an exam. Give them five minutes to do this. In pairs, they then do the role plays. You could move around, listening and helping.

¡Atención por favor! (page 166)

Main aim
Understanding and explaining announcements.

A The students read the instructions and ensure that they understand them.

B Play the first announcement and ask the students to say where they would hear it. Then play it again and ask them to explain to their partners, and to you, what the announcement said. Then play it once more and ask the students to try to write down any words which they had difficulty in understanding, and to look up these words in a dictionary. The ability to do this successfully can

UNIDAD 16

be extremely useful in exams and in real life. Repeat this process with the other recordings.

¡Atención por favor!
- Los señores pasajeros con destino a Sevilla vayan al andén número tres por favor.
- Se avisa a los señores pasajeros que no deben dejar su equipaje sin vigilar.
- Ultima llamada para el vuelo número IB206 de Iberia, con destino a Londres. Los pasajeros para este vuelo deben ir a la puerta número nueve.
- Se ruega al señor Smith, pasajero del Canadá, que vaya a la oficina de Air Canadá, donde le espera su colega señor Johnson.
- ¡Atención! Se ruega al conductor del coche matriculado M 7428 GD lo mueva en seguida pues está bloqueando la salida. Gracias.
- Atención por favor. Se ha encontrado un niño de unos dos años, vestido de rojo, ojos castaños y pelo moreno. Rogamos a los padres de este niño vayan a Información para recogerle. Gracias.
- ¡Barco once! ¡Barco once! Por favor regrese inmediatamente, se le ha acabado el tiempo.
- ¡Atención! ¡Atención, por favor! Avisamos al público que este parque de atracciones va a cerrar dentro de diez minutos. Por favor encamínense hacia las salidas. Gracias.

C Revise the unit so far to ensure that the students learn the key language, e.g.
Write ten key words on the board and give the class one minute to memorise them. Point to one of them and then rub it out. The students write the word. Repeat this with the other words. You could use phrases instead of words.
Prepare some cards, each with a word or a picture on it. A student chooses one, (e.g. with '*Una carta*' written on it), at random, and says what s/he did last night, involving what is on the card, e.g.
Comí una carta anoche.

Encourage them to say something unusual and unexpected. The others then guess why the student did this, e.g.

¿Tenías mucha hambre?
¿No habías comido nada?
¿Habías recibido una carta muy secreta?
¿Creías que era una tableta de chocolate?

¡Más reglas! (page 167)

Main aim
Understanding and explaining more signs and notices.

A Give the students just two minutes to read and understand these signs and notices, under exam conditions. To check their work, ask some students to explain some of them to you and clear up any problems. They then all explain all of them to their partners.

B Ask where each of these signs would be found and encourage the students to think of as many answers as possible for each. You could then reverse this. Say the name of a place and ask students to read aloud the notice(s) they might see there, e.g.

En la playa.
En el parque.
En una estación RENFE.
En un albergue.

Breves (page 167)

Main aim
Understanding newspaper reports of crimes.

Use this item to give important practice on how to tackle an exam question effectively, e.g.
1 Study the questions carefully and ensure you understand them.
2 Seek the answers in the texts and ignore anything in the texts not needed for the answers. Use communication strategies other than the use of a dictionary as much as possible, to save time.
3 Keep the answers as short and simple as possible. Use a dictionary, if there is time, to check spellings in the answers.

The students should aim to do the above in six minutes. Check their answers and clear up any problems.

UNIDAD 16

He oído en la radio (page 168)

Main aim
To develop reading and listening skills.

A Work on one article at a time. The students first read it, with the help of a dictionary, and a time limit of one minute. They then listen to the recording and note any differences. They listen again to check and then write their notes in full, checking their notes with a dictionary.

Vandalismo en el colegio
Newspaper: damage to the laboratory.
Radio: damage to the music room.
Newspaper: six children aged 9–10.
Radio: seven children aged 8–9.

Robo de joyas
Newspaper: door leading to offices forced.
Radio: window at back of shop forced.

Herido por arma blanca
Newspaper: attack took place on Sunday.
Radio: attack took place on Saturday.

Roba la moto que iba a comprar
Newspaper: Yamaha 200.000 pts.
Radio: Suzuki 210.000 pts.

B The students close their book and, using only their notes, respond to what the speakers on the recording say.

C Finally, the students listen again and write a short account of what happened, for their Spanish friend.

He oído en la radio
– Y ahora unos breves reportajes sobre incidentes que han tenido lugar en nuestra región:
– En el Colegio Nacional Luis de Góngora, Calle de Chantada, han sido causados muchos destrozos en la sala de música. Los autores de esta destrucción son siete chicos menores de edad; de ocho y nueve años. El director estima que los daños sobrepasan el medio millón de pesetas.
– Y en la Calle Costa Rica una joyería sufrió un robo de joyas valoradas en más de trece millones de pesetas. Fuentes de la Comisaría de Chamartín nos dicen que los ladrones entraron forzando una de las ventanas en la parte trasera del edificio.
– Un joven de 18 años, Pedro Luis Buiza Fernández, fue atacado el pasado sábado por dos desconocidos cerca de la vía del tren. Después se trasladó a un bar en la avenida de Entrevías a pedir ayuda, y desde allá fue trasladado directamente al Hospital Provincial.
– Y finalmente, ¡cuidado si Vd quiere vender su moto! Un señor residente en nuestra ciudad puso un anuncio en la prensa local para vender la suya; vino un joven que quería probarla. Y la probó, ¡que sí la probó! ¡No la devolvió! La moto era una Suzuki, y tenía valor de doscientas diez mil pesetas.
– Hay que ver, que la gente sí tiene chispa, ¿eh? Cuidado, cuidado.

El testigo (page 169)

Main aim
Understanding and writing an account of a crime.

A To give more important exam practice, work on this along the lines suggested for *Breves*, on page 167.

B Present the brief below on the board or OHP:
Dos amigos iban al partido de fútbol.
Vieron a dos hombres que salían de un banco.
Llevaban un bolso lleno de dinero.
Iban en moto. Llevaban pantalón y chaqueta de cuero.
Llegaron los policías.
Uno de los atracadores había dejado caer su billetero. Un amigo lo vio en el suelo.
Dieron el monedero a los policías.
Recibieron una recompensa.

The students adapt the letter to produce an account in line with this brief. This could be done orally first, with 'snowballing', and then written.

El atraco (page 170)

Main aim
Reporting an attempted theft.

A Give the students just two minutes to read and understand this, using a dictionary if they need to. Then give them three minutes to prepare their answers to the questions, again using a dictionary if they need to, but sparingly.

UNIDAD 16

B In pairs, they practise asking and answering the question, helping each other to produce good and accurate answers. You then put the questions to the class, using the 'snowballing' technique and clear up any problems. The students then practise these again, in pairs.

¿Y si eres tú la víctima? (page 170)

Main aim
Reporting a theft and describing the suspects.

A The students read this in three minutes and ensure that they understand it.

B They practise the model dialogue in pairs, playing each part in turns.

C In pairs, they adapt the model dialogue to report the thefts outlined in the notes.

D Each student writes an account of the two thefts. To help with this, where necessary, you could present a C–test of the first account on the board or OHP. You could work on this orally first, with the class, and clear up any problems. The students then write this account in full and then adapt that to write the second account.
Yo estaba en la cal_ cerca del merc_ . Un rat_ se acercó y cogió mi bol_ . Eran las tres de la tar_ aproximadamente y acababa de salir del ba_ . El rat_ era al_ y moreno y llev_ una chaqueta neg_ y vaqu_ .

La cuarta persona (page 171)

Main aim
Describing a suspect.

A The students read the description and compare it with the photograph. You could get them to do this orally first and clear up any problems before they write it, and ask some questions, e.g.
El chico de la foto, ¿llevaba la misma ropa?
¿Se vestía de la misma manera en la foto?

B As students complete the task above, they write the a brief list of the differences between the account and the photograph.

El retrato robot (page 171)

Main aim
Describing a suspect.

A Ask the students questions about the *ratero*, e.g.
¿Cómo es el hombre: joven o viejo?
¿Cuántos años tiene, más o menos?
¿Lleva el pelo largo o corto?
¿Tiene bigote o barba?
¿Es rubio o moreno?

B The students then ask each other questions in order to elicit the answers which would have been required for the composition of the identikit picture.

Una palabra conduce a otra (page 171)

Main aim
To develop communication strategies and to extend vocabulary.

A Work on this along lines which have previously proved successful.

B Present more examples on the board, e.g.
encantador, mirador, hablador, corredor, bebedor, liberador, narrador, limpiador.

Give the students five minutes to copy these, to write the English equivalent with each and the infinitive of the matching verb. They should try to do this without using a dictionary.

Ahora sé (page 172)

Main aim
To provide a summary of the *Unidad* and a basis for more practice and revision.

UNIDAD 16

A The students work on this, individually and in pairs, using their favourite techniques.

B Either now, or later for revision, you could use the following:

Give everyone a copy of **copymaster 147**. They could read this, and prepare their answers, at home. You could then ask the questions in class and discuss the answers. While working on this quiz, you could also use the distractors (e.g. with number 7), e.g.

¿Quién había escrito 'Don Quijote', en 1605?
¿Los discos de quién habían tenido un éxito internacional, en 1984?

You could use this opportunity to revise the pluperfect tense and have some verb circle practice based on, e.g.

Había escrito una carta.
Había visto un ladrón.
Habían bloqueado el camino.
Había pagado una multa.

Give everyone a copy of **copymaster 148**. They could work on this in class or at home.
N.B. *Martes trece* is the Spanish equivalent of Friday 13th.

Revision activities

1 Buying snacks in a café
(Libro 1, Unidad 6)

Play these recordings and ask the students to write the customers' orders.

Repaso: en el café

Número 1
- Buenos días.
- Buenos días.
- ¿Qué va a tomar?
- Un té con limón y un bocadillo.
- ¿De queso, jamón o atún?
- De jamón.
- Muy bien.

Número 2
- Camarero.
- Sí, señor.
- Una cerveza y una hamburguesa, por favor.
- Lo siento, no hay hamburguesas.
- ¿Hay perritos calientes?
- Sí.
- Entonces, un perrito caliente.
- Vale.

Número 3
- Buenas tardes. ¿Qué desea?
- Dos cafés con leche.
- Lo siento, no hay leche.
- Bueno, dos cafés.
- ¿Algo más?
- Sí, tráigame un vaso de agua.
- Vale, muy bien.

Número 4
- Camarero. Tráigame dos Coca-Colas y dos helados.
- Hay helados de vainilla, fresa, chocolate, café, limón …
- Uno de fresa y otro de chocolate.
- Muy bien.

Número 5
- Tráigame dos cervezas, un vino tinto y una agua mineral con gas.
- ¿Algo más?
- Sí, tres bocadillos de queso.
- Así que son una cerveza, dos vinos tintos …
- No, dos cervezas, un vino tinto y una agua mineral con gas.
- Sí.

2 Asking for, and understanding, information about hotels
(Libro 2, Unidad 5)

A Give each student a copy of **copymaster 149** to work on in class or at home.

B Give abler students a copy of **copymaster 150** for them to work on in pairs.

3 Eating at someone's house
(Libro 3, Unidad 6)

A The students revise *Unidad 6*. You could use now any activities suggested for the *Unidad* which you have not used before.

B Give everyone a copy of **copymaster 151**. They could work on this in class or at home and either write the answers or discuss them in class and in pairs.

UNIDAD 16

4 Using public transport
(Libro 3, Unidad 12)

A The students revise *Unidad 12* and you could introduce activities suggested with the unit which you have not used before.

B Give everyone one half of **copymaster 152** for them to work on in pairs.

C Give everyone a copy of **copymaster 153** for them to work on in pairs.

5 Describing past holidays
(Libro 3, Unidad 15)

A Revise *Unidad 15*, using favourite techniques and activities suggested with the unit but not previously used.

B Give students **copymasters 154** and **155** for them to work on at home.

UNIDAD 17

Los exámenes y después

Main aim
To talk about examinations and career plans.

Area(s) of experience
B – Personal and social life
D – The world of work
E – The international world

Materials
Cassette: Los exámenes y después, Hablan tus amigos, Necesitamos personal, ¿Qué harías tú?, Si no hubiera trabajo, Repaso: ¿tiene una habitación, por favor?
Copymasters 156–165

Tasks
Expressing opinions about school
Understanding, asking for and giving reasons for choice of study or training
Expressing hopes for the future, plans for the immediate future and after completion of study
Understanding and giving opinions about different jobs including advantages and disadvantages
Making a simple application for a job in Spain

Grammar
Conditional tense

Productive language
aire libre   ambicioso
apetecer   castigar
creativo   examen
ganar la vida   intelectual
rutinario   tener ganas de
variado

Receptive language
azafata   bachillerato
se busca   cajero(a)

carrera   cocinero
comprensivo   deportista
diseñador   enfermera
fotógrafo   informe
ingeniero   letras
lotería   maestra
músico   necesitar
paro/en paro   piloto
psicólogo   representante
sueldo   suspender
valorar

Revision points
Buying presents and souvenirs
(*Libro 1, Unidad 7*)
Booking into a hotel
(*Libro 2, Unidad 5*)
Using telephones and faxes
(*Libro 3, Unidad 7*)
Television and the media
(*Libro 3, Unidad 13*)
Crime and the law
(*Libro 3, Unidad 16*)

Los exámenes y después (page 173)

Main aim
To understand, and wish to achieve, the unit goals.

A Work on this along lines which have proved successful.

B The students listen to these recorded exchanges and categorise each one according to the language task it exemplifies.

Los exámenes y después

Número 1
– ¿Qué quieres hacer?
– Me gustaría ser profesor.

Número 2
– ¿Te gustaría ser mecánico?
– No, es demasiado sucio – el aceite, no, no me gustaría.

Número 3
– ¿Qué hace tu padre?
– Es periodista en Madrid.

Número 4
– ¿Qué vas a hacer después de los exámenes?
– Voy a ir a Escocia a ver a un amigo.
– ¿Cuánto tiempo vas a estar?
– Dos semanas.

Número 5
– ¿Te gustaría continuar tus estudios el año que viene?
– Sí, voy a continuar dos años más.
– Yo también.

Número 6
– ¿Es difícil encontrar trabajo en tu pueblo?
– Muy difícil: no hay fábricas; muchos jóvenes no trabajan.

C You could adapt the examples in the item on page 173 and encourage the students to do the same, e.g.

UNIDAD 17

Me gusta el colegio, sobre todo el sábado.
Los exámenes empiezan en dos meses.
Me gustaría ser taxista y viajar mucho.
Se necesita chico para trabajo de vendedor.

Estudiar o trabajar; ésa es la cuestión (page 173)

Main aim

To develop reading skills and to present some key vocabulary.

A Give the students one minute to read and understand the introduction, using a dictionary if they need to.

B Give the students four minutes to read the section on the ideal teacher and to pick out and note down the main features. Allow them to use a dictionary. Then ask students to tell you what they have noted down, discuss their ideas and clear up any problems. Repeat this procedure with the section on the ideal student.

C The students write the characteristics of the ideal teacher and student in order of importance. They compare and discuss their lists in pairs and then in class. The words they should pick out are:
Profesor – comprensivo, autoritario, didáctico, afectivo, cordial, entusiasta, organizador, atlético, fuerte, guapo, elegante, divertido, gracioso, optimista, original, abierto, cercano, democrático y exigente.
Alumno – normal, equilibrado, sincero, inconformista, participativo, inteligente, simpático, comprometido, responsable, amable, interesado, inquieto y preguntón.

The activity could develop in a number of ways. The class could discuss the findings and work out together what their ideal would be or individuals could be asked to write out a *retrato robot* of either the ideal teacher/student or the opposite.

Unas preguntas (page 174)

Main aim

Discussing plans for the future.

A Give the students two minutes to read and understand this, using a dictionary if they need to.

B You put the questions orally, to a few students, using the 'snowballing' technique. Then each student prepares her/his own answers and they practise asking and answering the questions in pairs, helping each other to produce the best possible answers.

C Put the questions to the class again and, from time to time, ask some unexpected questions relevant to this topic. This will help the students to expect to have to answer unplanned questions in a conversation. To give further practice in this, the students all prepare 6–8 relevant questions of their own on this topic and put them to each other.

La letra con sangre entra (page 175)

Main aim

Understanding and writing a letter about exams and future plans.

A In exam conditions, the students have eight minutes to read this and to find and write the answers. You could rehearse key strategies for doing this before they start, e.g. starting with reading the questions carefully, looking for the information needed to answer these and ignoring other parts of the text, using a dictionary only when necessary.

B Ask several students to say their answers. Discuss these and clear up any problems.

C Plan a reply to the letter with the class, again rehearsing appropriate exam techniques, e.g. using as much from the stimulus letter as possible, making sure to answer all the questions asked, asking a few questions of your own, including an opinion and a reason for it, and referring to past, present and future. Each student then writes an answer. This could be done at home.

UNIDAD 17

Unos jóvenes de categoría (page 176)

Main aim
Discussing the advantages and disadvantages of different occupations.

A The students begin by reading and understanding the introduction and questions, in exam conditions.

B They each select three or four texts to read, read them and write notes to answer the four questions. In class, ask students to say which jobs they chose to read about and to read out their answers. Ask all those who have read about the same job to compare and discuss their answers. Encourage them to respond personally and to discuss their own reactions to each job. They could soon do this in pairs along the lines suggested by the model dialogue.

C The students can then assume one of the roles and their partners can ask questions based on those posed in the book, e.g.
¿Cómo empezaste? ¿y cuándo?

D Finally, the students can discuss with their partners whether they would like to do any of the jobs featured.

Hablan tus amigos (page 176)

Main aim
To understand people discussing the future and expressing opinions about different jobs.

A The students read the instructions. Ensure that they have understood them and discuss appropriate exam strategies.

B Present this grid on the board or OHP and ensure that everyone understands it. Again discuss exam strategies relevant to completing a grid like this.

	Elena	Mónica	Pili	Alfonso
Edad				
Edad que va a dejar el colegio				
Carrera				
Calificaciones				
Más información				

C Play the interview with Elena and get the students to complete the grid for her, in exam conditions. Discuss their answers and clear up any problems. Work on the others in turn and aim to help the students to improve with each one. The exercise calls for certain communication strategies to be used to identify certain words which the students have not met, such as: *carrera, psicólogo/ psicología, periodismo, diseño gráfico, deportista, letras*. Some of the words have English cognates: *letras, psicólogo/psicología, diseño gráfico*. Others are derived from known Spanish words: *periodismo, deportista*. A third group of words can be worked out from the verbal context, for example, *carrera*.

Hablan tus amigos
– Elena, ¿qué quieres hacer?
– Pues, yo tengo quince años y voy a continuar aquí hasta los diecinueve años más o menos.
– ¿Qué quieres hacer en la vida?
– Hombre, pues yo quiero seguir estudiando.
– ¿Te interesa trabajar en una oficina, por ejemplo?
– No, ¡qué va! Me gustaría ejercer la carrera que he estudiado.
– ¿Qué carrera es?, ¿es en ciencias o en letras?
– Psicología.
– Te gustaría ser psicólogo?
– Sí.
– Y cuántos años de estudio te hacen falta?
– Cinco.
– Entonces tendrás como 23 o 24 años al terminar, ¿no?
– Sí, por ahí.
– Y, ¿no molesta estudiar tanto tiempo?
– Hombre, sí, me molesta pero hay que hacerlo.
– Mónica, y tú, ¿qué piensas hacer?
– Pues yo voy a continuar hasta que acabe, creo que será a los 18, 19 años y, después de eso, intentaré hacer una carrera o algo para luego trabajar. Lo malo es que hay mucho paro.
– ¿Qué tipo de estudios? ¿Ciencias o letras?

UNIDAD 17

- Quiero hacer letras.
- Y después, ¿qué te interesa hacer, periodismo?
- No sé, todavía no lo he pensado. A mí lo que siempre me ha gustado es pintar, dibujar.
- Entonces es diseño, diseño gráfico te interesaría quizás.
- Sí, sí.
- Y Miguel, ¿qué te interesaría a tí?
- Querría hacer una carrera en letras pero no sé qué.
- ¿Qué te apetecería?
- Estudiar idiomas, francés e inglés.
- Sí.
- Pero me sale muy mal.
- Es decir que no se le dan bien los idiomas.
- No, pero me gustaría estudiar inglés sobre todo.
- ¿Y estudias otros idiomas?
- No. A lo mejor podría estudiar francés más tarde pero no sé.
- Alfonso, ¿qué te gustaría hacer?
- Todavía no he elegido una carrera fija para estudiar, no sé más.
- Y, ¿hasta qué edad vas a continuar aquí?
- Hasta que termine a los dieciocho años.
- ¿Y qué piensas hacer después, salir de Madrid o quedarte aquí?
- No sé. Buscar trabajo.
- Y ¿qué tipo de trabajo te gustaría?
- El que salga.
- ¿Algo especial?
- No, bueno hombre ... me gustaría ser deportista.
- Ah, y ¿qué deportes se te dan bien?
- Judo y nada más.
- Y ¿qué importancia tiene una carrera?
- Depende de quien sea. Hay distintas opiniones. Para mi el trabajo, pues, no sé.
- ¿Trabajarás porque quieres trabajar o porque tienes que trabajar?
- Se tiene que trabajar porque si no ...

Cada oveja ... (page 177)

Main aim
Understanding job adverts and people expressing opinions about jobs.

A The students could again read the instructions in exam conditions and discuss appropriate exam strategies.

B They match the adverts to the people and then present and justify their choices.

C Ask the students to explain each advert, in English.

D Give out copies of **copymaster 156**. Ask them to read through the adverts and then to listen to Spanish people talking about what they would like to do. They have to find one or more suitable jobs for each person.

Necesitamos personal

Número 1
- Bueno, a mí me gustaría trabajar en una oficina, utilizar mis idiomas.

Número 2
- Me interesa la idea de viajar. Hablo francés e inglés y, a lo mejor, serían útiles para mí.

Número 3
- Mis padres son alemanes así que hablo bastante bien el idioma. Yo busco trabajo para ganar experiencia y poder seguir con mis estudios.

Número 4
- Yo querría ser representante. Tengo poca experiencia, casi ninguna si digo la verdad, pero tengo cierta ambición y estoy dispuesta a trabajar duro.

Número 5
- He trabajado en la electrónica como jefe de equipo y busco algo similar. Soy independiente y me gusta trabajar.

E To help the students to learn the key vocabulary for discussing jobs you could use the following activities:
Give each student a copy of **copymaster 157**. They could first complete the grid at home and then discuss particular jobs in class, with you and their partners.
Form groups of 4 or 5. Each group has a 6-sided pencil with the numbers 1 to 6 on the sides. In each group, a student rolls the pencil twice, the first for A and the second for B, on the board or OHP. Collectively, the group then selects a job which meets the two criteria. They write the jobs they choose. After five jobs, they give their list of jobs to another group. They try to guess the two criteria for each job.

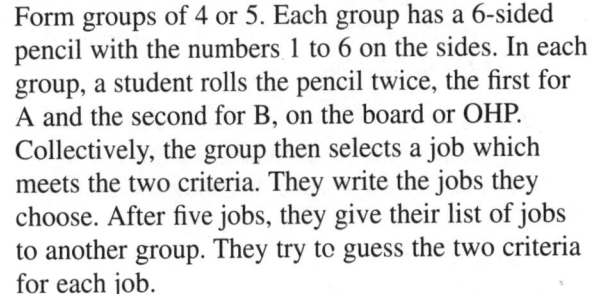

UNIDAD 17

A

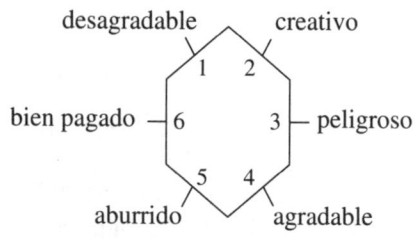

```
    desagradable    creativo
              \ 1  2 /
    bien pagado — 6   3 — peligroso
              / 5  4 \
       aburrido      agradable
```

B

```
        fácil     duro
          \ 1  2 /
    útil — 6   3 — privilegiado
          / 5  4 \
    independiente   difícil
```

Quiero ser ...   (page 178)

Main aim

Discussing plans for future career.

A Begin by working with the class on the list of key sentences, e.g.
The students read them and use a dictionary to understand them.
With the help of the class, produce some *Word Suns* on the board. Write the name of a job and, around it, words and phrases which relate to it, e.g.

```
              al aire libre
     dedicado      |      independiente
              \    |    /
    privilegiado — DEPORTISTA — bien pagado
              /    |    \
      ambicioso    |      duro
                 fuerte
```

Present some questions on the board or OHP for the students to answer by using and adapting the model sentences, e.g.
¿En qué quieres trabajar?
¿Qué harías si fuese posible?
¿Por qué?
¿Y dónde trabajarías?

B Work on *A ser detective*, page 216.

C Return to this item and revise the key sentences. The students answer the three questions and write them down. You then show them the solutions (*Escoger una carrera por ordenador*) in order to give them the jobs the computer recommends. The solutions can be put on the OHP or duplicated for the class. Some of the jobs mentioned are familiar. Some can be understood by using communication strategies: patterns of endings in Spanish (*frutero*), words which are similar to other known words (*periodista–periodismo*), words similar in spelling to the English form (*soldado, actriz*) and words similar in sound to the English form (*chófer*). However, there are some which the students cannot hope to guess: *abogado, azafata, revisor* and *fontanero*. For these, they can use a dictionary.

Escoger una carrera por ordenador
AAA pintor, jardinero
AAB hortelano, obrero agrícola
AAC torero, granjero, lechero, cartero
ABA ingeniero
ABB futbolista, obrero, marinero
ABC pescador
ACA guía turística
ACB policía
ACC limpiabotas
BAA programador de ordenadores, escritor
BBA actriz, cocinero
BCA profesor, peluquero, dentista, abogado
BAB secretaria
BBB director, técnico
BCB empleado de banco
BAC mecánico, ama de casa
BBC minero
BCC camarero, dependienta, frutero, tendero, pescadero, joyero, confitero, telefonista
CAA autor, artista, fotógrafo, carpintero
CAB representante, chófer, camionero
CAC electricista, fontanero
CBA músico, periodista, piloto
CBB modelo, hombre de negocios, bombero
CBC soldado
CCA arquitecto, doctor
CCB guía turística, azafata
CCC taxista, cobrador, revisor

D Ask two able students to adapt the model dialogue. Then ask other pairs to do it as a model for the class. The students can then all do this with their usual partners.

UNIDAD 17

E Give everyone a copy of **copymaster 158** as they complete the task above. This develops the work done so far on careers. The students do the survey individually and the results can be collated and compared with the survey carried out in a Madrid school among students between the ages of 15–18 taken from two classes.

N.B. 54 students took part in the survey, but in Questions 1, 4, 5 the number of reponses exceeds the total number. This is due to multiple responses.

Question 1
The responses were respectively: 7, 50, 28, 36, 43, 15.

Question 2
In the case of Question 2, the points given to the answers were added up and only the rank order is given: 6, 5, 7, 2, 3, 4, 1.

Question 3
For Question 3 the responses were as follows:
Hombre de negocios 5, Médico 5, Deportista 5, Veterinario 4, Ingeniero 4, Periodista 3, Diseñador 3, 'Turismo' 3, Derecho 2, Psicólogo 2, Ecólogo 2, Arquitecto 2, Científico 2, Relaciones públicas 2, Arqueólogo 1, Azafata 1, Mecánico 1, Programador 1, No saben 6

N.B. No teachers!

Question 4
The respective responses were: 18, 10, 0, 7, 30, 10.

Question 5
The respective responses were: 35, 1, 0, 1. 45.

Unas aspiraciones (page 179)

Main aim
Expressing hopes and discussing plans for the future.

A Ask the students to read what each of the young Spanish people would like to do and to try to pair them up with suitable jobs from the list given beneath.

B Ask them to take turns with their partners at being one of the young Spanish people. The other partner has to suggest suitable jobs.

C You could extend the activity by asking the students if any of them share the same views as any of the young Spanish people and whether they could suggest other jobs apart from the ones given that would be suitable for each of them.

D To help the students to learn some of the key vocabulary about future hopes and plans, you could use the following activities:
Give the students just two minutes to find at least one other person in the class with the same job ambitions as them. Write the following on the board for them to use:

Encuentra a alguien a quien le gusten las mismas asignaturas. Encuentra a alguien que busque el mismo trabajo que tú.

Ask several students what they would do if they won:

*10.000 pesetas
100.000 pesetas
1 millón de pesetas
10 millones de pesetas*

Encourage the students to talk about the jobs and career plans of people in their family.

¿Qué dices tú? (page 180)

Main aim
Talking about school and future career plans.

A Begin by revising the unit so far. You could use techniques suggested earlier in *¡vaya! nuevo* and also the following:
Choose some key sentences from earlier in the unit which your students need to learn. Write them on the board or OHP and jumble them up, e.g.

útil vida la en hacer quiero algo

The students write the sentences correctly. You could dictate the jumbled sentences.

Each student writes four things they like about school and work, and four things they dislike. You do the same on the board or OHP. Read aloud the first like on your list and then give an explanation for it, e.g.
Me gusta mucho el dibujo porque es creativo.

Then encourage the students to present their lists.

B The students read this item and prepare their answers. In pairs, they help each other to produce the best possible answers, and practise asking and answering the questions. As they become ready, they perform this for you.
This is a popular exam topic and the students would be well advised to learn by heart the answers to these questions.

UNIDAD 17

C Give one card from **copymaster 159** to each student. Make sure that you give out an employer's card to match each employee's card. The aim is for each employee to find a job and for each employer to find a suitable employee. So, the employers move around and interview the employees, taking on only those who are suitable.

¿Qué harías tú? (page 180)

Main aim
To develop listening skills.

A The students read the rubric carefully and ensure that they understand it. Discuss appropriate exam strategies with them.

B The students listen to the interviews and write notes. Ask several to tell you what their answers are and discuss their performance, suggesting how they could have done better.

¿Qué harías tú?
– Hola, ¿qué es lo que más te gustaría ser?
– Yo sería pintor o deportista. Pintor porque la pintura me gusta y además no dibujo muy mal.
– Y tú, tú ¿qué serías?
– Me gustaría ser profesora de gimnasia. Me importa tener una buena carrera para, en el futuro, poder viajar – ya que es lo que más me gusta.
– Y tú, ¿qué serías tú, si pudieras elegir?
– Yo ejercería la medicina, es decir sería doctora, puesto que es lo que me gusta.
– Y a ti, ¿a qué te gustaría dedicarte?
– Me dedicaría a algún trabajo que tuviera que ver con las telecomunicaciones.
– Y a ti, ¿en qué te gustaría trabajar más que nada?
– Haría farmacia y me gustaría trabajar en algún laboratorio.
– ¿Dónde te gustaría trabajar, si pudieras elegir?
– A mí me gustaría encontrar un buen trabajo en un banco u oficina.
– Y ¿a qué te dedicarías tú?
– Me dedicaría al deporte, en especial al fútbol u otro deporte.
– ¿Qué te gustaría a ti ser, si fuera posible elegir?
– Sería diseñador de automóviles y correría con un fórmula I.

¿Qué haría él o ella? (page 180)

Main aim
Discussing hopes and plans for the future.

A Ask the students to write down the answers to the questions. The imperfect subjunctive is necessarily used in this construction. It will be required only for receptive use.

B The students then tell their partners what they have written and discuss it.

C Further activities
Si no hubiera trabajo
The question of unemployment is extremely important both here and in Spain. Spain has a higher level of unemployment than most European countries and has been particularly affected by the decline of the heavy industries. About three-quarters of the unemployed receive no benefit whatsoever. Ask the students to listen to the tape and pick out the most important messages from the radio programme. Give them the following introduction:

Escuchas un programa en la radio sobre el paro en el cual gente en paro habla de sus problemas. Escucha lo que dicen algunos de los participantes y apunta lo más importante.

Si no hubiera trabajo
– Buenas tardes, señoras y señores. Esta tarde vamos a tratar un tema muy delicado, un problema nacional: el paro. Primero vamos a hablar con Carmen. Carmen, tu marido lleva casi un año sin trabajo, ¿verdad?
– Pues sí, y es difícil explicar cómo me siento. Solamente al ver a mi marido en casa todo el día ya me desespera. Porque mire, estamos acostumbrados a que los maridos salgan y luego vienen y eso; pero es que luego está todo el día en casa y, si sale, viene peor porque cuando sale no encuentra nada.
– Ya, ya veo. Y ahora vamos a hablar con Rosa. Rosa, tu marido también está en paro, ¿verdad? ¿Es tu situación parecida a la de Carmen?
– Pues sí. Es que piensas que no te va a ocurrir a ti. Y resulta que te va llegando y te llega. Me creo que nunca va a tener trabajo y, si lo tiene, si le sale un trabajo, pues creo que van a ser dos meses o así.

UNIDAD 17

– Es una situación muy, muy difícil. Y Pedro, Pedro está desempleado, es uno de estos padres de familia sin trabajo. Vamos a ver qué nos dice sobre su situación y cómo se siente.
– Yo ahora mismo me siento mucho más agresivo que cuando estaba trabajando. Yo creo que no valgo para hacer ninguna cosa ya. Estoy aquí como un parásito.
– Hay muchos hombres en esta situación. Francisco también, vamos a hablar con él.
– Pues mira, estamos perdidos. Las oficinas de empleo son inútiles, no sirven para nada. Lo que pasa es que nos tratan muy mal y te sientes humillado. Además, si hay una demora en los pagos, ¿qué?, da igual, no hacen caso.
– Es un tema del que tenemos que volver a tratar.

Un debate

On the subject of unemployment it is possible to generate an interesting group discussion introducing outline arguments and assigning different roles to each member of the group. The topic under discussion could be:

¿Qué soluciones hay al desempleo para los jóvenes?

The following suggestions could be given out in advance assigned to different people according to their role:

trabajar a mi-tiempo;
quitar el trabajo a las mujeres casadas;
introducir (prolongar) el servicio militar;
tener educación obligatoria hasta los 18 años;
retirar a la gente a los 50 años;
crear más puestos de trabajo;
limitar las mercancías importadas para en turno fabricar más en nuestro propio país.

The possible roles:
a woman engineer married with two children;
a 16–year old unemployed school leaver;
a 53–year old company manager;
an 18–year old student;
a factory worker at a foreign car assembly plant;
a teacher;
a single parent.

Desert island game

The students imagine they are being shipwrecked. They can salvage only ten items. They choose the items and must be able to explain what they would do with each, e.g.

Yo llevaría unas cerillas y así podría hacer un fuego.
Yo cogería unos libros para leer.

Individually, in teams or as a class activity, the students try to think of the items and their uses.

NASA game

Similar to the previous one, this game involves giving the students a list of objects (you can make up a list of basic items) and asking them to decide which would be most useful in space. Ask them to put them in order of importance and to give reasons. Then give them your opinions and see how close their ranking is to yours.

Consequences

Write down the first half of ten sentences on a piece of paper and ask the students to write the second half of the sentences without seeing the first. Sometimes the results can be very amusing.

'If' game

Ask the students the following type of question:

Si pudieses pasar una hora con una persona famosa, ¿con quién sería?; ¿qué harías?, ¿de qué hablarías?
Si fueses el Rey/la Reina de Inglaterra, el presidente de los EEUU, el director de tu instituto, ¿qué harías?
Si fueses arquitecto y si tuvieses responsibilidad para planificar un nuevo pueblo, ¿qué decidirías?, ¿tendrías fábricas?, ¿dónde?, ¿qué atracciones habría?

Ahora sé (page 181)

Main aim

To provide a summary of the *Unidad* and a basis for more practice and revision.

You could work on this along lines which have already proved successful.

UNIDAD 17

Revision activities

1 Buying presents and souvenirs
(Libro 1, Unidad 7)

A Play a game of *Categorías*. See how many presents and souvenirs the class can correctly categorise in one minute. Categories could include:
- presents suitable for adults, children, both;
- presents suitable for boys, girls, both.

You call out the words, e.g.

una muñeca roja, un cinturón marrón, un abanico amarillo, una chaqueta blanca, unas castañuelas, turrón, una guitarra, un bolso de piel, un monedero, zapatos, un abrigo, una camiseta negra, un CD de música clásica, unos sellos, un billetero.

B Each student writes what presents s/he would buy if s/he had 5,000 pesetas. Then, in groups, they tell each other what they would buy and for whom.

C This is a popular topic for oral exams. The students could prepare by working on **copymaster 160**.

2 Booking into a hotel
(Libro 2, Unidad 5)

A Play these recorded dialogues and ask the students to note the problems that arise and then the solutions. Check their answers and clear up any problems.

¿Tiene una habitación, por favor?

Número 1
- Buenos días.
- Buenos días.
- He reservado una habitación.
- ¿Su nombre, por favor?
- Hornsby.
- Lo siento, no hay nadie aquí de ese nombre.
- Pero llamé por teléfono ayer desde Madrid.
- ¿Cómo se escribe?
- H. O. R. N. S. B. Y.
- Ah, sí. Es una habitación individual, ¿verdad?
- Sí, para tres noches.
- Lo siento. Aquí tiene su llave, habitación 225.
- Gracias.

Número 2
- Buenas noches. ¿Tiene una habitación individual con baño?
- Lo siento, con baño no queda ninguna. Tenemos una habitación individual con lavabo y el cuarto de baño está al final del pasillo.
- No vale. Hay otro hotel por aquí.
- ¿Quiere que llame al hotel?
- Muchas gracias, sí.
- Ahora mismo.

Número 3
- Dígame.
- Oiga, le llamo desde la habitación 312.
- Sí. ¿Qué pasa?
- Es que en el baño no hay ni jabón, ni toallas ni papel higiénico.
- Lo siento, es domingo.
- Ya sé que es domingo pero tengo que lavarme los domingos.
- Subo en seguida. No se preocupe.

Número 4
- Oiga.
- Sí, señor.
- No hay vistas al mar desde mi habitación.
- Lo siento pero no todas las habitaciones tienen vistas al mar.
- Pero cuando reservé me prometieron una habitación doble con baño y con vistas al mar.
- Lo siento, no hay otra habitación hoy. Pero mañana habrá una habitación libre. ¿Vale?
- Bueno, sí.

B Give everyone a copy of **copymaster 161** for them to work on individually and in pairs.

3 Using telephones and faxes
(Libro 3, Unidad 7)

A Encourage the students to look back at *Unidad 7* and to revise it thoroughly.

B Give each student a copy of **copymaster 162**. They work on this in pairs.

4 Crime and the law
(Libro 3, Unidad 16)

A Encourage the students to look at *Unidad 16* (and then at Activity **3A** above).

B Give each student a copy of **copymaster 163**. They could work on this at home.

C Give each student a copy of **copymaster 164**. They work on this in pairs.

D Give each student a copy of **copymaster 165**. They work on this in pairs.